The Civil Power of the News

Jackie Harrison

The Civil Power of the News

palgrave
macmillan

Jackie Harrison
Department of Journalism Studies
University of Sheffield
Sheffield, UK

ISBN 978-3-030-19380-5   ISBN 978-3-030-19381-2 (eBook)
https://doi.org/10.1007/978-3-030-19381-2

© The Editor(s) (if applicable) and The Author(s), under exclusive license to Springer Nature Switzerland AG 2019
This work is subject to copyright. All rights are solely and exclusively licensed by the Publisher, whether the whole or part of the material is concerned, specifically the rights of translation, reprinting, reuse of illustrations, recitation, broadcasting, reproduction on microfilms or in any other physical way, and transmission or information storage and retrieval, electronic adaptation, computer software, or by similar or dissimilar methodology now known or hereafter developed.
The use of general descriptive names, registered names, trademarks, service marks, etc. in this publication does not imply, even in the absence of a specific statement, that such names are exempt from the relevant protective laws and regulations and therefore free for general use.
The publisher, the authors and the editors are safe to assume that the advice and information in this book are believed to be true and accurate at the date of publication. Neither the publisher nor the authors or the editors give a warranty, expressed or implied, with respect to the material contained herein or for any errors or omissions that may have been made. The publisher remains neutral with regard to jurisdictional claims in published maps and institutional affiliations.

Cover image: Towfiqu Photography/Getty images
Cover design by eStudioCalamar

This Palgrave Macmillan imprint is published by the registered company Springer Nature Switzerland AG
The registered company address is: Gewerbestrasse 11, 6330 Cham, Switzerland

To the Civil Sphere

Preface

Given the circumstances the factual media find themselves in today, and for the requirements of clarity, it is necessary to point out the two basic beliefs that hover above some of the main arguments of this book. They are, if you like, framing beliefs that provide some of the background context for my arguments concerning the civil power of the news. These beliefs are not the most important in this book (those are discussed ahead) nor are they systematically or logically related to each other in any strict sense. Rather, they form aspects of an overarching *Weltanschauung* about the role of the news, the nature of news journalism, journalism as a civil institution and the values it chooses to promote with regard to the civil sphere. They form part of the background to the book in what I hope is an obvious and self-evident way. I also believe they go some way to help to explain some of the assumptions and choices made in what follows with regard to what challenges confront the news today and my views on whether these can be regarded as in any way significantly different from challenges in the past. These basic beliefs consist of the following:

First, that advances in communication technology do not fundamentally alter the way the news exercises its civil power—that is its influence on the decisions we make about the nature and quality of civil life. The things that have changed over the last 150 years with regard to the news are the technical aspects of news gathering, dissemination, styles of writing and presentation and, via social media, the means through which public sentiment can express itself and decide to interact with the news cycle (or not). The fact that public sentiment is interested in and engages with the news hasn't changed and political and commercial pressures on the news remain. State and legal restrictions on the news are also debated in more or less the same pluralist and rights-based terms. And of course the news consuming public is still regarded as 'fed up', angry, outraged and clamouring for … (and here you can fill in the dots with just about any cause you care to name) or simply in need of entertainment and gossip, or (more rarely) it is regarded as consisting of discursive and enlightened intelligent citizens who need informing in terms of what is going on and who possess something called a 'right to know'. In short, the news is the sum total of how a news provider articulates and prioritises its role and responsibilities, how journalists choose to go about their profession and in what capacity the public engages with the news. Accordingly, and importantly, many of the non-technical aspects of news remain pretty much the same 'then and now'. Correspondingly, good and bad news journalism still coexists, as do good and bad regulatory regimes, just as good and bad news organisations do (even when some of them deny they are in the news business at all, preferring to describe themselves as technology companies) and of course the public is still perceived in myriad forms. Despite recurrent concerns about 'crises in journalism', the essential features of the news are the same and always will be, or at least until such time as there is no need for news. The key to this lack of fundamental change is the enduring persistence of self-interest narrowly conceived of and, opposing that, editorial and journalistic integrity and the preservation of a civil-minded journalistic culture of investigation and editing. Then, as now, the quality of news journalism in its broadest sense is absolutely critical to 'our' conception of entitlements, namely what we regard as our own freedoms and rights weighed alongside the freedom and rights of others. In effect, whether the news is a benign or malign influence on civil life is an enduring question to be asked of the news and one that this book tries to answer. Historically and currently, good and bad news is unchanging in its coexistence, mutual contestations and fundamental rivalry.

It's just that recently 'the bad' seems to be on the edge of winning—but so far it hasn't, and a history of survival is on the side of good journalism. The survival of good journalism is a civil necessity. Today, we face what seems like a surfeit of news which takes the guise of narratives of partisanship, exclusion/racism and blame/xenophobia, the systematic distortion of views via 'fake news' (here referring to false news, misinformation and disinformation), politically inspired viral hoaxes, hyper-partisan pleas and opinions, stories that escape the attention of non-human fact checkers/editors and the constant generation of idiotic memes. Yet these too have their equivalences in the past, news was particularly difficult to verify in the era of the invention of the Gutenberg printing press (circa 1439) and before the relatively recent development of the objective method of reporting, journalistic ethics and codes of practice. What remains true 'then and now' is how these fraudulent news activities succeed so successfully in engaging their audiences and are subsequently shared and recycled in no small part because they masquerade as real news. In short, and this is the second belief that this book rests upon, there is a good form of journalistic news which can be recognised and aspired to. It can also resist and expose the predations of the above. Indeed, as a matter of speculation, it is increasingly the case that techno-media companies and social media will become more and more regulated (possibly even self-regulated) in accordance with the demands for good journalism. Thus, this book presumes there is something called good journalism which can be realistically undertaken by all news organisations, that there are journalists who consistently believe in the value of being truthful and following that, that the truth can and should be known and where necessary, uncovered and disclosed for public benefit. This does not mean that good journalism follows a specific view of political and commercial outcomes; far from it, good journalism spans the political and economic divides. To be absolutely clear, anti-civil news can adhere to the precepts and values of good journalism. It is a categorical mistake to equate good journalism with civil sentiments and bad journalism with anti-civil sentiments (though recognisably much anti-civil journalism is also bad journalism). Good journalism is about judging events pragmatically, in situ and with an eye towards a comprehensive understanding and, with that, it does not rely upon or require the systematic and prejudicial denial of other people's civil standing. It does not engage in bigotry and hate speech of any kind but treats everyone with respect, nor does it simply copy and recycle nonsense and fictions derived from social media.

This book is also unembarrassedly attached to the virtues of news journalism that adopts a civil rather than anti-civil attitude, not only as an ideal but also as a way of going about doing a job. Simply stated, such news journalism values accuracy, sincerity and objectivity and requires news journalists to adopt 'the judge's outlook' and conform to the requirements of a fair and comprehensive understanding of events. Ultimately, there are no guaranteed outcomes with news journalism, neither is there an absolute standard for what constitutes civility and what is regarded as plainly anti-civil. The coexistence of the two is inevitable. Nevertheless, I am attached as a matter of preference to the kind of journalism that is truthful, interpretative and undertakes social criticism with integrity and has a civil disposition and outlook.

Sheffield, UK   Jackie Harrison

Acknowledgements

To the memory of my Dad—Ron and equally to the love and encouragement given to me by my Mum—Joan. Between them they taught me that much, if not all, is possible. As for other special individuals, a huge thanks to Maurice Roche who read and commented on an early draft and to Jeffrey Alexander whose work is the inspiration behind this book. A special thank you to all of those wonderful activists, researchers and scholars at the Centre for the Freedom of the Media—a toast to all of them for passions shared! I am grateful to my News and Civil Society students who asked just the right kinds of challenging questions and to the University of Bergen for providing me with a visiting professorship which provided much needed time to write and present my ideas. There are also two people who seem to be with me whenever I need them and who deserve a special thank you. My colleague and friend Stef who is testimony to the fact that a life is best lived when shared and whose support and input into this book has been so valuable, and when I find I have nothing left to say, there is always Neil on whom I can always rely and will always turn to.

Contents

Part I The Civil Power of the News Defined and Explained

1 Introduction to Part I   3

2 The Civil Ideal of the News   31

3 The Civil Ideal of the News and Political
   and Commercial Reality   65

4 Newsrooms and the News Cycle   105

Part II A Practical Demonstration of the Civil Power
         of the News Through an Analysis of the First
         British Railway Murder 1864

5 Introduction to Part II   145

6 The Reporting of the Murder and the Invariant Civil
   Concern of Identity   163

7 The Reporting of the Murder and the Invariant Civil
   Concern of Legitimacy   211

8	The Reporting of the Murder and the Invariant Civil Concern of Risk	265
9	The Reporting of the Murder as Type 3 Civil Boundary Maintenance: The Rejection of Change and the Endorsement of the Status Quo in Civil Society	303
10	Résumé	321
	Author Index	327
	Subject Index	335

List of Figures

Chapter 4

Fig. 1	The news cycle simplified	111
Fig. 2	News selection as a form of civil judgement	125
Fig. 3	The news cycle in greater detail (*keys* CJ: Civil Judgement; ACJ: Anti-civil Judgement; T: Tendentious; D1: Discursive; D2: Descriptive; CBT: Civil Boundary Type)	133
Fig. 4	News, the public and public sentiment	134

Chapter 5

Fig. 1	Research template	154

LIST OF TABLES

Chapter 4

Table 1	Civil and anti-civil selection criteria of the invariant civil concern of identity	122
Table 2	Civil and anti-civil selection criteria of the invariant civil concern of legitimacy	123
Table 3	Civil and anti-civil selection criteria of the invariant civil concern of risk	124

Chapter 6

Table 1	The civil lexicon of the invariant civil concern of identity in the news cycle	168
Table 2	The anti-civil lexicon of the invariant civil concern of identity in the news cycle	169

Chapter 7

Table 1	The civil lexicon of the invariant civil concern of legitimacy in the news cycle	215
Table 2	The anti-civil lexicon of the invariant civil concern of legitimacy in the news cycle	218

Chapter 8

Table 1	The civil lexicon of the invariant civil concern of risk in the news cycle	271
Table 2	The anti-civil lexicon of the invariant civil concern of risk in the news cycle	274

PART I

The Civil Power of the News Defined and Explained

CHAPTER 1

Introduction to Part I

1   Argument

The argument of Part I of this book can be simply stated. The civil power of the news resides in its relationship to public sentiment and the way the news reports our invariant civil concerns of identity, legitimacy and risk and subsequently how these invariant civil concerns are assembled and understood in the form of civil and anti-civil judgements. It is these judgements which contribute to the boundaries we[1] place and maintain around civil society with regard to whom and what we regard as civil and anti-civil. The demonstration of this argument takes a little longer and requires that I start with some terminological clarity, especially with regard to what I mean by civil society, from which all else follows.

2   A Very Brief Account of Alexander's CSI-CSII

In the 'Civil Sphere' (2006), Jeffrey Alexander argues that the term 'civil society' has gone through a particular intellectual history, which can be understood as consisting of three different understandings of civil society. He refers to these as CSI, CSII and CSIII. Briefly, CSI is a late seventeenth-century social and extensive understanding of the civil sphere, coinciding and emerging from the writings of Locke and Harrington, developed by Scottish moralists Adam Ferguson and Adam Smith and then by Rousseau, Hegel and finally used 'energetically' (Alexander 2006: 24) by Tocqueville.[2] In essence, according to

© The Author(s) 2019
J. Harrison, *The Civil Power of the News*,
https://doi.org/10.1007/978-3-030-19381-2_1

Alexander, CSI is an umbrella term for a 'plethora of institutions outside the state' (ibid.: 24) including the market, religious bodies and other cooperative bodies that created and utilised bonds of trust. Importantly, this conception of civil society had a 'moral and ethical force' (ibid.: 25) and an affinity with the development of capitalism. Indeed, at first CSI public life related to market life and capitalism was 'benignly conceived' of and viewed as an alternative to the excessive and repressive forces of aristocratic power (ibid.). However, this was to change as capitalism became more industrialised and followed the path of free trade and laissez-faire liberal economics.

By the mid-nineteenth century, the way of conceiving of society as CSI was supplanted by CSII, which held the view that capitalism was most definitely not a benign nor a progressive force. In short, civil society was no longer conceived of in associative and cooperative terms but was 'pejoratively associated with market capitalism alone' (ibid.: 26) and nowhere was this more so (for Alexander) than in the works of Marx who reduced the concept of civil society to an 'epiphenomenon of capitalism' (ibid.: 27). The critical concept now was the state and arguments (both radical and conservative) centred on the extent to which the state should be assigned the task of protecting the citizenry from the worst excesses of capitalism. From this, an intellectual polarity emerged which Alexander summarises accordingly: 'for the right, the capitalism-civil society identification suggested abolishing society; for the left it suggested abolishing markets and private property itself' (ibid.: 28). The concept of civil society had become bifurcated between understanding civil society through the diffuse inclusivity of CSI and the economic reductionism of CSII (ibid.: 31) neither of which addresses 'the empirical and normative problems of contemporary life' (ibid.: 32). In other words, for Alexander CSI and CSII are insufficient conceptual tools to enable us to understand civil society not least because 'To identify civil society with capitalism (CSII) is to degrade its universalizing moral implications' (ibid.: 33). Recognising this requires that the civil sphere and its independence from the market be conceptualised and defined in different terms. Accordingly, Alexander (2006: 3) suggests that we should envisage civil society as 'a world of values and institutions that generates the capacity for social criticism and democratic integration at the same time' and as based upon 'feelings of solidarity for others whom we do not know'. For Alexander, what we need to do is move beyond CSI and CSII into what he terms CSIII and it is this conception of civil society that this book uses throughout.

3 THE DIFFERENTIATION BETWEEN SPHERES AND THE INSTITUTIONAL BASE OF CSIII

In a very important passage, Alexander (2006: 31) writes that 'civil society should be conceived of as a solidary sphere, in which a certain kind of universalizing community comes to be culturally defined and to some extent institutionally enforced'. Accordingly, there is now a need to understand 'civil society as a sphere that can be analytically independent, empirically differentiated, and morally more universalistic vis-à-vis the state and the market and from other social spheres as well' (ibid.). Specifically, Alexander's conceptualisation of CSIII envisages civil society as existing as 'a sphere or subsystem of society that is analytically and, to various degrees, empirically separated from the spheres of political life, economic, family and religious life' (ibid.: 53) with each sphere having separate and identifiable goals and aspirations. The differentiation between these spheres: civil, political (where political is understood as the administration and power of the state), market, familial and religious, is important because it is, as Alexander notes, a 'dialectical' and 'functional' differentiation (ibid.: 203). By this he means that non-civil autonomous spheres have aims and concerns that contradict the solidarising aims of the civil sphere (social criticism, democratic integration, civility, justice, reciprocity, and mutual respect). He puts this point accordingly (and it is worth quoting at length): 'The goal of the economic sphere is wealth, not justice in the civil sense; it is organized around efficiency, not solidarity and depends more upon hierarchy than equality to meet its goals. Polities produce power not reciprocity, they demand loyalty, not criticism, and they seek to exercise coercive if legitimate forms of social control. The religious sphere produces salvation, not worldly just deserts; it is premised upon a fundamental inequality, not only between God and merely human believers but between God's representatives, his shepherds, and those whom they guide and instruct on earth; no matter how radically egalitarian or reformed the message, the very transcendental character of religious relationships demand mystery and deference not reciprocity or dialogue of a transparent kind. In the family, the species is reproduced not only in a biological but a moral sense; it is organized more by passion and unconditional love than self-control and critical questioning, and it depends fundamentally upon authority and deference' (ibid.: 203–204).

As to the differentiated relationship between the spheres, it is characterised by mutual 'input' and 'intrusion',[3] a never-ending clash of outlooks and values with varying degrees of outcomes. Indeed, Alexander puts the matter starkly, 'The privileged accumulations of goods in noncivil spheres are used to achieve power and recognition in civil society, to gain access to its discourse and control over its institutions, and to re-represent the elites of other spheres as idea participants in the interactive processes of civil life' (ibid.: 205). Correspondingly, and in order to maintain the democratic and just character of the civil sphere, it is necessary 'for the civil sphere to "invade" noncivil spheres, to demand certain kinds of reform, and to monitor them through regulation in turn' (ibid.: 34). Though to be fair to Alexander, this is not to say that there is nothing but endless conflict between the spheres, rather it is to recognise that 'Divisions between spheres and the antagonisms they create are continuously spanned by cultural and institutional bridges, sometimes for better, sometimes for worse' (Alexander 2015: 177). It is this structural and functional differentiation between the spheres and the corresponding constant clash between the civil and anti-civil in the civil sphere that forms the macro-sociological background to my arguments. On a meso-level, it is the clash between spheres at the institutional level and within the civil sphere that I wish to now focus attention on.

Alexander (2006: 31) notes that 'To the degree that this solidary community exists, it is exhibited and sustained by public opinion, deep cultural codes, distinctive organizations—legal, journalistic and associational—and such historically specific interactional practices as civility, criticism, and mutual respect'. To the extent that a civil community can exist as such (and to a large extent civility is an ideal), it can only be sustained to one degree or another, if 'the people' have 'teeth' (ibid.: 5) at their disposal in a form of 'communicative force' (ibid.) where the factual mass media 'select and reconstruct in civil terms what "actually goes on" in a society's life' (ibid.). In this way, 'Journalistic judgments thus possess an outsized power to affect the shape-shifting currents of contemporary social life' (Alexander 2016: 1). Importantly though, 'Real civil societies are contradictory and fragmented' (Alexander 2006: 7) and the civil sphere 'is always limited by, and interpenetrated with, the boundary relations of other, non-civil spheres' (ibid.: 31) and between the competing and different relationships that exist between communities, groups and publics within civil society.

In order for the civil sphere to be able to counter the non-civil power of those who hold different types of power either in non-civil settings or in civil settings, it requires that power holders act in a civil manner (using the resources of their office on behalf of others rather for themselves) regardless of what their own personal interests may be, to act in the public interest.[4] That is power holders must use their 'office' on behalf of the civil sphere. Accordingly, for Alexander (2006, 2008: 188), the use of 'office' in the interests of the civil sphere has the potential to act as a solidarising force and in this sense has 'become another major regulatory institution. Office obligations mediate between the concentration of wealth and power and the civil sphere's normative claims'. However, as noted above, the civil use of 'office' and the sustainability of the civil sphere both clash with the interests of other non-civil spheres.

Civil society itself is often dominated by endemic conflicts of interests which are played out (amongst other ways) at the institutional level of CSIII which Alexander divides into the regulatory institutions of law, political party organisations and free and fair elections, the communicative institutions of journalism and news media organisations, the public and its opinions, public opinion polls and civil associations. In other words, and empirically rather than analytically, modern democracies which lay claim to a civil sphere 'are filled with barbaric contradictions, and that the latter become lodged inside the sphere of solidarity itself' (Alexander 2007: 643). The point is that the civil sphere is a space of contestation where civil and anti-civil forces collide and compete for a form of hegemony in the institutions of civil society. He (ibid.: 651) expresses this idea in the following way: '*The Civil Sphere* does not, however, claim that symbolic understandings have trumped material concerns, and I affirm, rather than deny, that the institutions of the civil sphere, as those of other domains, are deeply self-interested and often profit seeking. What I do emphasize is that the civil sphere - both through its particular structures of symbolic discourse and through the distinctive qualities of its institutions, promotes solidarity in a manner that can, in principle and sometimes in practice, sharply curtail and control the hierarchies and instrumentalities of "material" life and those generated by the spheres of religion, politics, race, ethnicity, sex, and gender as well'. In short, whilst the distinction between civil and non-civil spheres is analytical, empirically the institutional basis of the civil sphere also houses 'the discourses, organizations, and goods produced by noncivil spheres: markets, states, parties, churches and sects, families and patriarchies, and groupings formed by ethnic, racial, and regional ties' (ibid.: 643). Alternatively expressed, the 'autonomy of civil society is continually compromised and consistently reduced. Noncivil cultural and institutional exigencies permeate civil society, and the discourse of repression is applied far and wide' (Alexander 2006: 194). Thus, 'anti-civil qualities—of space, time, and function—actually become lodged within the sphere of social solidarity itself, making at least a partial mockery of its emancipatory claims' (Alexander 2007: 643).

This analytical/empirical conceptualisation of CSIII importantly recognises that mature democracies require toleration and engagement with a plurality of interests and yet at its own institutional level the civil sphere is replete with an ongoing conflict of interests. In short, the civil sphere comes with no guarantee of liberal and democratic outcomes and its institutions represent contested civil spaces. Or to borrow yet again from Alexander, the civil sphere also has a 'dark side—the repressive and anticivil aspects of public opinion, fictional and factual media, civil associations, electoral systems, party conflicts, and law' (ibid.). Of all these contested spaces in the civil sphere, it is the civil institution of the factual media, or at least one element of it, the news, that I am interested in, and to be clear, it is only the civil power[5] of the news that I discuss. The analytical/empirical or, to put it another way, the normative and ideal character of CSIII and the reality of how the news denotes and reports CSIII is deeply influenced by anti-civil forces. On this, I leave the last word to Alexander (2006: 195) who points out that there is a 'necessity for functional differentiation and complexity, both in an institutional sense and in a moral one', but to 'avoid the idealistic fallacy, we must recognize that civil society is always nested in the practical worlds of the uncivil spheres, and we must study the compromise and fragmentation, the "real" rather than merely the idealized civil society that results'.

However, before proceeding to the ideal and real as regards the news as an institution of civil society in Chapters 2 and 3, two other concepts that the arguments made in this book rely upon need to be clarified: first, what I mean by public sentiment and second, what I mean by boundary maintenance in the context of the news. It is to the elaboration of these two concepts that I now turn.

4   Public Sentiment

The link between the news media and civil society,[6] which I wish to explore, is to be found in the relationship between the news and public sentiment, and as I said above, the arguments of this book seek to establish that the civil power of the news resides in its relationship to public sentiment. I use the term public sentiment as an umbrella term for three reasons: one, it covers the normative and factual composition of the public's views. Two, it emphasises the affective element of the public's views.[7] Three, it grounds the idea of the public's views as something everyday and ordinary, as a constituent feature of our 'lifeworld', our culture and our social experiences.[8] Let me elaborate. Too often, the cognates of public sentiment namely 'public opinion' (and related to that the 'court of public opinion', the 'public opinion tribunal',[9] the 'voice of public opinion', the 'formation of public opinion'), 'public will formation', 'public reason', 'will of the people', the 'democratic will', the 'democratic voice', etc., are used to imply that the public's views are or should be the product of a form of deracinated (sometimes proceduralist) and somewhat desiccated reasoning or opinion formation. Irrespective of the desirability of such rational detachment[10] and arguments for the exercise of some form of 'deliberative republican' civil responsibility,[11] in the context of an understanding of the constituent features of the civil power of the news, such a primarily rationally orientated approach will not suffice.[12] Quite simply, public sentiment stands in contradistinction to a 'we-perspective'[13] if it is exclusively a deliberative and rational conception of the public sphere. It is not the case that the 'unforced force' of the better—more rational and less selfish—argument will dominate in the public sphere. It is not the case that public sentiment is preoccupied with informed political decision-making but rather with the net effects of the allocation of primary social goods. An understanding of how public sentiment is responded to and reflected (or not) in the news is reliant on establishing to whom the majority of news reporters think they are reporting and what about. It is also a matter of understanding the way news reporters talk about themselves as individuals and what it is that they think they do and why; the way news organisations see themselves and articulate and deliver their remit and how they go about identifying, selecting and reporting the news. It is also about their customs and practices and importantly the way both news reporters and news organisations conceive of and regard their audiences. Indeed, all of this is very well documented both ethnographically through lengthy observation in newsrooms and empirically.[14] One of the important things that emerges from this literature is the recognition by those involved in the news that the 'public' simultaneously hold both rationally and irrationally, fair and prejudicial and calm and volatile views. The public when it expresses itself does so over the gamut of good and bad arguments, open and closed outlooks, and generous and mean attitudes.[15] Scholarship has shown us that this is understood by those involved in the production of the news even if they don't articulate it in those terms. Public sentiment is not a form of ideal speech nor is it systematic. While we might opine that the formation of public speech should attend to what Rawls calls the 'duty to civility', this is not the case; rather, it is a case of public sentiment articulating our 'civil passions'[16] sometimes passionately and sometimes calmly.

Given this understanding of public sentiment (as everyday, ordinary and contingent, as variously having a normative, factual and affective composition), it is not contradictory to go further and note that public sentiment exists as a regulating idea in the context of the news. That is, it exists, as I hope to show when discussing the news cycle in Chapter 4, both in the background and in the foreground of news reporting as something grounded in what is meant by an 'audience' and which is constantly attended to and subsequently regarded or ignored. In short, public sentiment is a fundamental part of newsroom subjectivity,[17] a point which also illustrates the fact that civil society is deeply communicative. By this, I mean the normative profile of civil society and the values it promotes and adopts are, in part, a result of mediated public debate, where the news produces public narratives and representations articulated via contestation in the news. The origin of this point is to be found in Dewey and his view that communicative democracy is the ideal form of democracy. He argues that democracy (understood as a social idea and not merely a political one) is to be conceived of as more than just majority rule (though this was undoubtedly an incontestable if rudimentary element of democracy).[18] Rather, it requires, in its ideal form, 'freedom of social inquiry and of distribution of its conclusions' (Dewey 1954 [1927]: 166). The latter assumes and requires publicity and systematically distributed communications.[19] Dewey is an optimistic communitarian who (like Lippmann) does not believe in 'omnicompetent' individuals (ibid.: 158), but (unlike Lippmann) believes in the possibility of 'communicative participation'[20] for the deliberation of shared interests and common concerns: 'communication of the results of social inquiry is the same thing as the formation of public opinion' (ibid.: 177). For Dewey, under the right democratic and communicative circumstances, public opinion is educable and potentially progressive. What helps to determine this is the extent to which the factual mass media in a democratic civil society are free and systematic and, more importantly (for my arguments ahead), the extent to which they are influenced by and reflect whatever form of 'social inquiry' groups within the civil sphere are concerned with. This is a matter of both understanding the constituent features of public sentiment and the playing out of civil and anti-civil forces in the setting of the news. I shall address the former below and the latter in Part II of this book.

It is a trite but necessary observation to say that civil society consists of many different associative groups. Indeed, the diversity of these associative groups goes some way to explain the plurality of views with regard to what 'we' regard as civil and anti-civil. While this plurality is a commonly observed and much discussed sociological fact, it is the case that public sentiment does express common civil interests. Indeed, I shall argue that such common civil interests are constitutive of the fundamental issues that define our version of civility and that they are best understood as invariant civil concerns. They are unchanging and ever-present in all civil societies. They are consistently held as simultaneous concerns by diverse civil associative groups and form the basis of the pluralism we take for granted in a modern civil society. The issues are the same, the answers different. Public sentiment represents a diversity of views, a heterogeneity and plurality around the way we address the same fundamental civil concerns. In other words, civil diversity and associated with that the plurality of views around common invariant civil concerns form the structural basis of the way I understand public sentiment throughout this book.

Correspondingly, my argument is that public sentiment consists of three basic invariant civil concerns constitutive of civil life which guide the principles and practices of civility we adopt and specifically the way 'we' attend to and define the civil values of social criticism, democratic integration, civility, justice, reciprocity and mutual respect. These three basic invariant civil concerns are identity, legitimacy and risk. Respectively, identity is a matter of who 'we' regard as tolerable and intolerable, who 'we' should be hospitable towards and who 'we' should not, who is like 'us' and who is not and so on. Legitimacy relates to what 'we' can justify and how 'we' do so, what is seen to be legally and ethically right and wrong, what is regarded as just and fair, what will withstand scrutiny, how and in what ways 'we' address issues of power and of who has it and how is it exercised. Risk relates to fear and the need for feelings of security and correspondingly, the risks we collectively perceive 'we' face. These three invariant civil concerns provide the basis for a form of architectural framework through which news journalism continually exercises its civil and anti-civil judgements. That is, public sentiment provides an architectural framework through which these civil and anti-civil judgements are manifest within the context of the stories news journalists and organisations report and vitally, how they report them. In this way, public sentiment is a constituent part of newsroom subjectivity and the conscious and unconscious choices, decisions and judgements made by news organisations and journalists in the news cycle. Consequently, in this book, I am concerned with public sentiment as it expresses a view of the workings (the principles and practices) of civil society. As such it can be likened to (but importantly is not the same as) Taylor's understanding of the public sphere as a social imaginary.

For Taylor (2007: 159), modern society is characterised by three primary social imaginaries that combine to envision and enable a 'modern moral order'.[21] They are the 'economy, the public sphere and the practices and outlooks of democratic self-rule' (ibid.: 176). Combined they form the 'generally shared background understandings of society, which makes it possible for it to function as it does' (ibid.: 323); that is, they enable social (and political) practices.[22] Of these three social imaginaries, the public sphere is the most relevant to my case. For Taylor, the public sphere exists as a 'common space'[23] of both face-to-face and mediated discussion about common interests, and the results of these discussions are 'public opinion', or in my sense of the term above, public sentiment. Taylor (ibid.: 187) puts it this way: 'we can speak of "common space" when people come together in a common act of focus for whatever purpose, be it ritual, the enjoyment of play, a conversation, the celebration of a major event, or whatever'. It is a space 'which is self-consciously ... outside [political] power' (Taylor 2007: 190). It would be tempting but misleading to refer to public sentiment as a civil imaginary, but in fact I am only appropriating certain features of Taylor's understanding of the public sphere and claiming that there is resemblance to my understanding of public sentiment. This resemblance can be demonstrated through the following shared features: both are concerned with the gamut of civil life, both combine principles and practices through 'common acts of focus', both are forms of a mediated space of competing views, both are outside the exercise of political qua state power and both provide a benchmark of legitimacy. Where I disagree with Taylor is that the public sphere can ideally be non-partisan and reflective and rational,[24] and that it comes with a guarantee that the principles it seeks to unite with the practices it envisions, endorses and enacts are commendable and desirable.[25] Rather, the public sphere manifest as public sentiment is a space of struggle where the reflective and rational, the solidarising and generous only and occasionally win over the bigoted, the self-interested views of partisan groups and widely held unreflective prejudices. To repeat Alexander's point (2006: 195): 'civil society is always nested in the practical worlds of the uncivil spheres'.

5   BOUNDARY MAINTENANCE

Boundary maintenance is contingent on the fact that there exists a 'we' that claims a commonly recognised, normative and symbolic attachment to a particular place and space, to a particular cultural and historical narrative and to a particular outlook replete with concepts, categorisations, beliefs, folkways, customs, mores, evaluative codes of behaviour, sanctions and penalties.[26] In short, boundary maintenance is made up of and sustained by many different things and experienced both at the group and at the personal level.

The two basic approaches to normative and symbolic boundaries are to be found in Durkheim and Weber.[27] For Durkheim,[28] normative and symbolic boundaries are contingent upon a moral order, whilst for Weber[29] they are contingent upon the formation of social status groups who lay claim to forms of social prestige, honour and operate restrictive barriers to membership of their particular group. Of the two, this work takes an essentially Durkheimian approach insofar as my argument is that the news contributes to the normative dimension of civil boundaries. More recently, such strong views on the nature and role of boundaries have been challenged by theories of cosmopolitanism, globalisation, technological advancements and what Thrift (1996) refers to as 'inhuman geographies'[30] all of which combine to create the increasingly widespread conditions of rootlessness and endless mobility.[31] At the same time, studies of the banal show the ubiquity of symbolic representations of identities and belonging.[32]

As boundaries are defined by culture, institutions, symbolic stories, historical narratives, a moral order and linguistic codes, they express who we are, what we do, who is seen to be civil and who is not, how we feel about the civil and the anti-civil and the level of tolerance and degrees of acceptable influence and otherness we can accord and accept. In a different way, but in a similar vein, Erikson (2003: 36) sees boundary maintenance to be occurring when, 'members [of a community] tend to confine themselves to a particular radius of activity and to regard any conduct which drifts outside that radius of activity as somehow inappropriate or immoral. Thus the group retains a kind of cultural integrity, a voluntary restriction on its own potential for expansion, beyond that which is strictly required for accommodation to the environment'. For Anderson (1991), boundaries are created by people who 'imagined' nations as being about people who created their own national identities through imagined communities, which came also to be bounded by the physical borders of the nation state. Boundaries are maintained around such communities through social comparisons that variously accommodate difference depending upon the extent to which a group and its views and its values are an in-group or an out-group (Tajfel and Turner 1979) and can lead to both exclusion and inclusion of diversity (Hall 1996). Where boundaries are drawn and maintained around those who are included and those who are excluded, the distinction between 'us' and 'them' is highlighted (Schlesinger 1991), and where boundaries of exclusion focus on difference or the other they are generally constructed in a negative way but when difference is not seen as a threat, it may be celebrated or seen as positive or enhancing (Woodward 1997: 35). Symbolic boundaries that place people into different groups can generate feelings of in-group similarity and group membership (Epstein 1992). Even though human behaviour can vary over a predictably eccentric range, each self-identifying community draws a set of symbolic and historically meaningful parenthesis around not only who is an insider and who is an outsider, but also boundary maintenance occurs in terms of what is seen to be acceptable and unacceptable behaviour, what is taboo and what is not, what is seen to threaten the community and what does not. This is no more than a sociological truism and evident in both Weber's and Durkheim's definitions above.

However, what is at issue from the point of view of reasonable coexistence (always) is the capacity or ability to which 'we' are hospitable, empathic, tolerant, fair-minded and can move beyond our self-interest. In Alexander's terms, it is our ability to engender a solidary civil sphere which 'unites individuals dispersed by class, race, religion, ethnicity, or race (sic)' (Alexander 2006: 43). It is this capacity and ability to engender a solidary sphere, while at the same time thinking of ourselves in multiple ways as 'multiply situated selves' (Sandel 2005: 34) that determines the extent to which we extend openness or closure to civil and anti-civil sentiments arising within civil society or coming from outside—and it is questionable.

For my purposes, I base my arguments on the view that boundaries are demarcation lines or borders that signify normatively, symbolically and physically spaces or territories of particular meanings and that the civil sphere is itself a bounded space. Concomitantly, the civil power of the news is exercised in the way it denotes and reports particular meanings given to 'our' invariant civil concerns of identity, legitimacy and risk as they are variously expressed in public sentiment. In essence, I shall argue ahead that when the news regards an event as significant for any of these invariant civil concerns, it will extensively cover it. This coverage generates and contributes to the normative dimension of our civil boundaries and the way they are maintained. In other words, it is this process in the news of denoting and reporting which influences the 'nature' of the boundaries surrounding civil society, particularly the extent to which these boundaries change, or are fixed or flexible, permeable or impermeable. Boundaries are therefore contingent on the situational context, but are fluid and under negotiation and may change and accommodate different values and ideas at different times (Guibernau 2013). Ultimately, boundaries are 'relational' (Cohen 1985; Delaney 2005; Massey 2005),[33] and following Lefebvre (1991), they are both imagined and lived. The relationships at issue here are between, on the one hand, the civil sphere and the non civil spheres, and on the other hand, the clash within the civil sphere itself of civil and anti-civil forces and how these are played out (denoted and reported) in the news and how they subsequently contribute to the boundaries we maintain around civil society.

Thus, my argument is that the particular meanings given to our invariant civil concerns as expressed in public sentiment are interpreted in the news as articulations of the kind of civil boundaries 'we' wish to maintain with regard to the identities 'we' prize, the 'order of things we most value' and the risk 'we' wish to ameliorate or avoid (see Chapters 4 and 8). These civil boundaries are articulated through the way the news interprets 'our' spatial stories and they serve to retell the particular cultural, historical narrative and beliefs 'we' hold most dear. These stories are also contested (see Part II passim). Such spatial news stories, the imaginative geographies they use and the extent to which they are fairly reported in the news are contingent upon the amount of investigative investment, open-mindedness, accurate judgement about sources' accounts and sincerity and honesty that the teller of the event brings to its telling and the willingness and ability to discern and understand the disputed nature of the stories' story. The ways in which distinctions and boundaries are drawn and engender exclusion or inclusion in terms of different social and cultural categories are relevant to the ways in which civil boundary relationships are assessed and monitored in the news and how civil boundary maintenance actually works and manifests itself in any given context. In short, the extent to which views, values, actions or sentiments are able to enter and/or flourish within civil society is based upon a complex series of decisions and judgements made by both members of civil society and also by the factual media institutions of the civil sphere. Such judgements illustrate the extent to which civil societies extend hospitality and tolerance and reflect upon what is deemed to be civil and the extent to which anti-civil sentiments are allowed to dominate or inform civil society discourses and moral choices. In turn, these judgements determine the extent to which the news media exercise civil narrowness, intolerance, inflexibility or prejudice from fear of the other, dislike of the new and of change and correspondingly, the extent to which such narrowness goes unchallenged in the news and in public sentiment. Ultimately, it is how the news relates to the different aspects of public sentiment that is at issue in the balance of judgements that is achieved or not between what is reported by the news as civil or anti-civil. The news journalists who select stories from the overlapping points in public sentiment may themselves have a range of goals and aspirations that lie in conflict with, or may be in agreement with, those of the non-civil spheres and this is why a recognisably objective method of reporting such stories (see Chapter 2) is an important element of the civil power of the news. News journalists have to be seen to be able to exercise judgement about the activities of the non-civil spheres (e.g. the correct use of a public office) and recognise that just because the analytical distinction can be made between the different aspirations of the distinct spheres, this does not necessarily mean that the non-civil spheres can be seen as simply a negative and antagonistic force always in conflict with the civil sphere. The boundary relations between the civil and non-civil spheres are continually in a state of flux and negotiation and, as we will see, news journalism has to take an objective approach when assessing these boundary relations. It is only through the deployment of an objective approach to reporting that news journalists can demonstrate fairness, balance and appropriate scepticism when receiving information from sources with conflicting interests.

As a distinct set of civil concerns belonging only to the civil sphere, the mediation of the three invariant civil concerns does not include events which remain solely within the non-civil spheres of politics and the state, the economy and markets, the police, family life, religion, etc. According to Alexander (2006, in particular), where there is an overlap between civil concerns and events in the non-civil spheres, it is because there is an incursion of the non-civil into civil society which is disputed or disapproved of by some or all members of civil society (when for example the police are seen to behave in a manner that is seen to go beyond their remit, or government actions are disputed, or organisations such as banks or hospitals affect or have the potential to affect peoples' lives). Where there is a welcome incursion of non-civil interests into civil society, this is generally where particular value sets or activities are in agreement around particular issues, for example, when religious organisations provide welfare or refuge, or in the realm of state/formal politics where welfare benefits are improved, or civil liberties increased, or where states exercise what are seen as appropriate measures to protect their citizens from harm. These interactions between civil society and the non-civil spheres presuppose an active and vibrant civil society and the inevitability of conflict and dispute between the civil and non-civil spheres and within civil society itself as our invariant civil concerns are articulated, resisted and ignored, or are addressed and dealt with by the news.[34]

The factual news media has the potential to foster civil independence of thought and action (which may on occasion sit uneasily with existing democratic processes and aspirations in any given context) as well as engage with what is seen to be just and what is unjust. Accordingly, at the centre of interest for my analysis of the civil power of the news are the detailed and specific characteristics and roles of particular factual communicative institutions of civil society, namely the news media which provide news through the practices of news journalism and which manifest themselves in different forms and arrangements.

Finally and as a matter of clarity, one caveat needs to be issued. News journalism in its myriad forms has generally been understood as emanating from traditional news media organisations; indeed, the vast majority of original news reporting still emerges from traditional news providers[35] (Newman et al. 2018) who publish across the platforms of print, broadcasting and online/mobile. In contemporary settings, these also include and incorporate online sources and so-called citizen journalism into their news, although the degree to which this done seems to vary from organisation to organisation.[36] Also highly relevant are alternative news media both traditional and new, relatively new news providers such as Vice News (launched in 2013 on YouTube) and Buzz Feed (which started out as a viral content company) and older online-only news providers such as Huffington Post (launched in 2005) as well as mobile first organisations such as Quartz, as well as sundry news-related blogs and vlogs, online videos and other material from a variety of sources such as Twitter and Facebook which become available to the public through the constant recycling of news provided by traditional and newer news providers. The recycling of news that is undertaken by the public via social media, through sharing, tweeting with commentary and retweeting, may even in theory demonstrate a new kind of 'audience power'. On this reading, the potential benefit of public intervention in the news is that it keeps journalists alert to mistakes, shortcuts and bad practices, as well as alerting them to public viewpoints and interests in relation to certain issues and events. Or in Alexander's (2016: 2) terms, 'new technologies can be, and are being, shaped to sustain value commitments, not only undermine them'. The recent concern for the dubious term 'fake news' has, amongst other things, demonstrated an abiding attachment to an ideal form of news journalism (discussed ahead) and in some quarters a demand for a genuine commitment to traditional journalistic practices of objectivity, truth telling and accuracy across all platforms. Though in all cases how we perceive our civil boundaries through the news is at issue.

6 Summary

The civil sphere is both deeply communicative and institutionally grounded. It is a space of contestation where the civil and non-civil spheres rival each other and clash, where its institutions are riven with civil and anti-civil forces. At its best, it is a bounded space which values social criticism, democratic integration, civility, justice, reciprocity and mutual respect; at its worst, it is dominated by selfishness, greed and fear. It has as its popular voice public sentiment and this too is riven between good and bad arguments, open and closed outlooks, and generous and mean attitudes. The civil sphere is a space constituted by 'we-ness' and 'we' have invariant civil concerns. These concerns form the basis of the civil character of public sentiment. The news is influenced by public sentiment and it also influences public sentiment in a cycle of mutual dependency. This cycle of mutual dependency needs to be properly understood.

To this end, Chapters 2, 3 and 4 are concerned respectively with: the civil ideal of the news and its interaction with the everyday reality of the newsroom, the public's invariant civil concerns and whether and when the news promotes civil or anti-civil values and what type of cardinal civil boundaries the news eventually endorses. Part II turns to a more empirical and methodological approach to demonstrate how the news actually arrives at this endorsement.

To begin to understand these compound and overlapping arguments, we start in Chapter 2 with the civil ideal of news.

Notes

1. Geuss (2016: 51) defines the meaning of 'we' in two distinct ways: First, as referring '*singillatim* to each individual in some notional group' (a characteristic of ethics) and second, as applied to '*cunctim*, that is, to a collective subject of some kind' (a characteristic of politics). In this book, the term 'we' refers to the collective 'we' of civil society, i.e. *cunctim*.
2. Tocqueville distinguishes between formal and informal democracy. The former comprises of political-democratic institutions and elections held every few years and is seen to prevent the people from getting what they want immediately. The latter, informal democracy, constitutes specific channels that enables people to get their way more quickly and outside of formal democratic procedures. For Tocqueville, informal democracy consists of three kinds of associations: First, permanent associations; second, political associations, that is voluntary groups in which citizens would come together to advance political causes and ideologies—the biggest political associations were political parties—and third, civil associations meaning religious, moral, intellectual, commercial groups and trade unions, the press and newspapers. Tocqueville believes that associations could provide an intermediate sphere between the central state and civil society. Through associations, citizens are enabled to participate in politics and to decide local affairs for themselves. The idea is that anything should be decided at the level—local, regional or national—that is most appropriate, that is closest to the decision that is to be taken. In contemporary terms, Tocqueville believes in the principle of subsidiarity. However, Tocqueville is also a frightened democrat who fears the 'cultural failings of mass society' brought about by democratic despotism and the tyranny of the majority which is a form of moral and intellectual despotism that is uniform, omnipresent and inescapable: 'It does not tyrannize, it hinders, compromises, enervates, dazes, and finally reduces each nation to being nothing more than a herd of timid and industrious

animals of which the government is the shepherd' (Tocqueville 2012 [1840]: 1252). On Tocqueville's understanding of civil society, see also Mansfield and Winthrop (2001), Villa (2006), and Ryan (2012).
3. And very importantly for Alexander's (2006)—but not as much for my argument—such intrusions can be 'repaired' often through the impetus emanating from social movements, political activism or civil protests.
4. Kant (1991 [1784]) distinguishes between a man's public use of reason and a man's private use of reason. The former is absolutely free in order to promote Enlightenment and the latter is narrowly restricted and is exercised by someone 'in a particular civil post or office' (ibid.). What this means is that those in office have to obey orders (whether they are disagreed with or not) when exercising this role and adhere to any protocols attached to it. When not exercising this role, man is free to question, debate and discuss any matter of interest. Waldron (2012) makes a similar point when he argues that freedom of speech in the form of racial epithets and discriminatory language can be restricted in the workplace (or on campuses) in order to preserve equality and collegiality.
5. Alexander (2006) uses the term 'civil power' to refer to the power and influence that civil society has regarding the non-civil spheres and particularly with the regard to the construction of state power.
6. Which as I hope to show includes both public and commercial news media. On the latter, see Alexander (2006: 583 n35).
7. Although Alexander (2006: 74) uses the term 'public opinion', he equally recognises that 'public opinion consists of factual accounts, emotional responses, and moral evaluations'.
8. Tocqueville (2012 [1840]) equally speaks about the need for newspapers to publish sentiments and principles, i.e. to engage with the readers. He is more optimistic about the contribution of public sentiment to democracy in Vol I and than in Vol II.
9. Bentham (1989: 283) believes in the progressiveness and maturity of public opinion. His idea of a Public Opinion Tribunal defined as '… a fictional tribunal the existence of which is (…) feigned under the pressure of inevitable necessity for the purpose of discourse to designate the imaginary tribunal or judiciary by which the punishments and rewards of which the popular or moral sanction is composed are applied' and based on the belief that public opinion was capable of engaging critically with issues of public interest. Lippmann (1993: 54) also recognises the existence of issues publics but argued 'that normally men as members of a public will not be well informed, continuously interested, nonpartisan, creative or executive (…) [and that they are] interested only when events have been melodramatised as a conflict'. In contrast, for Dewey (1954 [1927]: 137), the public is simply 'too diffused and scattered and too intricate in composition'.

10. Philosophers like Habermas and Rawls are quite aware of the limitations of thought experiments regarding ideal rational communicative and discursive settings and the true nature of public sentiment.
11. For a normative Republican theory of democratic control through public involvement and participation, see Pettit (1997, 2012). On civic virtue, see Sandel (1996). For a more sociological account of the value of civic virtue and reciprocal social relationships, see Putnam (2000).
12. I am not suggesting that political philosophy lacks realism regarding the issue of the constituent features of the public's capacity for argument and understanding.
13. Habermas (1995: 117) argues that in 'an inclusive and noncoercive rational discourse among free and equal participants, everyone is required to take their perspective of everyone else' and that it is from 'this interlocking of perspectives' that a 'we-perspective' emerges.
14. Empirical data gathering about journalistic practices has been growing exponentially over the last twenty years as journalism itself has emerged as a field of study. See Blumler and Cushion (2013) for a detailed overview.
15. A point well recognised by those who advocate public deliberation as an antidote or corrective to public ignorance and intolerance and, following on from such ignorance and intolerance, the usual combination of public prejudice and moral righteousness. See below Dewey (1954 [1927]) on communicative democracy and on democratic deliberation generally see Bohman and Rehg (1997), Cohen (1997, 1998), Dryzek (2000, 2008, 2012), Habermas (2006), and Held (2006). On the EU's attempts at deliberative democracy see Fishkin (2009), Saurugger (2010), and Pukallus (2016, 2019).
16. See Krause (2008) on the importance of considering 'civil passions' including the public's attachment to shared values. See also Berezin (2001, 2005) and Nussbaum (2013) on emotions in politics.
17. See Harrison (2010).
18. See Festenstein (1997, 2014).
19. Dewey (1954 [1927]: cf. 167) deeply believes in the need for full publicity and free and systematic communication as the means for a society in engage in anything worthy of the name social inquiry, a democratically undertaken community-based problem-solving that sought to confirm and check expert advice on public policies and to try and persuade publics.
20. See Lippmann (1922) and Festenstein (1997).
21. Grant (2014: 411) notes that 'A fourth [social] imaginary - bills and charters of rights - is cited by Taylor as a less mature addition to the first three'.
22. See Taylor (2004).

23. Taylor (2007: 187) further distinguishes the spatial characteristics of the public sphere into 'topical common space' (the same locale or venue) and 'meta-topical space' (mediated space) with the latter increasingly more significant for common understandings and normative evaluations in modern societies.
24. With regard to the essentially deliberative nature of the public sphere, both Habermas (2006: 94, citing Hoffmann and Levack 1949: 106) and Taylor (2007: 190 and 796–797 n32) cite Burke for his views on the 'private reflection of public affairs as rational' and that 'every man thinks he has a right to form and a right to deliver an opinion on them. They sift, examine and discuss them. They are curious, eager, attentive and jealous; and by making such matters the daily subjects of their thoughts and discoveries, vast numbers contract a very tolerable knowledge of them and some a very considerable one. … In free countries, there is often found more real public wisdom and sagacity on shops and manufactories than in the cabinets of princes in countries where none dares to have an opinion until he comes into them. Your whole importance, therefore, depends upon a constant, discreet use of your own reason'.
25. In so far as social imaginaries are both the background to our modern moral order and the way we assess practices as conforming (or not) to that modern moral order, there is little room for critique, radicalism or basic civil changes—on this see Grant (2014: cf. 413).
26. See Lamont and Molnar (2002) on the relationship between symbolic and social boundaries.
27. See Lamont et al. (2015).
28. Durkheim (1971 [1915]: 37–38) defines societies' symbolic boundaries as constituted by the sharing of a common definition of the sacred and the profane, of similar rules of conducts and a common compliance to rituals and interdictions that define the internal bonds within a community. In a similar fashion, Alexander and Smith (1993) regard the binary distinction sacred and profane as delineating emotionally charged symbols, which culturally frame what is ultimately regarded as good and bad.
29. See Parsons (1969) and Weber (2013 [1978]).
30. What I argue is that at its core the civil sphere is both a space of inclusion (of universalising solidarity) and exclusion (spaces of exclusion derived from Schmitt's (2007 [1931]) and subsequently Agamben's (2005) use of the phrase 'state of exception' which refers to the fact that for both thinkers political communities and government are based on exclusion. Gregory (2004) has adapted this phrase as 'spaces of exception' which helps to show how the spatial stories and imaginative geographies (Said 2003; Gregory 2004) and the stories 'we' tell about ourselves are as

important as ever and how exclusion from such space is an increasingly modern phenomenon.
31. See Urry (2010: 347) who attempts to develop a sociology of mobility which studies 'the diverse mobilities of peoples, objects, images, information, and wastes; and of the complex interdependencies between, and social consequences of, such diverse mobilities'.
32. Walls, for example, built by different regimes are legitimated in different ways but they can also amount to a lethal cartography (Gregory 2004) where borders become a matter of life and death or serve to starkly demarcate extremely different qualities of life and life chances (also Brown 2010; Thrift 1996). See also Billig (1995), Slavtcheva-Petkova (2014) for a critique of Billig (1995); Beall (2002) and Brown (2010) on walls as demarcations of identity; Delanty and Jones (2002), Goldberger (2009), and Wennberg (2015) on architecture and identity.
33. From the 1970s on space and boundaries were no longer understood as disconnected from human and social relations. Rather, it became increasingly accepted that the spatial and the social were intrinsically linked or, in other words, that 'space is a social construct' (Massey 1984: 3; also Morley and Robins 1995). Space and boundaries were therefore conceived of as contested, complex, fluid, dynamic, uncertain, mouldable and as imbued with historical, symbolic, social or cultural meaning (Lefebvre 1991). In this way, space is inter-relational and contains multiple identities and narratives which are 'always under construction' (Massey 2005: 9). See also Delanty's (2006, 2007) and Berezin and Schain's (2003) research on borders and Delaney's work on territory (2005).
34. Where a vibrant and active civil society does not exist because democratic cultures are absent or non-civil spheres are too dominating and boundaries between the spheres too weak that the people could not feasibly form a collective public (Perrin 2014), limited forms of civil action in the form of petition, mobilisation, strikes and protest may still be apparent around a limited number of events and issues.
35. See Newman et al. (2018).
36. Citizen journalism has been seen by some to challenge the traditional sole gatekeeping role of news selection (Cassidy 2007). Gatekeeping, which was first envisaged by Lewin (1947) and then adapted by White (1950), Shoemaker (1991), Shoemaker et al. (2001), and Shoemaker and Vos (2009), has moved in recent years towards something that has been termed a 'gatewatching' model (Bachmann and Harlow 2012; Bruns 2005; Yu 2011) where the control of information by traditional journalists is less routinised leaving them in a curating role, where they communicate what is judged to be the most relevant information rather

than gathering it all by themselves (Spence et al. 2013; Domingo et al. 2008; Harrison 2010; Hermida and Thurman 2008; Paulussen and Ugille 2008; Thurman 2008; Singer 2010; Singer and Ashman 2009: 18). News organisations' engagement with user-generated material, or citizen journalism as it is most often termed (Farinosi and Treré 2014; Hellmueller and Li 2014; Lewis et al. 2010), varies from story type to story type (i.e. across different news organisations), with some remaining cautious about the extent to which citizen material is judged to be trustworthy, relying on professional and traditional routines and remaining as primary gatekeepers (McConnell 2016). Other scholarship has indicated that in the case of crisis coverage online journalism may be reducing the news media's reliance on such sources relying more heavily instead on unofficial sources (Fontenot et al. 2009; Reynolds and Barnett 2003; Wigley and Fontenot 2009; Thurman 2015).

BIBLIOGRAPHY

Agamben, G. (2005). *State of Exception*. Chicago: University of Chicago Press.
Alexander, J. (2006). *The Civil Sphere*. Oxford: Oxford University Press.
Alexander, J. (2007). On the Interpretation of the Civil Sphere: Understanding and Contention in Contemporary Social Science. *The Sociological Quarterly, 48*(4), 641–659.
Alexander, J. (2008). Civil Sphere, State, and Citizenship: Replying to Turner and the Fear of Enclavement. *Citizenship Studies, 12*(2), 185–194.
Alexander, J. (2015). Nine Theses on *The Civil Sphere*. In P. Kivisto & G. Sciortino (Eds.), *Solidarity, Justice, and Incorporation: Thinking Through The Civil Sphere*. Oxford: Oxford University Press.
Alexander, J. (2016). Introduction: Journalism, Democratic Culture, and Creative Reconstruction. In J. Alexander, E. Butler-Breese, & M. Luengo (Eds.), *The Crisis of Journalism Reconsidered: Democratic Culture, Professional Codes, Digital Future* (pp. 1–28). Cambridge: Cambridge University Press.
Alexander, J. C., & Smith, P. (1993). The Discourse of American Civil Society: A New Proposal for Cultural Studies. *Theory and Society, 22*(2), 151–207.
Anderson, B. (1991). *Imagined Communities: Reflections on the Origin and Spread of Nationalism*. London: Verso.
Bachmann, I., & Harlow, S. (2012). Opening the Gates. *Journalism Practice, 6*(2), 217–232.
Beall, J. (2002). *The People Behind the Walls: Insecurity, Identity and Gated Communities in Johannesburg* (Crisis States Research Centre Working Papers Series 1, 10). London, UK: Crisis States Research Centre, London School of Economics and Political Science. Available at: http://eprints.lse.ac.uk/2932/. Accessed 20 July 2016.

Bentham, J. (1989). *First Principles Preparatory to the Constitutional Code* (S. Philip, Ed.). Oxford: Clarendon.

Berezin, M. (2001). Emotion and Political Identity: Mobilizing Affection for the Polity. In J. Jasper, J. Goodwin, & F. Poletta (Eds.), *Passionate Politics: Emotion and Social Movements* (pp. 83–98). Chicago: University of Chicago Press.

Berezin, M. (2005). Emotions and the Economy. In N. J. Smelser & R. Swedberg (Eds.), *Handbook of Economic Sociology* (2nd ed., pp. 109–127). New York and Princeton: Russell Sage Foundation and Princeton University Press.

Berezin, M., & Schain, M. (Eds.). (2003). *Europe Without Borders: Re-mapping Territory, Citizenship and Identity in a Transnational Age*. London: Sage.

Billig, M. (1995). *Banal Nationalism*. London: Sage.

Blumler, J. G., & Cushion, S. (2013). Normative Perspectives on Journalism Studies: Stock-Taking and Future Directions. *Journalism, 15*(3), 259–272.

Bohman, J., & Rehg, W. (Eds.). (1997). *Deliberative Democracy*. Cambridge: MIT Press.

Brown, W. (2010). *Walled States, Waning Sovereignty*. Cambridge: MIT Press.

Bruns, A. (2005). *Gatewatching, Not Gatekeeping: Collaborative Online News*. Available at: http://citeseerx.ist.psu.edu/viewdoc/download?doi=10.1.1.321.7516&rep=rep1&type=pdf. Accessed 11 February 2018.

Cassidy, W. P. (2007). Online News Credibility: An Examination of the Perceptions of Newspaper Journalists. *Journal of Computer-Mediated Communication, 12*(2), 478–498.

Cohen, A. (1985). *The Symbolic Construction of Community*. Chichester: Ellis Horwood.

Cohen, J. (1997). Deliberation and Democratic Legitimacy. In J. Bohman & W. Rehg (Eds.), *Deliberative Democracy* (pp. 67–91). Cambridge: MIT Press.

Cohen, J. (1998). Democracy and Liberty. In J. Elster (Ed.), *Deliberative Democracy* (pp. 185–231). Cambridge: Cambridge University Press.

Delaney, D. (2005). *Territory: A Short Introduction*. Oxford: Wiley-Blackwell.

Delanty, G. (2006). Borders in a Changing Europe: An Analysis of Recent Trends. *Comparative European Politics, 4*(2), 183–202.

Delanty, G. (2007). Peripheries and Borders in a Post-Western Europe. *Eurozine*. Available at: http://www.eurozine.com/articles/2007-08-29-delanty-en.html. Accessed 20 July 2016.

Delanty, G., & Jones, P. (2002). European Identity and Architecture. *European Journal of Social Theory, 5*(4), 453–466.

Dewey, J. (1954 [1927]). *The Public and Its Problems*. Athens: Ohio University Press/Swallow Press.

Domingo, D., Quandt, T., Heinonen, A., Paulussen, S., Singer, J. B., & Vujnovic, M. (2008). Participatory Journalism Practices in the Media

and Beyond: An International Comparative Study of Initiatives in Online Newspapers. *Journalism Practice, 2*(3), 326–342.
Dryzek, J. S. (2000). *Deliberative Democracy and Beyond: Liberals, Critics, Contestations*. Oxford: Oxford University Press.
Dryzek, J. S. (2008). *Discursive Democracy: Politics, Policy, and Political Science*. Cambridge: Cambridge University Press.
Dryzek, J. S. (2012). *Foundations and Frontiers of Deliberative Governance*. Oxford: Oxford University Press.
Durkheim, E. (1971 [1915]). *The Elementary Forms of Religious Life*. London: George Allen & Unwin.
Epstein, S. (1992). Gay Politics, Ethnic Identity: The Limits of Social Constructionism. In E. Stein (Ed.), *Forms of Desire* (pp. 239–293). London: Routledge.
Erikson, K. T. (2003). On the Sociology of Deviance. In P. Bean (Ed.), *Crime: Critical Concepts in Sociology* (pp. 32–50). London: Routledge.
Farinosi, M., & Treré, E. (2014). Challenging Mainstream Media, Documenting Real Life and Sharing with the Community: An Analysis of the Motivations for Producing Citizen Journalism in a Post-disaster City. *Global Media and Communication, 10*(1), 73–92.
Festenstein, M. (1997). The Ties of Communication: Dewey on Ideal and Political Democracy. *History of Political Thought, 18*(1), 104–124.
Festenstein, M. (2014). Dewey's Political Philosophy. In E. N. Zalta (Ed.), *The Stanford Encyclopedia of Philosophy* (Spring ed.). http://plato.stanford.edu/archives/spr2014/entries/dewey-political/. Accessed 5 April 2016.
Fishkin, J. (2009). *When the People Speak: Deliberative Democracy and Public Consultation*. Oxford: Oxford University Press.
Fontenot, M., Boyle, K., & Gallagher, A. H. (2009). Comparing Type of Sources in Coverage of Katrina, Rita. *Newspaper Research Journal, 30*(1), 21–33.
Geuss, R. (2016). *Reality and Its Dreams*. Harvard: Harvard University Press.
Goldberger, P. (2009). *Why Architecture Matters*. New Haven: Yale University Press.
Grant, J. (2014). On the Critique of Political Imaginaries. *European Journal of Political Theory, 13*(4), 408–426.
Gregory, D. (2004). *The Colonial Present*. Malden, MA: Blackwell.
Guibernau, M. (2013). *Belonging: Solidarity and Division in Modern Societies*. Cambridge: Polity Press.
Habermas, J. (1995). Reconciliation Through the Public Use of Reason: Remarks on John Rawls's Political Liberalism. *The Journal of Philosophy, 92*(3), 109–131.
Habermas, J. (1996). *Between Facts and Norms*. Cambridge: MIT Press.
Habermas, J. (2006 [1989]). *The Structural Transformation of the Public Sphere*. Cambridge: Polity Press.

Hall, S. (1996). *Questions of Cultural Identity*. London: Sage.
Harrison, J. (2010). User-Generated Content and Gatekeeping at the BBC Hub. *Journalism Studies*, 11(2), 243–256.
Held, D. (2006). *Models of Democracy* (3rd ed.). Cambridge: Polity Press.
Hellmueller, L., & Li, Y. (2014). Contest over Content: A Longitudinal Study of the CNN iReport Effect on the Journalistic Field. *Journalism Practice*, 9(5), 617–633.
Hermida, A., & Thurman, N. (2008). A Clash of Cultures: The Integration of User-Generated Content Within Professional Journalistic Frameworks at British Newspaper Websites. *Journalism Practice*, 2(3), 343–356.
Hoffmann, R. J. S., & Levack, P. (Eds.). (1949). *Burke's Politics*. New York: A. A. Knopf.
Kant, I. (1991 [1784]). *What Is Enlightenment in Kant Political Writings* (R. Hans Siegbert, Ed.). Cambridge: Cambridge University Press.
Krause, N. (2008). *Civil Passions: Moral Sentiments and Democratic Deliberation*. Princeton: Princeton University Press.
Lamont, M., & Molnar, V. (2002). The Study of Boundaries in the Social Sciences. *Annual Review of Sociology, 28*, 167–195.
Lamont, M., Pachucki, S., & Pendergrass, M. C. (2015). Symbolic Boundaries. In J. Wright (Ed.), *International Encyclopaedia of Social and Behavioural Sciences* (pp. 850–855). Oxford: Elsevier.
Lefebvre, H. (1991). *The Production of Space*. Malden, MA: Blackwell.
Lewin, K. (1947). Frontiers in Group Dynamics: Concept, Method and Reality in Science; Social Equilibria and Social Change. *Human Relations*, 1(1), 5–41.
Lewis, S. C., Kaufhold, K., & Lasorsa, D. L. (2010). Thinking About Citizen Journalism: The Philosophical and Practical Challenges of User-Generated Content for Community Newspapers. *Journalism Practice*, 4(2), 163–179.
Lippmann, W. (1922). *Public Opinion*. New York: Macmillan.
Lippmann, W. (1993). *The Phantom Public*. New Brunswick and London: Transaction Publishers.
Mansfield, H., & Winthrop, D. (2001). What Tocqueville Says to Liberals and Conservatives Today. *Perspectives on Political Science*, 30(4), 203–205.
Massey, D. (1984). Introduction: Geography Matters. In D. Massey & J. Allen (Eds.), *Geography Matters!* (pp. 1–11). Cambridge: Cambridge University Press.
Massey, D. (2005). *For Space*. London: Sage.
McConnell, S. (2016). *"This Place...!" Challenge and Change to Journalistic Identity in a Digital Age: A Study of Three London Local Newsrooms* (PhD thesis). University of Sheffield.
Morley, D., & Robins, K. (1995). *Spaces of Identity: Global Media, Electronic Landscapes and Cultural Boundaries*. London: Routledge.

Newman, N., with Fletcher, R., Kalogeropoulos, A., Levy, D. A. L., & Kleis Nielsen, R. (2018). *Reuters Institute Digital News Report 2018*. http://media.digitalnewsreport.org/wp-content/uploads/2018/06/digital-news-report-2018.pdf?x89475.

Nussbaum, M. (1996). Aristotle on Emotions and Rational Persuasion. In A. Rorty (Ed.), *Essays on Aristotle's Rhetoric* (pp. 303–323). Berkeley: University of California Press.

Nussbaum, M. (2013). *Political Emotions: Why Love Matters For Justice*. Cambridge, MA: Belknap Press of Harvard University Press.

Parsons, T. (1969). *Politics and Social Structure*. New York: The Free Press.

Paulussen, S., & Ugille, P. (2008). User Generated Content in the Newsroom: Professional and Organisational Constraints on Participatory Journalism. *Westminster Papers in Communication and Culture, 5*(2), 24–41.

Perrin, A. (2014). *American Democracy: From Tocqueville to Town Halls to Twitter*. Cambridge: Polity Press.

Pettit, P. (1997). *Republicanism: A Theory of Freedom and Government*. Oxford: Oxford University Press.

Pettit, P. (2012). *On the People's Terms: A Republican Theory and Model of Democracy*. Cambridge: Cambridge University Press.

Pukallus, S. (2016). *Representations of European Citizenship Since 1951*. Basingstoke: Palgrave Macmillan.

Pukallus, S. (2019). Single-Issue Ratifiers or Political Deliberators? The Strategic Interpretation and Application of the Participatory Norm and the Creation of Publics by the European Commission (1992–2009). *International Review of Public Policy, 1*(1:1), 88–103.

Putnam, R. (2000). *Bowling Alone*. New York: Simon & Schuster.

Reynolds, A., & Barnett, B. (2003). This Just in … How National TV News Handled the Breaking "Live" Coverage of September 11. *Journalism & Mass Communication Quarterly, 80*(3), 689–703.

Ryan, A. (2012). *On Politics*. London: W. W. Norton.

Said, E. (2003). *Orientalism*. London: Penguin Books.

Sandel, M. (1996). *Democracy's Discontent: America in Search of a Public Philosophy*. Harvard: Harvard University Press.

Sandel, M. (2005). *Public Philosophy: Essays on Morality and Politics*. Cambridge, MA and London: Harvard University Press.

Saurugger, S. (2010). The Social Construction of the Participatory Turn: The Emergence of a Norm in the European Union. *European Journal of Political Research, 49*(4), 471–495.

Schlesinger, P. (1991). Wishful Thinking: Cultural Politics, Media, and Collective Identities in Europe. *Journal of Communication, 43*(2), 6–17.

Schmitt, C. (2007 [1931]). *The Concept of the Political*. Chicago: University of Chicago Press.

Shoemaker, P. (1991). *Gatekeeping*. Newbury Park, CA: Sage.
Shoemaker, P., Eichholz, M., Kim, E., & Wrigley, B. (2001). Individual and Routine Forces in Gatekeeping. *Journalism & Mass Communication Quarterly, 78*(2), 233–246.
Shoemaker, P., & Vos, T. P. (2009). *Gatekeeping Theory*. London: Routledge.
Singer, J. (2010). Journalism Ethics Amid Structural Change. *Daedalus, 139*(2), 89–99.
Singer, J., & Ashman, I. (2009). 'Comment Is Free, but Facts Are Sacred': Usergenerated Content and Ethical Constructs at the Guardian. *Journal of Mass Media Ethics, 24*(1), 3–21.
Slavtcheva-Petkova, V. (2014). Rethinking Banal Nationalism: Banal Americanism, Europeanism, and the Missing Link Between Media Representations and Identities. *International Journal of Communication, 8*, 43–61.
Spence, P. R., Lachlan, K. A., Westerman, D., & Spates, S. A. (2013). Where the Gates Matter Less: Ethnicity and Perceived Source Credibility in Social Media Health Messages. *Howard Journal of Communications, 24*(1), 1–16.
Tajfel, H., & Turner, J. C. (1979). An Integrative Theory of Intergroup Conflict. In W. G. Austin & S. Worchel (Eds.), *The Social Psychology of Intergroup Relations* (pp. 33–37). Monterey, CA: Brooks/Cole.
Taylor, C. (2004). *Modern Social Imaginaries*. Durham, NC and London: Duke University Press.
Taylor, C. (2007). *A Secular Age*. Harvard: Harvard University Press.
Thrift, N. (1996). *Spatial Formations*. London: Sage.
Thurman, N. (2008). Forums for Citizen Journalists? Adoption of User-Generated Content Initiatives by Online News Media. *New Media & Society, 10*(1), 139–157.
Thurman, N. (2015). Journalism, Gatekeeping, and Interactivity. In S. Coleman & D. Freelon (Eds.), *A Handbook of Digital Politics* (pp. 357–374). Cheltenham: Edward Elgar.
Tocqueville, A. (2012 [1840]). *Democracy in America* (Vol. 2, E. Nolla, Ed.). Carmel, IN: Liberty Fund Inc.
Urry, J. (2010). Mobile Sociology. *The British Journal of Sociology, 61*(1), 347–366.
Villa, D. (2006). Tocqueville and Civil Society. In C. Welsh (Ed.), *The Cambridge Companion to Tocqueville* (pp. 216–244). Cambridge: Cambridge University Press.
Waldron, J. (2012). *The Harm in Hate Speech*. Cambridge, MA: Harvard University Press.
Weber, M. (2013 [1978]). *Economy and Society* (Vol. I, G. Roth & C. Wittich, Eds.). Berkeley: University of California Press.

Wennberg, H. (2015). *In Place: A Study of Building and Identity.* Adam Architecture. Available at: http://www.adamarchitecture.com/images/academic/books/In%20Place-INTBAU-2015.pdf. Accessed 20 July 2016.

White, D. M. (1950). The "Gate Keeper": A Case Study in the Selection of News. *Journalism & Mass Communication Quarterly, 27*(4), 383–390.

Wigley, S., & Fontenot, M. (2009). Where Media Turn During Crises: A Look at Information Subsidies and the Virginia Tech Shootings. *Electronic News, 3*(2), 94–108.

Woodward, K. (1997). *Identity and Difference.* London: Sage.

Yu, J. (2011). Beyond Gatekeeping: J-blogging in China. *Journalism, 12*(4), 379–393.

CHAPTER 2

The Civil Ideal of the News

1 Overview: The Civil Ideal of the News

The civil ideal of the news is significant because it provides the civil sphere with a powerful symbol of itself—a symbol based upon two critical and related elements (a) trustworthiness and (b) liberal ideals. It is a symbol manifest in a vocabulary that seems to naturally surround the ideal of news journalism: at one level specifically through the language and images of truth telling, fact finding and holding to account the powerful and at another, more general level, through the language and images of another equally attractive set of liberal ideals associated with democracy and justice, liberty and equality, solidarity and individualism. It is these two elements of the civil ideal of news that we must first investigate if for no other reason than to contextualise the actual civil power of the news and to show the contradictory tensions that reside within the civil power of the news as it is played out in reality (see Chapter 3). Of course, the usual caveats apply: the news can only ever fulfil its civil ideal when editorial integrity is observed and news journalism is independent from control by vested and selfish interests. It fulfils its civil ideal when it works to the benefit of a vibrant civil society and contributes both to civility and to civil identities; when it is believed in as truth telling and as objective and therefore trustworthy; when it is perceived to be serving liberal ideals; and finally when it is accepted as genuinely homologous to the world. And (depending on how pessimistic you are) we know that these conditions only happen occasionally if at all. In other words, the

© The Author(s) 2019
J. Harrison, *The Civil Power of the News*,
https://doi.org/10.1007/978-3-030-19381-2_2

civil ideal requires that news be solely orientated to citizens and their concerns and has as an outcome a solidarising intent and civilising effect. Naïve as this ideal may sound, within it (as I hope to show in the next two sections) lie the key elements of the news's actual civil power.

There exists in contemporary civil society a culture replete with a variety of highly charged normative symbols of civil life. Indeed, it is a curious fact that what immediately stands out when considering the role of the news is the diverse and different ways the civil ideal of the news is constantly alluded to. It is symbolically represented in the charters that founded public service broadcasting organisations,[1] the trappings of professional self-regard—notably the profession's own awards and prizes that recognise excellent 'public spirited' and 'public service' journalism, in some regulatory approaches and policies that aim particularly to serve 'the public interest' as well as in fiction and notably in films.[2] Finally, the civil ideal is found in news that is historically judged to have played 'a role in social and political struggles for justice and freedom' (Forde 2014: 573) for example in the context of the civil rights movement in 1960s America, or for political liberation. It is also to be found in global multi-stakeholder initiatives such as the 2012 UN Action Plan on the Safety of Journalists and the Issue of Impunity which, amongst other things, seeks to protect and prevent the normative force of journalism from being undermined. The civil ideal is also symbolised in the way news journalism presents and markets itself, how it represents its mission to the world and how it uses snappy phrases, titles and straplines.[3] These point to an essential, fundamental, basic and primordial sense of what news should be, namely that it is transparently homologous with the world (a mirror or window), important and historically relevant (paper of record, a first draft of history), a bringer of light and truth (shining light in dark corners, finding out what governments don't want you to know, watching the world, disclosing the world) as well as being honest and enduring (a fixed luminous point—like a star or a sun—that can be relied upon to help us find our way). Finally, other symbolic representations are to be found in the academy through the use of a morally evocative set of terms notably the fourth estate,[4] the public sphere, the public opinion tribunal and others.[5] Here, journalists are regarded as supervisors or stewards of liberal democracy. Overall, the normative force manifest in these symbolic representations typically emphasises serving 'the public interest' and sees in that a normative viewpoint which can go well beyond just the scrutiny of politicians and politics to include what we should value and preserve in the interests of civil solidarity, namely 'the kind of society in which people want to live, marked out by norms, values and achievements that they consider to be positive and important' (Edwards 2013: 8). Such symbols can therefore be read as encompassing the broader civil ideal of the news, namely the promotion and endorsement of civil values in liberal democratic political cultures. These civil values are solidarising in their force and intent and as such emphasise that civil interests are shared and that the formulation of collective publics who exercise civil independence in thought and behaviour is genuinely to be encouraged and desired.

Interestingly, these symbols are empirically incorporated in a professional ideal of news which is shared and believed in by many news journalists (even if articulated in a somewhat different way),[6] some politicians and many public intellectuals. It is a belief in an ideal of news which is in need of promotion or protection through the provision of public service communication channels; a merit good and wholly worthy of public subsidy[7]; a vital contributor to the stock of public knowledge or civic knowledge[8]; a redoubt against excessive commercialism that prizes the primacy of 'market efficiency' and 'consumer sovereignty'[9] as well as unscrupulous politicians and an increasingly corrupt and corrupting press.[10] Most impressively, and above all, it is valued by the public as something that should be adhered to, can be trusted and is anything but fake.[11]

For the public, the civil ideal of the news is premised on the desire, and it needs to be put no stronger than this, to simply know 'what is going on'. It is an explicit expectation that the public should be able to trust some organisation or someone in the news media to let them know about matters that concern them. In other words, people feel that there is a basic need or requirement to be able to trust some form of, and provider of, news[12]—that is, an organisation, an institution, a group of people that simply and straightforwardly acts as the 'people's witness' providing testimony which satisfies 'our unassuageable hunger to know what on earth is going on' (Inglis 2002: 376).[13] This is because one of the most basic facts of civil life is that 'for most members of civil society, and even for members of its institutional elites, the news is the only source of first-hand experience they will ever have about their fellow citizens, about their motives (…) the kind of relationships they form and the nature of the institutions they might potentially create' (Alexander 2006: 80, 2016: 1). To put the point negatively, the same demand to know what is going on is constantly opined in the numerous complaints and laments about the news's failures in calls for what the news should be, alongside what it is perceived to be, as numerous public opinion polls show. Public opinion polls also frequently provide evidence for the public's lack of trust in the news media to accurately report the news, and whilst the ideal of news may invite public trust, the opinion polls show a jaundiced view of partisan news. Finally, combining these different types of symbolic appeal and allusions to the value of the civil ideal of news, we can summarise accordingly: the civil ideal of the news coheres around its value in enabling 'us' to think in a more informed and critical way about things, and acts as an aid to conducting a 'civilised conversation'.[14]

I noted above that there are two key elements of the civil ideal of the news (a) trustworthiness and (b) liberal ideals. The former is achieved through the activity of truth telling and the use of an objective method, the latter is achieved when the news promotes the civil values of social criticism, democratic integration, civility, justice, reciprocity and mutual respect. Combined the two key elements form a completed picture of what the civil ideal of news journalism consists of and shows under which conditions it can be fulfilled. The civil ideal also clarifies how the news should understand its civil responsibility and obligations and how it should point 'us' in the right direction with regard to what 'we' should value and preserve in the face of non-civil and anti-civil interferences. Alternatively expressed, this ideal represents a way of selecting and producing a type of news that is trustworthy and it is how the news attempts to be seen as trustworthy that I now turn to.

2 Trustworthiness: Truth Telling and Objectivity

If there is a perception of a high level of correspondence between an event and its truthful mediation, then news may be seen as a reliable source of information through which one might make informed judgements (these informed judgements could of course be simply wrong, or open to criticism by those that disagree). If one believes the news account in question to be sufficiently homologous to the world and to be a reliable source of information, then there could be a correspondence between the news and one's own interests, views and concerns and one may withdraw or bestow trust on other institutions inside and outside civil society on the basis of such an account and be able to articulate the reasons for doing so. This is particularly the case if well-placed trust and mistrust grow out of shared knowledge and active inquiry rather than from blind acceptance. As O'Neill (2002: Lecture 4) argues: 'In judging whether to place our trust in others' words or undertakings, or to refuse that trust, we need information and we need the means to judge that information. To place trust reasonably we need to discover not only which claims or undertakings we are invited to trust, but what we might reasonably think about them'. The news invites our trust when it shows its ability to be truth telling and objective.

2.1 Truth Telling

In 1919, Weber wrote: 'Not everybody realizes that a really good journalistic accomplishment requires at least as much "genius" as any scholarly accomplishment, especially because of the necessity of producing at once and "on order", and because of the necessity of being effective, to be sure, under quite different conditions of production. It is almost never acknowledged that the responsibility of the journalist is far greater, and that the sense of responsibility of every honourable journalist is, on the average, not a bit lower than that of the scholar, but rather, as the war has shown, higher'. He was referring to the German press's critical reaction to the way the Kaiser, generals and politicians had conducted World War I. The extent of Weber's regard for such critical journalism extends to his recognition of political journalism's explanatory, investigative and truth telling role. For Lippmann (1920: 47), the news is 'the bible of Democracy' and news selection is 'priestly',[15] though he has been careful to separate news and truth as different things. For him (1922: 226), news is to signal an event, or make people aware of it, while 'truth is to bring to light hidden facts and to set them into relation with each other and make a picture of reality upon which men can act'. Of the two, my argument is more Weberian: in order to undertake truth telling in reports of the world, news should interrogate all claims and counterclaims, through the exercise of the practice of constative accuracy and interpretative sincerity. The constative force of news is that it reveals what is empirically the case and can easily be demonstrated as factually accurate, whilst the explanatory force of news is the interpretation of events undertaken sincerely and in a particular hermeneutic manner, one that, as I have argued elsewhere (Harrison 2007), is best understood as being driven by a simple 'logic of question and answer'. In other words, news has to be able to accommodate a range of contested views and accounts of issues and events. It is the extent to which news conveys these accurately and sincerely in a synoptic form that informs the perceptions the public have about the extent to which the news succeeds in achieving an homologous relationship to the world and which generates trust that the news is truthful. In this way, truth telling and trustworthiness are closely related. Of course, judgements about truth telling will be made by the public on a variety of criteria which form the basis by which a public does or does not trust that news reports are indeed truthful. However, perhaps the most important criterion is the public perception that a news organisation provides news which is consistently homologous to the world. If this is believed, then it is more likely that audiences will judge and treat news reports from this trusted source as an accurate and reliable source of information—one which provides the basis for civil or anti-civil judgements and for civil or anti-civil action (see ahead Chapter 4).

The pursuit of a truthful news account should be understood as a process or a continuing journey towards understanding, rather than reporting a series of unconnected (albeit accurate as far as they go) facts. In this vein, Rosenstiel (2013) reiterates that 'The Hutchins Committee on a free and responsible press [which] declared in 1947: "It is no longer enough to report the fact truthfully. It is now necessary to report the truth about the fact"'.[16] In short, the fact itself needs deeper consideration rather than for it to be taken as a given because it appears to be a simple fact. For Williams (2002), accuracy and sincerity are the core virtues of truth. Constative accuracy is the virtue of reporting how things are only when the report is the outcome of sufficient investigation—a sentiment we see expressed by journalists who argue that objective reporting is the best method to ensure that all facts and issues are fairly considered, weighed up and scrutinised. Achieving constative accuracy in any investigation 'lies in the skills and attitudes that resist the pleasure principle, in all its forms, from a gross need to believe the agreeable, to mere laziness in checking one's investigations' (ibid.: 125). It is a 'passion for getting it right' (ibid.: 126) and in relation to news journalism, 'getting it right' relies upon the news journalist's desire and ability to do so. The extent to which the journalist pursues accuracy is dependent upon what Williams refers to as 'attitudes, desires and wishes, the spirit of his attempts, the care that he takes' (ibid.: 127) and 'the methods that the investigator uses' (ibid.: 127); that is, the news journalist achieves accuracy through an effective investigation of contemporary events, which balances both the desire for truthfulness with an ethical justification of the methods that are used.

Interpretative sincerity, as part of truth telling, 'is the virtue of communicating only how you take things to be' (Blackburn 2007). Sincerity according to Williams 'merely implies that people say what they believe to be true' (2002, 2005: 154) and is 'centered on sustaining and developing relations with others that involve different kinds and degrees of trust' (2002: 121). At the very least, this involves journalists' expressing what they actually believe in the news report. It is 'trustworthiness in speech' (ibid.: 97), and by extension, in the written text or the online text. It is the disposition 'to make sure that any assertion one makes expresses a genuine belief' (ibid.). Sincerity is a disposition which, when shared, provides the grounds on which is built 'a modern understanding of what people deserve' (ibid.: 122) no matter how complicated or distant our relationship to another is. As Williams notes, sincerity is not out of place in 'social relations as they are constantly redefined in commercial society, those of privacy and intimacy as much as those of professional co-operation and rivalry' (ibid.).

Ideally and in order to be sincere, news reports should contain expressions of doubt when events or issues are not clear-cut. In other words, journalists and news providers should avoid misleading their audiences by withholding information or through excessive speculation. Instead of resorting to an assertive formula of reporting a set of disconnected facts and opposing viewpoints, a sincere interpreter should express her doubts in the news report itself and not stifle them, thereby indicating when all facts are not available, or where others' accounts are dubious. Sincerity also involves a certain type of courage to report what one believes to be truthful even when this may be discouraged or suppressed. Uncertainty, inability to express certain information and lack of clarity would therefore need to be shared with the audience. An important element of sincerity in this regard is the virtue of honesty in the exercise of reporting practices, whereby those who publish and provide news should not see themselves as having public sanction to act in illegal ways, or in ways that are deemed to go beyond acceptable levels of invasion of privacy, without a very strong public interest defence.[17] Interpretative sincerity in reporting therefore requires honesty and transparency in reporting practices, and when these are seen to have been transgressed audiences' distrust of the news media is likely to increase. Trust in the news media is easily lost. It is only by becoming a critical interpreter and by undertaking news reporting accurately and sincerely that news can distinguish itself from propaganda, which in part consists of the wilful distortion or suppression by the powerful of the spatial and temporal stories of the powerless. Equally, reporting details that contain only partial truths or cannot be confirmed as true, or where sources are dubious, where information is illegally obtained, or where the focus is on the private lives of individuals, for no other reason than for entertainment value, often results in news that cannot be distinguished from gossip—a fact that duly explains its popularity.

The two core virtues of truth—accuracy and sincerity—amount for news journalists, if they wish to be trusted as truth tellers, to an attitude towards their job. This attitude is one that guides their practices, grounding them in a careful balancing of (a) the desire to reveal facts and truths and (b) consideration of the way this is done and how it is expressed. News as a civil ideal requires news journalists to have a form of historical, anthropological and sociological imagination to allow them to combine the constative and interpretative[18] in a way that is most likely to lead to a truthful account that can be trusted to be homologous with the world that it reports.

This particular aspect of the civil ideal of the news is important. Since one of the self-evident and problematic aspects of news is that we, the audience, cannot know what we would have seen had we been involved, nor do we usually know what was actually seen, the news conveys information to us upon which we have no choice but to rely upon as civil actors. Where reliance on the news occurs and forms the basis for judgements and actions, it is based on the extent to which we place trust in the information we receive. This includes that we have at least some reasonable understanding of the motives of those who provide news to us—motives that can easily be brought into question and doubt. As Silverstone (2007: 120) puts it, 'disclosure and dissemblance are bedfellows. On the one hand a visible and trenchant expectation of truthfulness and disinterest in the reporting of the world. On the other hand a barely hidden gloss of at best disingenuous and most often an absence of context, an over-dependence on the immediate, a collusive oversimplification of the complexity of the event'. When trust in the news is withdrawn, it is because of its 'dissemblance' by which in this context I mean its inability to fulfil the basic requirement of truth telling. A basic requirement is the exercise of objectivity in reporting. Indeed, a lack of objectivity implies a failure to adopt a rigorous professional method and to collude in some form of dissemblance or other, and yet, at the same time, there is the typically plaintive cry that objectivity in news is impossible.

2.2 Objectivity

The claim to objectivity and the desire 'we' have for the news being as objective as possible still has genuine civil value with regard to what we believe and think, even though the mention of the word 'objective' seems to raise doubts about its possibility. Simply expressed the civil ideal of news requires that news journalism in all of its undertakings adopts the professional method of objective reporting which, when undertaken rigorously, meets certain professional procedural standards. These are standards which 'we' can legitimately regard as aimed at discovering the truth and which can also sensibly be regarded as trustworthy because they are motivated by an 'obligation not to deceive' (see, for example, O'Neill 2002 and Williams 2002). As I argue below, such procedural standards should not be discounted because of epistemological confusions or despairing claims with regard to how far from truth telling modern news journalism has descended—a view unwittingly supported by the faddish belief in some academic quarters that objectivity is impossible or is a form of delusional professional 'myth'. Objectivity, it is said, 'is a concept 'the majority [of journalism scholars] reject or denounce (...) in almost total unanimity' (Gauthier 1993). This view conflicts with the way in which some journalists regard 'their' professional method as desirable and as a feasible and correct way to bring together descriptions and judgements. In other words, objectivity is the application of professional standards which supports the reasonable expectation that newsgathering and reporting are undertaken in accordance with some form of 'methodological rigour'.

The objective aspects of newsgathering occur when all views and opinions that can be gathered are gathered, when all facts that can be known are accurately reported and when their explanatory value is weighed or judged in an impartial way. This form of objectivity carries with it an interest in the truth (and not deception) and an attempt to apply a disciplined professional method where views and evidence are not misrepresented or suppressed if they don't suit an opinion already held by the reporter or news organisation. Objectivity in news journalism thus implies that the reporter examines and challenges their own assumptions and prejudices as well as those of their readers or viewers if circumstances or events require it. This is to say that, ideally, 'we' can have a reasonable expectation of news journalism which is that it is more than the confirmation of particular world views or 'toeing the party line', pays attention to 'our' expectations and consciously avoids making unwarranted claims by engaging in deliberate deception and dissembling. Circumstances or events which challenge a news journalist's or an audience's outlooks and beliefs are simply occasions for reflection and judgement. In the case of news journalism, they are nothing other than the exercise of perspective, interpretation and truthfulness combined. Ideally, news journalism does not proceed in an epistemological vacuum, nor are news reports either isolated from or ignorant of each other[19]; they are compared, contrasted, discussed and judged with the reputation for professional rigour and objectivity being one of the most powerful bases for judging the adequacy of news suppliers and ultimately the placing of trust in them.

When wrestling with how to view objectivity in journalism, some researchers have focused on the definitional aspects of objectivity (Gauthier 1993) and others have chosen to examine the practical ways in which journalists use or evoke objectivity as a strategic ritual (Tuchman 1972), or as a professional ideology (Roshco 1975), or a routine element of good professional practice (Harrison 2000, 2006). For those who reject or denounce the concept altogether, one of the most serious charges made against objective journalism is simply that it is a case of being attached to a hopelessly naïve idealisation of knowing; that facts are socially constructed and views are contingent; and that cultural particularities require that we accept the inescapable relativism of located and socially constructed viewpoints. Sometimes, the charge is even spiced up with the concomitant accusation that such an idealisation is itself deeply political and ideologically motivated and that the reality of everyday journalistic practices is rather more grubby or sinister. However, such charges as above usually rest upon the view that we are not capable of 'arriving at a belief about how things are that is objectively reasonable, binding on anyone capable of appreciating the relevant evidence regardless of their social or cultural perspective' (Boghossian 2007: 130f.), combined with a basic epistemological confusion that objectivity requires a form of unconditional certainty with regard to the meaning and nature of the evidential circumstances the news journalists find themselves in. Only after removing this latter epistemological confusion can we understand what is meant by objective journalism and thereafter its place in relation to trustworthiness (Sect. 3 below) and following that the challenges facing the actualisation of the civil ideal of the news (Chapter 3).

Criticism of journalistic objectivity mainly takes the view that the way in which journalists understand objectivity is untenable for two reasons:

first, because news journalists are necessarily subjective and prejudicial actors who are not exclusively guided by the use of reason or empirical evidence when producing reports of events, this makes these reports more uncertain than is admitted to. Second, that the news selection and production processes exacerbate the problem of certainty further. This is achieved by only focusing on what are deemed to be, because of journalistic styles of writing such as the inverted pyramid approach,[20] the 'relevant facts' thereby ensuring that the report is both partial and provisional. Problematically, journalists tend to like to claim that they are certain about events or issues and they are very unlikely indeed to keep reminding us that they are not sure about what they are reporting on. Indeed, the clichés that are used to describe their role or purpose often appear to trade on a claim to certainty qua veracity, which simply further fuels the belief that journalistic objectivity is merely rhetorical or worse, culturally biased[21] and ideologically motivated. And yet these two charges of respectively the failure to acknowledge uncertainty and of only producing partial and provisional reports of events ignore what actually underlies journalistic objectivity.

Knowledge and certainty are not synonymous, and the abandonment of some form of foundationalism[22] does not mean that the traditional notion of the truth has been abandoned. From very different perspectives, both Karl Popper and Bernard Williams take great pains to remind us that truth is 'an essential regulative ideal'. Equating knowledge with certainty and certainty with objectivity leads to a confusion that can be expressed accordingly. If we believe all knowledge to be uncertain (i.e. no absolute foundational starting point) and if objectivity and certainty were the same thing, then subjectivity and uncertainty would be the same thing too—in which case all human knowledge is subjective. This is problematical for the academic gainsayer of journalism objectivity since it is manifestly the case that not all human knowledge is subjective or relative. More realistically and commonsensically, some views are more objective than others because of the way in which an inquiry has taken place and the evidential circumstances assessed. In short, objectivity can only be seen 'to be a label that we apply to inquiries that meet certain procedural standards, but objectivity does not guarantee the results of any inquiries have any certainty' (Phillips 1990: 23). Such procedural standards are best maintained by viewing objectivity as requiring the continual asking of the Popperian question—how best can we hope to detect and eliminate error (Popper 2002 [1968]).

Further adding to the epistemological confusion surrounding the meaning of objectivity is the failure by those who deny the plausibility of objective journalism to ask the question what is the purpose of attempting to be objective? Quite simply, as alluded to above, the answer lies in the relationship between journalistic objectivity and the endeavour for the news to be truth telling. It is in this that the purpose of objectivity is mostly clear, namely to maximise the amount of evidence pertaining to the attempt to try to understand a particular situation or event, thereby minimising error. This obviously requires that we can distinguish and judge between adequate and inadequate accounts. Alternatively expressed and to use a phrase of Williams (2002: 87), 'the investigative investment' has taken place in order to achieve an objective conclusion—even though we can never take for granted or be certain that the final conclusion will never be challenged in the future by new knowledge of the evidential circumstance being reported on.

Thus, if we wish to criticise journalists who claim to be objective and are not, we should not criticise them from the position that objectivity is impossible or mythical, but rather because their journalistic method, the 'investigative investment', is not up to a rigorous standard held to be a professional ideal. That journalists simply do not always have the time or the resources methodically to check and double check their work, or have it checked by others, is an unhelpful truism since the pursuit of objectivity is, like the quest for truth telling, a regulatory ideal. Such failures as there are should not prevent journalists from either being trained or educated in accordance with this method. And lest there be any confusion this is not a case of news journalism regressing to a simplistic formula of 'for' and 'against'. The reporting of evidential circumstances of situations and events requires more than this. Fortunately, many news journalists see objective reporting as entailing much more than just balancing two sides of a story. Rather, for news journalism to move closer to fulfilling the professional ideal of objective reporting, it is also necessary to separate facts from opinion and to cultivate an appropriately dispassionate manner. Here, being dispassionate is not an existential term but a practical one. It is an acquired skill or method (a professional approach) and should not be confused with being personally objective, disinterested in the world, cynical or uncaring. In other words, it is the case that the professional ideal of objectivity properly understood is nothing other than the use of a recognised and acceptable method for understanding to the maximum extent evidential circumstances and that reporting them entails a balanced representation of views combined with an appropriately dispassionate style (see ahead Chapter 4 on styles of news reporting).

Objectivity also elicits trust from audiences especially if the journalistic method of investigation and demonstration of objective methods of reporting are evident and if a reputation for objectivity has been built up and maintained over time. It may be possible then that the content of the news is seen by those who consume it as a reliable source and basis for making more informed judgements. Even if it remains the case that when discussing objectivity with regard to the news things still rapidly degenerate into claims that (a) there is no such thing, (b) it is impossible to undertake and (c) it is to be distrusted as a false idea (or an ideological obsession) which serves to encourage the mistaken belief in the neutrality of the news and its independence from vested interests and power holders. It is also the case that in spite of these views, objective news reporting has achieved the status of being a recognised professional ideal around the world.[23] News journalism emanating from modern Western liberal democratic conditions has gone to considerable lengths to establish that the routine application of being objective (in selecting and reporting news) is an essential feature of 'doing' good journalism.[24] However, it also has to be recognised that this aim is one which is not equally valued worldwide. Finally, it is sociologically correct to say that in most of the West journalists are still criticised by other journalists and academics if they are perceived to be falling short of objective standards by not adopting 'neutral' journalistic techniques when selecting and producing the news.[25] Indeed, in very high-profile cases, the 'rogue journalist' can see their professional standing traduced and their failings globally publicised.

The above understanding of objectivity seems to me to be sensible since it recognises that in practice objectivity is at best seen as a form of accuracy where mundane facts, plain or small truths or mini-narratives help to build up a fuller picture of the world. Kovach and Rosenstiel (2007) point out that when the concept of objectivity originally evolved in the USA, it did not mean that journalists were to undertake their work in a way that meant they themselves were free of bias. The term developed in part in recognition that journalists must have personal and cultural biases, but that these need not undermine their truth telling disposition, namely the accuracy of their work, or their self-knowledge about how sincere they are in terms of admitting how truthful their account actually is. In order to aid journalists in their work, objectivity as a desirable professional value entailed that journalists developed a method of testing information in a way that revealed their transparent approach to weighing up the evidence they had collected. In short, it is the method of journalism practice that is objective and not the journalist.

Once freed from the problematic linkages of objectivity with certainty, or from the understanding of it as an abstract journalistic goal, or as a characteristic of the individual journalist, we can see that in practice journalists who strive to be objective in their reporting can simply be considered as using a method which itself has value, virtues and problems. Consequently, such criticism that we should muster is better focused on the more or less successful application of a commitment to a professional method as a way of going about news selection and news production, and not from the perspective of falling short of some technical epistemological point of view, or as a goal grounded in a myth that should be heroically held onto and which is in perpetual danger of being undermined. Rather and in relation to the civil ideal of news, objectivity should be regarded as a journalistic method which has both value and shortcomings in relation to the role that news plays in civil society. Of value are the methods of reporting employed which require, in the name of objectivity, that journalists may be specifically trained in critical reflection, the checking of facts, triangulating sources, being edited (or peer-reviewed) and so on. The objective method manifests itself in particular practical skills such as achieving balance and even-handedness in presenting different sides of an issue, triangulating sources, presenting all the main relevant points, checking facts and separating them from others' opinions, but treating opinion as relevant, critical reflection or interpretation of complexity thereby minimising the influence of the writer's own attitude in the news report.

Its shortcomings can be found in the claim by news providers that it is enough to be producing news that uses a rigorous objective method of reporting. This is simply because such a claim is not sufficient in and of itself to stand for the whole of the civil ideal of news. In order to meet the demands of a civil ideal, news must also be seen in terms of the way it is primarily concerned with promoting and endorsing a version of civil values that have the potential to create a solidary sphere and is solidarising both in its force and in its intent. This requires that journalists are, in the name of truth telling and trustworthiness, not only employing a method that is rigorous and objective, but that news also fulfils a particular type of role which is explicitly informed by certain liberal values.

3 Liberal Ideals

The civil ideal of the news is based on and related to, but not the same as, the purely political idea (and desire) that the news needs to somehow serve the cause of—most notably in modern Western civil societies—representative and deliberative democracy. Attached to this comes the usual tetrad of liberal values: freedom, individualism, justice and equality[26] accompanied by some version of human rights, especially freedom of speech. More recently, this political view of the role of news has taken an optimistic view of itself with many public intellectuals, journalists and academics talking of the potential benefits of a wider discourse fostered by meaningful citizen engagement with news mediation processes through the rhetoric of 'citizen journalism', where passive audiences become active participants inspired by the so-called liberating power of new communication technologies. Optimist or not, it is typically concluded that generally the news has a liberal democratic role[27] in two broad ways. First, in actually promoting democracy (and in the West associated with this a mixture of 'liberal values') that is '*informing* citizens of what is happening around them', 'educating' them, providing a 'platform for public political discourse' and thereby facilitating the formulation of public sentiment, creating and facilitating 'space for the expression of dissent'[28] and 'giving publicity to governmental and political institutions. This also entails the independent monitoring of governmental power and to serve as a 'channel for the advocacy of political viewpoints' (McNair 2011: 18–19). Second, by expecting that news media institutions should also themselves be liberal and democratic in their structures and processes as well as being independent of one party or another and with that to avoid being so partisan as to obscure alternative views. In other words, they must serve the cause of a plurality of news viewpoints. This view is further disaggregated and refined as follows: free and independent journalism is one of the hallmarks of liberal democratic societies. It is the 'life blood' of democracy and the political public sphere and holds those in power to account through scrutiny and investigation (Brunetti and Weder 2003; Norris 2000). It requires the right of freedom of expression which it exercises in such a way that 'we' are able to possess the information we need to be both self-governing and free (Hanitzsch 2007; Kovach and Rosenstiel 2007), and has 'historically contributed' to the 'formation and conduct of civil societies' (Cottle et al. 2016: 1). In this light, the liberal democratic role of news entails that the news, in some way or another, contributes to a variety of expectations with regard to holding state power to account. Following this is the value we place (correctly) on the desirability of 'political deliberation'. This is no more than the idea that in any liberal democracy citizens are seen as being responsible for making better political choices and this requires an informed citizenry; and free and independent journalism is the handmaiden of an informed citizenry. In other words, according to this view, the role of news in Western liberal democratic states is that democratic arrangements require constant evaluation and debate by the public. Such a view tends to be derived from diverse intellectual sources which include for example Gramsci's articulation of civil society as a space within which hegemony and contestation develop, Dewey's view of public engagement and Habermas's theory of the public sphere. They overlap in their belief in the emancipatory power of more not less information, a view today that affirms that the free production, dissemination and availability of information are essential to liberal democracy and that this desire is confronted by state power holders who want to see it restricted in some way or other (usually through claims concerning national interest and security).[29]

There is much in these views to agree with and they are certainly part of the civil ideal of the news. However, it does not complete what the civil ideal of the news in a liberal democracy can be and what news should attain to. Rather, the political view above is for all its worth too narrow, too particularistic, too singular about the liberal democratic value of news journalism. It overlooks the extent and scope of the civil values of social criticism, democratic integration, civility, justice, reciprocity, and mutual respect and replaces it with a narrow conception of 'democratic duty'. In other words, it simply establishes journalism as a counterbalance to dirty politics. This 'condition of democratic life' perspective makes assumptions about the natural fix between a particular vision of journalism and a particular liberal vision of democracy, and although there is undoubtedly an important and ongoing relationship between the two (that simply is not at issue), the nature of that relationship is more complex than that sometimes occasioned in the academic lament that is levelled at journalism practice when it inevitably falls short of fulfilling its 'democratic duty' or that there exists a communication deficit.

What is missing in this view is an extension of the notions of democratic duty and of the communication deficit to include the civil necessity of the way the news should report on: the complexity of liberal democratic arrangements and the extent to which they are democratic in any way and if at all; the incommensurability of the various values paraded as desirable; the palatable and unpalatable aspects of plural democratic life; and the way that official power holders exercise their 'office' for the public good, which of course would require them to have a civil outlook (see Alexander 2006). Ideally, the news should evaluate competing claims about political legitimacy and authority, allow the demos to be heard, increase public knowledge, help to foster independent civil thought and action and influence decision-making in the non-civil political and economic spheres. It should engage robustly with our own hypocrisy and confused expectations about the nature and role of 'our' democracy and, as Tocqueville well understood, campaign on behalf of civil society and its values. Understood more widely, the civil ideal of news in its liberal democratic role is a 'shortcut to a set of norms against which journalism [and by extension its news product] could be measured' (Josephi 2013: 475). Understood too narrowly, it is not.

The problem with making such a linkage between a particular vision of news journalism and a particular political vision of liberal democracy is that the civil architecture at the heart of the civil ideal of the news has not been captured in terms of the relationship between conflicting liberal values, imperfect democratic institutions and the ideal civil values of social criticism, democratic integration, civility, justice, reciprocity and mutual respect. It is part of the civil ideal of the news that it exists to objectively and truthfully gather and interpret such evidence as is necessary to be able to sincerely and intelligently persuade and that requires an understanding of the way civil and anti-civil forces play themselves out within both the civil sphere and the non-civil spheres with regard to 'our' civil values. As Silverstone (2007: 187) puts it, 'We need to know about each other in a way that can only involve a constant critical engagement with our media's representation of the other'. And here the other needs to be understood in the widest sense of alterity.

However, it should also be noted that the ideal role of news comes with two further components: first, in relation to building new democracies and second (and related to that) in its relationship to public service communication.

With regard to the first, news can be used to 'bring about' more democratic settings. For some time in the USA, and by comparison quite recently in the UK, the democratic role of news has provided a rationale for journalism education and training. For American communication theorist Carey (1996), the third axiom of journalism is quite straightforwardly the following: 'Journalism is another name for democracy or, better, you cannot have journalism without democracy. The practices of journalism are not self-justifying; rather, they are justified in terms of the social consequences they engender, namely the constitution of a democratic social order'. [30] This strong linkage between journalism and the composition of democratic order, according to Carey, requires that care be taken in journalism education[31] because of the high expectations placed on journalism to 'create democratic communities'. The view that journalists play a role in creating democracy endures to some extent in scholarship today, though of course the fact that journalism also plays a role in bulwarking non-democratic societies is also well understood.[32] And yet it is the case that popular commentators, civil society organisations, international non-governmental organisations (INGOs) concerned with journalism safety such as the UN and UNESCO, the Council of Europe and many international journalists under threat endorse the idea that the more open a news media landscape, the more likely it is to strengthen the civil and democratisation processes and that policies and actions which reduce freedom of expression and allow intimidation and harassment of journalists as well as the development of large private news media oligopolies do have important negative consequences for those seeking to strengthen transitions away from autocracy. Perhaps this confidence in the relationship between journalism and burgeoning civil spheres and democracies is nowhere more clearly seen than in the use of news media (that explicitly accords with some form of public service communications outlook) in post-conflict resolution and/or reconstruction.[33]

This brings us to the second point, particular values, sometimes referred to by post-conflict practitioners and peacekeepers as the factual media's 'soft power', form a public service communication outlook and are based in the real history of the values and practices of traditional public service broadcasting. These values according to their founding charters encouraged a number of activities that were specifically orientated to the civil sphere and the public good, namely the recognition of the importance of independence from vested interests, increasing the stock of civic knowledge and being deserving of some kind of public funding. The civil ideal of the news was endorsed in the EU via its approach to public service broadcasting (PSB) evident in the protocol on public service broadcasting which emphasises the importance of PSB for member states, leaving the determination of its scope to them.[34] It was based on agreement by the member states and the EU that PSB has 'social, cultural and democratic functions'[35]; and vital for ensuring, amongst other things, pluralism and social cohesion[36] (Harrison and Woods 2007). The European Parliament has emphasised the importance of PSB as 'an aid to informed citizenship'[37] seeing it as having a role of fostering social cohesion and a sense of belonging to a community (Harrison and Woods 2000). The public service remit goes beyond informing citizens about politics towards fulfilling a democratic role through its civil ideal, although across Europe attacks from neoliberal agendas on public service values continue to restrict the supply of traditional public service journalism and, if anything, such agendas are on the increase.[38]

This is not to suggest that evoking the civil ideal of the news is a thing of the past, but rather that its evocation is increasingly found in the future of public service communication as 'not for profit' news sites establish themselves online. Such sites claim that traditional news journalism (including that provided by public service broadcasters) itself fails to fulfil its civil responsibility. Thus, for example, the stated and idealised principles of WikiLeaks assume a particular type of moral authority that is based upon the premise that freedom of expression is the single most important right and is one that cannot and should not be trumped by nationally based regulatory requirements or by appeals to national security or other forms of secrecy, as these undermine the people's ability to understand the world in which they live. Freedom of expression exercised by WikiLeaks is, according to its founder Julian Assange, what regulates government and law and pursues the truth where mainstream journalism has failed to do so. Its website for several years has emphasised the importance of the free flow of information 'to bring important news and information to the public' (WikiLeaks 2011) stating that: 'One of our most important activities is to publish original source material alongside our news stories so readers and historians alike can see evidence of the truth' and its anonymous 'high security anonymous drop box fortified by cutting-edge cryptographic information technologies' (ibid.) continues to be used as a way for sources to leak information to WikiLeaks without fear of reprisal. In this way, WikiLeaks has built upon and provided an outlet for the idea that moral authority necessitates the existence of an adherence to truth irrespective of the potential harm such truths can cause. The recent history of WikiLeaks throws considerable doubt on its vaunted ideals with regard to its democratic role, but nevertheless any WikiLeaks's fall from grace is being compensated for by the fact that information sites which meddle in elections and purvey 'fake news' (here referring to false news, misinformation and disinformation) are increasingly being addressed in terms of the need to protect and develop the civil ideal of the news across diverse digital news sites.[39]

The coalescence of various forms of civil activism, whistle-blowing and mainstream and non-mainstream journalism facilitated by new technology has undoubtedly challenged the power of non-civil spheres and actors on a global scale who seek to suppress information. Their claims that suppression of information is necessary to protect national security and rights to privacy and, even more compellingly, the safety of intelligence staff in the field are difficult to assess because it remains unclear to us, in the absence of information that is kept secret, just how serious such threats are. Unsurprisingly, there is growing disquiet within diverse groups within civil societies about the balance between legitimate levels of state secrecy and the right of the public to assess for itself the levels of risk it is willing to accommodate in order to know about the actions of those who governs it and in this sense how extensive the civil ideal of the news is. As new and intriguing questions are raised about the moral authority and power of those who disseminate information against the wishes of those who wish to keep it hidden and the moral authority and power of those who wish to share it, the civil ideal of the news will be evoked as the criterion for what should be the case in a liberal democracy.

4   Summary

What combines the two elements of the civil ideal of the news—trustworthiness and the news's liberal democratic role—is the unifying principle that audiences are constituted as comprising of citizens who matter and that both the providers of news and its 'citizen audience' should be able to a lesser or greater extent to play a role in building and maintaining civil freedoms through those news services which adhere to a shared civil ideal of news. Trustworthiness is derived from a public and journalistic belief in the value of truth telling and the adherence to an objective approach. The liberal democratic role of the civil ideal of the news is more expansive than is usually argued for—promoting the civil values of social criticism, democratic integration, civility, justice, reciprocity and mutual respect. From this, it follows that the civil ideal of the news recognises the diversity of incommensurate views (though not necessarily incompatible views) and values that exist in civil society, whilst also recognising its duty to be homologous with the world. The civil ideal of the news has a normative force that influences, shapes or reinforces preferences, choices, values, opinions and above all civil norms. This vein of thought can be seen in Silverstone's (2007) work and his ideal 'mediapolis', which should and can exist as a hospitable space for the working out of just choices. Mediapolis is a place of equal expression where for Silverstone (2007: 80–81), it is 'Within this cacophony of mediated voices, unheard and invisible in its totality for the most part, I see the possibility of a different kind of mediated environment ... Identifying the presence of the multiplicity of voices is, however, one thing. Finding a way of recognising their value and creating a framework for their viability and integration is clearly another... In both it is the same question. It is the question of how we might live together, and how the media in their capacity for hospitality and justice ... can be enabling rather than disabling of that rather basic project'. Silverstone's faith in the power of the media to create the conditions for both hospitality and justice represents, although he did not articulate it this way, a manifestation of the civil ideal of the news. Claims about the normative force of the civil ideal of the news can also be seen in peace journalism whose claims of tolerance, justice, the recognition of rights to welfare and dignity are supported by the belief in the moral superiority of peace over conflict, inclusive coverage with 'a voice for all'—no demonisation or, to put it positively, humanisation of all sides involved in conflict with each other, the naming of evil-doers, understanding the extent of casualties and victims (especially where there are attempts to hide them) and understanding the effects of cultural and infrastructural harm and damage. In short, a civil ideal of the news's liberal democratic role goes way beyond the traditional political formula noted above. Within Silverstone's 'mediapolis' and peace journalism's pledge for fairness and justice is an attempt to unleash the civil power of the news to address inequalities, injustices and secrecy that may otherwise remain invisible as inconvenient and unpalatable truths. The more the practical exercise of the civil ideal of the news is understood to reside in truth telling, objectivity and an expansive liberal democratic role, the greater its power to seek out and bring to light the hidden injustices and practices which harm the civil nature of societies such as cruelty to others, child abuse, human trafficking, rejection of asylum seekers and so on.

But of course the civil ideal of the news is only half the story.

Notes

1. Across Europe, there is an apparent consensus on the role and value of nationally based public service broadcasters as outlined by Harrison (2010: 111, drawing from Nikoltchev 2007). Descriptions include references to quality, diversity, plurality, education and innovation, democratic public debate and social integration as well as understanding, multiculturalism, cultural interaction and tolerance; citizenship, civil values and a right to information.
2. Fictional representations of news journalists frequently display a certain moral authority in terms of the way the civil ideal triumphs over corruption, deception and distraction. As heroes go, news journalists are seldom so flawed as to be genuinely fallen; see films such as Ace in the Hole (1951), The Front Page (1974), All the President's Men (1976), Live from Baghdad (2002), Veronica Guerin (2003), Shattered Glass (2003), Good Night and Good Luck (2005), A Mighty Heart (2007) and Spotlight (2015) as a display of the civil ideal of the news as one of triumph over abusive power. Ultimately, such films are palimpsests, a gloss on the question of competing power—civil, non-civil and anti-civil, but symbolically they matter.
3. Titles that some news organisations give to their products encapsulate authority, the bringing of light and important information, transparency, reliability and trustworthiness. Such titles include, for example, *The Daily Record*, *The Sun*, *The Times*, *The Herald*, *The Enquirer*, *Watch*, *The Mirror*, *El Mundo*, *The Citizen*, *The People*, *Die Welt* and *The Star*.
4. For Edmund Burke and Thomas Carlyle, the press actually represents a fourth power. Crucially, this fourth power is premised on freedom of expression, the exercise of which acts as a counterbalance to the other three estates, which in Britain between the seventeenth and nineteenth centuries were the Church, the aristocracy and the judiciary with each estate holding a distinct social role and a certain level of power.
5. Bentham (1990 [1843]) believes that a public opinion tribunal (POT) can take place in the newspapers and in fact argues that newspaper editors are were second only to the prime minister in the importance of their political function. Newspaper editors act like judges in the POT because they are able to undertake news selection, to decide which styles of reporting and tone to adapt and which civil and anti-civil judgements (to use the vocabulary of this book) to make. In the 'Securities against Misrule', Bentham (1990 [1843]) states that newspapers are the organ of the POT and that newspapers would feed into public opinion. Bentham understands newspapers as aspiring to fulfil what I have called the civil ideal of

the news, i.e. when he refers to newspapers he means those which report issues of public interest, expected editors to make the required investigative investment and to use the professional method of objectivity.
6. A range of scholars has highlighted in different ways a number of values that journalists seek to achieve. Such values are generally aligned to journalists' professional objectives of credibility, authority and authenticity (Singer 2003, 2010, 2015) or their role as independent operators (Born 2005), with an enthusiasm for the ideal of journalism as a form of public service (Aldridge 2007).
7. See, for example, Graham and Davies (1997), Graham et al. (1999), and Helm (2005).
8. Curran et al. (2009: 22) argue that 'media provision of public information does matter, and continued deregulation of the broadcast media is likely, on balance, to lead to lower levels of civic knowledge' which, in turn, reduce 'positive externalities' such as a better educated citizenry, or better informed voters. For similar studies/arguments, see Aalberg et al. (2013), Hahn et al. (2012), and Soroka et al. (2013).
9. On the difference between a citizen and a consumer, see Harrison and Woods (2007). Also Helm (2005).
10. The charge of corruption is not new. For example, R. G. Collingwood (2013: xxvi) in his autobiography refers to the *Daily Mail* as 'corrupting the public', 'corrupting the public mind' (ibid.: 156) and corrupting 'the electorate' (ibid.: 155). Weber (1919) makes a similar point about Lord Northcliffe, the pioneering co-owner of the *Daily Mail*.
11. Evidence for the value the public place on high-quality news suppliers that are regulated for quality news provision is found in the results of a range of annual surveys which, e.g., include the Reuters Report, the PSB Annual Research Report by the Office of Communication (OFCOM) and the annual.
12. Across the world, levels of trust in the news media are variable and in many instances are declining—see The Pew Research Center Report (2016) and The European Broadcasting Union's biannual trust in Media 2017 Report. On the question of trust in mainstream media, see also Harrison (2017) and Endnote 21 in Chapter 3.
13. Inglis (2006: 13) also explains that the 'journalist discovers what we could not possibly discover for ourselves, and tells us what it is. He or she is faithful to their science, which is the history of the present'.
14. Most versions of the public sphere, public reason and public discourse presuppose a 'background culture' (Rawls 1999: 134) of civil society that supports it.
15. Also cited in Alexander (2016: 8).

16. See greater elaboration at Rosenstiel (2013).
17. Safeguards to ensure that invasions of privacy should entail a strong public interest defence are in place, and greater emphasis on the importance of these has been evident since the Leveson inquiry into phone hacking in the UK in 2011 (see the Leveson Report 2012) and led to the creation of the Independent Press Standards Organisation (IPSO). A similar initiative has been the Australian Law Reform Commission Report (2014, ALRC Report 123) which was commissioned by the Australian Government following a number of privacy breaches in Australia and overseas. What is at stake is the challenge to find a balance between the public interest and the right to privacy. See, e.g., Axel Springer v Germany ([2012] ECHR 227) for how the European Court of Human rights makes a judgement call.
18. Alexander (2006: 580f.) uses the term 'constative/expressive' civil society.
19. See Williams (2002, cf. 261).
20. On the inverted pyramid technique, its history and various explanations for the adoption of it as a widespread technique, see Pottker (2003), McNair (1996), Allan (1997, 1999), Noelle-Neumann et al. (1989, cited in Pottker 2003: 503), and Schudson (2002).
21. On the implausibility of cultural relativism and objectivity being mistaken as being neutral, see Eagleton (2016).
22. On the standing of knowledge claims to truth, two broad schools of thought can be delineated: foundationalism—which assumes that knowledge is built on solid foundations (although there have been disputes about what constitutes those foundations exactly)—and coherentism which says that there is no absolutely secure and unshakable starting point for knowledge and as such no certainty about the foundations of knowledge.
23. This is for example illustrated by a study of the ethical views of the role perceptions of 1800 journalists from 18 countries points to detachment and non-involvement to be considered as core journalistic functions around the world (Hanitzsch et al. 2011) as well as by the largest evaluation of the world views of journalists to date, the ongoing Worlds of Journalism Study which currently undertakes research in 67 countries and has included interviews of over 27,000 journalists from 2012–2016.
24. On the value of objectivity, see Schiller (1981), Sambrook (2004) and Ball (2017).
25. Claims to objective reporting can be highly contested. For example, the BBC has been accused of favouring Palestinian views over those of Israel and was also labelled the Baghdad Broadcasting Corporation by a mixture of organisations and groups during the reporting of the first Gulf War. Fox News was launched to counter the claims of liberal bias of other

news organisations in the USA and Al-Jazeera to counter the Western bias in broadcasts about the Middle East.
26. As has been long recognised in political philosophy foundational ideas of freedom/liberty, justice and equality clash constantly with particular arrangements of democracy (Dunn 2005) because democratic states cannot (and perhaps do not want to) provide the material conditions for either liberty, justice or equality to be fully realised. Against those who see such liberal values as neutral and the best way to organise states, there are always those who argue that liberal values themselves embody a substantive moral and political view of the world which is contested and which is not compatible with world views held by many groups and individuals in different world states (Laclau and Mouffe 2001). The news media in their ideal civil role routinely encounter and engage with these contradictions.
27. Problematically, the starting point for much scholarship about the ideal political/democratic role of journalism is that democracy is normatively justified and an uncritical self-evident version of liberal democracy is imported into a good deal of academic scholarship of journalism. Of course, this is not the only normative role that has been envisaged for the news media—Lasswell's (1948) monitorial role of communications is another. For a detailed exploration of the normative roles of the news media, see Christians et al. (2009).
28. It is often noted that JS Mill was the most passionate of all defenders of free speech and with that freedom of the press even to the point of arguing that giving offence implied no real harm to a person. And yet related to this is the fact that Mill was also a 'frightened democrat' (Ryan 2012a: 716/717 and 727, 2012b: 259) caught between his admiration and hopes for 'government by discussion'—high journalism—and his fear of 'untutored public opinion' dominated by intellectual rectitude and rigid conformity.
29. However, there are larger demands that can be placed upon this expectation; namely, the potential benefits of new information technologies, public service journalism and community news media to empower publics to engage in deliberation, advocacy and protest are axiomatic. For liberal states, it is of course always useful to be able to point to their democratic qualifications and achievements by being seen to have a robust and possibly antagonistic press and to allow public debate and opinion to flourish via social media and other publication outlets. For many scholars (see Barnett, 1997, 2005; Barnett and Seaton 2010; Dahlgren 1995), the displacement of public service television by commercial channels signals that the pursuit of mass audiences with low-cost and low-quality programming may have negatively affected the audience's ability to make sense

of public affairs See also Curran (2009) on the diminishment of public knowledge.
30. Carey (1996) has been widely criticised for sentimentalising journalism, its past and its role which he sees in 'public conversation' (e.g. Josephi 2013).
31. Significantly, Carey (1996, no page number) does not warmly welcome a linkage between journalism education and social sciences which, so he says, leads to a different type of understanding of news journalism—one whereby 'alienated from its natural home, journalism education has sought refuge in technique or in science'.
32. Such high-level beliefs and expectations (that news should be free and have demonstrable public value) are also to be found in the 'best practice' approaches adopted in the syllabi of journalism education and training courses of many further and higher education institutions across the world as well as in critiques in academia of journalism practice. As for the extent to which neoliberal values have prevailed, it is still the case that there has been and remains a tradition of public and private investment in investigative journalism in the form of strong pockets of support for mainstream news organisations such as the BBC, Sky News, *The Guardian*, *New York Times* and *Washington Post*.
33. In 2015, the High-Level Independent Panel on UN Peace Operations (HIPPO) highlighted the importance of the factual media in delivering the operations' mandate of securing peace effectively via their use of digital media (para. 283) and especially radio (para. 284). There is, however, still a pressing need to develop a normative framework for UN peacekeeping media (Betz and Papper 2015). There are also recommendations that it is necessary to develop public service-level media standards for UN peacekeeping operations (Orme 2010) which can also be applied in post-conflict media environments (Harding 2015).
34. See the Protocol on Public Service Broadcasting which was annexed to the Treaty of Amsterdam which entered into force in 1999. For a comparative examination of public service obligations in six member states, see Katsirea (2008).
35. Council, Resolution of the Council and Representatives of the Governments of the Member States concerning PSB OJ [1999] C 30/1, para. B.
36. Council, Resolution concerning PSB; European Parliament, Motion for a Resolution on the future of public service television in a multichannel digital age, Committee on Culture, Youth, Education and the

Media 11/7/96 A4-0243/96; European Parliament, Resolution on the role of public service television in a multimedia society 19/9/96 A4-0243/96. See also Council of Europe, Recommendation of the Committee of Ministers to Member States on the Guarantee of the Independence of Public Service Broadcasting, R (96)10.
37. European Parliament, Resolution on the role of public service television in a multimedia society, 19/9/96 A4-0243/96, para. B.
38. Greece and Turkey are pertinent examples of this. For more information on Greece, see Hallin and Papathanassopoulos (2002), Iosifidis and Katsirea (2014), Pukallus and Harrison (2015), and Syllas (2014) and on Turkey's decline of media freedom and its move from the repression to oppression of news journalism see Pukallus et al. (forthcoming). The fast changing media environment (especially the rise of digital media) poses a challenge in various other democratic states such as Finland, France, Germany, Italy, Poland and the UK (see Sehl et al. 2016). Challenges to the mainstream media also come from highly successful corporations with huge audience reach such as Google and Facebook which have, despite their ambiguity in terms of their infotech/publishing status, become part of the news media ecosystem, taking virtually all the funding from advertising in the online context, with the added problem that changes to Facebook's algorithms can drive or significantly reduce traffic to mainstream news sites overnight (Ball 2017). Facebook's capacity for creating filter bubbles of like-minded opinion which can coalesce to form attacks on stories via social media and partisan news outlets can drive down the credibility of stories in the mainstream news media. In the USA, an anti-mainstream news agenda is inspired by and through the constant use of Twitter by President Trump to denigrate news organisations in extreme terms in an attempt to mitigate criticisms of his actions. By trying to delegitimise mainstream news media as civil institutions, Trump is attempting to limit the civil power of the mainstream news media in the USA—a tactic resonant of authoritarian regimes where only those news outlets that paint a consistently positive picture of the country's leader are allowed to be part of the national conversation.
39. Increasingly, opinion is turning to the view that social media companies should not be allowed simply to host extreme content without facing any consequences but that they should exhibit greater responsibility for content and how it is presented (fake news—that is false news or disinformation—placed against adverts and so on) and that they should face increasingly heavy financial penalties for posting 'illegal' content.

BIBLIOGRAPHY

Aalberg, T., et al. (2013). International Television News, Foreign Affairs Interest, and Public Knowledge: A Comparative Study of 11 Countries. *Journalism Studies, 14*(3), 387–406.

Aldridge, M. (2007). *Understanding the Local Media*. New York: Open University Press.

Alexander, J. (2006). *The Civil Sphere*. Oxford: Oxford University Press.

Alexander, J. (2016). Introduction: Journalism, Democratic Culture, and Creative Reconstruction. In J. Alexander, E. B. Breeze, & M. Luengo (Eds.), *The Crisis of Journalism Reconsidered* (pp. 1–30). New York: Cambridge University Press.

Allan, S. (1997). News and the Public Sphere: Towards a History of Objectivity and Impartiality. In M. Bromley & T. O'Malley (Eds.), *A Journalism Reader* (pp. 296–329). London: Routledge.

Allan, S. (1999). *News Culture*. Buckingham and Philadelphia: Open University Press.

Australian Law Reform Commission Report. (2014). *Serious Invasions of Privacy in the Digital Era*. ALRC Report 123.

Ball, J. (2017). *Post-Truth: How Bullshit Conquered the World*. London: Biteback Publishing.

Barnett, S. (1997). New Media, Old Problems: New Technology and the Political Process. *European Journal of Communication, 12*(2), 193–218.

Barnett, S. (2005). Opportunity or Threat? The BBC, Investigative Journalism and the Hutton Report. In S. Allan (Ed.), *Journalism: Critical Issues* (pp. 328–341). Maidenhead, UK: Open University Press.

Barnett, S., & Seaton, J. (2010). Why the BBC Matters: Memo to the New Parliament About a Unique British Institution. *Political Quarterly, 81*(3), 327–332.

Bentham, J. (1990 [1843]). *Securities Against Misrule and Other Constitutional Writings for Tripoli and Greece* (P. Schofield, Ed.). Oxford: Clarendon.

Betz, M., & Papper, H. (2015). UN Peacekeeping Radio: The Way Forward. In J. Hoffmann & V. Hawkins (Eds.), *Communication and Peace: Mapping an Emerging Field* (pp. 163–178). London: Routledge.

Blackburn, S. (2007). http://www2.phil.cam.ac.uk/~swb24/reviews/Williams1.htm.

Boghossian, P. (2007). *Fear of Knowledge. Against Relativism and Constructivism*. Oxford: Oxford University Press.

Born, G. (2005). *Uncertain Vision: Birt, Dyke and the Reinvention of the BBC*. London: Vintage.

Brunetti, A., & Weder, B. (2003). A Free Press Is Bad News for Corruption. *Journal of Public Economics, 87*(7–8), 1801–1824.

Carey, J. (1996). *Where Journalism Education Went Wrong*. Presentation at the 1996 Seigenthaler Conference at the Middle Tennessee State University. Available at https://lindadaniele.wordpress.com/2010/08/11/carey-where-journalism-education-went-wrong/.
Christians, C., et al. (2009). *Normative Theories of the Media: Journalism in Democratic Societies*. Urbana and Chicago: University of Illinois Press.
Collingwood, R. G. (2013). *An Autobiography and Other Writings: With Essays on Collingwood's Life and Work* (D. Boucher & T. Smith, Eds.). Oxford: Oxford University Press.
Cottle, S., Sambrook, R., & Mosdell, N. A. (2016). Introduction. In S. Cottle, R. Sambrook, & N. A. Mosdell (Eds.), *Reporting Dangerously: Journalist Killings, Intimidation and Security* (pp. 1–16). Basingstoke: Palgrave Macmillan.
Curran, J., et al. (2009). Media System, Public Knowledge and Democracy: A Comparative Study. *European Journal of Communication, 24*(1), 5–26.
Dahlgren, P. (1995). *Television and the Public Sphere: Citizenship, Democracy and the Media*. London: Sage.
Dunn, J. (2005). *Setting the People Free: The Story of Democracy*. London: Atlantic Books.
Eagleton, T. (2016). *Culture*. New Haven: Yale University Press.
Edwards, M. (2013). Introduction. In M. Edwards (Ed.), *The Oxford Handbook of Civil Society* (pp. 3–14). Oxford: Oxford University Press.
Forde, K. R. (2014). The Fire Next Time in the Civil Sphere: Literary Journalism and Justice in America 1963. *Journalism, 15*(5), 573–588.
Gauthier, G. (1993). In Defence of a Supposedly Outdated Notion: The Range of Application of Journalistic Objectivity. *Canadian Journal of Communication, 18*(4). Available at https://www.cjc-online.ca/index.php/journal/article/view/778/684.
Graham, A., & Davies, G. (1997). *Broadcasting, Society and Policy in the Multimedia Age*. Luton: John Libby.
Graham, A., et al. (1999). *Public Purposes in Broadcasting: Funding the BBC*. Luton: University of Luton Press.
Hahn, K. S., Iyengar, S., & Van Aelst, P. (2012). Does Knowledge of Hard News Go with Knowledge of Soft News? A Cross-National Analysis of the Structure of Public Affairs Knowledge. In T. Aalberg & J. Curran (Eds.), *How Media Inform Democracy* (pp. 119–137). Abingdon: Routledge.
Hallin, D. C., & Papathanassopoulos, S. (2002). Political Clientelism and the Media: Southern Europe and Latin America in Comparative Perspective. *Media, Culture and Society, 24*(2), 175–195.
Hanitzsch, T. (2007). Deconstructing Journalism Culture: Towards a Universal Theory. *Communication Theory, 17*(4), 367–385.

Hanitzsch, T., et al. (2011). Mapping Journalism Cultures Across Nations: A Comparative Study of 18 Countries. *Journalism Studies, 12*(3), 273–293.
Harding, P. (2015, October). *Public Service Media in Divided Societies: Relic or Renaissance*. Policy Briefing#15, BBC Media Action. Available at http://stmjo.com/en/wp-content/uploads/2015/11/psb-in-divided-societies-sept-2015.pdf.
Harrison, A. (2017, August 6). On the Question of Trust in Mainstream Media. *The Guardian*.
Harrison, J. (2000). *Terrestrial TV News in Britain: The Culture of News Production*. Manchester: Manchester University Press.
Harrison, J. (2006). *News*. London: Routledge.
Harrison, J. (2007). Critical Foundations and Directions for the Teaching of News Journalism. *Journalism Practice, 1*(2), 175–189.
Harrison, J. (2010). European Social Purpose and Public Service Communication. In C. Bee & E. Bozzini (Eds.), *Mapping the European Public Sphere: Institutions, Media and Civil Society* (pp. 99–116). London: Routledge.
Harrison, J., & Woods, L. (2000). European Citizenship: Can Audio-Visual Policy Make a Difference? *Journal of Common Market Studies, 38*(3), 471–495.
Harrison, J., & Woods, L. (2007). *European Broadcasting Law and Policy*. Cambridge: Cambridge University Press.
Helm, D. (2005). Consumers, Citizens and Members: Public Service Broadcasting and the BBC. In D. Helm, et al. (Eds.), *Can the Market Deliver? Funding Public Service Television in the Digital Age* (pp. 1–21). Eastleigh: John Libbey Publishing.
High-Level Independent Panel on UN Peace Operations Report (HIPPO) Presented to the UN Secretary General. (2015, June 16). *Uniting Our Strengths for Peace—Politics, Partnership and People*.
Inglis, F. (2002). *People's Witness: The Journalist in Modern Politics*. London and New Haven: Yale University Press.
Inglis, F. (2006). Universalism and Difference: The Separation of Culture and Politics. *British Journal of Canadian Studies, 19*(2), 165–176.
Iosifidis, P., and Katsirea, I. (2014). *Public Service Broadcasting in Greece in the Era of Austerity* (Working papers). Centre for Media Pluralism and Media Freedom (CMPF), EUI.
Josephi, B. (2013). How Much Democracy Does Journalism Need? *Journalism, 14*(4), 474–489.
Katsirea, I. (2008). *Public Broadcasting and European Law: A Comparative Examination of Public Service Obligations in Six Member States*. Austin: Wolters Kluwer.

Kovach, B., & Rosenstiel, T. (2007). *The Elements of Journalism: What Newspeople Should Know and the Public Should Expect.* New York: Random House.
Laclau, E., & Mouffe, C. (2001). *Hegemony and Socialist Strategy: Towards a Radical Democratic Politics.* London: Verso Books.
Lasswell, H. (1948). *The Structure and Function of Communication in Society.* New York: Harper & Bros.
Leveson Report. (2012). *An Inquiry into the Culture, Practices and Ethics of the Press.* London: The Stationery Office.
Lichtenberg, J. (1991). In Defence of Objectivity. In J. Curran & M. Gurevitch (Eds.), *Mass Media and Society.* London: Edward Arnold.
Lippmann, W. (1920). *Liberty and the News.* New York: Harcourt Brace and Howe.
Lippmann, W. (1922). *Public Opinion.* New York: Macmillan.
McNair, B. (1996). *News and Journalism in the UK* (2nd ed.). London: Routledge.
McNair, B. (2011). *An Introduction to Political Communication.* London: Routledge.
Newman, N., with Fletcher, R., Kalogeropoulos, A., Levy, D. A. L., & Kleis Nielsen, R. (2017). *Reuters Institute Digital News Report.* Oxford: Reuters Institute for the Study of Journalism.
Nikoltchev, S. (Ed.). (2007). *IRIS Special: The Public Service Broadcasting Culture.* Strasbourg: European Audiovisual Observatory.
Noelle-Neumann, E., Schulz, W., & Wilke, J. (Eds.). (1989). *Publizistik Massenkommunikation. Das Fischer Lexikon.* Frankfurt am Main: Fischer.
Norris, P. (2000). *A Virtuous Circle: Political Communication in Post-Industrial Societies.* Cambridge: Cambridge University Press.
O'Neil, O. (2002). *A Question of Trust.* Cambridge: Cambridge University Press.
Orme, B. (2010, February 16). *Broadcasting in UN Blue: The Unexamined Past and Uncertain Future of Peacekeeping Radio.* CIMA Report.
Pew Research Center. (2016). *The Modern News Consumer.* Available at https://www.journalism.org/2016/07/07/the-modern-news-consumer/. 7 July.
Pew Research Center. (2018). *Americans Still Prefer Watching to Reading the News.* Available at https://www.journalism.org/category/publications/survey-reports/. 3 December.
Phillips, D. (1990). Subjectivity and Objectivity: An Objective Inquiry. In E. W. Eisner & A. Peshkin (Eds.), *Qualitative Inquiry in Education: The Continuing Debate* (pp. 19–37). New York: Teachers College Press.
Popper, K. (2002 [1968]). *The Logic of Scientific Discovery.* London: Routledge.
Pottker, H. (2003). News and Its Communicative Quality: The Inverted Pyramid—When and Why Did It Appear? *Journalism Studies,* 4(4), 501–511.

Pukallus, S., and Harrison, J. (2015). If Media Freedom and Media Pluralism Are Fundamental Values in the EU Why Doesn't the EU Do Anything to Ensure Its Application: The Non-Use of Art. 7 TEU?'. In A. Koltay (Ed.), *Comparative Perspectives on the Fundamental Freedom of Expression* (pp. 368–387). Budapest: Wolters Kluwer.

Pukallus, S., et al. (forthcoming). From Repression to Oppression: Journalism in Turkey 2013–2018. *Journalism*, Under Review.

Rawls, J. (1999). *A Theory of Justice*. Harvard: Harvard University Press.

Riffkin, R. (2015). *Americans' Trust in Media Remains at Historical Low*. Available at https://news.gallup.com/poll/185927/americans-trust-media-remains-historical-low.aspx.

Rosenstiel, T. (2013). *The Danger of Journalism That Moves Too Quickly Beyond Fact*. Available at https://www.poynter.org/reporting-editing/2013/the-danger-of-journalism-that-moves-too-quickly-beyond-fact/.

Roshco, B. (1975). *Newsmaking*. Chicago and London: University of Chicago Press.

Ryan, A. (2012a). *On Politics*. London: W. W. Norton.

Ryan, A. (2012b). *The Making of Modern Liberalism*. Princeton: Princeton University Press.

Sambrook, R. (2004). *The Poliak Lecture Given at Columbia University, America—Holding on to Objectivity*. Available at http://www.bbc.co.uk/pressoffice/speeches/stories/sambrook_poliak.shtml.

Schiller, D. (1981). *Objectivity and the News*. Philadelphia: University of Pennsylvania Press.

Schudson, M. (2002). The News Media as Political Institutions. *Annual Review of Political Sciences, 5*(1), 249–269.

Sehl, A., Cornia, A., & Kleis Nielsen, R. (2016). *Public Service News and Digital Media*. Reuters Institute Reports.

Silverstone, R. (2007). *Media and Morality: On the Rise of the Mediapolis*. London: Wiley.

Singer, J. (2003). Who Are These Guys?: The Online Challenge to the Notion of Journalistic Professionalism. *Journalism, 4*(2), 139–163.

Singer, J. (2010). Journalism Ethics Amid Structural Change. *Daedalus, 139*(2), 89–99.

Singer, J. (2015). Leaning Conservative: Innovation and Presidential Campaign Coverage by U.S. Newspaper Websites in the Digital Age. *ISOJ, 5*(1), no page numbers.

Soroka, S., et al. 2013. Auntie Knows Best? Public Broadcasters and Current Affairs Knowledge. *British Journal of Political Science, 43*(4), 719–739.

Syllas, C. (2014). It's All Greek… *Index on Censorship, 43*(1), 28–33.

Tuchman, G. (1972). Objectivity as Strategic Ritual: An Examination of Newsmen's Notions of Objectivity. *American Journal of Sociology*, 77(4), 660–679.
Weber, M. (1919). *Politics as a Vocation*. Available at http://fs2.american.edu/dfagel/www/class%20readings/weber/politicsasavocation.pdf.
WikiLeaks. (2011). *What Is WikiLeaks?* https://wikileaks.org/About.html. Accessed 18 February 2019.
Williams, B. (2002). *Truth and Truthfulness: An Essay in Genealogy*. Princeton, NJ: Princeton University Press.
Williams, B. (2005). *In the Beginning Was the Deed: Realism and Moralism in Political Argument*. Princeton: Princeton University Press.

CHAPTER 3

The Civil Ideal of the News and Political and Commercial Reality

1 INTRODUCTION

The civil ideal of the news outlined in the last chapter does not simply evaporate when we confront the situations that contemporary news media organisations find themselves operating in and their attendant constraints. Nor does it hang over the modern world as some spectral presence. Rather it is the case that both journalists and audiences navigate a relationship between news as an ideal and its grounded reality. The civil ideal of the news remains as a promise of the news's contribution to civil life and liberal democratic culture and, as such, is an important part of both journalists' and audiences' imaginaries. The plain fact is that the civil ideal of news and the grounded reality of news coexist and constantly engage each other in different ways, in different conditions and under diverse circumstances both positively and negatively. It is the latter that is the other half of the story and which concerns this chapter.

The civil ideal of the news faces its greatest challenge at the hands of political power and commercial power which reduce people respectively to an audience of partisans or to an audience of consumers. In neither case are they treated as fully rounded citizens. In this chapter, I wish to look at political and commercial power and their anti-civil challenge as they are mostly expressed in Western-style news environments where opposition to the civil ideal takes an essentially ideational form.[1] In short, I focus on the political and commercial alternatives to the civil ideal of the news in non-totalitarian and non-authoritarian settings where the civil ideal of the news is negatively regarded by strong vested interests, but is sometimes positively endorsed and sometimes genuinely valued and somehow survives.

Within these non-totalitarian and non-authoritarian Western settings, there exist myriad contexts and places in which news journalism is undertaken—though they can roughly be divided into two camps. Camp A consists of those news organisations, news divisions, news channels, newspapers or news websites that produce news that is investigative,[2] that values journalistic integrity or has a public service remit to which they are legally or morally committed; that try very hard to overcome the constraints that are normally placed upon journalism by providing resources for lengthier investigations; that try to maintain their independence and reject the potential influence of vested interests; that develop detailed codes of practice; that include diverse views; and that seek to better serve the public interest. Camp B consists of those media and technology conglomerates (with news divisions), stand-alone news channels, newspapers and news websites that peddle political dogma and bigotry, prefer punditry and journalistic opinion, value market efficiency and regard themselves as simply in commercial competition with other news organisations. Importantly, they regard the numerical maximisation of audience engagement as a blanket justification for regarding people as consumers and nothing else. They also constantly evoke freedom of expression as the right that entitles them to do what they do, as well as news media pluralism as a desirable outcome.

But why should any of this matter? Does it really matter if some purported civil ideal of the news, which in partnership with other civil institutions enables civil society to flourish, is closely adhered to or is completely ignored in contemporary news journalism? What would be the cost to any of us if the news simply acceded to the values of whatever non-civil sphere you care to name? What would actually be lost and why would we be alarmed (assuming some of us would be) if all the news outlets in a particular setting were in the hands of those with a vested interest, say in a particular religion? The answers depend on whether or not you believe that in general the news media has any form of influence or power. It is to this question that I now turn since it is the question of the power of the news, civil or otherwise, that animates the competitive nature of the coexistence of the camps A and B and which determines how the civil ideal of the news is actually played out when confronted with the requisite demands of the state and the market and its own 'journalistic conscience'. It is Camp B that I wish to describe in its typical form later in this chapter. That is I want to focus on how it subverts and works against the civil ideal of the news with an alternative set of understandings about the value of news—namely its political and commercial value.

2 NEWS AND POWER

Sociology and related to this social psychology are usually regarded as the first academic disciplines to show an interest in the study of the news media and power. In the case of sociology, it was Robert Park who was the first to regard the systematic study of the news media as being worthy of genuine sociological interest.[3] For early social psychologists, the media's 'power' to modify or influence behaviour was mostly studied. In the commercial private sector, this was mainly centred on the power of advertising, while in the more publicly minded universities the social impact of media influence was looked at through questions of whether the media desensitise people to violence and whether it makes them more violent and so on. Accompanying these approaches the study of political communication began to develop its concerns with voter behaviour and intentions, opinion formation, gatekeeping and framing, from which evolved the cultural study of the media in the late 1960s and 1970s which brought with it media critical theory, feminism, the study of race and media consumption. More widely, the media came to be defined as a cultural industry with cultural structures dealing in cultural products or as a techno-political institution that seeks to persuade and whose products and language must be deconstructed to reveal their political intent.[4] Accordingly, interest in media power has spread to, on the one hand, the cultural nature and quality of their cultural products— how are they produced and constructed, what they represent, stand for and say about 'us'—and on the other hand the political economy of the industry—particularly who owns what, the commercial power of news media companies, the inequalities generated by the industry[5] and what political world view they stand for and promote, namely their outlook and bias. Today as the news media evolve, there is a continued focus on the audience and the question of media influence as well as the question of what is the appropriate policy response to any particular public concern, for example in relation to the effects of internet use on children and the impact of social media on politics.[6] Recently, another strand of research into news media power has emerged. It focuses on the idea of journalists themselves having a form of communicative power and exercising this power in an ethical or responsible way for example through peace journalism (Curran and Seaton 2009; Lynch 2008) and related to that how news journalism can facilitate post-conflict reconstruction and a sustainable peace in certain areas of the world.[7]

Overall, it is fair to say that the routine assumption now made is that 'in most societies the media do have power' (Corner 2013: 15), although the details of what this power amounts to, and subsequently how it can be judged, vary considerably. In large part, this may be accounted for by the fact that the analysis of coercive power tends to focus on normative questions about who should be able to use such power, to what ends, what limits should be placed on it and whether particular instances of the use of power are a positive or negative force. Today, the majority of studies into news media's power generally regard it as a form of 'soft' power (Nye 2004) if for no other reason than the fact that news media organisations manifestly do not have the legitimate coercive power of states nor, yet, the brute power of markets (though this is disputed by some). This does not mean that the factual media, and in particular the news media, have not routinely been studied by researchers in terms of different types and forms of power relationships. In fact, the two most commonly studied forms of power and their relationship to the factual media are political power and commercial power. It is these that I wish to focus on since in essence they represent the non-civil spheres of the state and the market and undermine or limit the civil ideal of the news. They do so by treating their audiences as either belonging to a partisan political group or as consumers (usually both) rather than as citizens. They regard the news as a product rather than as a (public) service and, as such, news and news journalism as an accessory to vested interests. The expression of political and commercial power varies across different geopolitical settings, political and regulatory arrangements and within different commercial and technological contexts. Nevertheless, we can provide an account of what they typically entail and how they judge their respective audiences—that is how they essentially stand in contradistinction and opposition to the civil ideal of the news. But first some clarity with regard to the concept of power is needed.

In essence, I take my understanding of power from Lukes (2005a, b) and follow his understanding of power generically as the pursuit of self-interest and as three-dimensional[8] in form. His work has gone a considerable way to achieving some form of broad consensus, although not an 'all-encompassing' one (Johal et al. 2014: 401), regarding the three dimensions of power. Briefly, the three dimensions of power Lukes identifies are as follows: One-dimensional power is where A can ensure that B does something that they may or may not want to do. This outcome is achieved through either influence or force. As such, this form of power is concrete, observable and measurable. As Lukes (2005a: 19) says, this form of power 'involves a focus on *behaviour* in the making of *decisions* on *issues* over which there is observable *conflict* of (subjective) *interests*, seen as express policy preferences, revealed by political participation' (emphasis in the original). Two-dimensional power lies in an ability to set agendas (including keeping items off the agenda) and to prevent issues being brought to public attention. It is a type of power which will bring benefit to certain actors, which cannot always be easily detected but which essentially resides in influencing decisions. Lukes (ibid.: 24f.) argues that two-dimensional power 'involves a *qualified critique* of the *behavioural focus* of the first view ... and it allows for consideration of the ways in which *decisions* are prevented from being taken on *potential issues* over which there is observable *conflict* of (subjective) *interests*, seen as embodied in express policy preferences and sub-political grievances' (emphasis in the original). However, as noted above, for Lukes power is best conceptualised as three-dimensional. Here, the exercise of power is not on the face of it coercive; rather, it consists of the production of narratives that influence people's desires and goals in a way that corresponds to the interests of those in power without publics necessarily being aware of it (a form of ideational hegemony). Thus, for example, the existence of prevailing social norms and attitudes that discriminate against particular groups and individuals or their ways of life, or where behaviour and beliefs (such as patriarchal power structures) are accepted as the norm, indicates that there are in any given social setting consistent asymmetrical power relations at play. Where these are amplified or reinforced through news mediation for example, the process may occur in such a way that individuals still feel that they have the freedom to form their own opinions and to make their own decisions. Consequently, unlike the more substantive nature of one- and two-dimensional power, three-dimensional power is potentially a more sinister and discreet force, particularly as it is the one that is unlikely to result in conflict as those being influenced do not necessarily feel coerced. Indeed, it is more likely the case that decisions, opinions and choices appear to them to be independent of any power relationships. It is a form of power through compliance. As Lukes (ibid.: 28) notes, 'the three dimensional view of power involves a *thoroughgoing critique of the behavioural focus* of the first two views as too individualistic and allows for considerations of the many ways in which *potential issues* are kept out of politics, whether through the operation of social forces and institutional practices or through individual decisions' (emphasis in the original).[9] Returning to the question of how the news and political power, the news and commercial power and related to both of them, their audiences, are typically played out across all three dimensions of Lukes's model of power, what follows shows how together they form limits to the civil ideal of the news.

2.1 Political Power

Any civil ideal of the news as manifest in journalism practice is constantly challenged by the daily reality of political power by those in power, those who support the politically powerful and those who seek political power. The exercise of political power ranges from suppression of free and independent news media with impunity[10] to undue editorial influence and agenda setting, to the active collusion of a news organisation in their support of the politically powerful. Accordingly, political power in the news spans all three of Lukes's dimensions of power. Though, as noted above, in this book, I am not concerned with the violent suppression of free and independent news media, but here, the more subtle expression of political power through editorial control, more subtle forms of agenda setting, the production of particular news narratives and forms of news media collaboration or even collusion with power holders. These are the dominant modes of the expression of political power in news organisation in the West, and it is the case that we are increasingly witnessing the rise of these expressions across news platforms of the politically partisan news groups that can be exploited by populist leaders to help them to spread exaggerated information or misinformation which helps them to get elected (Mounk 2018). Sadly, it must also be admitted that we are also seeing some signs by some countries in Europe of an increasing use of state coercion, and sometimes the use of demeaning language[11] or actual violence against news journalists and news organisations.[12]

To capture how political power in the news is played out through editorial control and agenda setting, we can extend an old journalistic metaphor. News organisations range from lapdogs that comply with and collude with political power, yapping dogs that have both a version of the civil ideal of the news, but engage in mutually beneficial relationships with political power and watchdogs which try actively to protect the civil ideal of the news as truth telling, demonstrably employing an objective method of inquiry and gaining a reputation for being trustworthy. In short, the orientation of news organisations to the expressions of political power is simply a matter of how independent the civil sphere is and accordingly how independent the factual media are.

2.1.1 The Lapdog
The pursuit of political power undermines the liberal democratic role of the news and with that the civil ideal. This occurs when news providers become partisan and provide succour to whomever they support in the form of trying to use the news to confirm a person's outlook, or to channel and reinforce discontent in a certain direction, and to do both by reinforcing or seeking to influence what Schutz and Luckmann (1973) call a person's 'natural attitude' and therefore how they understand the world.[13] It is nothing other than a totalising approach to news where everything must conform to a specific ideology or world view and what does not is simply ignored (edited out). Such news presents itself as a form of populism which, as Müller (2016: 101) notes, is not only anti-elites but also anti-pluralist and claims for itself to represent *the* people, that is a people defined by the right criteria working towards promoting a 'single common good', and 'whose will cannot err'. Operating like this and knowingly under the influence of partisan political power, news journalism works in accordance with Lukes's third dimension of power. In other words, the appearance of the exercise of freedom of choice is maintained through news reports which frame everything towards the support of a particular political outlook and, correspondingly, a political agenda which actively delimits choice while masquerading as representing the voice of the people. Such news ceases to undertake or even have a civil role, and it certainly cannot function as a fourth estate. Instead, it is news that defines itself as representing a natural way of life that is historically justified, socially superior and ethical or in some cases Godly in character. The illusion of free choice is always maintained by the claim that the news only represents what the people have already chosen. This possibly explains why this form of news tends also to be trusted and regarded as offering an accurate account of events by certain partisan audiences.[14] The net effect of this is that the

civil ideal of the news is, alongside open public discussion, simply displaced by news that is based on a combination of political certainty and moral intolerance. Nowhere is the partisan news method better summarised than by Michael Carlson (2017) in his obituary of Fox News founder Roger Ailes: 'If his on-air formula had been honed at MSNBC, it was perfected at Fox. Every programme, whether news bulletin, opinion or talk show, stayed on message, keeping to the same talking points, reinforcing then (sic) repeatedly throughout the news cycle. Panels were always weighted toward the in-house viewpoint; any token "liberal" … was browbeaten, talked over and dismissed'. At its most invidious, political power manifests itself in the West in the production of systematic naturalistic news narratives that correspond to the interests of those who wish to gain or retain political power and that resonate with their particular audience as truthful and believable. And nowhere is this clearer than in the audiences for 'alt right' news channels in the USA.[15]

As I have argued elsewhere the emergence of these partisan channels has been put down to a variety of reasons, notably because politics itself is less consensual, that politicians themselves have debased public discourse and the media reflect this, that technology has facilitated the proliferation of opportunities for extreme views to be disseminated and that regulators have failed to moderate what is said.[16] What emerges is an antagonistic setting for news and news journalism in which sides are taken where attention-grabbing stories and the pursuit of emotional engagement in news means that it is more likely to deal in binaries of good/evil and black and white judgements which avoid complexity or shades of grey, all too easily feeding off and contributing to public feelings of disempowerment. In such an antagonistic environment, the net result is that 'facts' are constantly disputed and substituted for 'alternative facts', or 'our facts',[17] and without the sharing of 'a common baseline of facts' (Kakutani 2018: 14) attempts at discursive rationality are deemed somewhat pointless.

A partisan news service has four dimensions. First, it regards the public sphere as a battleground. Second, the battle is intensely political (specifically populist) being conceived of in terms of 'real people',[18] 'the common good', 'the unrepresented' (or the 'left behind' and the 'forgotten') versus dominant elites, pluralists and liberal democrats. As Schmitt (2007: 90) observes: 'in enmity a person who has lost his right seeks to regain it, in enmity he finds the meaning of his cause and the meaning of right when the framework of protection and obedience within which he formerly lived breaks up'. Third, partisan channels encourage interactivity, involvement and, above all, the mobilisation of their audiences to affirm their message and to protest against those perceived to be part of 'the occupying army' across all forms of media. Fourth, partisan news channels are usually tied to an organised party or some formal (usually corporate or charitable) source of funding. With these four criteria, partisan news is the antithesis of public service journalism and, according to some, its greatest threat.

Although highly partisan news is to be found in the West in the form of alt-right and left-wing news sites,[19] this explicit form of partisan news is not (yet) the dominant model for news organisations in the West. There are occasions when political power and its expression in the news are at its most recognisable and in its most traditional form, meaning that the expression of support for a particular political position is explicit and overt in news reports. This is visible when particular news media outlets celebrate a decision, claiming success when 'their' political party wins a general election or when they regard themselves as having changed a political policy they opposed. Here, the news organisations themselves become or claim to have acted as (representative democratic) political agents openly seeking to influence readers (or tell them what they like to hear), explicitly trying to set a political agenda, advertising political parties or advertising their leaders. In these instances, politics and the news organisation may be seen to be 'too close' and news journalism simply becomes the lapdog to a particular set of interests (Lukes's second dimension of power). This is no more than taking sides. The net result is that this explicit manifestation of political power over the news is simply seen as slanted reporting which results in biases in the coverage of political disputes, i.e. where one side is favoured over the other (Entman 2010). Here, the news colludes with political power by operating a form of what Starkman (2014) calls 'access reporting'. Access reporting is driven by relationships between journalists and their sources. Here, journalists tend to wilfully frame a story in accordance with the leads and leaks provided by sources, even if those sources are themselves 'political elites [that] are framed with suspicion' (Dahlgren 2009: 51). For Paterson (2014), the problem is not collusion but compliance, specifically compliance to government diktat or fiat on what can be covered and increasingly how it should be covered. Such compliance ranges across diverse forms of government controlled access to politicians, military personnel and experts of various kinds. Paterson duly highlights the way in which journalists are treated instrumentally by the US government, for example in relation to its growing obsession with military information control and embedding journalists in conflict zones.[20] The effect of this, according to Paterson, has been to elicit a compliant press which just goes along with the Pentagon and fails to sufficiently interrogate the US's thinking behind its policies.

To conclude, the lapdog response to the exercise of political power can be understood as twofold: (a) to offer naturalistic accounts and systemic narratives about a certain way of life as superior to others and (b) be blatant, obvious and invite audiences to 'take sides'. It moves along a spectrum of third- and second-dimensional power, and in both cases, the deleterious effect of lapdog news journalism is the gradual and corrosive undermining of civic knowledge, public discourse, liberal ideals and some audiences' trust in journalistic practices and political institutions.[21]

2.1.2 The Yapping Dog

The yapping dog form of news media may or may not take sides, though it usually tries to appear as if it does not (see below). Its *forte* is that it is engaged in an increasingly mutually dependent, but largely unrecognised, relationship with all aspects of political power and with all of those who wish to obtain it. It is not therefore a question of which side but of all sides of the political process engaging with the news media based on the recognition that politics now exists in a state of 'permanent campaigning'.[22] A consequence of this is that political power needs to work with the news media in increasingly mutually beneficial but different ways. There is now an increased understanding of the performative nature of political events. For example, elections are as constructed and designed as news media events; there is a perceived need for symbols and metaphors to be produced and the communicative necessity for meaning to be created (often out of the most vapid pronouncements) and to attempt to ensure control of the corresponding dissemination of these messages. To live in a political system of permanent political campaigning and 'reality-TV politics' (Luce 2017: 79) requires that the various representatives of political power now compete for: dominating and achieving total coverage for its particular manifesto, of maximising reach and exposure and of 'shouting' down the other side. News organisations know this only too well, and as such, news and politics exist in a kind of negotiated mutual dependency as to how they can facilitate these political outcomes. As Dahlgren (2009: 53) observes, politics has increasingly been 'organised as a media phenomenon, planned and executed for and with the co-operation of the media' and in the process, this may change the nature of politics and with that the nature of political journalism. For Alexander (2016), politics is now performative and choreographed around 'cultural reconstructions', 'compelling stories', 'plot points', 'symbolic domination' and their various coverage and representation in the news media.[23] Political power is, in short, shared at the level of the mediated campaign.

The news media and politicians and political parties are seen to need each other to combine their respective strengths and to create news media spectacles out of political events and to enable politicians to become 'personalities with stories'. While this may entertain and/or persuade, it reduces the news media to that of being complicit in 'packaging politics' (Franklin 2004) and simultaneously engaging in the charade that both are independent of each other. The unwritten 'rules of engagement' between the two are well understood by all, that is editors, news journalists and pundits, politicians, spin doctors, campaign managers and message gurus et al. Politicians routinely work to the rhythm of the news cycle and the type of audience they want to reach. They systematically feed stories to favoured news journalists and pundits, dovetail their schedule and events to accord with maximum or most flattering exposure, do the news rounds and so on. Occasionally, they may appear to be independent of the news media (not undertaking to join in a debate or not giving a press conference), but the essential rhythm of the relationship remains undisturbed. Equally, news organisations must appear independent of these political considerations, though not so independent as to incur some form of political sanction. This results in political commentary becoming routine and anodyne. It is anodyne in three ways: first, it adopts the appearance of being clever and insightful by claiming that it is exposing politics as it is really practised, its 'dirty side' and what that really means. Second, it routinely expresses moral disapproval when it exposes politicians as having 'dirty hands', as being unsuited for something or as being hypocritical.[24] Third (and as a result of one and two), it engages in trivial punditry, which produces a narrative of who can and cannot be trusted with political power. Anodyne commentary is not based on scrutiny; rather, it serves to achieve two things: first, the appearance of independence and second, to provide the reasons for deciding whom 'we' should support. While they may appear contradictory, they are not: both serve the relationship of mutuality between the news media and political power.

With regard to the first, it establishes a (faux) independence between the news media and political power, one that delights in the appearance of scrutiny and presents its commentaries as in-depth analysis or exclusive insight because it must achieve a patina of balance. The culture of balance is particularly conducive to the rapprochement between the news media and political power since it plays to the concept of fairness, which is perceived to be a democratic virtue. In this case, however, 'fairness' is reduced to the application of a ritualistic formula which can be easily achieved and where different points of view are merely juxtaposed. In such an event, the news 'stages' a setting which consists of 'talking heads' and which is devoid of the genuine richness and ambiguity of ordinary and daily discussions about politics. This staging frequently involves the allocation of 'an equal amount of time' given to each participant. Such simple measuring of the time accorded to different views is maintained as an artificial arithmetic balance which mimics the appearance of objectivity.[25] The ritualistic display of balance and even-handedness simply serves to showcase the appearance of independence.

With regard to the second, to help 'us' to decide whom to support it trivialises the criteria for the reasons for support. Consider the example of the coverage of the UK General Election in 2015 which resulted in a Conservative Party victory. The reporting was dominated by the 'the horse race' between the two party leaders—Ed Miliband and David Cameron—who were being judged according to morals, character and suitability as determined by their particular personalities rather than on their political expertise and their parties' take on policy issues.[26] Ultimately, the press reported particularly negatively on Ed Miliband (then the Labour Party leader) via a sustained commentary about his eating habits, fashion style, his father, his relationship with his brother and other similar matters. In essence, the news media reported the UK elections like a presidential election replete with all the noise that comes with such a personality-focused type of election where substantive issues of the parties' policies often don't make headlines.

In short, anodyne commentary turns non-events into news media events and genuine political disagreement into non-events. The net result is that the news media make a lot of noise but actually do not scrutinise policies; rather, they produce 'process' news. What 'we' witness is the packaged routinely conflictual but polished exchange between news media trained actors and the trivialisation of decision-making. Political packaging now matters more than ever and comes with the recognition that the news media also now matter more than ever to politicians. What has emerged is a symbiotic relationship of mutual dependency where the news media and political power put up the appearance of independence from each other while settling for the fact that mediated politics consists of a fundamentally shared agenda that politics is spectacle and performance and not decision-making or policy advocacy of any detail. In essence, the yapping dog news media lives with its own form of hypocrisy—the appearance of independence—while attending to the demands of politics as a permanent campaign and informing 'us' of the trivial criteria, which should guide our political decisions.

2.1.3 The Watchdog
The role of a watchdog journalist is an old cliché. It expresses the ideal news journalist as some form of 'protector' or 'guardian' who supplies 'us' with the information 'we' need to prevent abuses of power and to enable us to prosecute those who are causing us harm. In short, to undertake a watchdog role news journalists have to be free to investigate political power, to scrutinise and challenge it. It is the news media as a fourth estate which holds power to account and exposes wrongdoing—this is how the watchdog role is widely understood. It is also where the civil ideal of the news is at its most proximate and real because it is a form of news where critique and criticism of politicians and their actions reveal areas of genuine contestation with regard to policy implementation, wrongdoing or failures and where audiences are treated as citizens with rights that must be upheld. At such times, the news becomes a watchdog whose very presence acts as an important deterrent to the misuse or abuse of political power in democratic cultures. It displays its power through its ability to maintain editorial independence from all forms of political power and control its own news agendas free from political whims and wants. It is an expression of the second dimension of power which exists in and through the way it holds political power to account by effectively scrutinising what power holders seek to impose on civil society without a public warrant or mandate. In this way, the news contributes to the possibility of a civil debate and a deliberative culture.

News journalists spend more time advocating that this is what they do in practice than anything else. It is a mantra, an uncontentious article of faith, integrity and professional pride. It is what they say they actually undertake consistently. Importantly and in defence of these claims, news journalism does indeed produce some civil outcomes of consequence.[27] However, in order to achieve civil outcomes watchdog journalism has to live with the recognition that liberalism expresses incommensurable values, that 'other' political ideas can be attractive, that the civil sphere is complex and riven with diverse views and that the public sentiment we express with regard to our invariant civil concerns precludes easy formulaic news journalism. As such, it represents the extent to which 'indignation ripples through the communicative institutions of the civil sphere' (Alexander 2008: 188) and reflects the degree to which the news media effectively seek to control and subordinate political will where it departs from the values of civil society. It is often said that what constrains watchdog journalism is not so much political power—though this is certainly true when state violence is deployed—but is rather nothing other than commercial power.

2.2 Commercial Power

Commercial power is mainly expressed in terms of Lukes's first and second dimensions of power. Commercial power colludes with political power typically in terms of commercial necessity and commercial priorities, which further typically involve commercial organisations in demanding to be unregulated or deregulated. At the same time, commercially minded (private and public) news organisations seek market dominance and treat the public as an audience—many audiences in fact. News organisations engage in competitions about which one manages to address which audience, wins a particular ratings war and, related to that, hits their advertising revenue targets. In this competitive market, audiences are not seen as citizens rather they are consumers to be 'fed and led', to be entertained and their tastes catered for (Harrison and Woods 2007). As such, there is an explicit behavioural as well as a hidden persuasive element to commercial power in that it seeks to attract as big an audience as possible, influence its commercial decisions and accord with its expectations while all the time pursuing the simple aim of maximising revenues. Two things need to be noted: first, news organisations are very attractive commercial propositions in their current cross-platform formats and as such are targets for a variety of other commercial groups because of the way they can drive particular agendas. Second, this attractiveness takes two forms: either non-news commercial interests buy extant news organisations, or seek to form their own. In both cases, the production of the news becomes more complicit in libertarian and commercial values and thereby undermines civil interests.

2.2.1 News Media as Targets and Drivers of Commercial Interests and the Production of Contemporary Commercial Journalism

As already noted in Chapter 2, Weber admired critically independent news journalism. Yet, his admiration was not so naïve as not to come without a warning: commercial power and interests corrupt news independence. For Weber (1919: 12), the risks to critically independent journalism are easily identified with the commercial power of 'chain newspapers' that breed and encourage political indifference, the loss of editorial independence, editors who are party officials or proselytisers, the demand for sensationalism (his word: ibid.: 13), the power of advertising and the political power of owners. In particular, he refers to Lord Northcliffe as a 'capitalist press magnate' (ibid.: 12) whose own influence 'gains more and more political influence', while 'apparently the journalist worker gains less and less' (ibid.). Old-fashioned newspaper barons—such as Northcliffe, Rothermere and Beaverbrook in Britain, Randolph Hearst in America and Axel Springer in Germany—have largely been replaced by corporate managers of large transnational conglomerations who are often involved across a wide range of media, sometimes with a diverse range of products and interests.

Nevertheless, it still remains the case that newspaper owners retain an interest in influencing political outcomes, or at least enjoy claiming that this has been the case, that is until they are confronted by a lawyer.[28] The potential commercial power of some news media organisations and of their owners (who may in turn also be owners of large media conglomerates) lies in the degree of success they have in their attempts to use their influence and commercial power to be overtly or covertly involved in politics for commercial gain, i.e. to drive particular agendas.[29] Commercial news media owners may seek explicitly to influence politicians and their decisions and see their news outlet as a mouthpiece to amplify their own views. In these cases, the relationship with political power is more likely to be one of commercial expediency than ideological attachment, though of course some ideologies are more commercially attractive to news media owners than others (see next section). Related to this is the increasing commercial attractiveness for media owners found in establishing cultural hegemonies usually through the fictional media, but increasingly with the support of factual media which consistently promotes a certain way of life as superior (see above). Such commercial interests lead to a contemporary form of corporate journalism which, in all its aspects, systematically responds to commercial imperatives in ways that past newspaper barons could only ever have dreamed about.

More specifically, news organisations today are now more likely to be owned by techno-media companies, which embrace both fictional and factual outputs, or by international technology companies which see the value in diverse forms of media content. The net effect of this is that establishing or acquiring a news organisation in this kind of setting entails that news organisations are increasingly subject to (and the target of) the commercial imperatives of maximising revenues and forms of cost control that take little account of the cost of the 'investigative investment' necessary to produce reliable news journalism or that attends to the complex nature of audiences.[30] News aggregation systems and editorial algorithms[31] are just two of the most obvious forms of cost control on newsgathering and reporting that are on the increase because, as more than one commentator believes, social media is (for the time being) the most common way news is shared and consumed. Further, and as Luce (2017: 65) notes, 'Reporters are losing jobs to algorithmic content farms that write news reports based on keywords that push them to the top of the Google search page'. It appears likely that techno-media companies will increasingly dominate the news business and with this arise open-ended political questions about the necessity for global and national regulatory control, the management of false news and the extent of fact-checking which now has to extend beyond the written word to anticipate content produced by 'a new breed of video and audio manipulation tools, made possible by advances in artificial intelligence and computer graphics' (Solon 2017). Editorial independence dominates factual media policy and regulation and relationships with political power—whichever type of company dominates and whatever new mergers and acquisitions appear. Techno-media companies may or may not internally subsidise the news operation or place it under very strict cost management with an emphasis on the news organisation breaking even or of being self-financing,[32] Under the influence of such companies where there is a requirement for news to maximise online clicks and shares, the newsroom is reduced in scope, breadth and capacity for investigative journalism exemplifying with greater force what (Schlesinger 1987: 84) once described as a 'stop-watch' culture.

Indeed, working to a deadline, competing with rival news organisations and working quickly have been constant elements of journalism as has the need to maximise audience revenue. In response, news organisations have made increasing use of market research about their audiences, incorporating their findings into management decisions about how the newsroom operates (Hamilton 2006) and to find ways to harness new technology to try better to attract audiences and advertisers (Curran et al. 2009; Ghersetti 2014). Increased competition with other news providers in the digital environment has placed news providers under ever-growing pressure to get the story published as quickly as possible—sometimes immediately—as the use of portable devices such as mobile phones and laptops encouraged audiences to access the news at any time and in almost any location (Dimmick et al. 2011; Westlund 2013). Publishing as quickly as possible in order to be the first to 'break' the story has been and remains a key newsroom priority since the 1980s and accordingly, the process has had to speed up. A prioritisation of speed allows less time for the more methodologically rigorous aspects of professional journalistic practice to be applied. The demands of 24/7 news of constant commentary, updates, piecemeal and rolling narratives, an unceasing demand for 'experts' and 'witnesses', maximum use of visuals (pictures, graphics and video) are all supported by a lexicon of disclosure where we, the audience, become witnesses of events as they happen. Ongoing developments can actually prove to be rather exciting for the audience and may even produce in some way a sense of being involved in the story, and the more that audiences are drawn in and stories go viral or begin to trend on Twitter, the more news becomes a valuable commodity. It is part of a trend towards realising the commercial value of the news as a form of news that people will want to be updated on, to share and perhaps to comment on and with which advertisers will want to be associated. In this frenetic environment, being first is often seen as a more important factor than being right, but where corrections occur (if they occur), they can be easily missed or lost in the overwhelming torrents of information.

The sheer diversity of news produced in different institutional settings now enables it to take many saleable forms, notably ways in which to integrate different media platforms in a variety of different ways and to involve audiences directly. Attempts to produce cross-platform news that conforms to 24/7 demands has led to a widespread and general view that the news must be dumbing down simply because of the inability of newsrooms to adequately respond to and manage the volume of information now at journalists' disposal—a volume that is simply overwhelming, resorting to a flat earth news approach that is too heavily reliant on public relations press releases and other forms of persuasive and distorted content (Davies 2009). In addition, the practices of some journalists and the news products of many news organisations have been criticised for handling such volume and seeking to entertain their audiences by marginalising analytical news out of peak time schedules[33] or off the home pages of their websites and encouraging the growth of tabloid values which change the focus of news selection away from the 'serious' (politics, public policy, social issues, economics, international affairs, etc.) to human interest news focused on show business, celebrities and scandal. News providers have been accused of providing a less accurate or incomplete account of events than in previous less competitive eras. In other words, they have been accused of producing news that may become less homologous to the world as it is selected, diced and sliced to fit in with fickle audience interests and the intention first and foremost to sell the news at all costs. The pressure on all news organisations in the hyper-competitive 'new attention economy' (Baldwin 2018: 249) that now dominates the contemporary media ecosystem is to provide their audiences/users with instant gratification. Their task is both variously aided and hindered by social media as increasingly 'news journalism is caught up in and being bounced around businesses which make their money by selling its users' attention to advertisers' (Kakutani 2018: 259). Overall, the competitive drive to acquire audiences/users/readers and advertisers has increased the propensity of some, but not all, news organisations to prioritise salacious and entertaining news that appeals to the 'emotional, impulsive, identity-based outrage' (Baldwin 2018: 249) of its audiences/users/readers above the measured and the considered, to shout louder and louder to gain attention and even to break the law in order to create stories from people's private lives and secrets.[34] Nonetheless, events are still selected as newsworthy because they fit into what a news supplier regards itself as standing for and the consumer audience/users/readers it serves and consequently accords with the news supplier's own a priori commercial values (Harrison 2008).

Linked to the pressure of news having to match audiences'/users'/readers' express expectations and preferences, there has been an increasing drive to encourage the participation of audiences in sourcing news and some have suggested that there is now an altered landscape between the professional journalist and the audience.[35] This involvement, it is argued, has emerged because of digitally facilitated developments such as social media and online resources, which are equally available to both news journalists and audiences. The net result of this, it is further suggested, is a reduction in the journalists' monopoly of newsgathering and news production, which, in turn, is accompanied by a potential chipping away at traditional journalistic boundaries of professionalism and exclusivity in the form of progressive activities such as user-generated content (UGC) or 'collaborative journalism' (Canter 2013: 1106). Collaborative journalism extends to instances such as the incorporation of citizen activist video into a professional news organisation's material in what Wall and El Zahed (2015: 720) have referred to as a 'pop-up news ecology'. For Wall (2015: 807), citizen involvement in news 'is now so intertwined with the workings of the professional news media that it is hard to imagine citizen journalism—or whatever one wants to call it—disappearing', reminding us that 'journalism is merely one set of practices within a network of activities that make up society'. It has also been noted that ordinary citizen voices are finding their way into the news more than before (De Keyser and Raeymaeckers 2012). In such developments, Wall (2015: 807) finds a link to civil aspirations in citizen journalism which she argues 'has become the touchstone term for the last decade precisely because it reflects an ongoing normative belief that news is connected to a potentially positive form of civic behaviour'. In other words, it is being strongly argued in some quarters that a form of audience power exists, albeit in pockets, that could be seen positively and should be welcomed with some degree of optimism about the ability of both traditional and non-traditional news media to play a role in global social activism and to undertake a democratic role by holding repressive regimes to account. In this vein, the growth of citizen journalism, network journalism[36] and crowdsourcing has been seen as a way to (a) hold other types of power to account[37] and (b) allow the public to speak in ways it has never been able to before. The exposure by citizens of state secrets to the press[38] and also to Wikileaks[39] has meant that the idea has taken hold that the public should be made privy to more information than the mainstream news providers routinely provide in order to make its own judgements about what should be kept secret and what should not. The view of digital technologies in this kind of reading is they have and are helping to create a more democratic space where the relationship between citizens and journalists is more interactive (Blumler and Gurevitch 2001) facilitating greater representational power for citizens (Coleman 2005) and possibly even an alternative type of public sphere (Guo 2017). Such claims to audience power undoubtedly have some form of civil significance (activism, involvement, participation and so on) and potential, particularly to those who are affected by them or participate in making them. However, this picture appears to be somewhat rosy given that such journalistic engagements with audiences remain patchy (Ghersetti 2014) and uneven (Canter 2013) as most journalists do not want to leave behind their traditional routine practices and are not particularly keen to share their professional authority with non-journalists (Lewis 2012; Singer and Ashman 2009; Blaagaard 2013; Örnebring 2013). In fact, other studies have shown that professional journalists still continue to employ means to control citizen content seeing it as unprofessional or poorer quality, needing verification, and in mainstream news media tends to require editorialising in what has been called a 'playground' model or the 'UGC ghetto' (Ghersetti 2014; Harrison 2010; Jönsson and Örnebring 2011: 135; Pantti and Bakker 2009). Notably, some of those supplying UGC or citizen journalism have said that they have felt somewhat exploited by the mainstream news organisations (Borger et al. 2013). Furthermore, there is evidence to show that citizens' voices are still not routinely heard in mainstream news simply because routines such as those determining who journalists contact as sources of information remain largely unchanged (Domingo et al. 2008; Kleemans et al. 2017; Paulussen and Ugille 2008).

The commercial imperative behind the encouragement of audience engagement is however self-fulfilling consumerism whereby news providers find up-to-date ways to engage audiences who, in turn, increasingly expect interesting and exciting, informative, personalised, interactive, instantaneous, bite-sized and customisable news to be available to them 24/7, that is for news to fit in with consumers consumption patterns of any time, anywhere and anyhow—and always according to the preferences of a particular audience. As Eagleton (2016: 144) puts it: 'The fact that the newscasters are selected among other things for being easy on the eye, as well as for the resonant pitch of their voices, the faux-genial banter between them, the abrupt leaping from one news item to another, the sensationalised presentation, the monosyllabic scripts, the fact that camera shots in film footage are rarely sustained for more than a few seconds, the absence of in-depth analysis so as to not bore less sophisticated viewers, the relentless focus on home-grown news even if a nuclear war has just broken out in Yorkshire – all this bespeaks the overriding imperative of securing the largest possible audience for the sake of the greatest possible profit'. In particular, the libertarian and commercial instincts of technology-driven media companies see news as an accoutrement to customisation and with that comes personal recommendation profiling and personalised advertising. This is far from a return to the 'Daily Me',[40] even though audiences have for a while been fragmented into smaller groups with niche interests (Hamilton 2006) and some possibly even into 'different communication universes' (Kakutani 2018: 14). While some audience involvement may make inroads into traditional news media power structures, claims about the power of technological change to empower some audience action, activism or engagement or democratising news media power to any significant extent can easily be overstated. In fact, those who view audience participation as potentially democratic need to engage with the fact that much participation occurs in what are increasingly known as 'echo chambers', 'information cocoons' and 'filter bubbles' which can even create audiences' 'own realities' which operate 'with their own facts' (Kakutani 2018: 88), as these environments can hardly be seen to be deliberative.[41] The involvement of audiences in the news process at different levels has undoubtedly created a range of tensions and problems for journalists who seek to reconcile their traditional values of quality, impartiality and balance with audience participation. Consequently, it is still largely the case that news organisations appropriate material from the public on their own terms and within their own editorial guidelines to enhance and add value and interest to their own provision, while keeping a close control on the content.

2.2.2 The Libertarian Commercial Ethic and the News
Assuming it is plausible to talk about a commercial ethic, then the dominant one for the news is provided by the libertarian commercialism of Silicon Valley. While it is true that Silicon Valley has managed to find for itself both a reputation for sponsoring progressive causes and for promoting social and environmental concerns, it has at the same time promoted libertarianism.[42] There is no real contradiction here since the libertarianism in question is simply of the commercial variety and not necessarily the political philosophical kind that Nozick espouses, though both attend to issues of the maximisation of rights. More widely conceived of, libertarian commercialism is a mishmash of views about freedom of choice and consumer sovereignty, personal autonomy and opportunities for maximising preferences, individual liberty and the limited role of the state (except as a customer)—all in all an ideology of how markets should be dealt with, left alone or minimally regulated and how

the consumer benefits from all of this. More narrowly conceived of, libertarian commercialism of the techno-media kind advocates the view that the space and location for the maximisation of certain rights are to be found in the free market, and of all the rights to be maximised the most commercially valuable is freedom of expression, and accompanying this, news media pluralism, albeit of a very specific kind.

At an individual level, this is easy to see why. Being able to express yourself freely and without restraint quickly and to whomever you want to send your views to (and of course whomever they send them to and so on) is the staple diet of giant social media companies. They provide nothing other than a series of privately owned public spheres (Garton-Ash 2016) freely joined (and enjoyed) by billions. Equally, this freedom of expression enables a more coherent profile of whom you are to be drawn up. This provides an opportunity for closed platforms to build a profile of your likes and dislikes in order to then sell that information on and/or to target you with personalised adverts, recommendations of services you might be interested in and of places where you may meet like-minded people. The more often I freely express myself the more it is possible for a techno-media company to get to know me. If the gathering of such information seems to infringe on other rights I might have, the reply is: (a) I voluntarily agreed to such profiling, and therefore, no rights have been infringed or (b) if the platform I use is free, then such profiling is the commercial price I must pay for it being free at the point of use and this too is contractually assented to as a condition of use. Freedom of expression constantly reflects its commercial value the more we use the media to air our views. However, at another level these privately owned public spheres also house groups who claim to be dealing in news. At which point, freedom of expression is used to justify the expression of extreme and sometimes abhorrent views and algorithmic or human (in-house or outsourced) 'moderators', 'content deciders' and 'fact checkers' are deployed to supply content control services for the techno-media company. These then routinely remove the odd transgressor or remove content from their platform if they are deemed to have violated their internal guidelines. Unfortunately, such guidelines (dominated as they are by an extreme form of freedom of expression) are proving to be either inadequate or inconsistent.

An illustration of this can be found in Facebook's problematic relationship with the news as it struggles with its own identity as a technology company or a news media organisation. It is notable that the pressures that the company has come under to explain and justify itself are based on the civil ideal of the news (see Chapter 2), namely the responsibility that is seen to come with the provision of news. Facebook's somewhat ambiguous status as variously a content recommendation engine, techno-media company or news organisation has drawn it into debates about the extent to which it is part of the global news ecology for several reasons. First, its sheer size and market domination mean that Facebook both competes with news organisations for advertising and has shaped the format news takes in order for news organisations to ensure that Facebook recommends their stories to its users. Second, Facebook's environment of social sharing and recommendations among friends and families has meant that false and hyper-partisan news that is likely to be exciting, encourages an emotional response, panders to our susceptibility to enjoy 'confirmation bias' (Vaidhyanathan 2018: 94) is widely circulated along with information and views that may be 'liberating, energising and transformative' but are also just as likely to be 'toxic, divisive, poisonous and dangerous' (Rusbridger 2018: xix). Third, Facebook provides a user profile that can be specifically targeted by advertisers and other purveyors of information. In recognition that it brings niche news organisations, fake news suppliers (those who deliberately provide false information, misinformation and disinformation) and mainstream news media their audience traffic, as well as simultaneously hosting fake, distorted and accurate information on its site, in 2016 Facebook began to address the need to fact check. The company partnered with ABC News, FactCheck.org, Politifact and Snopes[43] to flag and check stories that are circulating widely on its network and has added a tool which allows users to flag up any stories that appear to be fake (Ball 2017). While Facebook calls itself 'a friend of journalism' (Ball 2017: 141) because it drives traffic to mainstream news media sites, it also deprives them of online advertising thereby seriously affecting their revenue streams. The addition by Facebook of a feature called 'trending' to users' home pages entailed the employment of a small group of journalists at Facebook. The stories that were picked gave a massive boost of traffic to different news organisations' websites. Leaks by the trending teams about the power of these curators of news and their ability to blacklist topics put Facebook under scrutiny about its news selection process. At that point, Facebook faced the dilemma of any news organisation, namely how to ensure that news selection processes were fair, transparent and neutral. Facebook's response was to remove its curators and to develop an algorithm. Problematically for Facebook, this algorithm is just as likely to distort the selection process by amplifying false and hyper-partisan news along with other news. The sharing of distorted news in so-called filter bubbles has meant that stories that appeal to users of Facebook will be spread among trust communities of family and friends whether it is faked or not. Equally, political groups make use of Facebook to target specific groups with particular messages favourable to their candidate. While fact-checking may address some of the stories that are circulating through Facebook, it remains the case that it is far harder and much more time-consuming to debunk a made-up story than to make one up. The effort and investment put into fact-checking are not tackling the problems, rather addressing them as they crop up. The creation of false stories and misinformation for some is a lucrative occupation and based on a basic business model of the higher the number of views/shares the more income is generated, meaning there is a financial incentive to provide stories that stand out from the mainstream and target and reinforce people's opinions and prejudices—a trend that looks set to continue. Even so techno-media companies still persist in creating the impression that the defence of freedom of expression is responsibly undertaken and that our guardians in this matter are to be thanked for their integrity and ability to responsibly control content.

Of course, techno-media companies have the added advantage of evoking their defence in terms of ubiquitous declarations of freedom of expression,[44] and they can also afford to take part in the legal debates that surround questions of what such things as group libel, race and gender defamation, libel, slander and hate speech actually are.[45] All of this conspires to ensure that very few transgressors are actually found out, let alone barred from the network. First amendment fundamentalism covers a lot of sins and has been eloquently espoused by distinguished legal scholars who justify 'Freedom for the Thought That We Hate' (Lewis 2007).[46] Techno-media companies know their jurisprudence.

Media pluralism is also like freedom of expression—a double-edged sword. It can be appealed to as a democratic necessity, but paradoxically, it is more likely to be used in the modern news ecology to provide a justification for techno-media companies to engage in cross-media deals or acquire more of the supplier-content-consumer value chain. For commercial libertarianism media, pluralism is not about democracy. Rather it has a more specific meaning—commercial diversity. As such contemporary media pluralism is increasingly judged according to guarantees with regard to diversity of suppliers, content and outlook. These guarantees are assessed according to a local determination of whether any form of news media concentration breaches extant local competition rules. Take for example the EU news landscape in which the choice of news is becoming increasingly stark: authoritarian political power interfering with local news services and a single market favourable to libertarian commercial values. Not unexpectedly, the EU conceives of itself as a representative democracy and, attendant upon this, values news media freedom and media pluralism.[47] The latter is seen to be a vital element of democracy and therefore to be protected. However, its value-laden discourse has so far proved to be largely symbolic and little has been done in terms of implementing its own principles of news media governance or via its power of direct intervention.[48] With the net result that the authoritarian control of the news by neo-liberal autocrats is bizarrely seen as somehow not infringing free competition rules nor of limiting media pluralism and hence does not require any form of intervention. Across the EU, the increasing concentration of ownership of the news media supply chain proceeds unabated and in this way appears to be judged not to be detrimental to media and news diversity.[49] For the EU, there is no contradiction between the concentration of control and/or ownership and news media diversity achieved by fulfilling the requirements of consumer choice. Simply put, what all techno-media companies have to do is undertake to guarantee commercial diversity which to say the very least is an undemanding quality threshold. It is not difficult for libertarian commercial values to be used by techno-media companies to prove that they conform to the EU competition rules of the single market. The commercial dynamic at play in the EU and around the globe is simply between claims that market acquisitions guarantee commercial criteria of diversification. This is because techno-media companies simply value a marketplace where there are no barriers to entry, no undue regulation and no prior restraint (censorship) to content.

By contrast, markets, which constrain techno-media companies by some form of meaningful regulatory supervision on news services and freedom of expression, are regarded as unduly restrictive and this forms part of the backdrop against which their own news organisations operate in, whereby libertarian news organisations are passionate advocates of freedom of expression (and with that commercial diversity). Contemporary news ideology is replete with the widespread acceptance of this libertarian outlook and its associated commercial and corporate norms. The result of this is that the news owning giant techno-media companies enter public spaces while seeing themselves as either minimally compliant to generous rules of competition or beyond the command of international regulatory regimes and nation states. In other words, they see themselves as ultimately beyond accountability while valorising individual freedom and their own form of news media pluralism. Support for freedom of expression and news media diversity when tied to commercial libertarianism produces what Garton-Ash (2016) refers to as a corporate language which effortlessly vacillates between high-minded free speech rhetoric and salesmanship. The latter for no other reason than as noted above audiences are consumers, there to be maximised and to talk about what they have bought or wish to buy.

Critics see the influence of libertarian values as variously: reducing the quality and reliability of news content (McManus 1994), having a trivialising and corrosive effect on meaningful democratic discussion (Hanitzsch 2007; Postman 1996), requiring that news journalism surrender to market demands (Bourdieu 1996), reducing the likelihood of any challenge to 'the economic elite' which, given the greater focus on political power by journalists, 'basically gets edited out of discourses about power' (Dahlgren 2009: 33). As Couldry (2010: 2) notes, such a practice 'formally, practically, culturally and imaginatively' marginalises some types of voices, thereby diminishing public knowledge. It is difficult, however, not to agree with Chomsky's summary (1989 in Mitchell and Schoeffl 2003: 15)—and it is worth quoting him at length: 'Well, essentially in Manufacturing Consent what we were doing was contrasting two models: how the media ought to function, and how they do function. The former model is the more or less conventional one: it's what the New York Times recently referred to in a book review as the "traditional Jeffersonian role of the media as a counter-weight to government" – in other words, a cantankerous, obstinate, ubiquitous press, which must be suffered by those in authority in order to preserve the right of the people to know, and to help the population assert meaningful control over the political process. That's the standard conception of the media in the United States, and it's what most of the people in the media themselves take for granted. The alternative conception is that the media will present a picture of the world, which defends and inculcates the economic, social, and political agendas of the privileged groups that dominate the domestic economy, and who therefore also largely control the government'.

3 Summary

As noted above, all three dimensions of power (following Lukes, influence, agenda setting and adjusting choices and expectations) are concerned with what is left out in the news, what is excluded, what is omitted and what views and outlooks remain unchallenged. In this way, politically and commercially inspired anti-civil values seek to provide the context for all news. It makes no difference if this is political or social news: single mothers are tax burdens, welfare policy is antithetical to free enterprise, free health care distorts the health insurance market, asylum seekers need to prove their market utility, and so on. There is built into politically and commercially inspired anti-civil values a hostility towards the value of accurate and sincere news journalism or a public service ethos in news reporting. This type of ideological framing is constant, and the above criticisms are sometimes left unanswered. Exacerbating the problem of the survival of the civil ideal of the news is how political and commercial power diminish the civil standing of their audiences/users/readers by conceiving of them as partisans from whom is demanded their blind loyalty, or consumers from whom is demanded their undivided attention, rather than citizens and the regulatory landscape generally supports this view (Harrison and Woods 2007). Both political power and commercial power prefer an instrumental relationship to their audiences/users/readers. Accordingly, audiences/users/readers are seen as more 'useful' or 'beneficial' to the news providers when they are regarded as having some form of political power to help bring about and endorse a political outcome or have the commercial power to spend on services and goods promoted or supportive of the news channel. All of this is very well understood, and yet the civil ideal of the news survives. It survives as a background challenge to journalism conceived of as a purely political or commercial venture and as a rationale for journalism conceived of as a public service. In this, it still can influence styles of reporting and through that the type of boundary maintenance the news ultimately endorses. The ideal and the real belong together and more often than not are in a state of tension. In order to explain what news is, we must recognise how this tension is played out and thereby recognise that in this, the real and the ideal cannot be practically separated.

NOTES

1. In totalitarian or authoritarian states, power expresses itself in every part of the world (and with alarming and increasing regularity in Europe) with brutal and vicious hostility against journalists (see Bennett [2013], Davies and Crawford [2013], Horsley and Harrison [2013], and Paterson [2014]). In these cases, where attacks against journalists include, e.g., murder, abductions, harassment and arbitrary detention, and are often undertaken with impunity (Harrison and Pukallus 2018), the civil ideal of the news is nothing if not a forlorn hope. On the dangers of being a journalist, see Hudson and Stanier (1997), Katovsky and Carlson (2003), Knightley (2004), Lisosky and Henrichsen (2009), Paul and Kim (2004), Smyth (2009), and Tumber and Webster (2006).
2. One particular type of investigative news is what is called 'alternative news' that engages with non-elite sources (Harcup 2003, 2011a) and is a form of 'oppositional reporting' that 'speaks up for the powerless against the powerful' (Harcup 2014: 575, also Harcup 2011b).
3. Jacobs (2009: 151) shows how Park's sociology of the news media initially focused on news and the power of the press and argues that '[w]hile the conceptual vocabulary was different, this work was clearly engaged with questions that today would invoke the language of news media and public sphere' and that Park had developed a theory of factual media and the public sphere by 1941: 'In essence, Park distinguished between an elite public sphere and a popular public sphere, and linked each to a specific part of the newspaper (...) [and that particularly] during periods of change and social transformation, Park's theory of press and public sphere pointed to the importance of the news column and the way it organised political discussion among ordinary citizens'. In short, news reporting as a form of civil power.
4. On the cultural power of the news as a form of symbolic power, see Hall (1973 [2006]), Schudson (1995), Thompson (1997) and more recently Alexander et al. (2016).
5. Inequalities here range from the 'digital divide' to international media conglomerates' use of cheap labour.
6. For more general discussions about some of the problems of media effects research, see Buckingham (1998), Gunter and Harrison (1998), and Livingstone (1996).
7. See Note 32, Chapter 2.
8. Corner (2013) also considers Lukes's work but applies it more generally to an understanding of media power rather than news power.
9. The intellectual roots for one-dimensional power lie in the work of C. Wright Mills' The Power Elite (1956) and Dahl's response

(1957, 1958, 1961) regarding the capacity to exercise sovereign influence over the outcomes of overt decisions in which parties had revealed different sets of preferences. Lukes's two-dimensional power is reminiscent of Bachrach and Baratz (1962, 1963) who illustrate that the power to dominate can be exercised through the ability to manipulate agendas. Lukes points to a gap which he terms third-dimensional power. For a helpful historical summary, see Johal et al.(2014).
10. See Harrison and Pukallus (2018).
11. President Donald Trump has used a variety of tactics to attack both individual journalists and journalism itself, ranging from the use of the term fake news to try to discredit the accuracy of news stories from mainstream news media organisations, labelling journalists as the 'enemies of the people', mocking journalists and excluding them from White House briefings.
12. See Pukallus and Harrison (2015a, b). More recent examples of attacks on news journalists within the EU are Sloavkian journalist Ján Kuciak shot dead in February 2018 and Maltese journalist Daphne Caruana Galizia who investigated the corruption and money laundering in Malta and was killed in a car bomb in October 2017.
13. For Schutz, the 'Natural Attitude' is the acceptance by an individual that the world is historically constituted and ordered, socially and intersubjectively arranged and can be taken for granted in an unreflective way. However, it is also malleable in the sense that what appears unreflectively natural can be altered by alternative narratives of what a person should be able to take for granted and can reasonably expect.
14. Hyper-partisan news has recently gained audiences who are only too eager to enter into a 'filter bubble' (Pariser 2012) or echo chambers that simply reinforce their own prejudices by producing 'polarised and largely untrue narratives' (Ball 2017: 9).
15. For analyses of the recent development of alt-right news media in the USA, see Brock and Rabin-Havt (2012), Green (2017), and Sherman (2017), for a historical overview since the 1940s see Hemmer (2016).
16. See Harrison (2018, 2019).
17. The term 'alternative facts' was used 22 January 2017 by Ms Kellyanne Conway (at the time Counsellor to President Trump) when defending the then President's press secretary.
18. For a clear statement on the role of 'real people' in populism, see Müller (2016: 101–103).
19. Baldwin (2018: 202) identifies a new media ecosystem in the USA where right-wing news sites such as Reddit and 4 Chan 'orbit around Fox News and Breitbart'.
20. In June 2015, the US Pentagon announced that it had produced its first Law of War Manual. Smyth (2015), Senior Adviser for Journalist Security at the Committee to Protect Journalists, raised the concern that the Law

of War Manual allows the USA to classify journalists as 'unprivileged belligerents' in certain situations. Problematically, the new categorisation 'does not emerge from case law or treaty' which 'may allow military officials to detain journalists without charge, and without any apparent need to show evidence or bring a suspect to trial'.

21. Hammond (2017) shows that data from 28 countries suggests that people have less trust in four key institutions: government, factual media, business and non-government sector. More specifically, the British Social Attitudes Report 30, 2013 shows how trust in government had declined from 38% in 1986 to 18% in 2013. According to the Pew Research Centre (2017), only 20% of Americans today say that they can trust the government in Washington to do what is right 'just about always' (4%) or 'most of the time' (16%).

22. Gutmann and Thompson (2014) argue that political campaigning no longer stops after elections but is continuously undertaken throughout terms of office.

23. On politics as performance and as a spectacle, see Alexander (2011, 2012), Alexander and Jaworsky (2014), and Edelman (1985, 1988).

24. According to Runciman (2008: 21), political hypocrisy can be defined mainly as 'an ill-intended act dressed up to look like a well-intended one'. Whereas one might argue that journalists need to fully understand all layers of hypocrisy—Runciman speaks of first-order and second-order hypocrisy—in order to fulfil the civil ideal, Shklar (1984) argues that the excessive concern we have for hypocrisy is misplaced and our attachment to sincerity and with that our fear of being deceived is also excessive, leading as it does to a desire for a form of purity in politics which is both unrealistic and unrealisable (also Shklar 1976).

25. This is also common for televised debates between politicians competing for office such as the French presidency.

26. On this point, see Jackson and Thorsen's (2015) analysis of the UK General Elections 2015.

27. There are many examples of news reporting having civil consequences ranging from the Washington Post and its investigation into the Watergate scandal in 1972, the Panama Papers in 2016 conducted by the International Consortium of Investigative Journalists and the German newspaper Süddeutsche Zeitung and more recently The Guardian led Cambridge Analytica/Facebook stories.

28. An example of this is News Corporation chairman Rupert Murdoch who during the Leveson Inquiry appeared to be contrite when he described the 'Sun Wot Won It' headline of 11 April 1992 as 'tasteless and wrong for us' and said that he gave Mr. MacKenzie, editor of the Sun at the time 'a terrible bollocking' (see Dowell 2012).

29. Silvio Berlusconi of Italy combined being prime minister with ownership of commercial television channels.
30. The commercial imperative is not a new phenomenon, see, for example, McManus (1994) who argues that economic considerations control decisions made in commercial news media organisations, changed the news media audience into customers, news into a product and the area in which the product circulates into a market.
31. It is worth noting that such algorithms can be manipulated and that as such, they can't replace reliable fact-checking as a means to avoid the spread of fake news (false news, misinformation and disinformation) contra to what Google claims. See Levin (2017).
32. Interestingly, commercial news organisations are not averse to expressing corporate principles or codes of conduct, which can be read as a parody of 'civil' values. For example, Axel Springer's corporate principles include five aspects: (a) the defence of liberty, rule of law, democracy and a united Europe, (b) the support of the Jewish people and the defence of the right to existence of a Jewish State, (c) solidarity with the USA as regards common values, (d) the endorsement of a free social market economy and (e) a rejection of all forms of political or religious extremism. Axel Springer equally endorses independent journalism—how this endorsement is upheld in practice is a matter of conjecture. Such grandiloquent sentiments live cheek by jowl with commercial reality and ambition, and for those of a suspicious nature, are merely rhetorical.
33. However, the BBC announced in January 2017 that it was going to dedicate more space to slow news, i.e. news that provides audiences with in-depth analysis.
34. In the UK, this led to the Leveson Inquiry of 2011–2012 into the Culture, Practices and Ethics of the Press in the UK as a response to illegal intrusion into the private lives of particular victims of crime where a public interest defence was not valid.
35. This altered landscape includes changes by journalists on their perceptions about their areas of professional authority and autonomy and who constitutes insiders and outsiders (Carlson 2015; Carlson and Lewis 2015; Lewis 2012); the maintenance of journalistic boundaries, routines and values (Gieryn 1983); the processes of verification (Hermida 2015); the development of participatory media platforms (Robinson 2010; Wahl-Jorgensen 2015); the nature of journalist-source relations (Revers 2014) and the impact of data journalism (Boyles and Meyer 2016; Coddington 2015; Fink and Anderson 2014; Gynnild 2014; Karlsen and Stavelin 2014).
36. Network journalism involves mainstream journalism outlets, bloggers, journalists who operate independently of journalism outlets and citizens/providers of content.

37. For examples of crowdsourcing investigations in partnership with journalists, see Vehkoo (2013).
38. Ed Snowden, former CIA employee and NSA contractor, disclosed classified details of several top-secret USA and British government mass surveillance programmes to The Guardian newspaper (among others) in May 2013.
39. There have been numerous leaks released by Wikileaks since 2008. These include the Afghan War documents leak on 25 July 2010 as well as the Iraq logs, Guantanamo Bay Files, US diplomatic cables and the Democratic National Committee leaks.
40. Daily Me refers to the idea of a virtual newspaper completely customised to the reader's taste. It is a term coined by Negroponte who founded the MIT media lab in 1985. In an article for the magazine Wired, Fred Hapgood (1995) records that it was in the 1970s that Negroponte first considered an interactive news media environment. Since then and in one form or another the pursuit of web-based retail opportunities, based on personalised knowledge of the consumer, has inspired information, communication and technology companies (ICTs) to enter the news market and to challenge the previous supremacy of traditional news media companies by offering more and more sophisticated versions of the 'Daily Me' replete with customised adverts. Sunstein (2007) uses the Daily Me as a metaphor for the excesses of consumer sovereignty and argues for its debilitating and ultimately deleterious consequences for democracy and the Daily We (Sunstein 2001).
41. See Sunstein (2006, 2009).
42. On Silicon Valley's tarnished image, see Morozov (2017). Related to this, Foer (2017) describes the rhetoric of the Silicon Valley ethic as a personal liberation platform in the spirit of the 1960s: 'Everyone has the right to speak their mind on social media, to fulfil their intellectual and democratic potential, to express their individuality'.
43. All the organisations were members of the Poynter International Fact-Checking Network attempting quickly to fact check and identify hoaxes.
44. The Universal Declaration of Human Rights is the enduring statement of human rights to which all people are entitled. The International Covenant on Civil and Political Rights (Article 19), the African Charter on Human and Peoples' Rights, the American Convention on Human Rights and the European Convention on Human Rights are the key human rights treaties protecting freedom of expression.
45. Waldron (2012) goes some considerable way to answering this question.
46. Alongside Anthony Lewis are Ronald Dworkin and C. Edwin Baker who provide the most brilliant defences of hate speech.

47. See Art. 10 TEU and Art. 11 of the EU Charter of Fundamental Rights. The EU has attempted to access the European Convention of Human Rights (ECHR). However, the draft accession Treaty was rejected by the European Court of Justice (ECJ) on 18 December 2014 for incompatibility with EU law. Whereas a discussion of the rejection is beyond the scope of this chapter, it is nevertheless important to remember that (a) the attempt to access the ECHR testifies to the fact that the EU values fundamental rights including freedom of expression and media freedom and (b) an accession to the ECHR would have meant that the ECJ could have applied European Court of Human Rights jurisprudence directly; see Harris (2013).
48. See also Pukallus and Harrison (2015b).
49. On the problems of media concentration and its detrimental effect on media pluralism and/or media diversity, see Gálik (2010).

BIBLIOGRAPHY

Alexander, J. (2008). Civil Sphere, State, and Citizenship: Replying to Turner and the Fear of Enclavement. *Citizenship Studies, 12*(2), 185–194.
Alexander, J. (2011). *Performance and Power*. Cambridge: Polity.
Alexander, J. (2012). *The Performance of Politics: Obama's Victory and the Democratic Struggle for Power*. Oxford: Oxford University Press.
Alexander, J. (2016). Introduction: Journalism, Democratic Culture, and Creative Reconstruction. In J. Alexander, E. Butler-Breese, & M. Luengo (Eds.), *The Crisis of Journalism Reconsidered: Democratic Culture, Professional Codes, Digital Future* (pp. 1–28). Cambridge: Cambridge University Press.
Alexander, J., & Jaworsky, B. (2014). *Obama Power*. Cambridge: Polity.
Alexander, J., Butler-Breese, E., & Luengo, M. (Eds.). (2016). *The Crisis of Journalism Reconsidered: Democratic Culture, Professional Codes, Digital Future*. Cambridge: Cambridge University Press.
Bachrach, P., & Baratz, M. S. (1962). Two Faces of Power. *The American Political Science Review, 56*(4), 947–952.
Bachrach, P., & Baratz, M. S. (1963). Decisions and Nondecisions: An Analytical Framework. *The American Political Science Review, 57*(3), 632–642.
Baldwin, T. (2018). *Ctrl Alt Delete: How Politics and the Media Crashed Our Democracy*. London: Hurst and Company.
Ball, J. (2017). *Post-truth: How Bullshit Conquered the World*. London: Biteback Publishing.
Bennett, D. (2013). Exploring the Impact of an Evolving War and Terror Blogosphere on Traditional Media Coverage of Conflict. *Media, War & Conflict, 6*(1), 37–53.

Blaagaard, B. (2013). Shifting Boundaries: Objectivity, Citizen Journalism and Tomorrow's Journalists. *Journalism*, *14*(8), 1076–1090.

Blumler, J. G., & Gurevitch, M. (2001). The New Media and Our Political Communication Discontents: Democratizing Cyberspace. *Information, Communication & Society*, *4*(1), 1–13.

Borger, M., et al. (2013). Constructing Participatory Journalism as a Scholarly Object: A Genealogical Analysis. *Digital Journalism*, *1*(1), 117–134.

Bourdieu, P. (1996). *On Television and Journalism*. London: Pluto Press.

Boyles, J. L., & Meyer, E. (2016). Letting the Data Speak. *Digital Journalism*, *4*(7), 944–954.

Brock, D., & Rabin-Havt, A. (2012). *The Fox Effect: How Roger Ailes Turned a Network into a Propaganda Machine*. New York: Anchor Books.

Buckingham, D. (1998). Media Education in the UK: Moving Beyond Protectionism. *Journal of Communication*, *48*(1), 33–43.

Canter, L. (2013). The Source, the Resource and the Collaborator: The Role of Citizen Journalism in Local UK Newspapers. *Journalism*, *14*(8), 1091–1109.

Carlson, M. (2015). The Robotic Reporter: Automated Journalism and the Redefinition of Labor, Compositional Forms, and Journalistic Authority. *Digital Journalism*, *3*(3), 416–631.

Carlson, M. (2017, May 18). Roger Ailes Obituary. *The Guardian*.

Carlson, M., & Lewis, S. C. (Eds.). (2015). *Boundaries of Journalism: Professionalism, Practices and Participation*. London: Routledge.

Coddington, M. (2015). Clarifying Journalism's Quantitative Turn: A Typology for Evaluating Data Journalism, Computational Journalism, and Computer-Assisted Reporting. *Digital Journalism*, *3*(3), 331–348.

Coleman, S. (2005). New Mediation and Direct Representation: Reconceptualizing Representation in the Digital Age. *New Media & Society*, *7*(2), 177–198.

Corner, J. (2013). *Theorising Media: Power, Form and Subjectivity*. Manchester: Manchester University Press.

Couldry, N. (2010). *Why Voice Matters: Culture and Politics After Neoliberalism*. London: Sage.

Curran, J. P., & Seaton, J. (2009). *Power Without Responsibility*. London: Routledge.

Curran, J., Iyengar, S., Lund, A. B., & Salovaara-Moring, I. (2009). Media System, Public Knowledge and Democracy: A Comparative Study. *European Journal of Communication*, *24*(1), 5–26.

Dahl, R. A. (1957). The Concept of Power. *Behavioral Science*, *2*(3), 201–215.

Dahl, R. A. (1958). A Critique of the Ruling Elite Model. *The American Political Science Review*, *52*(2), 463–469.

Dahl, R. A. (1961). *Who Governs? Democracy and Power in an American City*. New Haven: Yale University Press.

Dahlgren, P. (2009). *Media and Political Engagement: Citizens, Communication, and Democracy.* New York: Cambridge University Press.

Davies, K. H., & Crawford, E. (2013). Legal Avenues for Ending Impunity for the Death of Journalists in Conflict Zones: Current and Proposed International Agreements. *International Journal of Communication, 7*(1), 2157–2177.

Davies, N. (2009). *Flat Earth News: An Award-Winning Reporter Exposes Falsehood, Distortion and Propaganda in the Global Media.* London: Vintage.

De Keyser, J., & Raeymaeckers, K. (2012). The Printed Rise of the Common Man: How Web 2.0 Has Changed the Representation of Ordinary People in Newspapers. *Journalism Studies, 13*(5–6), 825–835.

Dimmick, J., Feaster, J., & Hoplamazian, G. (2011). News in the Interstices: The Niches of Mobile Media in Space and Time. *New Media & Society, 13*(1), 23–39.

Domingo, D., et al. (2008). Participatory Journalism Practices in the Media and Beyond: An International Comparative Study of Initiatives in Online Newspapers. *Journalism Practice, 2*(3), 326–342.

Dowell, B. (2012, April 25). Rupert Murdoch: 'Sun wot won it' Headline Was Tasteless and Wrong. *The Guardian.*

Eagleton, T. (2016). *Culture.* New Haven: Yale University Press.

Edelman, M. (1985). *The Symbolic Uses of Politics.* Chicago: University of Illinois Press.

Edelman, M. (1988). *Constructing the Political Spectacle.* Chicago: University of Chicago Press.

Entman, R. (2010). Media Framing Biases and Political Power: Explaining Slant in News of Campaign 2008. *Journalism, 11*(4), 389–408.

Fink, K., & Anderson, C. W. (2014). Data Journalism in the United States. Beyond the "*Usual Suspects*": *Journalism Studies, 16*(4), 467–481.

Foer, F. (2017, September 19). How Technology Is Making Our Minds Redundant. *The Guardian.*

Franklin, B. (2004). *Packaging Politics: Political Communications in Britain's Media Democracy.* London: Bloomsbury Academic.

Gálik, M. (2010). Regulating Media Concentration Within the Council of Europe and the European Union. In B. Klimkiewicz (Ed.), *Media Freedom and Pluralism: Media Policy Challenges in the Enlarged Europe* (pp. 229–244). Budapest: Central European University Press.

Garton-Ash, T. (2016). *Free Speech: Ten Principles for a Connected World.* Yale: Yale University Press; London: Atlantic Books.

Ghersetti, M. (2014). Still the Same? Comparing News Content in Online and Print Media. *Journalism Practice, 8*(4), 373–389.

Gieryn, T. F. (1983). Boundary-Work and the Demarcation of Science from Non-science: Strains and Interests in Professional Ideologies of Scientists. *American Sociological Review, 48*(6), 781–795.

Green, J. (2017). *Devil's Bargain: Steve Bannon, Donald Trump and the Storming of the Presidency*. London: Penguin Press.

Gunter, B., & Harrison, J. (1998). *Violence on Television: An Analysis of Amount, Nature, Location and Origin of Violence in British Programmes*. London: Routledge.

Guo, L. (2017). WeChat as a Semipublic Alternative Sphere: Exploring the Use of WeChat Among Chinese Older Adults. *International Journal of Communication, 11*, 408–428.

Gutmann, A., & Thompson, D. (2014). *The Spirit of Compromise: Why Governing Demands It and Campaigning Undermines It*. Princeton: Princeton University Press.

Gynnild, A. (2014). Journalism Innovation Leads to Innovation Journalism: The Impact of Computational Exploration on Changing Mindsets. *Journalism, 15*(6), 713–730.

Hall, S. (1973 [2006]). Encoding/Decoding. In M. G. Durham & D. M. Kellner (Eds.), *Media and Cultural Studies: KeyWorks* (2nd ed., pp: 163–173). Oxford: Blackwell.

Hamilton, J. T. (2006). *All the News That's Fit to Sell: How the Market Transforms Information into News*. Princeton, NJ: Princeton University Press.

Hammond, E. (2017, January 24). Deteriorating Trust in Government. Centre for Public Security. https://www.cfps.org.uk/trust-in-government/.

Hanitzsch, T. (2007). Deconstructing Journalism Culture: Towards a Universal Theory. *Communication Theory, 17*(4), 367–385.

Hapgood, F. (1995, January 11). The Media Lab at 10. *Wired*. https://www.wired.com/1995/11/media/.

Harcup, T. (2003). 'The Unspoken—Said': The Journalism of Alternative Media. *Journalism, 4*(3), 356–376.

Harcup, T. (2011a). Alternative Journalism as Active Citizenship. *Journalism, 12*(1), 15–31.

Harcup, T. (2011b). Questioning the 'Bleeding Obvious': What's the Point of Researching Journalism? *Journalism, 13*(1), 21–37.

Harcup, T. (2014). "News with a Kick": A Model of Oppositional Reporting. *Communication, Culture & Critique, 7*(4), 559–577.

Harris, M. (2013, December 12). Time to Step Up: The EU and Freedom of Expression. *Index on Censorship*. https://www.indexoncensorship.org/2013/12/eureport/.

Harrison, J. (2008). Exploring News Values: The Ideal and the Real. In J. Chapman & M. Kinsey (Eds.), *Broadcast Journalism: A Critical Introduction* (pp. 60–68). London: Routledge.

Harrison, J. (2010). User-Generated Content and Gatekeeping at the BBC Hub. *Journalism Studies, 11*(2), 243–256.

Harrison J. (2018, November 7). *UNESCO Chair Inaugural Lecture: Diminishment and Resistance—The Civil and Anti-civil Power of News and*

News Journalism. https://www.unesco.org.uk/news/diminishment-and-resistance-the-civil-and-anti-civil-power-of-news-and-news-journalism-2/.
Harrison, J. (2019). *Public Service Journalism.* Oxford Research Encyclopedia of Communication: Oxford University Press. https://doi.org/10.1093/acrefore/9780190228613.013.867.
Harrison, J., & Pukallus, S. (2018). The Politics of Impunity: A Study of Journalists' Experiential Accounts of Impunity in Bulgaria, Democratic Republic of Congo, India, Mexico and Pakistan. *Journalism,* Published online, pp. 1–17.
Harrison, J., & Woods, L. (2007). *European Broadcasting Law and Policy.* Cambridge: Cambridge University Press.
Hemmer, N. (2016). *Messengers of the Right: Conservative Media and the Transformation of American Politics.* Philadelphia: University of Pennsylvania Press.
Hermida, A. (2015). Nothing But the Truth: Redrafting the Journalistic Boundary of Verification. In M. Carlson & S. C. Lewis (Eds.), *Boundaries of Journalism: Professionalism, Practices and Participation* (pp. 37–50). London: Routledge.
Horsley, W., & Harrison, J. (2013). Censorship by Bullet. *British Journalism Review, 24*(1), 39–46.
Hudson, M., & Stanier, J. (1997). *War and the Media: A Random Searchlight.* Stroud: Sutton Publishing.
Jackson, D., & Thorsen, E. (Eds.). (2015). UK Election Analysis 2015: Media, Voters, and the Campaign. Report, PSA and CSJCC. https://www.psa.ac.uk/sites/default/files/page-files/UK%20Election%20Analysis%202015%20-%20Jackson%20and%20Thorsen%20v1.pdf.
Jacobs, R. N. (2009). Culture, the Public Sphere, and Media Sociology: A Search for a Classical Founder in the Work of Robert Park. *The American Sociologist, 40*(3), 149–166.
Johal, S., Moran, M., & Williams, K. (2014). Power, Politics and the City of London After the Great Financial Crisis. *Government and Opposition, 49*(3), 400–425.
Jönsson, A. M., & Örnebring, H. (2011). User-Generated Content and the News: Empowerment of Citizens or Interactive Illusion?. *Journalism Practice, 5*(2), 127–144.
Kakutani, M. (2018). *The Death of Truth.* London: William Collins.
Karlsen, J., & Stavelin, E. (2014). Computational Journalism in Norwegian Newsrooms. *Journalism Practice, 8*(1), 34–48.
Katovsky, B., & Carlson, T. (2003). *Embedded: The Media at War in Iraq—An Oral History.* Guilford, CN: Lyons Press.
Kleemans, M., Schaap, G., & Hermans, L. (2017). Citizen Sources in the News: Above and Beyond the Vox Pop? *Journalism, 18*(4), 464–481.
Knightley, P. (2004). *The First Casualty: The War Correspondent as Hero and Myth-Maker from the Crimea to Iraq.* Baltimore, MD: The Johns Hopkins University Press.

Levin, S. (2017, October 2). Facebook and Google Promote Politicized Fake News About Las Vegas Shooter. *The Guardian*.
Lewis, A. (2007). *Freedom for the Thought We Hate*. New York: Basic books.
Lewis, S. C. (2012). The Tension Between Professional Control and Open Participation: Journalism and Its Boundaries. *Information, Communication & Society, 15*(6), 836–866.
Lisosky, J. M., & Henrichsen, J. (2009). Don't Shoot the Messenger: Prospects for Protecting Journalists in Conflict Situations. *Media, War & Conflict, 2*(2), 129–148.
Livingstone, S. (1996). On the Continuing Problems of Media Effects Research. In J. Curran & M. Gurevitch (Eds.), *Mass Media and Society* (2nd ed., pp. 305–324). London, UK: Edward Arnold.
Luce, E. (2017). *The Retreat of Western Liberalism*. London: Little, Brown.
Lukes, S. (2005a). *Power: A Radical View*. Basingstoke: Palgrave Macmillan.
Lukes, S. (2005b). Power and Battle for Hearts and Minds. *Millennium: Journal of International Studies, 33*(3), 477–493.
Lynch, J. (2008). *Debates in Peace Journalism*. Sydney: Sydney University Press.
McManus, J. H. (1994). *Market-Driven Journalism: Let the Citizens Beware?*. Thousand Oaks, CA: Sage.
Mitchell, P., & Schoeffl, J. (Eds.). (2003). *Understanding Power: The Indispensable Chomsky*. London: Verso.
Morozov, E. (2017, September 3). Silicon Valley Has Been Humbled: But Its Schemes Are as Dangerous as Ever. *The Guardian*.
Mounk, Y. (2018). *The People vs Democracy*. Cambridge: University of Harvard Press.
Müller, J. W. (2016). *What Is Populism?*. Philadelphia: University of Pennsylvania Press.
Nye, J. (2004). *Soft Power: The Means to Success in World Politics*. New York: Public Affairs.
Örnebring, H. (2013). Anything You Can Do, I Can Do Better? Professional Journalists on Citizen Journalism in Six European Countries. *International Communication Gazette, 75*(1), 35–53.
Pantti, M., & Bakker, P. (2009). *Beyond News: User-Generated Content on Dutch Media Websites*. Proceedings of the Future of Journalism Congress. Cardiff, Wales: Cardiff University.
Pariser, E. (2012). *The Filter Bubble: What the Internet Is Hiding from You*. London: Penguin Press.
Park, R. (1941). News and the Paper of the Press. *American Journal of Sociology, 45*, 669–686.
Paterson, C. (2014). *War Reporters Under Threat: The United States and Media Freedom*. London: Pluto Press.
Paul, C., & Kim, J. J. (2004). *Reporters on the Battlefield: The Embedded Press System in Historical Context*. Pittsburgh: RAND Cooperation, National Security Research Division.

Paulussen, S., & Ugille, P. (2008). User Generated Content in the Newsroom: Professional and Organisational Constraints on Participatory Journalism. *Westminster Papers in Communication and Culture, 5*(2), 24–41.
Pew Research Center. (2017, December 14). *Public Trust in Government: 1958–2017.* http://www.people-press.org/2017/12/14/public-trust-in-government-1958-2017/.
Postman, N. (1996). *Amusing Ourselves to Death.* New York: Penguin Books.
Pukallus, S., & Harrison, J. (2015a, March). Journalists Die: Who Cares. *British Journalism Review, 26*(1), 63–68.
Pukallus, S., & Harrison, J. (2015b). If Media Freedom and Media Pluralism Are Fundamental Values in the EU Why Doesn't the EU Do Anything to Ensure Its Application: The Non-use of Art. 7 TEU?. In A. Koltay (Ed.), *Comparative Perspectives on the Fundamental Freedom of Expression* (pp. 368–387). Budapest: Wolters Kluwer.
Revers, M. (2014). The Augmented Newsbeat: Spatial Structuring in a Twitterized News Ecosystem. *Media, Culture and Society, 37*(1), 3–18.
Robinson, S. (2010). Traditionalists vs. Convergers: Textual Privilege, Boundary Work, and the Journalist—Audience Relationship in the Commenting Policies of Online News Sites. *Convergence: The International Journal of Research into New Media Technologies, 16*(1), 125–143.
Runciman, D. (2008). *Political Hypocrisy: The Mask of Power, from Hobbes to Orwell and Beyond.* Princeton: Princeton University Press.
Rusbridger, A. (2018). *Breaking News: The Remaking of Journalism and Why It Matters Now.* Edinburgh: Canongate.
Schlesinger, P. (1987). *Putting "Reality" Together: BBC News.* London: Routledge.
Schmitt, C. (2007). *Theory of the Partisan.* New York: Telos Press Publishing.
Schudson, M. (1995). *The Power of News.* Cambridge, MA: Harvard University Press.
Schutz, A., & Luckmann, T. (1973). *The Structures of the Life-World.* Evanston: Northwestern University Press.
Sherman, E. (2017, May 23). Trump *Budget Cuts Social Security and Medicaid, Breaking Major Promises.* Forbes. Available at: http://bit.ly/2u2PTkd.
Shklar, J. (1976). *Freedom and Independence: A Study of the Political Ideas of Hegel's Phenomenology of Mind.* Cambridge: Cambridge University Press.
Shklar, J. (1984). *Ordinary Vices.* Harvard: Belknap Press of Harvard University Press.
Singer, J., & Ashman, I. (2009). 'Comment Is Free, But Facts Are Sacred': Usergenerated Content and Ethical Constructs at the Guardian. *Journal of Mass Media Ethics, 24*(1), 3–21.
Smyth, F. (2015, July). In Times of War, Pentagon Reserves Right to Treat Journalists Like Spies. Committee to Protect Journalists Blog. https://cpj.org/blog/2015/07/in-times-of-war-pentagon-reserves-right-to-treat-j.php.

Smyth, M. B. (2009). Subjectivities, 'Subject Communities', Governments, and the Ethics of Research on 'Terrorism'. In R. Jackson, M. B. Smyth, & J. Gunning (Eds.), *Critical Terrorism Studies: A New Research Agenda* (pp. 194–215). London: Routledge.

Solon, O. (2017, July 26). The Future of Fake News: Don't Believe Everything You Read, See or Hear. *The Guardian*.

Starkman, D. (2014). *The Watchdog That Didn't Bark: The Financial Crisis and the Disappearance of Investigative Journalism*. New York: Columbia University Press.

Sunstein, C. (2001). *Republic.com*. Princeton: Princeton University Press.

Sunstein, C. (2006). *Infotopia*. Oxford: Oxford University Press.

Sunstein, C. (2007). *Republic.Com 2.0*. Princeton: Princeton University Press.

Sunstein, C. (2009). *Going to Extremes*. Oxford: Oxford University Press.

The Express. (2017, January). BBC News to Offer Audiences More In-depth Analysis Says Director-General.

Thompson, J. (1997). *The Media and Modernity: A Social Theory of the Media*. Cambridge: Polity Press.

Tumber, H., & Webster, F. (2006). *Journalists Under Fire: Information War and Journalistic Practices*. London: Sage.

Vaidhyanathan, S. (2018). *Anti-social Media*. Oxford: Oxford University Press.

Vehkoo, J. (2013). *Crowdsourcing in Investigative Journalism*, Report, Reuters Institute for the Study of Journalism, August.

Wahl-Jorgensen, K. (2015). Resisting Epistemologies of User-Generated Content? Cooptation, Segregation and the Boundaries of Journalism. In M. Carlson & S. C. Lewis (Eds.), *Boundaries of Journalism: Professionalism, Practices and Participation* (pp. 169–185). London: Routledge.

Waldron, J. (2012). *The Harm in Hate Speech*. Cambridge, MA: Harvard University Press.

Wall, M. (2015). Citizen Journalism: A Retrospective on What We Know, an Agenda for What We Don't. *Digital Journalism, 3*(6), 797–813.

Wall, M., & El Zahed, S. (2015). Syrian Citizen Journalism: A Pop-Up News Ecology in an Authoritarian Space. *Digital Journalism, 3*(5), 720–736.

Weber, M. (1919). *Politics as a Vocation*. Available at: http://fs2.american.edu/dfagel/www/class%20readings/weber/politicsasavocation.pdf.

Westlund, O. (2013). Mobile News: A Review and Model of Journalism in an Age of Mobile Media. *Digital Journalism, 1*(1), 6–26. https://doi.org/10.1080/21670811.2012.740273.

Wright Mills, C. (1956). *The Power Elite*. Oxford: Oxford University Press.

CHAPTER 4

Newsrooms and the News Cycle

1 Introduction

In the reality of daily life in newsrooms, the civil ideal and the claims made by political and commercial realism generate conflict, partial coexistence and overlap to produce within the news ecology a news reality that is anything but straightforward. Camp A and Camp B coexist and news journalists constantly change camps, or work for organisations that try to be in both camps at the same time (see Chapter 3). Few adamantly stick to one camp. The clash between the civil ideal of the news and the vicissitudes of political and commercial pressures, combined with the demands of the newsroom are constant and take many forms. There are the never-ending arguments over resources, news agendas and priorities, what constitutes responsible journalism and what comes closest to the civil ideal and who does or does not fulfil it, what 'rivals' and the 'opposition' are doing, what audiences (sometimes citizens) really want and how to engage or involve them and so on.[1] Realistically, in non-totalitarian or non-authoritarian states there is no such thing as a completely positive or negative news environment for the pursuit of the civil ideal of the news though, of course, some places are better than others. Nor is there a completely negative context or setting (yet) that rejects every single aspect of the civil ideal of the news. However, some places are making a determined effort to do just that.[2] Ultimately how strong is the civil ideal is a matter of different 'newsroom cultures' and in order to understand why the civil ideal of the news survives it is important to

© The Author(s) 2019
J. Harrison, *The Civil Power of the News*,
https://doi.org/10.1007/978-3-030-19381-2_4

examine what the resistance to the complete acceptance of political and commercial values consists of as well as to what extent these are resisted. The answer is fairly straightforward. The civil ideal survives by virtue of those newsroom cultures that attempt to contribute to upholding it by resisting, to various degrees, political and commercial power, as well as by rejecting the trivialisation of the audience.[3]

Newsrooms are physical or virtual centres for decision-making processes with regard to the publication of news. They are according to Randall (2000: 16) 'the moral atmosphere of a paper' (or of whatever platform is used). Some techno-media companies have internal newsrooms that superintend editorial decisions for their news divisions, other companies outsource decision-making to external newsrooms (Google for example). However manifested, newsroom cultures are highly significant with regard to what is judged acceptable and what is not for publication (Harrison 2000). The crisis facing social media companies in terms of acceptable and unacceptable content ('toxic' content) is down to the lack of coherent guidelines of the kind found in those newsrooms that have a tradition and culture of editorial responsibility, integrity and concern for public interest. These newsrooms stand in contrast to those that pander solely to and replicate the interests of political and commercial power.

Newsroom cultures are diverse in the extent to which and the way in which they endorse, accept and uphold certain journalistic values and standards. When newsrooms are being studied they may be regarded either as places simply deemed to be the accidental happenstance under which the conditions of doing a job takes place, or are regarded as part of a conspiracy designed to avoid the truth, and/or promote a particular bias that serves vested interests. However, this is too simplistic as all newsrooms, even the most virtual, operate within a cultural background that brings with it a history of attachment to certain values, a priority or hierarchy of beliefs and ethical standards. These attachments reside within the ideational background of different newsroom cultures and help to form the taken-for-granted nature of any particular newsroom's set of outlooks and reasons for making the decisions about news in the way that they do (Harrison 2010). Overall these background values shape any particular newsroom's attachment (or not) to the civil ideal of the news. Sometimes they are dominated by a broad homogeneity of views and values which fails to challenge the status quo and to question extant social political or economic arrangements—essentially an outlook of conformity and conservatism. Sometimes these background values may embrace and accept a plurality of values and welcome the debate and arguments surrounding the diversity of social, political or economic arrangements. Of the two, the latter is more conducive to and offers more promising circumstances for the fulfilment of the civil ideal of the news. Reality however is much more prosaic since most modern newsrooms culturally fall between the narrowness of the homogeneous newsroom and the openness of the pluralistic newsroom. The cultural reality of most, if not all, newsrooms in a modern democratic setting is that they are contested spaces where civil and anti-civil forces are played out. The net result is that the forms of civil boundary maintenance promoted and endorsed by the news vary over time, according to events and to how public sentiment regards the civil sphere itself—for example as in need of protection, development or advocacy.

The location of this contestation resides in the daily practicalities of what we might call the 'foreground' of the newsroom. The foreground is where the articulation of the civil ideal of the news is operationalised (if at all), where a specific editorial policy and its attendant decisions shape the particular practices of newsgathering and where routines and rituals are used to report the news. These activities combine to determine whose voices are heard and whose are not, what issues are covered and which are not, what angles of news reporting are taken and what are not. They also determine the extent to which audiences are involved; that is whether people are invited to give their views or to supply content for a particular story, and if they do the extent to which these views are reported or responded to by the particular newsroom and how their content is used and framed (Harrison 2010). By making these kinds of decisions—selecting stories and choosing the format these stories are reported in and the ways in which they are told—news journalists can be seen to be exercising a form of journalistic power.[4] This power is most clearly (and mundanely) expressed in the daily practices of news journalists and news organisations. It is through the exercise of this power that news journalists may knowingly or unwittingly undermine the civil ideal of the news. More specifically this occurs through the exclusion of those voices that are uncomfortable or too challenging, by undertaking unjustifiable intrusion into private lives, or by buying into dominant narratives and discourse without question. Newsrooms select and report issues, which they 'locate, perceive, identify and label' (Goffman 1974: 21).

They take daily life experiences and either represent them accurately or distort them through the stigmatising of people and groups. The output that is produced is well known and understood through the study of news media representations[5] as well as inquiries into the legality of newsroom behaviour,[6] and serves to illustrate and reinforce the view that newsrooms are spaces and places of contested meanings and values. Individual news reports represent the playing out of a continual flow of contested meanings and must endlessly navigate between civil and anti-civil values, and ultimately endorse one or the other but not both. By endorsing civil values, political and commercial power may sometimes be challenged by the news media which seek to contribute to the articulation of a civil outlook which endorses solidarity, inclusion and hospitality (see, e.g., Silverstone 2007).

It is in the choices made in daily activities of the newsroom that the capacity of news providers to select and report particular events and issues while ignoring others is revealed. In other words, news providers have the power to decide what makes it into the news cycle to become news and it is within the news cycle that editorial decisions are simultaneously made as to whether to amplify, to ignore or to listen to public sentiment about the event or issue at stake. It is in this way, through the news cycle, that the news expresses its relationship to public sentiment, particularly when judgements are made relating to our invariant civil concerns of identity, legitimacy and risk. The decisions about how to engage with our invariant civil concerns in news selection (and always following selection in the subsequent forms of reporting undertaken) come with what I refer to as civil and anti-civil judgements. These judgements combine to endorse and promote a particular normative form of civil boundary maintenance. More specifically, I argue that there are three cardinal types of normative civil boundary maintenance and that it is through these that news ultimately contributes to the boundaries we place and maintain around civil society with regard to whom and what we regard as civil and anti-civil and also to the way in which we maintain, reconsider and possibly change the current and particular form of these boundaries. It is through and within the news cycle that the news exercises its civil power by making civil and anti-civil judgements as a particular normative form of civil boundary maintenance. These civil and anti-civil judgements are made in all newsrooms and found in all types of news reports and, correspondingly, are the way news ultimately endorses a particular view of 'our' civil boundaries.

Because the news cycle occurs 24/7, the news has the ability to pervade the everyday, to become part of our everyday consumption patterns and often to inform aspects of our conversations and the views we share with others. In this way, the news can also be said to have a form of capillary power. Such power is part of the everyday reality of life and as Foucault (1991: 194) observes, it is important to recognise and understand its significance: 'We must cease once and for all to describe the effects of power in negative terms: it "excludes", it "represses", it "censors", it "abstracts", it "masks", it "conceals". In fact power produces; it produces reality; it produces domains of objects and rituals of truth'. Leaving aside the problem of dispensing with the 'negative' language of domination, agency or regarding people as docile, the point I wish to make here is to emphasise the extent of the scope and reach of the news, its everydayness[7] and its relationship to public sentiment (see below). If we accept that the civil power of the news is three dimensional, a constituent feature of our 'lifeworld' (that is our everyday social experiences) and an integral aspect of our culture of communication then exactly what is the outcome of this civil power and towards what is it directed?

Civil boundaries are relational and are contested in two settings: first, at a macro-level; that is between the civil sphere and the non-civil spheres and second, at a meso-level; that is the clash within the institutions and associative groups of the civil sphere itself. So far I have suggested nothing other than that the news uses its civil power through civil and anti-civil judgements to influence the normative aspect of civil boundary maintenance via public sentiment. It is time to qualify this and to examine what sort of influence the news actually seeks and what it attempts to do with the boundaries surrounding civil society and those within civil society and what the role of public sentiment is.

Civil society is, to borrow a concept from political psychology, an idealised collective self grounded in a unity of universalising shared sentiments and values which bestows the pronouns 'we', 'us' and 'other' 'them' and ultimately the adjectives 'civil' and 'anti-civil' with meaning. This is not to say that civil society is not real rather it is, to agree with Alexander's (2006: 195) point, 'instantiated in the real'. Such instantiation though needs to be understood in the context of the fact that the civil sphere is not instantiated in some ideal or perfect form. Rather the civil sphere is always instantiated as incomplete—if for no other reason than it never provides a form of boundary maintenance that permanently reconciles our invariant civil concerns to everyone's satisfaction. There is no agreement on an ideal type of civil sphere. Reconciliation as a permanent form of social stability may be what 'we' aim for, but any particular forms of reconciliation are always disputed and correspondingly so are the types of boundaries 'we' variously advocate. The manifestation of the civil power of the news is to be found in the types of civil boundaries it endorses and represents.

Accordingly the news, via its attention to public sentiment in and through the news cycle, also constantly defines the meaning and significance of the competing civil and anti-civil judgements it makes in the processes of news selection. But these judgements, too, are only provisional and vary according to 'our' response to events. Thus identity concerns are reconciled in the news by what Chernobrov (2014: 78) calls the 'granting of self-identity', ('they are just like us') and 'the withdrawing of self-identity' (they are 'other' than us); legitimacy concerns are reconciled by advocating or not supporting justifications based around the formal and informal exercise of authority. Risk concerns are reconciled by the provision of 'ontological security'[8] or by the issuance of warnings. Combined, these three forms of reconciliation provide some of the building blocks for the type of civil boundary 'we' want to place around the civil sphere. As I develop these arguments and show below, there are three cardinal types of civil boundary instantiated in the news: first, an endorsement of civil values and the promotion of change in accordance and consistent with those values in civil society; second, an endorsement of anti-civil values and the promotion of change in accordance and consistent with those values in civil society; and third, the rejection of change and the civil or anti-civil endorsement of the status quo in civil society. In each case, a normative order is advocated. In short, the news selects and reports news in terms of the civil and anti-civil judgements made about our invariant civil concerns which, when combined (aggregated together), reveal the type of civil boundary the news endorses and promotes and which 'we' may wish to accept and maintain.

The news cycle consists of news providers listening to, being influenced by, responding to, ignoring or amplifying public sentiment through the continuous activity of selecting the news and within it representing our invariant civil concerns. It can be represented diagrammatically accordingly (Fig. 1).

As can be seen, the news cycle hinges on a two-way relationship between news selection and reports as forms of civil and anti-civil judgements (undertaking the task of reconciling our invariant civil concerns)

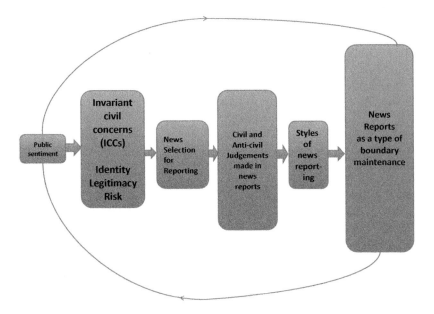

Fig. 1 The news cycle simplified

and the forms of any boundaries 'we' desire to maintain, with public sentiment as a vehicle of expression for the specific nature of our invariant civil concerns. It is appropriate to understand their general features and specific place in the news cycle more clearly before addressing news selection and news reporting as well the different types of civil boundaries and their normative aspects. To do this we must return to our invariant civil concerns since it is these that animate public sentiment and that are at the heart of what the news attends to in the processes of selection.

2 INVARIANT CIVIL CONCERNS: IDENTITY, LEGITIMACY AND RISK

Invariant civil concerns are unchanging and generic. They are continuously manifest in public sentiment. They are frequently emotionally felt, pre-reflectively, prejudicially and intuitively believed in, occasionally rationally articulated, sometimes progressive and sometimes oppressive, and whatever else they are, they come with no guarantee of increased human enlightenment or liberal outcomes. Importantly, they should be regarded as an unchanging shared set of concerns whose expression is entirely context-dependent; that is they are both a shared background of common concerns and yet manifest in news reports and public sentiment in a variety of particularistic ways—though these ways are mutually intelligible. As such, they are not to be understood as theoretical concepts but as common dispositions found and articulated in all civil societies. In fact and as expressed by Isaiah Berlin, 'more people in more countries at more times accept more common values than is often believed' (Lukes 2003: 42, also Garton-Ash 2016). Accordingly and even though there may be disagreement among members of civil society about the detail of the nature of civil society's activities and priorities, 'our' invariant civil concerns are the constituent parts that come together to provide the kind of solidarising sentiment that we hold. Civil society has aspirations towards a universalistic sense of 'we-ness' that can, when it is civil in its intentions and sentiment, overcome the anti-civil tendencies of racism, religious and ethnic intolerance, misogyny, corruption and cronyism, injustice and the unchecked tyranny of expert knowledge. How we express our invariant civil concerns defines our response to these anti-civil tendencies. As we saw in Chapter 3, both civil and anti-civil sentiments always circulate within civil society (more recently they have become more evident to most of us through social media). Importantly, these common dispositions, common values and disagreements—civil and anti-civil sentiments—can be empirically accounted for. In fact, they form definable and real areas of concern that can be methodologically collated as expressions of one of the three invariant civil concerns we share (see Part II). At a general level, the three invariant civil concerns can be briefly described as follows.

First, the invariant civil concern of identity seeks to answer the question of who has civil status and who does not. It is expressed through the language of who and what I am/we are in the context of a particular set of material, cultural and political circumstances. The language of identity reveals each person's conception of their individuality and their group affiliations and articulates such things as the right to be considered in equal terms, to achieve equality of representation or equality of opportunity. Claims about civil identity form the basis from which who or what is viewed as civilised and who or what is seen as uncivilised. From such a distinction, determinations are made as to who can and cannot make valid identity claims, the acceptance of which permits a person to inhabit a civil space with dignity—'dignity in the sense of a person's basic entitlement to be regarded as a member of society in good standing' (Waldron 2012: 105).

Second, legitimacy involves the acceptance of justifications based around the formal and informal exercise of authority. It is the acceptance of a civil warrant. Typically the invariant civil concern of legitimacy is expressed through consideration of what the formal and informal criteria are by which we judge and hold to 'our' standards of legality and justice. This is expressed in two ways, formally through the regulative institutions of civil society as a formal legal code adjudicated upon by a judiciary and, informally through the standards of 'natural justice' that we hold, and which we are constantly debating, within and through the communicative institutions of civil society. As such, the invariant civil concern of legitimacy relates to what we can justify—namely the conduct of civility based on what is seen to be legally and ethically right and wrong, what is fair and what will withstand scrutiny. In short, it reflects the process of how Geuss's (2008: 25) universal question relating to power relations of who in practice '<does>what to whom for whose benefit' is answered.[9] In the context of the civil power of the news such a question can be reformulated as one which asks on civil society's behalf: what will they do, what could they do or what are they doing to whom in whose interests? The process of asking and exploring these questions engaging with the way that they are disputed and/or implicitly or explicitly consented to is both a symbolic and a practical way of exploring the limits and constraints of power, both present and future, and of considering over and over again the legitimacy of action with the potential to interrogate overt and hidden intentions. Where concerns arise in relation to the legitimacy of a claim, belief or action there is the process of civil scrutiny in which the news can often play an important leading or supplementary role and that may give rise to the expression of public sentiment in terms of what is seen to be legitimate and which may on some occasions lead to what Alexander (2006) calls civil repair through the use of legal counter-power (the courts), or collective action of civil mobilisation and performance (civil association).

Third, the invariant civil concern of risk is underpinned by fear and danger and the attendant need for 'feeling secure' (ontological security). It is centred on the risks we face and reflects how we worry about things and the people who we think may threaten our world. This self-centred world is formulated via our own interpretation of the kind of risk we face (which may affect me and my own family) in parallel with the collective we that underpins our sense of belonging and solidarity and relates to constant interpretations we all make over the extent of the threats of risk and the levels of security and insecurity to our civil society and our civil lives. It is expressed in the language of our concerns about our safety and the sustainability of our environment, as well as our need for reassurance and a sense of security. Such concerns may range from economic risks, risks to health, safety, environmental problems, information security, job security, financial security and so on. The reporting of our invariant civil concern with risk is and will continue to be a central and enduring element of news and is one that can lead to problematic outcomes.

In the context of the civil power of the news, these three invariant civil concerns can be simply labelled as matters of 'our' historical and cultural identity, as questions over what constitutes justice and civil legitimacy and as issues to do with the extent and nature of risks and threats we perceive we face. As such each of the three invariant civil concerns has its own set of concepts, a language of use and a specific range of concerns and meanings (see Chapters 6–8). In this way, they provide a means through which to examine the many ways in which the news makes civil and anti-civil judgements and as such contributes to the boundary maintenance of civil society.

Ultimately at issue, with regard to the way the three invariant civil concerns are utilised in news reports, is what we come to accept when considering the nature of otherness and the extent of the influence we accept in relation to others' identity claims; the legitimacy of civil/legal procedures and of claim and counterclaim as to what is and what is not just and how we feel about things and people who may threaten our own world of security and familiarity. Though one caveat needs to be made, it is important to understand that the three different invariant civil concerns overlap and coexist in everyday life. Indeed news stories can carry matters exclusive to one concern just as easily as matters relevant to all three concerns. News reports do not operate to a particular formula, rather and in reality these invariant civil concerns overlap. For example, a news story about concerns arising from rising immigration speaks to a public feeling of risk, encompasses issues relating to the identity of those being classified as 'other' and begs the question of whether or not those grounds for classification are legitimate. The separation between the three invariant civil concerns is simply used in this book as an analytically useful heuristic device as it allows for a closer scrutiny of the news's civil and anti-civil judgements.

The defining feature of the three invariant civil concerns is that they can, and sometimes do, represent and reflect the solidarising sentiment that is persistent and underpins civil society and what we act upon, talk about and what we believe in, such as the extent of inclusivity of hospitality and so on. In this way, the invariant civil concerns represent, at a normative level, civil values of social criticism, democratic integration, civility, justice, reciprocity and mutual respect. In the news cycle, 'our' invariant civil concerns are constantly addressed with the net result that the news can ignore or respond in various ways to public sentiment through news selection. It is then in the variant forms of reporting that the three invariant civil concerns can be discerned as forming the deep architecture of the civil power of the news.

The expression in the news of these diverse articulations of our invariant civil concerns is today undertaken in complex modern societies that are essentially defined through increasing scale, 'massification' and structural differentiation. The modern news institutions of communication including social media have replaced the face-to-face communication and debate of the Greek agora, the Roman fora, the medieval plaza, the seventeenth- and eighteenth-century coffee houses and dining clubs, the hustings and the stump of the nineteenth century and now play a vital role in communicating a range of civil representations backwards and forwards between the civil and non-civil spheres. Nonetheless the news continues to report stories that (a) are newsworthy because of the issue they address and (b) have a bearing on our invariant civil concerns—one, two or all of them. Both (a) and (b) ensure that the news reports are of relevance to the public and have the potential to engage public sentiment in various ways.

3 News Selection

Even in the most modern and virtual newsroom news selection and agenda setting occur and are still associated with the traditional problem of the extent of the influence over newsrooms by representatives of commercial and political power. As already noted in Chapter 3, Weber (1919: 12) recognises that the risks to critically independent journalism are obvious and easily identified with the establishment of 'chain newspapers' that breed and encourage political indifference, the loss of editorial independence, editors who are party officials or proselytisers, the demand for sensationalism (his word), the power of advertising and the political power of owners (he cites Lord Northcliffe who is usually regarded as one of the British pioneers of tabloid journalism). Similarly Dewey (2008 [1935]: 270) when considering the liberty of the press writes, with wonderful prescience, that 'The only really fundamental approach to the problem is to inquire concerning the necessary effect of the present economic system upon the whole system of publicity; upon the judgment of what news is, upon the selection and elimination of matter that is published, upon the treatment of news in both editorial and news columns. The question, under this mode of approach, is not how many specific abuses there are and how they may be remedied, but how far intellectual freedom and social responsibility are possible on any large scale under the existing economic regime'. While Dewey opines that only a complete change of economic circumstances into something much more 'co-operative' could ensure that the 'irresponsible journalism engaged in by William Randolph Hearst' be rendered 'impossible', both he and Weber also recognise the achievements of the press, its capacity for public service and fairness and its enabling potential. Today the debate over news selection and agenda setting has shifted ground but has not really changed so much in substance. We are more inclined to talk, with regard to news selection and agenda setting, of the implicit cultural bias/prejudices of social media and the Internet, the combination of specifically American neoliberal economic values with libertarian social values and the risks from corporate techno-media superpowers (news manipulation, distortion and censorship) associated with the ownership of the architecture and software of the manifold platforms that carry the news. We are now more likely to ask the following questions: Who controls the news on social media and the Internet? How free and independent is it? How trustworthy (accurate and sincere) is it? In point of fact, all these questions can be summarised by asking the question that Dewey was intimating: What are the problems associated with privately owned public spheres? Equally unchanged is the character of the answers we now console ourselves with—a combination of optimism and pessimism over the extent of the risks to the survival or creation of a free and independent news media. But all of this is by way of context to the issue I wish to focus on; the mechanics of news selection in the news cycle as it occurs daily in the newsroom. To put the matter directly: Does news selection accord to the routinised pursuit of vested interests, or is it rather more complex than that? Below I attempt to distinguish between two different but related forms of news selection: first, routine selection and second, selection as a form of civil or anti-civil judgement and what they both mean for news reporting.

3.1 The Routine Selection of News in the Newsroom

For the purpose of clarity, I am assuming that a functioning newsroom receives a variety of news alerts and content that is newsworthy, engages in some form of approval process with regard to one or a combination of all of the following: news dissemination, broadcasting, publication and distribution and in some cases decides on how a news report looks (its news tone and style) and where and when it appears. In a large newsroom, these decisions are made by a collection of individuals with overlapping roles who work in accordance with some form official decision-making hierarchy, in smaller news operations the tasks may be vested in only a few people or even one person. In short, news selection in this wide sense begins and ends in the idea of the newsroom and circumscribes what is ultimately reported.

A wide range of empirical evidence suggests that newsrooms are replete with tensions and pressures, conflicting views and priorities and, in common with all organisations and institutions, they have their own codes and conventions (Altheide and Rasmussen 1976; Born 2005; Epstein 1973; Fishman 1980; Gans 1979; Harrison 2000; Küng-Shankleman 2000; Ryfe 2012; Schlesinger 1978; Tuchman 1978; Soloski 1989). Over the last two decades, news providers have undoubtedly faced a range of new challenges as technological developments have driven them to change the way in which the news is presented to the audience and to accommodate and build upon opportunities from changes in the ways in which audiences access and even engage with the news. In the context of high levels of competition for audiences, news providers have become increasingly focused on attracting and maintaining them. In the online environment, this focus on engaging audiences has led to greater emphasis on interactivity, hypertexts, multimedia and immediacy as new elements that now distinguish online journalism from print (Bardoel and Deuze 2001; Dahlgren 1995; Deuze 2004; Mitchelstein and Boczkowski 2009; Oblak 2005; Steensen 2011).

Technological developments coupled with greater competition between news providers for audiences have meant that for some the exercise of news selection is increasingly audience-led and has become an exercise in drawing audiences into 'have their say', to provide user-generated material and for the news provider to ensure their news stories are popular because it is incumbent upon them to keep and grow their audiences by understanding and pandering to their preferences.[10]

Despite these technological challenges and different approaches to meeting audience demands, there still remain regularities and consistencies of routines in journalistic practice which are manifest in the selection of the news. A variety of studies of newsrooms over the years have highlighted similar types of practical procedures in news selection processes, for example: identifying structures, routines, pressures and constraints on journalists (Burns 1969; Epstein 1973; Harrison 2000; Schlesinger 1987; Tuchman 1978). Indeed as far back as 1965, Gold and Simmons found that news selection patterns among daily newspapers in Iowa were remarkably similar, and Buckalew (1969) and Clyde and Buckalew (1969) showed that news editors' judging patterns in US newspapers were nearly unanimous. Somewhat more recently Altheide and Snow (1979: 10) identify these similarities in selection practices to be based upon activities that determine 'how material is organised, the style in which it is presented, the focus or emphasis on particular characteristics of behaviour, and the grammar of media communication', in short there is what the following authors refer to as a 'media logic' in journalistic practices (Altheide and Snow 1979) which can also be found in their activities in what Dahlgren (1995: 59) then referred to as 'cyberspace'. In later studies, an emphasis has been placed on the more technological and institutional aspects of newsroom activities (Ryfe 2006a, b), with the discovery that the processes of news production themselves have not changed markedly (Mazzoleni 2008; Ryfe 2006b, 2009) and the values that journalists share largely continue to endure, manifest in the similarities in a range of newsroom settings (Harrison 2000). Deuze (2005) considers journalistic selection practices as more or less universal traits and values and as an expression of shared occupational ideology among newsworkers. Consequently, it is still possible to see evidence of regularities, consistencies and similarities of practice at work in all newsrooms. Although the public adds its opinions, views and sometimes concrete facts into the mix and user-generated material has become part of the routine processes of news selection and is built into newsroom structures, public tip-offs and information have long been part of the journalistic process and much evidence exists to show that at the moment editorial control still largely remains vested with the news provider.

From this, it follows that the adoption of routine practices within the process of newsgathering results in particular conventional selection norms which determine why stories are reported or not deemed worth reporting and that this is generally and mainly done on the basis of professional journalistic news values. These conventional and routinised news selection criteria emphasise basic (or immediate) qualities of newsworthiness. Here such basic qualities of newsworthiness include information that is provided by prominent members of society who are trusted and have credibility (Berkowitz 2009; Grabe et al. 2000; Shoemaker and Reese 1996; Sundar 1998; Tuchman 1978) and who become routine sources of information. These sources such as the police, officials, members of elite groups and institutions (Berkowitz 2009; Davis 2000; Manning 2001) identify events and issues that may be newsworthy (Ericson et al. 1987, 1991; Schlesinger and Tumber 1994) and push their versions of events and issues onto the news agenda. In this way, what is determined to be newsworthy is contingent on the idea that some voices are more worth hearing than others (Dimitrova and Strömbäck 2009; Manning 2001; Tuchman 1978).

Contacting certain types of sources routinely results in a patchwork selection of newsworthy events and issues, eliciting uneven coverage of world regions (Wallis and Baran 1990). Inevitably the determination of what is newsworthy through the routine use of sources results in a lack of homologous fit to the world, something that has been seen to be a form of unwitting bias (Golding and Elliott 1979). When a story is newsworthy it 'is not made in the echoing of anything: it is made in the telling' (Hartley 1989: 45). To make events and issues newsworthy, news providers have to tame and interpret them so that they can be told, which for Schudson (2008: 88) means that they have to 'socially reconstruct' them. News providers do this using a range of professional methods such as the organisation of work (Bantz 1985); exercising control over the constraints of time (Schlesinger 1978); via the use of routines (Tuchman 1972, 1973, 1978), depending 'on available cultural resources, treasure house of tropes, narrative forms, resonant mythic forms and frames of their culture' (Schudson 2008: 88), using objectivity norms; routinely using particular sources (such as the police, courts, local councils, gossip websites) and narrative frameworks to construct a story and using journalistic precedents to tell stories (Harrison 2000). Through these types of professional practice devices news providers are able to absorb, and deem newsworthy, the sudden and unexpected and even the unprecedented as they tame them into familiar ways of telling a story. News reporting is nothing if not interpretative and judgemental. It is, as Schudson (2008: 61) notes, caught up in 'a set of complex institutional relations that lead them [reporters] to reproduce day after day the opinions and news of established figures' and they do so while enmeshed in numerous organisational constraints (notably power relationships, newsroom cultures and daily and contingent constraints) and by recourse to a range of 'literary forms and narrative devices journalists regularly use to manage the overwhelming flow of events' (Carey 1986: 180).

What is at issue here is exactly what events to bring to the attention of the public. One theory is, as Galtung and Ruge (1965)[11] suggest, that newsworthiness resides in the properties inherent in a contemporary event itself which 'tell' the journalist that it is newsworthy. And it is this, rather than the news organisations' newsroom ideology or value system, that determines if an event is to be reported. Thus for newsrooms and news providers events are deemed to be self-evidently newsworthy because they have certain characteristics that make them recognisably news to both journalists and to the news audience: they chime with some aspect of public sentiment and are considered to be of public relevance. But how are these 'self-evident' criteria to be met? While a focus on the intrinsic nature of news value is useful for showing us how 'a property of an event … increases its chance of becoming "news"' (Sande 1971: 222) and that news does tend to cover certain types of stories, the content-based studies about news values do not tell us enough about the meeting of those self-evident criteria that are acceptable within particular newsrooms (Harrison 2000, 2006, 2008a).

Where the story is not so obviously and routinely newsworthy and is of interest to some news outlets and not others, we see important levels of differentiation of conceptions of newsworthiness which leads to different selection choices. Sometimes the event is of greater interest to one news outlet than another, sometimes the story will be picked up on by particular programmes, newspapers or other outlets because news editors 'know' their audiences and what kinds of stories are likely to interest them. It is in this respect that those selecting news have a qualified two-dimensional power. It is qualified because at the individual level journalists can rarely exercise the freedom to choose stories that do not fall within the organisational remit and news agenda of the institution for which they work. Freelance journalists and those who set up their own journalistic endeavours though might find that they are freer than their counterparts in traditional news media to select stories based on their own interests and preferences (although freelance journalists still need to be able to sell their story).

However this level of news selection only shows and reflects a certain form of taken-for-granted daily activity, intelligible to all within and across diverse newsrooms. A news event is interpreted in the newsroom as being both routinely newsworthy and as one which requires and affords civil and anti-civil judgements which, in turn, are expressed in and supported by a specific style of news reporting. In many ways, this immediate form of news selection proceeds automatically—without too much attention at this level to systematically pursuing specific vested interests or working to an incorrigible news agenda. To move our understanding of the news cycle and the news's capacity for civil and anti-civil judgements on we also need to step back and look at the selection of news stories regarding our three invariant civil concerns, to look at the relations between the civil sphere and the non-civil spheres as well as the diverse agendas within civil society itself.

3.2 News Selection as a Form of Civil and Anti-Civil Judgements

Newsworthy events are evaluated in the newsroom in terms of their civil or anti-civil significance at two levels. First, as to what significance an event has at a macro-level—that is between the non-civil spheres and the civil sphere. Second, as to what significance an event has at a meso-level—that is only within the civil sphere. The former arises from the boundary relationships of the civil sphere with the non-civil spheres where non-civil interests have a bearing on any one or a combination of the three invariant civil concerns. The latter arises from the competing agendas and values that are in a constant state of tension and negotiation within the civil sphere itself and which contest what is civil and what is not. In either case, those news stories that derive from events and actions in the non-civil sphere and the civil sphere itself will be judged via the same editorial processes noted above namely at the appropriate editorial 'meeting' (virtual or physical) where their newsworthiness and significance is determined. News coverage requires planning and if it is decided to report and disseminate a particular story then resources will be subsequently allocated in terms of human and technical support (obviously the amount differs from news provider to news provider). If an event is deemed newsworthy in terms of its significant civil impact it is because, to repeat the point, it has been editorially evaluated to have such impact in terms of its priority and significance regarding (a) its impact upon relationships between the civil and non-civil spheres and (b) its impact upon institutional and associative relationships intra civil spheres. In short, it is about how an event deemed newsworthy impacts upon our invariant civil concerns. In this way, the selection of which event to report can be understood as a form of civil or anti-civil judgement. This is shown schematically in Tables 1, 2 (p. 123), and 3 (p. 124):

It is important to understand how news selection as just described fits into the news cycle, is related to public sentiment and newsroom agendas. In other words, it is necessary to put news selection back into the wider context of the newsroom, newsroom agendas and their relationship to public sentiment. These relationships are shown in Fig. 2 on p. 125. In fact, Fig. 2 shows that news selection and agenda setting are undertaken according to something deeper and more complex than the routine recognition of the basic qualities of newsworthiness. It aims to show the way a news event has a relationship to our invariant civil concerns. It is precisely in the way that a news event is seen to impact upon one or a combination of any of the three invariant civil concerns that the news starts the process of forming civil and anti-civil judgements which will also, explicitly or implicitly, determine the way in which the story is written. In other words, through the news selection process the

Table 1 Civil and anti-civil selection criteria of the invariant civil concern of identity

Evaluation of boundary relations civil disposition

Inputs from the non-civil spheres and from within civil society where they have a bearing on the invariant civil concern of **identity** may be selected as being civil, welcome and worth reporting when they are:	• Supportive of existing approved of political power structures and state intervention, profit motives and market successes, particular types of family values and actions • Statements from religious institutions that are seen as civil in intent

Evaluation of boundary relations anti-civil disposition

Inputs from the non-civil spheres and from within civil society where they have a bearing on the invariant civil concern of **identity** may be selected as being anti-civil and worth reporting when they are:	• Imposing non-solidarising action, policy or values into civil society and its institutions that are seen as anti-civil in intent and damaging to civil society

Table 2   Civil and anti-civil selection criteria of the invariant civil concern of legitimacy

Evaluation of boundary relations civil disposition	
Inputs from the non-civil spheres or from within civil society where they have a bearing on the invariant civil concern of **legitimacy** may be selected as being civil, welcome and worth reporting when they are:	• Exhibiting legitimate authority and acting justly • Supporting a need for a change in the law via non-civil intervention for greater national or personal security to protect a particular civil freedom • Indicating the need for justice and its correction via non-civil intervention such as new legislation that protects civil life and civil action • Emphasising the importance of liberty that is achieved by non-civil intervention or mobilisation • Emphasising the importance of greater democracy achieved through non-civil intervention or mobilisation • Emphasising the desirability of public trust in non-civil and civil institutions that hold power
Evaluation of boundary relations anti-civil disposition	
Inputs from the non-civil spheres or within civil society where they have a bearing on the invariant civil concern of **legitimacy** may be selected as being anti-civil and worth reporting when they are:	• Exhibiting non-legitimate authority and abuse of power • Exhibiting unjust actions and processes • Advocating a change in the law that may reduce civil freedoms and democratic processes and where there is insufficient justification • Engendering a reduction in public trust in the institutions that hold power

newsroom becomes a judge in terms of the nature of the relationship between the three invariant civil concerns and of the way the goals of non-civil spheres, and the clash between competing values within civil society itself is seen to affect them.

It is through the judgements made in news selection and subsequently the news reporting process that each newsroom provides its own representation of the world, one that each claims to be homologous.[12] In other words, given the variety of possibilities that arise in the selection of an event, and the possibility of variant forms of expression of the event, news can only provide a fragmented or selective view of the world and mediated events are contingent on the form, slant or tone adopted

Table 3 Civil and anti-civil selection criteria of the invariant civil concern of risk

Evaluation of boundary relations civil disposition	
Inputs from the non-civil spheres (non-solidarising) or from within civil society where they have a bearing on the invariant civil concern of **risk** may be selected as being civil, welcome and worth reporting when they are:	• Interventions and actions that are required to reduce risk • Measures are undertaken by civil or non-civil institutions which are perceived as necessary to increase personal safety in the face of risk • Intervention from the non-civil spheres from politicians, the state and the police are seen as proportionate, including the declaration of a state of emergency
Evaluation of boundary relations anti-civil disposition	
Inputs from the non-civil spheres or from within civil society where they have a bearing on the invariant civil concern of **risk** may be selected as anti-civil and worth reporting when they are:	• Emphasising the problems with scientific, medical, technical and engineering research (undermining) • Emphasising the need for caution against engaging in risk-taking behaviour (retrenchment rather than progression) • Emphasising the need to be cautious towards that which is unfamiliar and to those who are unfamiliar to us (increased isolationism) • Emphasising the need to be cautious about extending civil freedoms • Amplifying the nature of risk(s) without giving full explanation of its precise nature or scale • Failing to put the nature of risk into a wider context. • Emphasising ambiguity and complexity • Emphasising a need for greater vigilance and a need for watchfulness and without explanation of why this is necessary

by those engaged in their own particular telling of the selected event (Crossley and Harrison 2013). Once the event has been reported it is generally possible to identify when facts are not reported correctly and in theory these should be easy to correct, although, as we are seeing in an era of 'fake news' (false news, misinformation and disinformation) and hyper-partisan news this is not always the case, but nonetheless it is still the selection of which facts to report and the way in which they are reported that produces a particular representation of the event as civil or anti-civil. In this way, news stories are not actually homologous to the world. In fact, each news report represents a different view of the world,

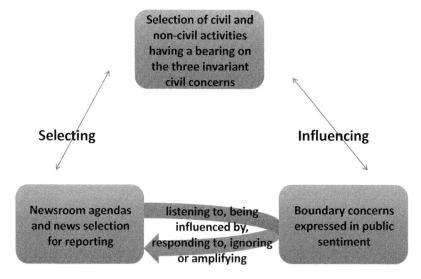

Fig. 2 News selection as a form of civil judgement

adopts a different style of reporting and in many cases carries within it civil and/or anti-judgements that combine to represent a particular type of civil boundary maintenance. It is the particular nature of these judgements that I turn to next.

4 News Reporting and the Three Cardinal Types of Civil Boundary Maintenance

Once the news event which is to be reported has been selected with due consideration to public sentiment, the news exercises its civil power through combining (a) which civil and anti-civil judgements it makes and subsequently what cardinal type of civil boundary these judgements represent or point to and (b) the particular news style of reporting adopted (see Sect. 5 below).

With regard to (a) these civil and anti-civil judgements come together and combine in news reports. Nevertheless, news reports do ultimately endorse one type of normative civil boundary maintenance rather than another, though again in varying combinations. Sometimes news reports unequivocally endorse a particular normative civil boundary and at other times they qualify such support with ideals derived from another type of civil boundary. To be precise a civil boundary is a composite of normative views and outlooks and represents a values profile of how 'we' regard whom and what is civil or anti-civil. If a news event is of significant newsworthiness it is extensively covered and in the coverage, the nature of the civil judgements generates one of the three particular types of civil boundary:

4.1   Type 1: The Endorsement of Civil Values and the Promotion of Change in Accordance and Consistent with Those Values in Civil Society

The endorsement of civil values and promoting change in civil society is where the news actively upholds its civil ideal, or is at least more proximate to that ideal than not. It is here that it uses its civil power in an attempt to (a) enable what is civil to flourish and (b) help bring about some form of civil repair. At a macro-level, the news can judge that some developments and inputs from the non-civil spheres (state, politics, economics, family, gender, race, scientific knowledge and so on) may amplify or develop civil life and be helpful. Equally civil repair can occur in the restoration of something or correcting an injustice. Both typically occur against a background of intellectual and emotional demand articulated in and through public sentiment when public sentiment advocates that current civil boundaries should be more open in order to encourage new ways of thinking and behaving within civil society. In this way, the news judges that there is a need for boundaries to change. At a meso-level (from within the civil sphere), institutional reform might well be supported by the news because it is seen to reinforce civil values, or conversely civil institutions adversely affected by non-civil or anti-civil intrusion (and expressed within their own organisational setting) may require some form of civil repair to reinstate certain civil values.

4.2   Type 2: The Endorsement of Anti-civil Values and the Promotion of Change in Accordance and Consistent with Those Values in Civil Society

The endorsement of anti-civil values (expressed either at a macro-level by the non-civil spheres, or at a meso-level within the institutions of civil society itself) and promoting change across civil society in accordance with these anti-civil values typically occur where the news falls away from its civil ideal, is non-solidarising and exercises a more instrumental form of its civil power and actively promotes political or commercial vested interests. Here anti-civil sentiments and values are judged in the news to be in some way more beneficial to 'our way of life' than those values and ideas endorsed by extant civil society and accordingly, the news judges that it is necessary for boundaries to change either by returning to 'how things used to be' or 'what the future requires is that we change'. To achieve this, the selection and reporting of the news shapes or reinforces preferences, choices, values, opinions, social norms and views within civil society. The news's judgement about the need for anti-civil values to be adopted and boundaries to change accordingly resides in its ability to engender or allow anti-civil sentiment to shape public sentiment and the social narratives or the lexicon we use to talk about events and issues that the news has mediated. It is the advocacy of change and of retooling civil society in some way or another—for example to make it more individualistic, less or more politically active, or more commercially inclined.

4.3 Type 3: The Rejection of Change: The Endorsement of the Status Quo in Civil Society

Here the news may or may not conform to its civil ideal—it simply depends upon the nature of the status quo and what is being promoted at the macro- and meso-level to alter the boundaries of the civil sphere. In short, the news can be upholding its civil ideal and solidarising or protecting vested interests (non-solidarising). The assessment made here is that current levels of civility are sufficient for a civilised and just society and that there is widespread agreement that the status quo should be maintained and preserved. The news actively rejects change of what is currently agreed to be civil by, for example, judging that the social narrative with regard to the constitution of the private, the public, or what is taboo is right; that established forms of behaviour and manners are both functional and aesthetically acceptable and endorsable, while modish forms are unacceptable; that linguistic innovations break the rules and should be avoided. Overall the assessment made is that current levels of civility should be maintained as they are. This has both a conservative and progressive element. Conservatively, such assessments are at odds with the fact that as attitudes and values change, boundaries shift and challenging cultural artefacts, language or behaviour may become more acceptable. The progressive element is reflected in what has been achieved against reactionary forces and what is judged as non-solidarising is resisted or criticised by the news media.

Of course the simplicity of this triadic typology jars at the level of a pluralistic news environment where we take for granted that the news should undoubtedly pick up on and remark on civil and anti-civil sentiments both within and outside civil society and that it is vital for a civil society and for the right to freedom of expression that such sentiments are not simply ignored or hidden away. Indeed, freedom of expression in a pluralistic context requires that such sentiments are voiced and debated if it is in any way to be consistently applied. The point being that the civil power of the news can be identified and analytically abstracted from the cacophony of any debate and correspondingly the typology above can be found through content analysis. The loss of subtlety or the ironing out of ambiguity within any given position within any particular debate is not at issue here since the news is both critical, in an evaluative sense, and critical insofar as it raises objections to any given position in any given debate.[13] It has always done so and always will. In this way, the news's role in any particular debates or disagreements is central and the extent to which the news 'reflects' civil society in all its antagonisms is at the heart of the civil role of the news. Consequently, these three cardinal types of civil boundary maintenance by the news are in reality never clear-cut (though I repeat they can be uncovered and analytically disaggregated, see Part II), but exist in a state of constant contestation and are the defining instances of where the civil ideal of the news is constantly challenged by the realities of journalistic practices, changing public sentiment and the pursuit of vested interests. And although the civil ideal of the news ensures that the news continues to endure as an essential institutional feature of vibrant civil life, its limitations and flaws are often visible as the quotidian reality of news production and news consumption lays bare the civil ideal of the news as something pure and unadulterated (see Chapters 2 and 3). Indeed as a matter of daily routine the civil power of the news to undertake any one of these three cardinal types of civil boundary maintenance relies upon both journalists and audiences being able to negotiate between the civil ideal of the news and its real shortfalls. News providers get to know their audiences through various types of audience research, interactions with viewers and readers and by tracking public opinion polls and changing views as well as more recently by inviting their audiences to comment on their news stories and to engage in different types of dialogues with the news organisation.

The intention is twofold: first, the news by its very nature must be and wants to be up-to-date with events and issues and news providers must also be sensitive to the zeitgeist, the counter-zeitgeist and the changing values and mores in society. Second and equally however, they must be and want to be sensitive to the views, likes and dislikes of their viewers, interlocutors or readers to ensure that they do not lose them to rivals by challenging them too much. Consequently, news journalism must be sensitive not only to the non-civil interests of the non-civil spheres, but also to the range of civil and anti-civil sentiments articulated around every issue in order to reflect a plurality of viewpoints within the institutions of civil society itself. It must do this while equally being sensitive to the needs of their own audience and the commercial and other priorities of the news organisation within which they work. These contingencies and considerations will influence (both knowingly and unknowingly) the news provider's story selection—namely its news agendas—but also the particular ways it tells its stories, which elements it emphasises and which it ignores to meet audience expectations.[14] It will also influence, as noted above, what kind of news style is used in the reporting.

5   Three Styles of News Reporting

If there are three cardinal types of civil boundary maintenance in news reports, there are also three ways in which these assessments on boundary maintenance are conveyed. To be precise there are three styles of news reporting in which a civil or anti-civil judgement can be made. These styles are discursive, descriptive and tendentious (Harrison 2008b; Crossley and Harrison 2015). These styles influence the way in which expressions about who or what is seen to be civil or anti-civil are articulated and which determine the extent to which each type of news report can be seen to convey its civil and anti-civil judgements and interpretations of the world.

The analysis of news styles looks at the way news reports look and feel, how they are laid out and designed as well as their para-textual qualities (photographs, diagrams, drawings, use of multi-screen features and chyrons, etc). Such things are increasingly important in the digital packaging for all news formats. Though not as significant for the case study in Part II of this book as for the study of a modern newsroom—where design and layout are constantly considered in terms of their rhetorical and aesthetic force—they provide for an extra aspect of our understanding of how a particular cardinal type of boundary maintenance was endorsed. To put the matter slightly differently, and to borrow two terms from Richards (1965 [1937]), news styles provide for both the 'tenor' and 'vehicle' of meaning given to the event being reported on.[15] The 'tenor' is the subject of the news report and the 'vehicle' is the way a particular style of news report rhetorically reimagines and attributes qualities and significance to the subject. In other words, news styles provide an affective register that needs to be included into our reaggregated account. They are rather like a musical score where the notation indicates how loud a passage of music is to be played. The discursive news style is written *piano*, the descriptive style is written *mezzo piano* or *mezzo forte* and the tendentious style is written *forte, fortissimo* and occasionally (though occurring more frequently) *fortississimo*.

The discursive style of news reporting is used to convey both civil and anti-civil expressions in an apparently serious, well-researched or sourced manner. Reports in the discursive style offer analysis and commentary, use experts and are written by specialists. Such reports are often independent of 'official versions of events' although sources are used to express a variety of civil or anti-civil views. Nevertheless, the perception of such news reports is that of a balanced or fair account. The greater the number of viewpoints presented the greater the effort that is required from the reader (or viewer) to evaluate and judge the conflicting views and varied positions. News reports which reflect a plurality of views necessarily contain values that may not be approved of by many and risk audience disapproval for giving them airtime or space. Such news reports may also seek to expose the limited character of 'official accounts', or offer up different possible accounts. The discursive approach can be described as an overtly objective method of reporting (see Chapter 2) and is produced for audiences perceived to be capable of understanding and following many lines of an argument and who do not require that everything be explained to them. The language and style is of equals talking to equals. The discursive style of news seeks to serve the public interest rather than only to interest the public and it does not seek to reassure through distortion, or by distilling only those views that express civil values. The discursive style of reporting usually accompanies a hard news agenda that includes and covers intellectual or technical issues and is the most likely style to be adopted for traditional investigative reports that seek to present (or the investigative journalist has considered) the different aspects of an issue or an event in order to evaluate and assess them in an even-handed manner. The discursive style is what Gregory (2004: XVII) refers to as 'critical reporting and writing', which without 'the privilege of presence', consumers of news rely upon to know 'about "there" from "here"' (in this vein, see also Inglis 2002: 3).

The descriptive style of news reporting focuses on the reporting of facts in a clear and intelligible way. Events that are complex are reduced to simplicity by a process of paring down a news event to its core or essential facts. In stylistic terms, the appearance of this type of news is one of studied neutrality although, in practice, descriptive news also coexists with different narrative styles in the same news outlet. Reports in the descriptive style are usually summative without comment or opinion and heavily reliant upon the material it describes usually through extensive quotes (from a report, a public document or a transcript, where sometimes the whole transcript is included verbatim) and they are often accompanied by descriptive graphics and photographs. Reports in this style may be expressed in a short bulletin–style piece, sometimes referred to as 'news in brief' (NIB), factoids or one-minute news-bites. Such news reports can be very instructive where the news consumer is seen as requiring no more than a minimum report or accurate summary and has little time (or attention) to spare, when the complex facts need to be simplified, or when an event is deemed less important than others. The guiding motif is that the facts must speak for themselves. These reports represent one of the most valuable functions of news journalism, which is to simply describe events as they are and not to interpret them as one would like them to be or to be what one might approve of. This style of news reporting is generally associated with such mottos as 'Comment is free, but facts are sacred' (Scott 1921), whereby the primary role of a newspaper is accurate reporting.[16] Using a descriptive news style that lets the facts speak for themselves does not necessarily mean that the descriptive news form (especially in its longer form) is always neutral. Rather, such a news style can also produce evaluative news reports that are judgemental about who or what is civil or anti-civil. The use of graphics, statistics and facts and figures can be very powerful, for example when a graphic shows the number of nationals in the armed forces that have been killed in conflict abroad or a row of photographs of the dead. Factual, descriptive and accurate reports can elicit shock, outrage, sadness and civil protest. This descriptive style of reporting is overt rather than discreet and is not dishonestly or surreptitiously undertaken; rather it is the employment of a perspective, a type of reporting, civil or anti-civil depending on the context, which is judged to accord with the news consumers' invariant civil concerns.

The tendentious style of news reporting can be identified where news becomes the direct advocate of a specific cause, or offers to explain events in terms solely of the personal in so-called human-interest stories where it appeals to emotions and feelings. Tendentious news reports generally adopt a campaigning and universalistic style. Their judgements are substantively made and are aimed at persuading audiences. The cause is clearly and stridently announced—often by using a didactic tone—and the news report seeks actively to elicit support and the objective method of reporting is not adhered to. Evidence is marshalled to support a particular viewpoint and those facts or views that do not accord may be ignored, sidelined or even mocked or ridiculed. Tendentious news reports use language that is emotive and its pursuit has led on some occasions to unlawful attempts at phone tapping, entrapment and 'stings'. Tendentious news reports engage with the news consumer at the emotional level and require little more than a response of moral approval or moral disapproval. The tendentious style is not new: R. G. Collingwood (1939: 55) argues that Victorian news values were being corrupted by the *Daily Mail* 'the first English newspaper for which the word "news" lost its old meaning of facts which a reader ought to know if he was to vote intelligently', although in what is to follow in Chapters 6–8 I would argue that the tendentious style (as well as the discursive and the descriptive) were alive and well in the earlier Victorian era. In order to emphasise a point, the news story may be given a prominent position in the paper, on the website or mobile device, or in a news programme. Campaigns in newspapers have a long history and can range from those that fulfil a civil purpose, to the sentimental and mawkish, to the genuinely unpleasant. The tendentious style of news reporting may support both civil and anti-civil views and actions, can be highly sensational, prurient or voyeuristic, or may deliberately be billed as trivial and fun and often strike a populist note.

News styles accord with a reader's affective and rational disposition and degree of concern towards a particular subject. More specifically, the discursive news style anticipates a reader who is perceived to be capable of understanding and following an argument; that is a deliberative reader persuaded more by reason that emotion; the descriptive style anticipates a moderately attentive reader, interested in a factual synopsis and who requires no more than a minimum report or accurate summary; the tendentious news style speaks to a reader who is to be persuaded who is to be turned into an advocate of any given particular point of view or is already predisposed to the point of view being tendentiously reported on.

If we amalgamate the findings of the above Sects. 3, 4 and 5 and apply it to our understanding of the news cycle (Fig. 1) we can now add three more pieces of information to the way the news cycle can be represented in terms of including: (a) how news selection is undertaken and contributes to the civil judgements made in the newsroom (Sect. 3), (b) the nature of the three cardinal types of civil boundary maintenance endorsed by news report (Sect. 4), and (c) and the styles of news reporting used (Sect. 5). These adjustments provide a more complete schema of the workings of the news cycle and the civil power of the news as influencing 'our' civil boundary maintenance, as can be seen in Fig. 3.

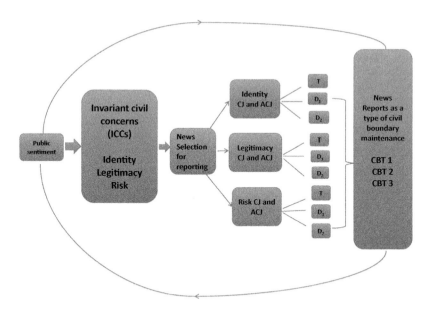

Fig. 3 The news cycle in greater detail (*keys* CJ: Civil Judgement; ACJ: Anti-civil Judgement; T: Tendentious; D1: Discursive; D2: Descriptive; CBT: Civil Boundary Type)

6 Summary

While it is true to say that many concerns of civil society have been fixed and agreed upon through historical, political and social arrangements, namely there are many important things on which we all agree, there still remain events and developments that are disputed and contested and the news has the ability to report stories as both civil and anti-civil and to amplify or reduce the impact of the story through the different styles of news reporting that are adopted. Mediated news both in relation to its production methods and its final news products is not simply a neutral conduit of events, but rather it has a form of civil power which is judgemental and which engages with public sentiment as can be seen in Fig. 4 below:

The civil power of the news is located in the news cycle with its endless relationship between news reports and public sentiment. The relationship between the two (lineally expressed) is, as noted above, that a news event is regarded by public sentiment as relevant to 'our' invariant civil concerns with regard to the civil sphere and the nature of civil society. As such this news event is interpreted in the newsroom as being both routinely newsworthy and as one which requires and affords civil and anti-civil judgements which are expressed in and supported by a specific style of news reporting. In turn, the news report engages with public sentiment by ignoring, reporting or amplifying our invariant civil concerns. In this endless circularity, the civil

Fig. 4 News, the public and public sentiment

power of the news is exercised in three ways: first in the choice of whether to select a news event for reporting; second, through its civil and anti-civil judgements and third via the use of different news styles which are discursive (D_1), descriptive (D_2) and tendentious (T) which serve to produce a varied number of types and styles of news reports on any given invariant civil concern-related event or issue. Combined they form the way we seek to maintain the type of civil boundaries 'we' value and want. At the same time, public sentiment expresses our invariant civil concerns and comes to the attention of the newsroom in a variety of ways, via a range of social media, public opinion polls, audience research, public protests, 'letters to the editor', UGC, interviews, reports, knowledge from previous events, referenda/election results, vox pops and so on, all of which attend to how 'we' feel about our civil society, how 'we' regard the non-civil spheres and what 'we' do about those internal and external forces that seek to influence and change civil society from within. These mediated public sentiments are constantly recycled and replayed both within and outside the civil sphere as expressions of social and cultural solidarity about those matters that have a bearing on our invariant civil concerns. Sometimes civil and anti-civil sentiments that are expressed in public sentiment become part of the story itself, for example when the news media pick up on public outrage at a particular event and where public sentiment is amplified by the news media it may engender some kind of response from those holding office in the non-civil spheres. Public sentiment, whether expressed via social media or within different non-virtual settings, can contain rational and emotional expressions of a range of civil and anti-civil views which are generally challenged both within civil society itself and from outside civil society. Where there is contestation about an issue or an event within public sentiment those views that are anti-civil for some may be seen as civil by others and the justifications that follow are generally an attempt to establish a prominent position that holds within it a rationale built upon a variety of motivations that may not be articulated completely truthfully. The different motivations of the expressers of public sentiment range from vested and instrumental self-interest through to expressions of public interest and public good as well as many shades of grey in between.

NOTES

1. This has been done (a) by journalists being expected to develop and respond to audiences using a range of social media, as well as to understand how to write stories that are clear and straightforward enough to stand out when audiences conduct searches for news and (b) through user-generated content, blogs and other types of 'citizen journalism' see Chapter 1, endnote 36.
2. For example, the alt-right news media has recently flourished by offering a systematic set of counter-narratives to the 'mainstream news media' that they seek to discredit.
3. For an example of how three London newsrooms attempt to uphold editorial standards such as objectivity and professionalism, see McConnell (2016).
4. See Curran and Seaton (2009) and Corner (2013) on the idea of responsible journalistic power.
5. The key areas of representation scholarship relate among other things to the 'symbolic annihilation' of certain types of people in the factual media through their exclusion which is usually based on race, class, age, gender and sexual orientation (see Tuchman 1978, 2000) and the mediation of key markers of identity in the news such as gender (Carter et al. 1998; Ross and Carter 2011); social class (Butsch 1992), race and ethnicity (Dixon 2007; Dixon and Azocar 2007; Dixon and Linz 2000; Dixon and Williams 2015; Gilens 1996) and even to the use of media representations in the development of a global imagination (Orgad 2012).
6. Inquiries into the behaviour of news journalists are not new, as a series of reports and Royal Commissions (1947–1949; 1961–1962; 1974–1977), the Calcutt Reports 1990 and 1993 on the UK press testify. These commissions and inquiries have had as their focus (variously) the democratic role of the press, the commercial nature of the press, the abandonment of responsible reporting and preventing unjustified press intrusion into people's private lives. A recent example is the independent inquiry undertaken by the Australian Government into Media and Media Regulation in 2011 led by Mr. Ray Finkelstein QC (see Berg 2012).
7. Johal et al. (2014: 402), when talking about public participation in economic life and responding to the discipline of the market, refer to this aspect of power as the capillary 'power of learned self-discipline'. The potency of expert knowledge from a wide range of aspects of public life is that it reaches into our quotidian lives in ways which are often unacknowledged or are simply taken for granted. They are often largely unnoticed and therefore remain unchallenged. The news can be complicit in this.

8. This term is R. D. Laing's (2010 [1960]) used as a contrastive to anxiety. It was subsequently developed sociologically by Giddens (1991) to refer to conditions of continuity, routine, consistency and order and to form a contrast to 'postmodern' conditions of uncertainty and insecurity.
9. Geuss (2008: 25) reformulates Lenin's fundamental question of 'Who, whom?' as 'Who <does> what to whom for whose benefit?'. For Geuss this reformulation requires one to think about agency, power, and interests, and the relationships between them; a process which requires political philosophy to cease to be abstract in order to adopt a realist approach to understanding the exercise of power (among other things).
10. See Garton-Ash (2016: 13).
11. See Harrison (2000, 2006: 136–137 for a summary of Galtung and Ruge's news values). These news values were reassessed and updated by Harcup and O'Neill (2001), discussed in some detail by Harcup (2004: 30–39) and updated further in Harcup and O'Neill (2017). See also Bell (1991), Harrison (2000), Ostgaard (1965), Rosengren (1977), Sande (1971), Sparkes and Winter (1980), Tunstall (1971), and Rosengren (1977).
12. A news homology has three broad features: first there is a normative base for the common understandings that 'we' (civil society, which includes both the 'newsroom' and audiences) regard as compatible or incompatible with the ideals and shape of things we believe in, where the degree of correspondence between our beliefs and those reflected in news accounts will be significant in relation to the level of trust placed in those accounts. Second, there must be a certain kind of correspondence to reality which consists of both a constative and explanatory dimension. Third, it is through these common understandings, and our agreements and disagreements we hold about them, that a news homology makes a contribution to public sentiment via truth directed synoptic reports which can then be discussed, scrutinised and tested in public settings and via the critical aspects and sites for discussion and contestation (and agreement and reinforcement) including those that social media now bring through sharing and liking, blogs and twitter. The correspondence between events and the way in which they are recorded in news outputs varies as particular news homologies often differ in substance and content from news provider to news provider thus taking variant forms.
13. I take this use of 'critical' from Geuss (2016).
14. See Harrison (2000) for an overview of the similarities and differences in news selection and presentation practices in a range of newsrooms.
15. For the sake of clarity, it needs to be noted that Richards's (1965 [1937]) use of the terms 'tenor' (subject) and 'vehicle' (an object borrowed from which the subject is ascribed meaning) serves to describe the twofold structure of a metaphor. Thus the metaphor 'Nancy was as brave as an

African lioness' has Nancy as the subject (tenor) and the African lioness as the object (vehicle) from which attributed meaning is derived and applied to the subject.
16. In the same essay in the Manchester Guardian centenary edition May 1921, CP Scott also recognises the role of editorial comments as fairness and goes on to recommend good newspaper business practices. Nonetheless, the dictum stands as a leitmotif for the descriptive form of newspaper news.

Bibliography

Alexander, J. (2006). *The Civil Sphere*. Oxford: Oxford University Press.
Altheide, D. L., & Rasmussen, P. K. (1976). Becoming News: A Study of Two Newsrooms. *Work and Occupation, 3*(2), 223–246.
Altheide, D. L., & Snow, R. P. (1979). *Media Logic*. London: Sage.
Bantz, C. (1985). News Organisations: Conflict as a Crafted Cultural Norm. *Communication, 8,* 225–244.
Bardoel, J., & Deuze, M. (2001). Network Journalism: Converging Competences of Media Professionals and Professionalism. *Australian Journalism Review, 23*(2), 91–103.
Bell, A. (1991). *The Language of News Media*. Oxford: Blackwell.
Berg, C. (2012, March). *The Finkelstein Report into Media and Media Regulation: Licensing, Censorship and Accountability* (Institute of Public Affairs Briefing Paper). Melbourne, Australia.
Berkowitz, D. (2009). Journalism in the Broader Cultural Mediascape. *Journalism, 10*(3), 290–292.
Born, G. (2005). *Uncertain Vision: Birt, Dyke and the Reinvention of the BBC*. London: Vintage.
Buckalew, J. K. (1969). A Q-Analysis of Television News Editors' Decisions. *Journalism Quarterly, 46,* 135–137.
Burns, T. (1969). Public Service and Private World. *The Sociological Review Monograph, 13*(1), 53–73.
Butsch, R. (1992). Class and Gender in Four Decades of Television Situation Comedy: Plus ça Change. *Critical Studies in Mass Communication, 9*(4), 387–399.
Carey, J. (1986). The Dark Continent of American Journalism. In R. Manoff & M. Schudson (Eds.), *Reading the News: A Pantheon Guide to Popular Culture* (pp. 144–188). New York: Pantheon books.
Carter, C., Branston, G., & Allan, S. (Eds.). (1998). *News, Gender and Power*. London: Routledge.
Chernobrov, D. (2014). The Spring of Western Narcissism: A Psychoanalytic Approach to Western Reactions to the 'Arab Spring'. *Psychoanalysis, Culture & Society, 19*(1), 72–88.

Clyde, R. W., & Buckalew, J. K. (1969). Inter-Media Standardisation: A Q-Analysis of News Editors. *Journalism Quarterly, 46,* 349–351.
Collingwood, R. G. (1939). *An Autobiography.* Oxford: Oxford University Press.
Corner, J. (2013). *Theorising Media: Power, Form and Subjectivity.* Manchester: Manchester University Press.
Crossley, J. G., & Harrison, J. (2013). The Mediation of the Distinction of "Religion" and "Politics" by the UK Press on the Occasion of Pope Benedict XVI's State Visit to the UK. *Political Theology, 16*(4), 329–345.
Crossley, J. G., & Harrison, J. (2015). Atheism, Christianity and the British Press: Press Coverage of Pope Benedict XVI's 2010 State Visit to the UK. *Implicit Religion, 18*(1), 77–105.
Curran, J. P., & Seaton, J. (2009). *Power Without Responsibility.* London: Routledge.
Dahlgren, P. (1995). *Television and the Public Sphere: Citizenship, Democracy and the Media.* London: Sage.
Davis, A. (2000). Public Relations, News Production and Changing Patterns of Source Access in the British National Media. *Media, Culture and Society, 22*(1), 39–59.
Deuze, M. (2004). What Is Multimedia Journalism? *Journalism Studies, 5*(2), 139–152.
Deuze, M. (2005). What Is Journalism? Professional Identity and Ideology of Journalists Reconsidered. *Journalism, 6*(4), 442–464.
Dewey, J. (2008 [1935]). *The Later Works of John Dewey, 1925–1953*(Vol. 4) (J. A. Boydston Ed.). Carbondale: Southern Illinois University Press.
Dimitrova, D. V., & Strömbäck, J. (2009). Look Who's Talking: Use of Sources in Newspaper Coverage in Sweden and the United States. *Journalism Practice, 3*(1), 75–91.
Dixon, T. (2007). Black Criminals and White Officers: The Effects of Racially Misrepresenting Law Breakers and Law Defenders on Television News. *Media Psychology, 10*(2), 270–291.
Dixon, T., & Azocar, C. (2007). Priming Crime and Activating Blackness: Understanding the Psychological Impact of the Overrepresentation of Blacks as Lawbreakers on Television News. *Journal of Communication, 57*(2), 229–253.
Dixon, T., & Linz, D. (2000). Overrepresentation and Underrepresentation of African Americans and Latinos as Lawbreakers on Television News. *Journal of Communication, 50*(2), 131–154.
Dixon, T., & Williams, C. (2015). The Changing Misrepresentation of Race and Crime on Network and Cable News. *Journal of Communication, 65*(1), 24–39.
Epstein, E. J. (1973). *News from Nowhere: Television and the News.* New York: Random House.
Ericson, R. V., Baranek, P. M., & Chan, J. B. L. (1987). *Visualising Deviance.* Toronto: Toronto University Press.

Ericson, R. V., Baranek, P. M., & Chan, J. B. L. (1991). *Representing Order: Crime, Law and Justice in the News Media*. Milton Keynes: Open University Press.
Fishman, M. (1980). *Manufacturing the News*. Austin, TX: University of Texas Press.
Foucault, M. (1991). *Discipline and Punish: The Birth of a Prison*. London: Penguin.
Galtung, J., & Ruge, M. (1965). The Structure of Foreign News. *Journal of Peace Research, 2*(1), 64–91.
Gans, H. J. (1979). *Deciding What's News*. Evanston, IL: Northwestern University Press.
Garton-Ash, T. (2016). *Free Speech: Ten Principles for a Connected World*. New Haven and London: Yale University Press and Atlantic Books.
Geuss, R. (2008). *Philosophy and Real Politics*. Princeton: Princeton University Press.
Geuss, R. (2016). *Reality and Its Dreas*. Harvard: Harvard University Press.
Giddens, A. (1991). *Modernity and Self-Identity: Self and Society in the Late Modern Age*. Cambridge: Polity Press.
Gilens, M. (1996). Race and Poverty in America: Public Misperceptions and the American News Media. *Public Opinion Quarterly, 60*(4), 515–541.
Goffman, E. (1974). *Frame Analysis: An Essay on the Organization of Experience*. Boston: Northeastern University Press.
Gold, D., & Simmons, J. L. (1965). News Selection Patterns Among Iowa Dailies. *Public Opinion Quarterly, 29,* 425–430.
Golding, P., & Elliott, P. (1979). *Making the News*. Harlow: Longman.
Grabe, M. E., Zhou, S., Lang, A., & Bols, P. D. (2000). Packaging Television News: The Effects of Tabloid on Information Processing and Evaluative Responses. *Journal of Broadcasting and Electronic Media, 44*(4), 581–598.
Gregory, D. (2004). *The Colonial Present*. Malden, MA: Blackwell.
Harcup, T. (2004). *Journalism: Principles and Practice*. London: Sage.
Harcup, T., & O'Neill, D. (2001). What Is News? Galtung and Ruge Revisited. *Journalism Studies, 2*(2), 261–280.
Harcup, T., & O'Neill, D. (2017). What Is News? News Values Revisited (Again). *Journalism Studies, 18*(12), 1470–1488.
Harrison, J. (2000). *Terrestrial TV News in Britain: The Culture of Production*. Manchester: Manchester University Press.
Harrison, J. (2006). *News*. London: Routledge.
Harrison, J. (2008a). Exploring News Values: The Ideal and the Real. In J. Chapman & M. Kinsey (Eds.), *Broadcast Journalism: A Critical Introduction* (pp. 60–68). London: Routledge.
Harrison, J. (2008b). News. In B. Franklin (Ed.), *Pulling Newspapers Apart* (pp. 39–47). London: Routledge.

Harrison, J. (2010). User-Generated Content and Gatekeeping at the BBC Hub. *Journalism Studies*, 11(2), 243–256.
Hartley, L. (1989). *Understanding News*. London: Routledge.
Inglis, F. (2002). *People's Witness: The Journalist in Modern Politics*. London and New Haven: Yale University Press.
Johal, S., Moran, M., & Williams, K. (2014). Power, Politics and the City of London After the Great Financial Crisis. *Government and Opposition*, 49(3), 400–425.
Küng-Shankleman, L. (2000). *Inside the BBC and CNN: Managing Media Organisations*. London: Routledge.
Laing, R. D. (2010 [1960]). *The Divided Self: An Existential Study in Sanity and Madness*. London: Penguin books.
Lukes, S. (2003). *Liberals and Cannibals: The Implications of Diversity*. London: Verso.
Manning, P. (2001). *News and News Sources*. London: Sage.
Mazzoleni, G. (2008). Media Logic. In W. Donsbach (Ed.), *The International Encyclopedia of Communication* (Vol. III, pp. 2930–2932). Malden, MA: Blackwell.
McConnell, S. (2016). *"This Place…!" Challenge and Change to Journalistic Identity in a Digital Age. A Study of Three London Local Newsrooms* (PhD thesis). University of Sheffield.
Mitchelstein, E., & Boczkowski, P. J. (2009). Between Tradition and Change: A Review of Research on Online News Production. *Journalism*, 5(10), 562–586.
Oblak, T. (2005). The Lack of Interactivity and Hypertextuality in Online Media. *International Communication Gazette*, 67(1), 87–106.
Orgad, S. (2012). *Media Representation and the Global Imagination*. Cambridge: Polity Press.
Ostgaard, E. (1965). Factors Influencing the Flow of News. *Journal of Peace Research*, 2, 39–63.
Randall, D. (2000). *The Ethical Journalist* (2nd ed.). London: Pluto Press.
Richards, I. A. (1965 [1937]). *The Philosophy of Rhetoric*. New York: Oxford University Press.
Rosengren, K. E. (1977). Four Types of Tables. *Journal of Communication*, 27(1), 67–75.
Ross, K., & Carter, C. (2011). Women and News: A Long and Winding Road. *Media, Culture and Society*, 33(8), 1148–1165.
Ryfe, D. (2006a). Guest Editor's Introduction: New Institutionalism and the News. *Political Communication*, 23, 135–144.
Ryfe, D. (2006b). The Nature of News Rules. *Political Communication*, 23(2), 203–214.
Ryfe, D. (2009). Broader and Deeper: A Study of Newsroom Culture in a Time of Change. *Journalism*, 10(2), 197–216.
Ryfe, D. (2012). *Can Journalism Survive: An Inside Look at American Newsrooms*. Cambridge: Polity Press.

Sande, O. (1971). The Perception of Foreign News. *Journal of Peace Research, 8,* 221–237.

Schlesinger, P. (1978). *Putting 'Reality' Together: BBC News.* London: Constable.

Schlesinger, P. (1987). *Putting 'Reality' Together: BBC News* (2nd ed.). London: Constable.

Schlesinger, P., & Tumber, H. (1994). *Reporting Crimes.* Oxford: Oxford University Press.

Schudson, M. (2008). *Why Democracies Need an Unlovable Press.* Cambridge: Polity Press.

Scott, C. P. (1921, May 5). *A Hundred Years. Essay.* Available at: http://backup.gmgplc.co.uk.s3.amazonaws.com/wp-content/uploads/2010/10/CP_Scott_leader.pdf.

Shoemaker, P. J., & Reese, S. (1996). *Mediating the Message: Theories of Influences on Mass Media Content.* USA: Longman.

Silverstone, R. (2007). *Media and Morality: On the Rise of the Mediapolis.* London: Wiley.

Soloski, J. (1989). News Reporting and Professionalism: Some Constraints on the Reporting of the News. *Media, Culture and Society, 11*(2), 207–228.

Sparkes, V. M., & Winter, J. P. (1980). Public Interest in Foreign News. *Gazette, 20,* 149–170.

Steensen, S. (2011). Online Journalism and the Promises of New Technology: A Critical Review and Look Ahead. *Journalism Studies, 12*(3), 311–327.

Sundar, S. (1998). Effect of Source Attribution on Perception of Online News Stories. *Journalism and Mass Communication Quarterly, 75*(1), 55–68.

Tuchman, G. (1972). Objectivity as a Strategic Ritual: An Examination of Newsmen's Notions of Objectivity. *American Journal of Sociology, 77*(4), 660–679.

Tuchman, G. (1973). Making News By Doing Work: Routinizing the Unexpected. *American Journal of Sociology, 79*(1), 110–131.

Tuchman, G. (1978). *Making News: A Study in the Construction of Reality.* New York: Free Press.

Tuchman, G. (2000). The Symbolic Annihilation of Women by the Mass Media. In L. Crothers & C. Lockhart (Eds.), *Culture and Politics* (pp. 150–174). Basingstoke: Palgrave Macmillan.

Tunstall, J. (1971). *Journalists at Work.* London: Constable.

Waldron, J. (2012). *The Harm in Hate Speech.* Cambridge, MA: Harvard University Press.

Wallis, R., & Baran, S. (1990). *The Known World of Broadcast News.* London: Routledge.

Weber, M. (1919). *Politics as a Vocation.* Available at: http://fs2.american.edu/dfagel/www/class%20readings/weber/politicsasavocation.pdf.

PART II

A Practical Demonstration of the Civil Power of the News Through an Analysis of the First British Railway Murder 1864

CHAPTER 5

Introduction to Part II

The purpose of Part II is to demonstrate the civil power of the news analytically and to show that such power is not simply a contemporary phenomenon, but that as the word 'invariant' signals, civil power has always been a key part of the deep architecture of news. With this argument in mind, I have chosen to analyse the ways invariant civil concerns were reported in the news and the press's reactions and engagement with public sentiment when reporting the first murder which occurred in a first-class railway carriage in Britain in 1864.[1] What may seem like a rather eccentric choice for analysis revealed rich seams of reportage, which, while historically contextualised, is notable for its familiarity and relevance in contemporary settings. It includes the same matters that would be covered or addressed in the reporting of a murder today. Such matters include those of nationality/immigration, social class, technological progress, legal processes, policing, the role of the political sphere as well as writing in ways that cater for all perceived audience tastes—then as now. Equally, then as now, the types of civil judgements about what is newsworthy and what aspects of a story is of concern to the public as well as what kind of information may be relied upon from particular non-civil and civil sources remain remarkably relevant to a contemporary setting. That is they are historically consistent with today and the way in which the civil power of the news works and continues to work in the context of the news cycle. Thus, and as I shall demonstrate, the choice of the first British railway murder doesn't restrict or weaken the relevance of the analysis of the civil power of the news in any way. Rather the analysis testifies to the timeless and continuing validity of the civil power of the news.

© The Author(s) 2019
J. Harrison, *The Civil Power of the News*,
https://doi.org/10.1007/978-3-030-19381-2_5

1 The Murder

1.1 The Events

The first murder on a train[2] on the British Victorian railways occurred on Saturday 9 July 1864. The victim was Thomas Briggs, a sixty-nine-year-old chief clerk at Robarts, Curtis Bank in Lombard Street, a bank located in the City which was then as now the financial district of London. He was travelling home to Clapton Square as a first-class passenger on the 9.45 p.m. train from Fenchurch Street to Hackney, on the North London Railway line. Hackney station was at a halfway point between Fenchurch Street and the train's final stop at Chalk Farm on the outskirts of London. Two passengers, who coincidentally were clerks at the same bank as Thomas Briggs, raised the alarm shortly after 10 p.m. upon the discovery of a blood-soaked seat in an empty carriage compartment on the train.[3] The full significance of the blood in the compartment was not evident until about twenty minutes later when another train driver discovered Briggs lying between two railway tracks further down the line 'with his head towards Hackney Wick and his feet towards London'.[4] A quick examination of Briggs revealed he had been very badly beaten on and around the head by a blunt instrument.[5] He died later that evening. Detectives established a timeline of events, noted the discovery of a hat in the compartment which did not belong to Briggs. They also set about cataloguing what they regarded as Briggs's missing items. These included his own hat,[6] his gold watch[7] and a chain. This made it look like the motive for the killing was robbery.[8]

The fact that Thomas Briggs died without having regained consciousness and that no one had witnessed the murder made the investigation difficult. Accordingly, the relatively new detective force[9] had very few clues to base their subsequent investigation on. Moreover, the detective work at the time was not anything like today's forensic crime scene analysis. For example, blood type analyses (except to establish that the blood was most likely to be human), the taking of fingerprints (this was introduced in the early 1900s) and DNA analysis were impossible. Rather crime scene routines were, by today's standards, chaotic—it wasn't even routine to gather forensic evidence such as hair samples. Overall, the evidence that could be used to identify and catch the killer was circumstantial rather than scientific and forensic. This gap in scientific knowledge and expertise was to leave key details about the murder of Briggs ambiguous and open to public and press interpretation and speculation.

On 18 July (nine days after the murder), suspicion fell on a young man, Franz Müller,[10] a German tailor, when evidence emerged that he had swapped a gold watch chain similar to the one stolen from Briggs for another chain and a ring at a jeweller pawnbroker's owned by John Death. Müller could be identified because Death explained that the customer who had swapped the jewellery had received it in a small box which had the name and address of the jeweller's printed on the lid. Accordingly, when a public appeal (with a reward of £300) to identify the person who had traded the gold watch chain at the jeweller's had been issued, a cab driver, Jonathan Matthews[11] came forward to claim the reward saying that Müller—who was Matthews's friend—had given Matthews's ten-year-old daughter an empty jewellery box from John Death's shop to play with when he visited Matthews's widowed sister-in-law at his home on Monday 11 July 1864, just two days after the murder. Matthews also claimed to recognise the hat that had been left in the bloodstained carriage as Müller's.

Apparently, Matthews recognised the hat because he had it made for Müller by Mr. Walker, a hat maker in Crawford Street, after Müller had admired one of Matthews's own hats.[12] Matthews also provided a photograph of Müller. By the time Müller had been identified and the detective force was in possession of his photograph, Müller had left London for New York travelling in the steerage class of a sailing ship, named Victoria.[13]

On 19 July, the day after Matthews came forward, depositions were hurriedly taken from six witnesses at the Magistrates Court at 4 Bow Street, London[14] and an arrest warrant for Franz Müller was issued. The detective in charge, Detective Inspector Tanner, another police officer, Sergeant Clarke, as well as two witnesses who had given depositions, John Death (the jeweller pawnbroker) and Jonathan Matthews (the cab driver) all left London for Liverpool and boarded a more modern and faster steamship, called the City of Manchester. The steamship arrived in New York on 5 August 1864, three weeks before Müller's ship. On arrival Detective Inspector Tanner began the difficult process of setting up an extradition hearing and met with the man who was to act as the US arresting officer.[15] Despite Tanner's own anxieties and concerns that Müller may be rescued or escape,[16] Müller was successfully arrested relatively quietly off the Victoria sailing ship as it docked in New York on 25 August 1864. Müller's possessions were searched and he was found to possess a watch, which was identified by Sergeant Clarke as belonging to

Thomas Briggs from the serial numbers given to him by the watchmaker in London. Also found in Müller's possession was a top hat, cut down by about one to one and a half inches.

Müller's extradition hearing was held in New York at the US Circuit Court House on the 26 and 27 August. Despite the spirited defence from Müller's defence lawyer Mr. Chauncey Schaffer, Commissioner Newton decided that Müller was to be extradited and brought back to the UK on the steamship Etna by the British team. They arrived in Liverpool to huge crowds that had gathered to try to get a glimpse of the arrested man, who was already a 'celebrity villain' as a result of earlier and ongoing press coverage. Müller was taken to London and charged at Bow Street. His magisterial hearing on 19 September and the Coroner's jury verdict of wilful murder on 26 September led Müller to be committed for trial at the Central Criminal Court in October 1864. The trial began on 27 October 1864, where Müller, as a German citizen, was supported by the German Legal Protection Society (GLPS).[17]

A prostitute who Müller claimed to be with at the time of the murder provided his alibi. However, both the prostitute and the alibi she provided were discredited in court. The prosecution emphasised the fact that the prostitute was unreliable and self-evidently immoral and therefore an unworthy witness—a view very much in tune with Victorian moral conventions of the time.[18] A further problem for Müller was that the Solicitor General had a right of reply to the defence, meaning that the final words the jury heard were his severe dismissal of the evidence that had been called for the defence and he 'reiterated the great strength of the case that had been made out by the Crown' (Knott 1911: xxix). The jury, which declined the offer from the judge to read out once more all the circumstantial evidence, took just fifteen minutes to return its verdict of guilty of murder. On 29 October 1864, Müller was sentenced to death by public hanging.

Müller's trial as 'an exercise in jurisprudence … was a rather routine business' (Fox 1998: 286) as the law in 1864 only had two categories by which to judge unlawful killing: murder or manslaughter. This meant that provocations that might today be taken into account as reasons for committing a murder were not relevant at the time in English law and there was no right of appeal despite the fact that all the evidence against Müller was circumstantial.[19] The junior judge, Baron Martin, effectively classified the unlawful killing of Thomas Briggs, arising from a robbery, as premeditated murder and passed the sentence of death. Outraged by a sense of injustice, the GLPS presented a Memorial on 10 November 1864 to the Home Secretary, Sir George Grey, requesting a commutation of the sentence to life imprisonment.[20] Other memorials were also submitted, but none of the appeals were successful. The Home Secretary wrote to the GLPS on 12 November declining to interfere with the sentence[21] and Müller was hanged outside Newgate Prison in London on 14 November 1864.

1.2   Press and Public Reactions

The murder of Briggs was a prominent event in the news cycle throughout July to November 1864. The first reports appeared on 11 July (a Monday) and all took on tones of outraged horror and alarm, declaring that this particular murder was 'one of the most atrocious crimes that has probably ever disgraced this country'. The press's focus on the audacious nature of the murder elicited public fascination and obsession with the question of who could have possibly committed this crime. Further, the press recognised and amplified the public's interest in the murder, skilfully drawing its readership into its reporting of the murder, the subsequent trial and execution. The more the story was reported, the more newsworthy it became and the greater the public's engagement.[22] The Leeds Mercury exemplified the extent to which the press labelled the crime as especially important when it reported that 'It would be impossible to convey an adequate idea of the excitement which prevails in the neighbourhood of the murder. Thousands of persons have visited it this morning, and all sorts of speculations are, of course, indulged in'.[23] The newspaper report went on itself to speculate about the way in which the crime must have unfolded, skilfully setting the scene with a number of dramatic embellishments, 'the struggle between the murderer and the victim must have been short and desperate' in the 'wild' and 'unbuilt upon' neighbourhood of Bow.[24] The idea of the murder occurring as the train flew by an unlit wilderness emphasised the brutal, violent and sinister nature of the crime. Added piquancy was provided by the fact that it took place in a *first-class* railway carriage, which should, according to the Victorian hierarchical and class-based social outlook, have been a safe middle- and to a lesser extent upper-class enclave secure from the dangers of the 'outside' uncivilised world (see this chapter and Chapters 8, 9).

The murder, the search for Müller, the trial and the public hanging attracted widespread coverage both within the national and the regional press. The latter had notably expanded its readership in the previous decade. Numerous members of the public wrote to the press, to the police and to the Home Office. Public sentiment was stirred by a combination of factors: the novelty of a murder on a train; the contradictory locations—an 'unbuilt' wilderness and a first-class carriage; the perceived brutality and savagery of the violence; the excitement of the chase over the Atlantic Ocean in pursuit of the alleged killer; the extradition back to the UK; the close reporting of the legal proceedings as well as the finality and spectacle of a public hanging all ensured that the story 'had legs' and that it ran for several months,[25] all of this the press tapped into and exploited. Ultimately and over the course of events the press's and the public's interest in the story became distilled and focused mainly on the murder suspect. With the growth of cheaper newspapers and more accessible and popular journalism following the abolition of the Stamp Duty in 1855,[26] competition for readers had increased among all of the press which 'was alive to the commercial importance of sensational crime reporting' (Chibnall 1981: 205).[27] Correspondingly, the volume of press coverage about Müller, the villain, soon overshadowed that of the murdered man.

As with any press coverage of a high-profile murder, reporting about the victim and the villain was the focus of timeless questions: Is the villain an insider or an outsider? Is he/she or they one of us, part of our community, or not one of us, a stranger? Is the victim innocent or especially vulnerable? Was it a case of being in the wrong place at the wrong time? Could it have happened to any of us? The proximity of the crime was evident in that somehow the murder 'occurred close to home' and was expressed as a feeling of being physically threatened and fears about the despoliation of secure private places, or being psychologically cowed, with fear and alarm directed at moral decline, social fragmentation and national vulnerability. All of these concerns were evident in the press reports as well as among the public in its own letters to the newspapers and to the Home Office. Public sentiment and press reports became inextricably linked when facing these intractable questions and anxieties.

1.3 The Relevance of the First British Railway Murder for the Demonstration of the Civil Power of the News

The direct relevance of the press coverage of the murder to the civil power of the news is fivefold: first, the fact that the story was reported for over four months demonstrates its intrinsic newsworthiness and that it contained aspects of perceived public concern about threats to the civil sphere. Second, it was a story with which the public actively engaged. Evidence of this exists in both the press and in Home Office archives and files. Third, the press coverage of the murder demonstrates that historically (and like today) the press continuously responds to public sentiment in the news cycle sometimes engaging with it, seeming to listen and consider it, sometimes amplifying it by taking a particular stance on behalf of its readers and sometimes dismissing it. Fourth, the press coverage of the story serves to demonstrate how, through its engagement with the three invariant civil concerns and public sentiment, the news arrives at its civil and anti-civil judgements. As an extension of this point and fifth, the press coverage of the story provides some historical evidence that the three civil concerns of identity, legitimacy and risk are indeed invariant.

2 A Note on Method

2.1 Sample

Three kinds of data were used: first, newspaper articles in the regional and national press reporting the Briggs's murder between 10 July and 31 December 1864; second, letters written to both the police and the press and the home office[28] and third, Home Office archival files.

First and with regard to the news sample, it comprised of all the news coverage of the case by the following nine national newspapers: *Lloyds Weekly London Newspaper, The Daily News, Reynolds Newspaper, The Evening Standard, The Times, The Daily Telegraph,* Illustrated *London News, The Sunday Times, Morning Post* and the following thirty regional newspapers: *The Leeds Mercury, The Carlisle Journal, The Belfast Newsletter, The Belfast Morning News, The Stirling Observer and Midland Counties Advertiser, The Western Gazette, The Westmorland Gazette and Kendal Advertiser, The Burnley Gazette, The Leicestershire Mercury, The Kendal Mercury, The Sheffield Daily Telegraph,* The Weekly Supplement to the *Sheffield Telegraph, The Era, The Preston Chronicle and Lancashire Advertiser, The Hereford Times, The Huddersfield Chronicle, The Dublin Evening Mail, The Cork Examiner, The North Wales Chronicle, Woolmer's Exeter and Plymouth Gazette, The Cheltenham Chronicle, The Leeds Intelligencer, The Birmingham Daily Post, The Grantham Journal, The Staffordshire Advertiser, Hampshire Telegraph and Sussex Chronicle, The Manchester Courier and Lancashire General Advertiser, The Bury and Norwich Post, The North Devon Journal and Newcastle Courant.*

These newspapers were obtained via the British Newspaper Archives and represent the entirety of the sample under the search terms of 'Briggs', 'Mr Briggs', 'Franz Müller', 'Franz Muller', 'railway murder'. Articles from *The Daily Telegraph* were collected using the same search terms from the Telegraph Historical Archive 1855–2000 via the Gale News Vault. In total there were 486 separate articles ranging in length from six lines to six columns depending on the amount of coverage given to the story on any one day. The coverage in the regional newspapers was generally verbatim reporting from one of the nationals so there was some significant overlap in content between the different newspapers. Within the newspaper sample, fourteen letters from the public on the subject were also analysed.

With regard to the general features of the news reports themselves, they were of the same combination of lengths as today ranging from a few lines to full front pages of several columns. The newsprint was smaller and reports often adopted a formal style of writing which entailed a denser vocabulary than today and longer multi-clausal sentences. There was also a greater usage of transcript material (especially court reports) and interestingly, regional newspapers often cited national newspaper reports verbatim. By today's standards, the reports were more difficult to read (presuming a reader with a greater reading age than that presumed by a UK tabloid newspaper today). And in mid-Victorian 1860s reading a news report aloud at work or home was not uncommon as such the longer reports would have required the audience to pay attention. Though, as a matter of background and more generally, the sense of the reader being spoken to is middle class. This is, however, not to say that the newspapers did not reach the working class but just that they tended to (in our sample) ignore working-class concerns and sensibilities. Indeed as Brown (1985: 273) argues, 'In the second half of the nineteenth century the newspaper became established as part of the normal furniture of life for all classes; and "newspaper" would have been understood as a paper purchased by the reader (possibly shared) and most probably appearing weekly and daily'.[29]

Second, the sample of news reports has been complemented by an analysis of 214 letters written to the police and the Home Office by members of the public. They were used in two ways: (a) when published in the news articles themselves as part of the news reporting analysis and (b) as background evidence to support my analysis of how the news coverage relates to public sentiment. Overall the letters, where it could be identified, appeared to be written by members of the middle class or to put the matter negatively no letter appeared to be written by members of the working class. The tone and overall content of the letters show an attachment to a specific social status (letters written from a specific class-based outlook) and were concerned with what the murder indicated as risk to a particular way of life (see Chapter 8). Some letters concerned themselves with whether Müller had been treated fairly, several advised on how to solve the crime and some were interested in emphasising that English procedural justice must be undertaken (see Chapters 6–8).

Third, Home Office files (opened to the public in 1964) were analysed. These contain correspondence between the detectives involved in the case and reports by Detective Inspector Tanner to the Home Secretary, Sir George Grey. They also contain a range of public pamphlets, selected news clipping and responses by the Home Secretary to letters sent by the public and provide context and background as well as some apposite quotations.[30]

2.2 *The Research Template*

The research adopted can be divided into two main stages (see Fig. 1, p. 154). The first concerns the story selection and the determination of the context of the story, which takes into account relevant political, social, cultural or economic aspects[31] that the press noted and engaged with in the reporting of the murder story which had a bearing on the three invariant civil concerns. This is important as it recognises that when the news engages with all or any of the three invariant civil concerns it does so within the particular defining spirit or mood of a particular period of history and its attendant associated ideas and beliefs replete as they are with ever-changing sets of dominant norms, cultural dispositions, modish outlooks and justificatory rationalities. In other words, the ideas and beliefs of the time represented in the news stories are relevant to both *selection* of events and issues and the news's civil and anti-civil *judgements* about them. It is in this way that news journalism may be seen to merit, in some respects, its claims about being 'a mirror on the world', namely that in the process of making sense of contemporary contingences the news *reflects* back to civil society both the civil and anti-civil nature of that civil society, which can make for uncomfortable reading. This is the case whether it be a conflictual and nasty Presidential election campaign, debates about the constitutional requirements needed to leave the European Union, a terrorist attack, natural disasters and accidents, refugees, migration and immigration, war and conflict, crises of any flavour, murder, threats and attacks, state

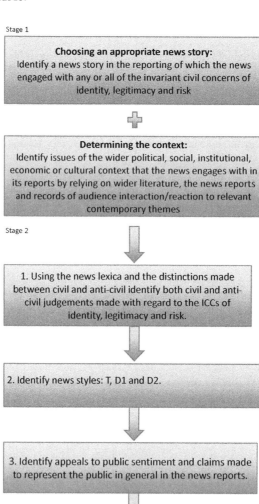

Fig. 1 Research template

visits, court cases and rulings, health and anxiety, tragedies or indeed, a murder committed in 1864 which cut into the heart of Victorian values, identity and sense of security. As the news engages with difficult and complex issues that have a bearing on the three invariant civil concerns, news reporting elicits sentiments that can be generous and ungenerous, progressive or reactionary, kind and compassionate or unkind and unforgiving. The engagement with our invariant civil concerns is continuous while at the same time the civil and anti-civil judgements made are plural and often incommensurate.

The second stage concerns the analysis of the news reports. This is undertaken via the four steps schematically represented below. Importantly these four steps can be used for the analysis of the civil power of the news in any news story whether historical or contemporary, irrespective of the form of journalism or the distribution platform utilised. In this second stage, the first step consisted of the following: each of the newspaper articles was read in their entirety and then manually colour coded using a different colour to first identify text that related to each of three invariant civil concerns, and second to then identify numerically the particular lexicon used (see the lexical tables[32] in Chapters 6–8), to lead to the civil and anti-civil judgements made. In a second step, the styles of news reporting used—tendentious (T1), discursive (D1) or descriptive (D2)—were identified. Following on from this approach the code I/CL/CJi/D1 means: *invariant civil concern of identity (I), the civil lexicon (CL), civil judgement category: (i) Civil values, status and citizenship (CJi), which was written in a discursive style (D1)*. Each article generally had within it more than one invariant civil concern, several lexical codes and possibly more than one style of reporting.

In a third step, appeals to public sentiment in the news reporting and claims made to represent the public in general were identified. The information from each newspaper article was then disaggregated into the different categories to form a separate document which then formed the body of evidence (quotations) which underpins the analysis under each of the lexical headings in Chapters 6–8.

Finally and in a fourth step, the analysis of the civil and anti-civil judgements made for all three invariant civil concerns, the appeals to public sentiment and the styles of news reporting were brought together in order to determine ultimately what cardinal type of civil boundary was endorsed and promoted by the press coverage and public sentiment. This is done in Chapter 9.

2.3 The Structure of Part II

For the sake of analytical clarity in the forthcoming Chapters 6–8, the three invariant civil concerns have been disaggregated to show how each one is constituted around its own particularities as well as to show how the press engages with each invariant civil concern utilising different civil and anti-civil lexica. In reality, the three invariant civil concerns overlap in news reports and their various particularities are effortlessly combined or presented side by side in any particular story reported and, correspondingly, in any different style of reporting undertaken. With this last point in mind, the next three chapters seek to show *how* in fact the civil and anti-civil reporting of all three invariant civil concerns is simultaneously part of the news cycle and often coexists and interrelates in different ways within the same story and even within the same newspaper article. What is subsequently revealed is, hopefully, the levels of complexity and tensions in the way in which civil and anti-civil judgements are articulated in the news and what those judgements mean for the way we address our invariant civil concerns. Chapter 9 reaggregates the news coverage of the murder by bringing together the main civil and anti-civil judgements made for each invariant civil concern in order to show the overall type of cardinal civil boundary maintenance that was endorsed by the press.

Notes

1. In popular culture, the murder has been picked up by Madame Tussaud's that hosts a waxwork model of Müller in the Chamber of Horrors in London, in a well researched book by Colquhoun (2012) and a BBC documentary, see also Arkell (2013). For other studies of notorious Victorian murders, see Gordon and Nair (2009) and Rieley (2018).
2. The next notable murder would not happen for another seventeen years. For a brief summary of other murders on trains or on the railway tracks and convictions, see Knott (1911: xxxiii–xxxvi).
3. Briggs couldn't have asked for help or signalled an emergency when he was attacked as the compartments were all closed and there was no means to communicate between them. As a result of this particular murder, the communication cord safety device was introduced in passenger carriages by the Regulation of Railways Act 1868. This allowed passengers to communicate with the conductor.
4. These words were spoken by Lord Chief Baron, one of the judges at the trial in his summing up of the evidence. The complete transcript of the

trial of Franz Müller is reprinted in Knott (1911: xiiv–147), the citation is on page 136.
5. It was generally assumed by the police, the press and both the defence and the prosecution that the murder weapon was Thomas Briggs's own walking stick which had a rounded handle. Traces of human blood were found on it, but it was never conclusively proven that this was the murder weapon. A bloodied stone near the scene was never examined or admitted as evidence.
6. The victim's hat played an important part in the case as the same or a similar hat was eventually found in the possession of Franz Müller who was tried and convicted of the crime. It was made by Digance hat makers in London, where Briggs also bought his own hats, and was originally a black silk top hat with a white silk lining which had been cut down to make it lower as was the fashion among some young men at the time. Testimony made later by a representative from Digance confirmed that the cutting down had not been done by them as they would have glued it, whereas this had been stitched by hand. Given that Müller was a tailor, that the hat was cut even slightly lower than usual and Digance were in the habit of sometimes writing the owner's name inside the hat, the alteration seemed to confirm the suspect's guilt, namely that he cut the hat down to remove the name. Another hat, found inside the empty train carriage where the attack had taken place, also played an important part in the case. This hat was quickly identified as not belonging to Thomas Briggs and the conclusion was drawn that the killer had accidentally left it behind and picked up Briggs's hat by mistake. The second hat was soon after identified by Jonathan Matthews a cab driver as belonging to Franz Müller and that he had one 'very similar'. Although neither hat was ever conclusively proven to belong to the victim and the suspect, testimony from several witnesses who claimed to recognise the hats was enough to provide the hats with a status and importance. Two pieces of circumstantial evidence seemed, when added together, to provide proof of guilt.
7. Thomas Briggs's Hackney watchmaker was able to provide a description of the watch and provide two serial numbers, one of the workings of the watch and another for the gold case.
8. This motive was questioned in the newspapers and in letters from the public as a diamond ring was still worn on Briggs's little finger and four sovereigns, some loose change and a silver snuffbox were found among other items (keys, half a first-class return ticked and a bundle of letters) in Thomas Briggs's pocket when he was examined after the attack had taken place.
9. The detective force in England originated in 1842 when eight new elite police officers were chosen to form the plain clothed Detective Branch.

Unlike the existing police officers who were entrusted with keeping law and order, these men were tasked with a new remit, that of investigating and solving murders.
10. I have used the correct spelling of Müller's name, with an umlaut over the 'u' when discussing him but retained the incorrect spelling of his name by the press. All the newspapers quoted omitted the umlaut from their copy.
11. The claim for one of the rewards offered at the time by Jonathan Matthews was to become controversial and a talking point in the press. Sergeant Parry for the Defence spent a good deal of time at the trial trying to discredit Matthews's motive for coming forward, the soundness of his testimony which kept changing and also attempted to raise the idea that Matthews might also have played some part in the crime. Despite press and public misgivings, Matthews was eventually awarded the reward in April 1865 in accordance with the rules at the time and he was seen to have been the first person to provide the evidence that led to a successful conviction.
12. In particular, Matthews's account of his knowledge of Franz Müller's hat was questioned both at the trial and in the press and by the public in its letters to the Home Office. The main question concerned the likelihood that a person would send someone else to get a hat made for them when it required careful fitting. This question was never really fully addressed but evidence about the particular lining of the hat was deemed to point to it being Müller's despite the evidence given by Matthews that the lining of the hat was *similar* to that found in the bloodstained carriage.
13. After having bought his ticket on 13 July (four days after the murder), Müller left for New York on 15 July. Although Müller's departure for New York seemed suspicious at the time, it later transpired through depositions and evidence given from several of the people close to him that Müller had started talking about the trip two or so weeks before the murder.
14. Witness statements were taken from characters who would later give evidence at Müller's trial and whose names began to crop up in newspaper articles, like characters in a play. The soundness of their evidence and their characters would be played out in the press and in public sentiment in October 1864. The witnesses were: John Hoffa, a work colleague and friend of Müller's; Jonathan and Eliza Matthews, the cabman who eventually claimed the reward of £300 for correct evidence and his wife; Thomas James Briggs, the son of the victim; the train guard, Benjamin Ames, who had discovered the bloodstained empty train carriage and John Death, the pawnbroker jeweller who identified the gold chain. Back in the UK, two remaining police officers, Sir Richard Mayne and Inspector Frederick Williamson, continued to work on the case.

5 INTRODUCTION TO PART II 159

15. Although England and America had an extradition treaty in place, relationships between the two nations were volatile and there was some uncertainty that Müller would be safely apprehended from the Victoria. America was in a state of civil war and many immigrants were encouraged, or forced by material circumstances, to join the fighting and to die for someone else's cause. In a letter to Sir Richard Mayne, Tanner explains how press coverage of the case in America was more sympathetic to Müller than the UK press and he was afraid that an attempt to save Müller may be undertaken (MEPO 3/75; Letter from Richard Tanner to Sir Richard Mayne, 28 August 1864). As an English detective had no jurisdiction in America, Tanner was careful to make sure that he contacted and worked with Mr. Edwards, the Consul 'who placed the law in the hands of Mr. Marberry lawyer to the Dutch Consulate', and with Mr. Kennedy the Chief of Police. Tanner went on to explain to his superior officer back home, the 'arrest must be made by an officer deputed to the USA Marshall' (MEPO 3/75; Letter from Richard Tanner to Sir Richard Mayne, 9 August 1864, received 25 August 1864). In the same letter, Tanner anticipated the processes of arrest and extradition, explaining that after Müller's arrest in New York off the Victoria 'the prisoner will then be taken before a Commissioner and upon a petition from the Dutch Consul stating that the prisoner is a fugitive from England charged with murder'.

16. Tanner's deep anxiety was evident in the letters he wrote to Sir Richard Mayne, Commissioner of the Metropolitan Police where he let him know that he was in severe pain having fallen down a ladder on the ship and that he could not immediately confirm that Müller's ship, the Victoria had not already arrived or been intercepted at sea. Once Tanner was able to ascertain that the Victoria had not arrived he let Sir Richard Mayne know of his extensive preparations for the arrest of Müller but that he was concerned that because of the extensive coverage of the case in the American newspapers, which meant that readers knew 'of all my movements there is a possibility of Müller escaping' (MEPO 3/75, 9 August 1864). A week later Tanner reported that 'up to this date the Victoria has not yet arrived, or since the 25th July been heard of' signing off 'We are all well but suffer somewhat from the very great heat' (MEPO 3/75, 16 August 1964). Three days later Tanner reported that 'up to this day we have no tidings of the ship "Victoria" altho [sic] she is now hourly expected' (MEPO 3/75, 19 August 1864).

17. The German Legal Protection Society (Deutscher Rechtsschutz-Verein, also referred to in the UK as the German National Verein) provided legal assistance to German immigrants in need, 'who in this country may not be able to obtain it from the authorised representative of their respective

Governments' (*Daily Telegraph*, 5 September 1864: 7). The legal aid provided by the GLPS offered Müller some legal support, but it is unlikely that his defence had the resources of the prosecution.

18. The Solicitor General in his address to the jury following the close of the argument for the defence went so far as to say the following directly to the jury: 'We next come to the alibi which my learned friend has been instructed to set up. Now, gentlemen, I must confess to some doubt as to the wisdom and the prudence of setting up that defence, for a more unsatisfactory and a more dangerous alibi was never set up in a Court of justice', he then went on to explain why it was unsatisfactory by reference to 'The clock of a brothel, the keeper of the house, and the statement of one of the unfortunate women who reside in it' (Knott 1911: 128). He went on to ask 'Do you suppose that the proceedings of that respectable and well-conducted establishment are regulated by clockwork? Why, it is preposterous' (ibid.: 129).
19. The right to appeal wasn't introduced into law until 1907.
20. See HO12/152/63. The GLPS made strenuous attempts to obtain a reprieve. The society prepared a Memorial which was received by the Home Office on 10 November 1864. It ran to some 41 pages. The GLPS also wrote to the Home Secretary in a letter received by the Home Office on 12 November. The note made by the Home Office clerk receiving the letter refers to the letter as calling 'attention to newspaper paragraphs respecting the convicts [sic] guilt or innocence'.
21. The Home Secretary's response was reprinted in several newspapers, but the papers in the National Archives in London (HO12/152/63401) reveal that the Home Secretary made several handwritten drafts before he settled on his response. He also made pencilled notes on the back of another Memorial, received by the Home Office on 14 November 1864 (HO12/152/83401) sent to him by John Thomas Percival in favour of Müller's innocence. In his notes Sir George Grey said, 'Act not and inform him that the memorial from the GPS [sic] was fully and carefully considered and that after such consideration and after personal [illegible] with the counsel judges who had the memorial I felt that it was inappropriate for me consistently with my duty to advise any interference with the commission of the law'.
22. As Diamond (2003) shows very clearly, the Victorian public was fascinated and enthralled by murder stories.
23. *The Leeds Mercury*, 12 July 1864: 5.
24. Ibid.
25. Then as now the press's and public's salacious appetites and constant desire to appeal to them are both commented upon and criticised by

those who expect the press to behave better and for the public to be more restrained in its response.

26. During the 1860s newspapers were becoming increasingly commercialised and rationally organised—offices were becoming more adept at the management of information (duplication, storage and retrieval) and securing advertising revenue was also becoming more and more professional. At the same time readership was expanding, in part driven by an expanding regional press.

27. Popular newspapers such as *Reynolds Weekly Newspaper* and *Lloyds Weekly* were owned by G. W. M Reynold and Edward Lloyd, both of whom had originally worked for 'penny dreadfuls' in the UK which produced weekly sensational popular serial literature, crime, gothic, supernatural and horror fiction costing one penny. *The Telegraph* was the first paper to reduce its cover price to one penny, building a circulation 'of 200,000 among its mainly middle class readers' (Chibnall 1981: 205) by the 1870s. Also Cranfield (1962) and Williams (1998).

28. All the quotes taken from these three forms of documentary sources and used in Chapters 6–8 are presented in their original form. This means that spellings, misspellings and emphases have deliberately been left unaltered.

29. The point being that the majority of newspapers in mid-Victorian England in the 1860s may well have been read by some of the working class but that the style, format and content of newspaper of the 1860s were designed and written as if all readers were middle class. On this and the relationship between readership, the price of the newspaper and the abolition of the newspaper tax, see Ensor (1936 [1966]), Altick (1957), and Lee (1976).

30. The letters and Home Office files were located in the British National Archives, the official archive and publisher for the UK government based in Kew, London. They have mainly been used as background documents, but also have been cited where appropriate and include: Metropolitan Police (MEPO 3/75 and 3/76), Minutes of evidence (CRIM 10/53) and a historical railway file (RAIL 529/113). The Home Office files contained correspondence and warrants 8 July 1864–13 June 1866 (HO13/108); execution of criminals (HO45/681); rewards 1860–1864 (HO45/7078); old criminal papers 1849–1871 (HO12/152/63401), which included a number of letters, both signed and anonymous, from the public and Memorials requesting a reprieve of execution to the Home Secretary, Sir George Grey, numerous penny pamphlets, telegrams and other correspondence. The correspondence to the Home Office generally contained a stamp of receipt by the Home Office and often notes from

the Home Secretary and other officials about how to deal with them could be found on the back.
31. The readers, then as now encountered prejudice, civil intolerance and hypocrisy alongside a 'sweeping social commentary and call for various reforms' (Fox 1998: 273).
32. These lexica were developed by the author over a five-year period of empirical investigation, though this is not to suggest that they are definitive.

Bibliography

Altick, R. D. (1957). *English Common Reader: A Social History of the Mass Reading Public 1800–1900*. Chicago: University of Chicago Press.
Arkell, H. (2013, February 15). Murder on the Hackney Express: The First Class Train Killing That Terrified the Victorian Middle-Classes. *Daily Mail Online*.
Brown, L. (1985). *Victorian News and Newspapers*. Oxford: Clarendon Press.
Chibnall, S. (1981). Chronicles of the Gallows: The Social History of Crime Reporting. *The Sociological Review, 29*(1), 179–217.
Colquhoun, K. (2012). *Mr. Briggs' Hat: A Sensational Account of Britain's First Railway Murder*. London: Abacus, Little, Brown Book Group.
Cranfield, D. (1962). *The Development of the Provincial Newspaper 1700–1760*. Oxford: Oxford University Press.
Diamond, M. (2003). *Victorian Sensation*. London: Anthem Press.
Ensor, R. C. K. (1936 [1966]). *England, 1870–1914*. Oxford: Clarendon Press.
Fox, W. (1998). Murder in Daily Installments: The Newspapers and the Case of Franz Müller (1864). *Victorian Periodicals Review, 31*(3), 271–298.
Gordon, E., & Nair, G. (2009). *Murder and Morality in Victorian Britain: The Story of Madeleine Smith*. Manchester: Manchester University Press.
Knott, G. (1911). *The Trial of Franz Müller*. https://archive.org/stream/trialoffranzmull025046mbp#page/n9/mode/2up.
Lee, A. J. (1976). *The Origins of the Popular Press in England, 1855–1914*. Lanham, MD: Rowman & Littlefield.
Rieley, A. (2018). The Convict Kirwan. *Media History, 24*(3–4), 306–319.
Williams, K. (1998). *Get Me a Murder a Day! A History of Mass Communication in Britain*. London: Arnold.

CHAPTER 6

The Reporting of the Murder and the Invariant Civil Concern of Identity

1   The Scope of the Invariant Civil Concern of Identity

There are many approaches to understanding identity,[1] all focusing on various aspects of self-identity, collective identity and identity formation. In this book, I only address the extent to which identity is reported in the news as an invariant civil concern. As an invariant civil concern, identity is mainly concerned with the constituent features of self-identification and group membership, more specifically it focuses on questions of who and what I am, who and what we are and who and what they are. Alternatively expressed, it is a concern for who or what is viewed as civil and who or what is viewed as anti-civil. It is about who and what has civil status and who and what does not. It is also about who gets to speak as upholders of the civil orthodoxy, or who we listen to on the issue of civil change as well as who does not get to speak and whose ideas we reject. In this way identity, as a civil concern, is about expressing both our individuality, the extent of our group membership and our group affiliations and loyalties. It is by reporting and judging in a particular way that identity, in terms of defining the 'we' and the 'they', is played out in the news. As with the other invariant civil concerns, the news is here engaged with both interpretation and judgement.

To understand the news's engagement with our invariant civil concern of identity and the subsequent reporting of it, it is possible to draw some insights from a range of scholarship which illustrates how humans understand similarity and difference through processes of classification, identification and comparison with others (Becker 1963; Cornell and Hartmann 1998; Jenkins 2000; Tajfel and Turner 1979). We categorise others and objects to understand and identify them via social categories such as gender, skin colour, nationality, religious affiliation, occupation and social standing and we define appropriate behaviour by reference to the norms of groups we belong to. There often exists an emotional significance to our identification with a group, and our self-esteem may become bound up with group membership (Hogg 2006; Hogg and Abrams 1988) as we tend to compare our group to other groups (Turner 1975), probably in the hope that our own group compares favourably. The processes of competition for identity may be highly discriminatory resulting in negative stereotyping of particular out-groups, which involves overemphasising the differences between groups as well as overemphasising the similarities of things or attributes that exist within the same group. As history repeatedly shows us in zones of conflict, competition for identity can lead to greater fragmentation between groups (Dinc 2016) and concomitantly, hostility between competing identities can easily escalate from expressions and attitudes of civil prejudice and intolerance towards 'others' to overt expressions of hatred in highly emotive and violent hate speech. The news media may also be complicit in fostering incitement to discrimination, hostility or violence acting in contravention of international law.[2]

Where identity claims are made in the news, news reports may also endorse civil change by reporting discussions about identity within civil societies in a way which focuses on exposing social injustice and inequalities. From time to time, such news reports may have some success in challenging majority but discriminatory identity claims, leading to the recognition of the need for civil status for those who are not seen as being one of us. When undertaking this type of reporting the news opposes the exclusive and anti-civil tendencies identity claims can take when there is a refusal to accept difference. It challenges the anti-civil tendency that exists in all societies that fail to recognise and value the stranger by seeking to make him or her similar to ourselves and/or emphasising in a pejorative way their difference from ourselves. At other times, however, the news becomes compliant and appears frequently to affirm majority and relatively uncontested beliefs, norms and values, and in this way resists any change. The news in this way implicitly and/or explicitly makes assumptions and judgements about who belongs and who does not. Such assumptions and judgements made in news reports are expressions of civil affiliations and values and can be understood as emanating from and contributing to wider moral codes of conduct, mores, norms and traditions articulated in and through public sentiment.

The invariant civil concern of identity is manifest in the news specifically in the range of civil and anti-civil judgements made by the news about who or what is viewed as being civil and as such as civilised, and who or what is seen as anti-civil and as such uncivilised. From these judgements, issues of self-identity, group membership, wider local loyalties (and the changes accepted as necessary or unnecessary to them) are contextualised as well as provided with a salient performative reality. To be clear, the civil and anti-civil judgements about identity made by the news may be almost hidden from view or alternatively may be expressly articulated—in either case they have a form of saliency (and authority) that is both an interpretative representation of public sentiment and a response to it. As will be shown, in the context of the invariant civil concern of identity the news's implicit or explicit civil and anti-civil judgements are generally made through the lens of age, gender, sexuality, class, religion, ethnicity or sometimes about lifestyle choices. These judgements can be found in stories relating to a wide variety of matters and concerns ranging from the nature of murderers, suicidal fanatics, job thieves, undeserving welfare claimants, representatives of non-national values, believers in unacceptable norms and customs that encroach on 'our way of life', to more homespun stories of gay marriage, the ordination of women priests and so on. At the heart of these stories are civil and anti-civil judgements about who we are and correspondingly what particular form of identity is at risk of being lost or overwhelmed. It is these judgements which can influence public sentiment and its regard for what and who has a civil identity and the extent of the liberty that I have to sustain my own particular identity.

Of course, such liberty may be restricted in scope depending on the nature of the press and how independent it is from vested interests (see Chapter 3). Usually such restrictions occur when there is an expanding non-civil sphere—usually the state or the market—which attempts to dominate the civil sphere. Here we may experience the gradual diminishment of the 'securities against misrule' that the press and public sentiment might have provided us with in more progressive times and that accommodate more expansive visions of identity (cf. Bentham and J. S. Mill); or it might be that the public mood is encouraged to become one of 'individualism' or 'consumerism' with an attendant retreat from civil life and loss of interest in participating in public discourse and civil openness (cf. Tocqueville); or more straightforwardly (and frequently) through the amplification and validation of an orthodoxy that effectively silences the 'antagonism of opinions' through the establishment of what has been described as 'soft' or 'quiet despotism' (cf. J. S. Mill). For each of these three thinkers but particularly for Tocqueville and Mill the relatively uncontested views of the majority were problematic and could lead to mass society cultures with strong homogeneous tendencies engendering norms of public conformity which leave those who are not heard or who are misrepresented feeling marginalised and peripheral and democracy empty of debate. And yet, in spite of this influence from other spheres, at the heart of even the most restricted form of news coverage lies a constant concern for the appropriate interpretative perspective to be taken by which to judge identity claims. Even under excessive totalitarian conditions competing identity claims are constantly made in the name of the 'true orthodoxy'. Even if such claims are hidden behind code and nuance they reveal the futility of trying to impose a non-interpretative form of news journalism on news providers. From this follows that the truism, that one person's civil defence of civil freedoms can be recast as another person's intolerance of other people's values, just happens to be true. The news engages with the complexity of adopting an appropriate interpretative perspective in different ways (and as noted in Part I for different reasons), sometimes allowing different voices to articulate particular viewpoints in a way that appears balanced or neutral, or sometimes by overtly guiding the news consuming public towards a viewpoint about who or what is civil or anti-civil, or sometimes by responding to and incorporating public views and ideas into the very fabric of the news stories' narrative. Whatever approach is taken, the question of interpretative perspective is recognised and understood by audiences and goes some way to explaining the delineation of the news media into popular versions which reflect 'their own bias', as seen in the development of 'news echo chambers'. In short, some judgements made by some news outlets are nothing more than predictable, although it is a far cry from actually saying that such predictable responses as there are form the basis of a hegemonic outlook with regard to claim and counter-claim about civil identities,[3] nor can the news be seen to be responsible for the creation of new civil identities.[4]

2 News Lexica of the Invariant Civil Concern of Identity

Given the above it is inevitable that the language of identity is simultaneously about both outsiders and insiders with a preponderance for reports about those who are not seen to have or merit civil identity and who are seen as 'the other', rather than the 'inclusive we' or the 'belonging I' of those individuals and groups who take for granted their right to have a voice in civil society. Such distinctions are crucial as they determine who (belonging to a particular group or association) is able to make civil identity claims, who is able to inhabit the civil space of public sentiment and whose views are regarded as valid and valuable and should be reported and whose are not. There are many complexities inherent in the formation of identities and the hostile and open competition between identities and the differing types of prejudice that this may engender is often a corollary of complex multicultural civil societies where freedom of expression of difference and open disagreement are permitted. Given that conflict and disagreement is a staple of news content, we will see in the example of the Thomas Briggs murder just how many of these hostile exchanges were played out in different ways in the mediation of the civil identity of the victim and the perpetrator (see below Sect. 2).

However before that it is necessary to identify *both* a civil and anti-civil lexicon that the news uses in its reporting of the invariant civil concern of identity (see Table 1, p. 168 and Table 2, p. 169).

The civil lexicon of identity is found when news reports emphasise the need and desirability to extend civil hospitality to others by indicating the commonality of civil values and the civil requirement to exercise tolerance and respect for difference. There is a sense that those civil values accord civil status and citizenship as they are representative of a civil society and the language of we/us/our cements the idea that there is a sense of belonging created by the similarities that a civil society shares. While the focus of reporting is on the protection of the values of the civil sphere, there may also be a recognition that from time to time that there is agreement and compatibility between the civil and non-civil spheres, where the actions of the non-civil spheres bring a welcome change to civil society by enhancing and protecting its civil values, such as policy recommendations for improvements in welfare provisions,

Table 1 The civil lexicon of the invariant civil concern of identity in the news cycle

Civil lexicon	Expressions of the civil lexicon of identity: The focus is on solidarising identity
Civil values, status and citizenship	• Emphasises civil values such as honesty, tolerance, decency, respectability, bravery, selflessness, benevolence, compassion, humanitarianism, civil pride • Emphasises civil status and citizenship and claims to be representative of civil society. • Focuses on similarities • Uses the language of we/us/our
Civil hospitality and attitudes	• Focuses on approved types of civil behaviour, such as civil hospitality, and attitudes such as neighbourliness, charitable giving, diligence, good parenting, sobriety, expressing remorse, spontaneous helping, acts of altruism and kindness, active citizenry, such as assembly, mobilisation, protest and passive citizenry, such as appeals to public opinion, 'the public', the people, the majority, common sense • Focuses on civil hospitality accorded to difference/others by showing that there exist some common civil values, or through calls for the exercise of tolerance and respect for difference
Protecting the values of the civil sphere	• Criticises non-civil and anti-civil input and intrusions that are harmful to civil society by reporting their desire to restrict, curtail or limit civil discourse in some way • Emphasises compatibility with the non-civil spheres by showing where and when some common civil values between different spheres exist • Approves of the non-civil spheres of family life, police activity, political change and the work of religious institutions when they are seen to have or seen to foster civil virtues

or the protection of vulnerable groups in society by non-civil actors such as religious organisations, or the timely and speedy response of emergency services in moments of national crisis. Approval or acceptance of the actions of non-civil organisations and actors is often expressed in the news through the use of direct transcripts and of direct quotations or a specific narrative supplied from non-civil sources.

Any overt or tacit approval accorded to non-civil intervention in matters of the civil sphere does not however extend to tolerating those non-civil and anti-civil values or actions that are seen to be harmful to civil

Table 2 The anti-civil lexicon of the invariant civil concern of identity in the news cycle

Anti-civil lexicon	Expressions of the anti-civil lexicon of identity: The focus is on alterity and the state of being different (not sharing a common identity)
Anti-civil attitudes and behaviour	• Identifies and labels unacceptable attitudes and behaviour • Criticises what are seen to be unacceptable attitudes and behaviour such as extremism, unexpected strangeness, non-conventional lifestyle choices, unwarranted laziness, vanity and greed, not being respectable enough, not conforming to majority moral, social and cultural expectations
Non-compatibility	• Focuses on difference emphasising and possibly amplifying the danger of difference • Criticises the other for non-acceptance or conformity with established civil values, attitudes and beliefs • Non-acceptance of different customes/cultures, fads/trends and beliefs • Non-acceptance of the norms, values, attitudes, appearance and beliefs of others
Civil intolerance	• Rejection of 'the other' as pure alterity, in order to protect majority values and dominant identities • Uses casual racism, accusations about the betrayal of 'our' hospitality by being overly accommodating of difference • Uses claims about unnecessary and absurd political correctness or positive discrimination to reject greater accommodation of and respect for others/difference • The term 'citizen' is used to differentiate and exclude those who are identified as 'non-citizens' • May encourage moral panics, where a person or group are labelled as a threat to fundamental civil values and interests • Uses stereotyping, scapegoating and stigmatising

society, meaning that the exercise of civil toleration is contingent on each particular context. The solidarising aspects of the civil lexicon and its expression by the news in a civil disposition entail the use of an inclusive and rights-based language of 'we', 'our' and 'us' to focus on similarities without excluding others on the basis of identity traits. Citizenship rights and duties are not seen to be compromised or undermined by others, but rather guide 'our' civil behaviour and attitudes towards them.

In contrast, the anti-civil lexicon of identity (see Table 2) addresses many of the same issues in the news from a different perspective as well as raising other concerns about threats to civil identity. The anti-civil lexicon often exists in news stories in parallel with the civil lexicon (stories that are completely civil or anti-civil are rare). This is particularly the case in stories that are told in a balanced (discursive) way with different views expressed. The anti-civil lexicon may be subordinate, or it may dominate depending on the orientation of the news producer when it deals with contemporary issues and events in the context of the invariant civil concern of identity. In either case, it can be summarised accordingly.

The anti-civil lexicon of the invariant civil concern of identity in news reports is found in expressions of disapproval of others' attitudes, behaviour, customs, cultures, norms and values. Such expressions may be taken further to stress the non-compatibility of the other with civil society, where the focus intensifies from one of disapproval to one that highlights the impossibility of reconciling differences and lack of acceptance of differences. Sometimes, an anti-civil disposition in news reporting is hidden from view and sometimes it is overt and openly stated. In this way, a racist or nationalistic attitude may be implicit or explicit and the alterity of the other can be expanded to a point where he or she or a group come to be placed 'beyond the pale'. The exercise of civil intolerance can result in the use of casual racist language, stereotyping, scapegoating and stigmatising in ways that stress alterity, raises suspicion, engenders moral panics and which taken to extreme may serve to incite hatred, or even to incite harm. Anti-civil reporting focuses on the impossibility of reconciling difference and emphasising 'the alien other' as pure alterity. Here, the news report builds on disapproval and non-acceptance of different customs/cultures, fads/trends, values, attitudes and beliefs of others to emphasise where a person or group are a threat to fundamental civil values and interests. Anti-civil observations in news reports (by journalists or the experts they quote) may tendentiously seek to persuade the public that this is in order to protect the status quo of a shared and solidarising common identity, casting themselves as civil actors and their observations as having a civil intention. In this way, a stress on alterity in the anti-civil lexicon may also make use of the language of 'we', 'our' and 'us'. Unlike the use of those same words in the civil lexicon, the anti-civil lexicon's use of these words is designed to signal exclusion from a particular type of collective 'we' or common citizenship. At the same time, anti-civil sentiments confirm and criticise what are deemed to be unacceptable behaviour or actions by using the language and sentiment of them versus us.[5] Sometimes the eliding of two aspects of people's identity—'the victim of persecution' with the 'would-be terrorist' for example—is used in a way that is destructive and designed to undermine any potential solidarising sentiment for those in distress and who may need our help.[6]

Tables 1 and 2 show how one can identify the expressions of civil hospitality and civil intolerance in news reports that approve of or criticise implicitly or explicitly different norms, values, attitudes, behaviours and beliefs.

3 The Context of Identity of the Murder: Newspapers, Social Class and German Nationality

Civil and social standing in the form of 'like us' or the 'best of us' is at the heart of the positive endorsement of our solidarising tendencies; just as the opposite is at the heart of our non-solidarising tendencies. The Franz Müller case was riven with the issue of the bestowal and withdrawal of identity. Judgements of who is like us and what represents us and who and what is anti-civil—in part or completely—constantly changed throughout the press coverage. These changes were particularly notable at the time of the identification of Müller as a suspect and through the arrest, trial and the execution. In the context of the murder of 1864 the press's engagement with the invariant civil concern of identity was related to two main aspects: first, social class and second, nationality and, related to both, behaviour and appearance. As such the coverage of the murder was for many readers 'a means through which the social world was represented and understood' (Hampton 2004: 19) and public sentiment played its part in influencing the type of press coverage that emerged.

3.1 Newspapers and Social Class in 1864

By the 1860s, newspapers in the UK had become cheaper, more widely read and increasingly diversified in terms of political views and social attitudes. News reports and interviews were becoming more and more common and accepted. In short, the public wanted more news. There were more newspapers than ever before with many tied to one or other political party or trade union. In some way, the distribution of newspapers across the political spectrum reflected the fact that the social class system in 1864 was rigid and clearly stratified around wealth and privilege and related to that social and political outlook. Categorisations about the number and types of classes varied but broadly speaking, and following Marx, classes represented sets of social relationships which when combined with the forces of production (the means by which we produce and provide for our material needs) became what he called modes of production, and these were the basis of social class. Classes existed in terms of what mode of production they represented and coalesced around and this went much of the way to explaining their fundamental different social and political viewpoints and rivalries. The upshot of this was that classes competed against each other in ever-changing temporary sets of alliances of mutual benefit and/or disunions of mutual antipathy. What is apparent from the newspapers of the 1860s is how different social classes were represented in terms of different and very well-understood (by newspaper owners, editors and journalists) world views. Indeed the newspapers from this time appear to regard that the way to secure readers lay in both adopting and attacking competing class-based world views. This meant, in part, taking different stances about the role of the state and the role of government and its relationship to the economy and law and order—even the most rustic and rudimentary of journalists understood this. There is ample evidence that shows that 'attack journalism' then was very much like 'attack journalism' today: utterly partisan. The reason for the existence of this earlier form of differentiated press outlooks (and the tendencies it displayed towards taking sides) lay in the fact that attached to the class system of the 1860s was a set of moral views specifically related to the period of Queen Victoria's reign (1837–1901) which sought deliberately to differentiate the so-called Victorian period from the previous Georgian era which was vilified by the Victorians as a period of loose morality, wasteful expenditure and weak leadership. This is especially relevant when considering the context in which the murder of Briggs took place.

During the reign of Queen Victoria, there was excessively low tolerance of all forms of crime and there existed strict codes of moral conduct. Victorian moral values were embedded into all areas of living and Godliness,[7] elitism, hard work and improvement[8] were all highly valued virtues. The Victorians cultivated outward appearances of dignity and virtue while at the same time presided over gross inequality, child labour and destitution leading to prostitution.[9] Correspondingly, there existed a plethora of political and social movements which attempted to improve the harsh life for many under this rigid class system. The 'progressive' call to improvement of the poor ran in parallel with the continued abuse that many received from those who saw them as little more than cogs in a profit-making machine with little sympathy for those who fell into poverty. While it has been suggested that learned respectability rather than class was a sound basis on which social relations were founded (Thompson 1988), it has also been argued that there was 'an entrenched middle-class mid-Victorian prejudice against the character and behaviour of manual workers as a class, a prejudice which was embodied in the civil law and which has exerted a powerful long-term influence on class relationships and self-perceptions' (Johnson 1993: 147).

This rigid class system was certainly embodied within the railway system. From the first steam railway line from Stockton-upon-Tees to Darlington which opened in 1825, railway companies had largely avoided catering for working-class travellers, running trains that only offered second- and first-class carriages if possible and that only stopped at selected stations. The controversial (at the time) Section VI of the Railway Regulation Act of 1844 had required that a train should include third-class carriages, which for the first time would be roofed and contain seating rather than simply being an open goods wagon within which passengers had to stand. These challenges to the elitist approach to railway travel for the higher middle and upper classes required that at least one train each day would stop at every station, bringing new types of connectivity between people of different class. There was resistance to this and railway companies were quick to find loopholes in the new legislation. Given that the time of the day for these new stops was not specified in the Act, peak time travel was still generally only available to and from the more respectable neighbourhoods. Nonetheless, by 1864 larger numbers of people could afford to travel both for work and for leisure in relative comfort. This factor played a part in the development of tourism and in the public's growing confidence about the ability to be mobile (Mathieson 2015). The railways grew exponentially in size and scale from the 1830s and linked towns and cities for the first time. This expansion of the railways had a major and visible impact on the fabric of those cities as it led to large-scale evictions which occurred usually in poorer areas where it was easier to get planning permission and to create space for railway lines and stations (Kellett 1969). Nonetheless, the segregation of railway carriages into different and unconnected compartments still allowed for the class system to be strictly adhered to. In 1864, first-class travellers enjoyed plush and luxurious carriages with armrests whereas the third-class travellers were cramped into carriages with small wooden benches. These travel arrangements symbolised position, wealth and status in society and reflected prevalent and inflexible attitudes about the differences in social standing. It was this representation of the class system and its symbolic despoliation by a murder in a first-class carriage that was to provide a long-running social and political theme to the press coverage of the Briggs murder.

3.2   *German Nationality*

Newspapers were never tired of pointing to their own patriotism, or at least their version of it. Press criticisms of the day thought nothing of declaring the government to be unpatriotic, for whatever reason was to hand, and of betraying the country and what it stood for. Patriotism was a well-understood journalistic leitmotif of social and political journalism. In 1864, British attitudes towards Germany were complex. The failed revolutions in 1848–1849 in the states of the German Confederation were seen as evidence of widespread German political malaise. The progressive elements of the German middle and working classes advocated greater liberalism and pan-Germanism, but were quickly and brutally repressed by the conservatives of all classes who wanted the autocratic governments of the thirty-nine 'independent' German states to remain as they were. Many of the social and political progressives were as a consequence forced into exile and went to the USA and to England. The chaos of 1848 lent itself to a form of patriotic press smugness and it was an easy trope to compare superior British democratic governance to both German autocracy and cruelty on one side and political incompetence and ineptitude on the other side. For the press, it was a case of a 'plague on both your houses'. Indeed there is some evidence that this sense of superiority facilitated negative feelings towards German immigrants and by 1864 émigrés from Germany comprised around forty per cent of the foreign community in mid-nineteenth-century London.[10] The press of the day was not above comparing life in the British Empire with that of life across the German states and by extension pointing out the inferior status and criminality of the German immigrant. The Second Schleswig War between Denmark, Austria and Prussia received attention in the UK press which supported Denmark's policy but was critical and disapproving of the behaviour of Prussia. *Lloyd's Weekly London Newspaper's* retrospective of the previous year on 1 January 1865 reflected this anti-German sentiment, 'The Germans were advancing into the duchies, and most people saw, in this German invasion of Denmark, the beginning of a European war … The Germans … were bent on the conquest of the dutchies. They advanced under cover of shameless subterfuges and falsehoods, and their bearing was so defiant and insolent, it was hardly possible to believe that peace could be maintained with them… The German invaders showed their customary cruelty and bravado. Their numbers, and not their courage, had given them the victory'.[11] The Treaty of Vienna to end the war was signed on 30 October 1864, a few days before the trial of Franz Müller.

In this context and with regard to German habits and culture, one example from the year of the murder, 1864, will suffice to show the cultural context in which Müller found himself in at his trial. Henry Mayhew's (1864) two volume work inelegantly but comprehensively titled *German Life and Manners as Seen in Saxony at the Present Day: With an Account of Village Life--Town Life--Fashionable Life--Married Life--School and University Life, &c., of Germany at the Present Time* was highly critical of German manners and lifestyles. Mayhew lampooned the German diet as being comprised largely of 'liver-sausage, and red-sausage, and Savoyard-sausage, and hard-sausage, and roast sausage' (Mayhew 1864: 40) and he expressed concern about the quality of Saxon meat that might find its way into England.[12] For him, English food represented vigour, vitality and empire. He concluded that 'Germans delight, in the jealousy, to make sport over the number of beggars that are to be met with in the British dominions; but we can tell them … that an English beggar, living in his "padding-ken," and faring upon the broken victuals which he collects from house to house, is better bed and better fed than even some of the best German mechanics or gentry' (ibid.: 206). The theme of British intellectual, moral and racial superiority as well as the emphasis on the superior character and civilised nature of the British imperial realm (Byrne 2007) continues and Mayhew was not above delivering more personal remarks about the appearance of Germans and their obsession (in his view) with eating: 'as we have said, you have but to look at the countenances of these potato-fed and half-clad German folk to know what long strides the race has yet to take, in order to keep pace with the rest of civilized Europe; and yet, like half-starved people, they are always eating' (Mayhew 1864: 207) to which he added: 'There is but one explanation for that utter want of muscular power, and manly energy, as well as bold enterprise, which is the peculiar characteristic of the entire Saxon and Rhenish people. Enlightened Germans tell you very candidly, that Englishmen are ever foremost in all matters of progress' (ibid.: 209f.). Notably sentiments similar to those expressed by Mayhew were reflected in the reporting of the murder.

4   Civil Judgements Made in the News Reports

4.1   Civil Values, Status and Citizenship: Thomas Briggs' Superior Status and Franz Müller's Social Class

Thomas Briggs was reported as embodying the civil values and civil status of a Victorian middle-class gentleman-professional and was described in these terms in all of the press coverage immediately following the murder. The newspapers took pains to stress that 'His family were of the middle class and members of the Church of England … he was well qualified for the important duties of his post, as well by his long experience as by his calmness of judgement and his frank and cordial manners … Mr Briggs was in his domestic and social arrangements very happy … head of a large family … Always affectionate and kind'.[13] Alongside a picture of respectability Thomas Briggs was also noted for his diligence and hard work in an era when men were expected to provide for their families and to be unequivocally the head of the family. Not only had Briggs been diligent and hardworking, he had also risen within the, by then, highly respected profession of banking, which had enabled him to move his family away from the industrialised city centre to the London suburb of Hackney, where he had 'by the steady performance of his duties, and his spotless character, raised himself to the highest post in the establishment'[14] of Messrs. Robarts, Curtis and Co, a bank on

Lombard Street. Briggs in this way was approvingly portrayed as an ideal Victorian citizen who worked so hard that the 'severe toils and responsibilities of his post ... proved too great for his strength'.[15]

More details about Thomas Briggs unfolded in the press coverage of the Coroner's Inquest on 18 July 1864, when it was revealed that he was born in 1795 in the village of Cartnell, a tranquil village, educated at grammar school and began his career at the banking house of Sir John Lubbock when he was sixteen years old. Because he was seen to be a worthy representative of his class, his murder elicited a reaction of anger and shock in the press which, on this occasion, spoke with unanimity on behalf of middle-class values and a 'civilised public' in condemning this 'frightful outrage of which this amiable man was the victim' which had, it claimed, 'roused public sympathy with the bereaved family, an abhorrence of the crime which destroyed a most useful life in a degree seldom in our experience surpassed'.[16] In short, the nature of the crime was made all the worse because 'in the courtesies of social life no one could better play his part'[17] and because it was felt that this 'man of a singularly benevolent heart and genial manner'[18] had fallen victim to one of the 'most atrocious crimes that probably ever disgraced this country'.[19] He was 'a gentleman'[20] who 'was highly esteemed by a very large circle of friends'[21] and was 'murderously assailed, plundered and thrown out of the train'.[22]

The outrage that was expressed took for granted that being a member of the gentleman-professional middle class brought to Briggs an entitlement to a first-class carriage on the train. His social standing and privilege engendered an unquestioned expectation that he should therefore be free from harm from others not of his class and to be in the company of his own class who would certainly not commit such a crime. The shock expressed by the press was not so much that a murder had been committed—they were commonplace in Victorian London—but that a violation had occurred to someone whose social identity entitled him to a particular type of bounded territory and security. The headlines emphasised this expectation almost in unison, proclaiming the murder to be of a special and highly significant nature.[23] 'The railway murder'[24] occasioned a sense of specific violation and *The Daily Telegraph* summarised this in a most forceful way: 'If we can be murdered thus we may be slain in our pew at church or assassinated at our dinner table'.[25] The use of the collective 'we' here is telling, as the newspaper very effectively closes ranks and excludes all those others who are not seen as one of 'us' and who do not belong to the civilised classes and elements of Victorian society. The representation of Briggs as someone just like 'us' allows the press to speak to its like-minded readers and to construct a narrative 'in which "tens of thousands" of London's citizens, or "all of us" … could see themselves at the centre' (Fox 1998: 275). In this case, the murder was seen in many of the newspapers as an 'attack on bourgeois respectability' (ibid.). The press's focus on gentleman-professional middle-class identity in the coverage in the immediate aftermath highlights the way in which its self-perceptions and their performative expressions and presentations sought to make the press qualitatively similar to their own readers and to differentiate them from others. Interestingly, in this particular case the sentiment of 'all of us' referred only to those of us 'who actually possesses something which is worth taking' (ibid.) which was true of middle-class readers generally who feared property theft and associated acts of violence as the most heinous form of anti-civil behaviour. Overall Briggs was personified in terms of his contribution to decency and civility. He was seen as the finest expression of his class and his social standing was, for the press, unimpeachable.

Rather unusually some of Franz Müller's values were classed in the press as being civil in character. Whereas the majority of the reporting about him was anti-civil in tone, civil aspects to his character were highlighted approvingly in a variety of different ways in the coverage. His manners, his demeanour or aspects of his respectability were seen in some respects to point to his innocence by virtue of them being, at the time, highly valued by the Victorian middle class. This did not make him middle class in the eyes of the press but merely signalled that he had a sensibility and demeanour which it appeared could be approved of. This meant that within the news reporting Müller was not always seen as a likely or typical villain: 'The murderer, as we now know, was Franz Müller, a young man who passed among his few acquaintances for a steady, industrious, kindly, humane person, and against whom no antecedents, up to the hour of this deadly deed, have yet been found pointing him out as a likely man to commit so desperate a crime',[26] and 'Dr Juch, in supporting the prayer of the memorial, stated that he saw Müller the day after his arrival in England, and affirmed that he never met a man giving a more straightforward and consistent account of any matter on which he was questioned, always telling the same story in a simple, honest way'.[27] Müller himself was reported to have said, 'that he was never in a police station before, and the sooner he got out of this one the better'.[28]

Throughout the reporting, the press appeared to be somewhat disconcerted about these contradictory qualities regarding Müller's status as a villain, but also as a respectable man. *Lloyd's Weekly London Newspaper's* coverage of the inquest reported that a photograph of Müller 'was handed round to the jury, and his gentlemanly attire and appearance seemed to denote him to be a person of a class decidedly superior to that to which Müller belonged'.[29] In this way, he appeared at times to be beyond the categorisation and typifications used by the press to discern class and social standing or esteem. And it was notable that they sometimes dealt with his civil qualities by linking them to the acquisition of a British identity. In short, Müller was perceived to be taking on the characteristics of an Englishman and in this way was 'disconcertingly British'.[30] Müller's apparently acquired 'British' values were approved of. When his trial began on 27 October 1864 and he rejected the opportunity to be tried by a jury comprised of fifty per cent foreign nationals opting for an exclusively English jury, there was some admiration for this choice.[31] Similarly it was reported approvingly that 'After his removal to his cell Mr Burnsby [Chief Clark] asked him if he wanted anything, and during this brief interview Muller said if he had to speak he should prefer doing so in the English language, as he could express himself more clearly than he could in his native tongue'.[32] Unlike Briggs's unequivocal sense of belonging, the civil dimensions of Müller were seen through the lens of adaptation and socialisation into British culture and the class system, where he was becoming more like 'us'. The fragility of press approval or sympathy for Müller, even when strong doubts about his innocence were later expressed, meant that it was easy for the press to default to a recasting of some of his so-called civil virtues into anti-civil vices (see below). The fact that the GLPS supported Müller and attempted to get his death sentence commuted was held against him. *The Evening Standard* noted that the GLPS should be careful not wrongly to raise Müller's hopes, having 'never once hinted [to Müller] even at the fact of their getting up a memorial [a publication advocating clemency] on his behalf, and have sought by every means possible to keep it a secret, as far as the prisoner is concerned'.[33] By reprinting its Memorial to the Home Secretary in full[34] the press displayed partial willingness to demure from their default position. Indeed *The Daily Telegraph* actually published a letter to the Editor outlining 'the views of a German national'. In this letter, the writer argued that the evidence against Müller was being constructed and that he had in fact acted openly (i.e. that his character was not furtive or untrustworthy). The writer then signed himself (assuming it was a man) 'A GERMAN WHO WILL WATCH'.[35] Ultimately the press was by no means so partisan as not to provide space for views that expressed support for Müller, even if this support was only accorded for his neonate English sensibilities, demeanour and his display of English manners.

4.2 Civil Hospitality and Attitudes: Franz Müller's Behaviour and Appearance

Müller was sometimes reported as being a civilised man as the press scrutinised his behaviour and appearance throughout the inquiry, his imprisonment and the trial. Where the press agreed with particular aspects of Müller's behaviour (in its eyes the acquired Englishness) the more it exhibited a degree of civil hospitality towards him. As such, the extent of the press's civil hospitality was specific and occasional. It reported for example that while in England he was 'good and even gentlemanly … He was not known to be in liquor; he generally returned home straight from work and it is said that he never frequented public houses' and in this respect the paper also expressed the view that Müller was 'disconcertingly British'[36] in his behaviour. Müller was also described as hardworking and able to pay his rent as well as 'quiet and composed'[37] and even when subjected to public and press scrutiny in court he was observed to be 'quite calm and collected'.[38] The press further acknowledged that he did not look and act like a common criminal or murderer and that accordingly attributing blame for the murder to Müller was difficult: 'there are rather complicated accounts as to Müller's disposition'[39] and behaviour 'which made him a complex character'.[40] This type of judgement was supported by *The Daily News* which reported that, 'After viewing the prisoner again carefully, we see nothing to alter in our former description of him. He is certainly not such a thorough going pugilist and ruffian as most of his photographs represent'.[41]

When cast in civil terms, Müller's behaviour and appearance were seen to be virtues, notable because 'Without the slightest touch of bravado his demeanour at this time was quiet and self-possessed in a remarkable degree'.[42] Or as *Lloyd's Weekly London Newspaper* put it, 'Indeed, as far as outward appearances went, it may be said he was the most unconcerned and the least excited person present in the court. His behaviour, however, was quiet and respectful with an entire absence of bravado or a desire to create a sensation. Indeed his whole bearing was quite in keeping with his appearance, that of a mild and inoffensive man'.[43] In even more benevolent moments, some elements of the press went further: 'Looking at MULLER'S behaviour since his apprehension, we cannot but wish that he might have proved himself innocent. Unquestionably he has behaved well, and now that his guilt is so distinctly proved we cannot but feel that in this unpretending and unprepossessing looking youth there must be a greater depth of character than was originally supposed'.[44] In these expressions of sympathy, there lies some degree of commonality as well as the clear indication that a civilised press knows its 'duty'—to remind us of who and what is civil in any given context and how 'we' are civil in the way we extend hospitality and, occasionally sympathy.

In the view of the press, Müller's highest civil values were exhibited through his piety—something the press thoroughly approved of: 'He attends the morning service in the chapel daily …. He spends much of his time reading - the Bible principally'.[45] Related to this, *The Times* expressed praise for Müller's Lutheran pastor Dr Cappel, when giving an account of an investigative interview with Müller which Cappel attended: 'During the interview, which lasted nearly two hours, the convict frequently clung to him and embraced him, observing with tears in his eyes, that he was the only friend he had then in the world, and expressing his fervent gratitude for all the kindness that he had shown him'.[46] Dr Cappel's support of Müller provided Müller with another patina of credibility, one which once again led the press to report his case in a sympathetic manner. The *Reynolds's Newspaper* reported Müller's physical condition in prison by using Müller's own words: 'I feel weak and bad; I am sick' to which the news journalist added in a note of sympathy 'the poor fellow's appearance sustained his words'.[47]

However, sympathy for Müller came with a warning. The *Reynolds's Newspaper* portrayed Müller as a gentle and friendless victim to whom 'we' (the British, the readership, the public) were extending civil hospitality while simultaneously emphasising his lowly condition as an animal now at bay after having being hunted down by the hounds of justice. He was rendered part human and part animal, rightly trapped and restrained. 'For seven long hours he stood at bay, a hare surrounded by hounds, and whatever might be his amount of criminality, it was impossible not to feel some sympathy for the wretched human animal far away from home and kindred, and frowned upon by hundreds of hostile strangers'.[48]

4.3 Protecting the Values of the Civil Sphere: The Murder and Victorian Society

The murder struck at the heart of a widespread middle-class world view that they were privileged and close to God. Their ideology came with a belief that they were secure and protected by governments, which for the most part respected them, needed their support and also provided the apparatus of security. A first-class railway carriage was seen as 'off limits', a space that didn't require special security measures as it wasn't known to be intruded by feckless and dangerous members of an underclass. Rather it was seen as the natural domain of gentleman-professionals and therefore a safe thoroughly middle-class space. As such the murder represented something dangerous to the Victorian version of civil life and the security of middle-class identity (see also Chapter 8). The impact of the murder was amplified by the numerous reports which were focused on reflecting public concern, thereby generating even more interest from the public, which was then duly reported. The extent and depth of public sentiment was perceived by journalists to be evidence of the public's genuine interest in the story as well as of its concern that the values of the Victorian civil sphere had been fundamentally challenged. In this, press and public sentiment were aligned and the civil judgement was made that our values must not and will not be damaged by events such as these. The tendentious claim that 'No event has excited such intense interest among the public, for years past, as the murder on the North London Railway. The generation has not been violent …; it has not shown itself in outburst, and then died away, but it grows keener as well as deeper each hour; and the reasons are obvious; the blow has struck more than one moral home',[49] evokes a sense of violation and righteous indignation and a need for protection. The reference to the 'moral home' reflects the expectations of the time that Victorians should behave with outward dignity and restraint. Strict codes of conduct within society were publicly respected and publicly protected by the middle class. Such public conduct and values were regarded as exemplary ones and served the self-appointed imperial role of civilising the rest of the world.[50] In this vein, *The Daily Telegraph* lamented that 'If we boasted of our advanced civilisation, this ferocious and fantastic yet sordid and vulgar tragedy is an humiliating commentary on our pride'.[51]

When protecting civil values in this way the press was sometimes caught between humanely condemning the murder of a man with a spotless character a gentleman-professional, protecting more widely held middle-class identity while simultaneously reassuring both itself and public sentiment that the wrong man was not hanged on the basis of the incompetence of the police or courts, or any kind of anti-civil prejudice against him (see also Chapter 7). Related to this, a further and important concern was the fear, expressed by the press, that Müller might go to the gallows 'an unconfessed sinner', unrepentant and not having had the chance to express remorse for his actions. This was deeply unpalatable to the public. Victorian values were Christian values and public sentiment reflected these concerns very clearly in numerous letters to the press. It was felt that Müller's death must conform to a form of Christian (qua civilised) behaviour that protected the values of the Victorian civil sphere. Accordingly, close to the time of execution members of the public wrote to the Home Office to say that given the atrocious nature of the crime they prayed that 'the convict may be allowed time to repent'.[52] Müller's last-minute confession to Dr Louis Cappel, Müller's German-speaking Lutheran pastor at the point of execution, was seen as most welcome and entirely compatible with the Christian values of the Victorian civil sphere which required that he expresses remorse as well as atone for his sins. A sense of relief was evident in the press in its reporting of his confession 'Happily for him that even with his last breath he has atoned for his heavy sin to God, to men, and to his friends, through the acknowledgement of his guilt'.[53] A letter from Cappel to the Editor of the Hermann describing Müller's confession and reporting the words he used was reprinted in several newspapers and Cappel was reported as being overcome by emotion in *The Times*. 'So greatly relieved was Cappel by the confession, that he rushed to from the scaffold exclaiming "Thank God! Thank God!" and sank down in a chair, completely exhausted by his own emotion'.[54] Müller's confession also allowed the press to celebrate the civilised nature of the processes (which it had judged throughout) and which had led to what was seen to be the correct outcome. *The Times* made the observation that, 'Viewed from this aspect, and only as a solemn warning and example, it is to be wished that this last and saddest offering to man's justice could have been made less hideous than yesterday',[55] lamenting the nature of the punishment, while approving of its necessity as a way of maintaining Victorian Christian and civil standards.

Indeed, accompanying expressions of sympathy and commonality was also a self-evident delight in describing the horrors of the public execution and judging the behaviour of those who attended the execution who were reported as enjoying it. *The Times* took the view that although 'It is very cheap morality to go to the "Ring's" side and proclaim the brutality of prize fights, or from beneath the gallow-tree to preach forth upon the demoralising effect of public executions; but still the truth is the truth, and how the mob of yesterday behaved must be told'.[56] The growing concerns about the uncivil nature of public hanging were acknowledged. At the same time, the press expressed pride about changes that had occurred recently which were welcomed as indicating a more civilised and enlightened approach to any necessary public executions, 'The time has been, and very lately too, when the dress in which a felon died, or even a cast of his distorted features, would have been worth their weight in gold. But nothing of this catering for the wretched curiosity of the gallows is permitted now'.[57] This sense of satisfaction extended to the observation that 'We do not hang a man in the same hurry that our forefathers did, and one object of this clemency is doubtless that the murderer shall have time for repentance'.[58] Such sentiments resonated and acknowledged the changing and more progressive ideas expressed in public sentiment about the abolition of public hanging (see Chapter 7). Following Müller's confession, and the reprinting of Dr Cappel's letter as evidence that he was indeed a repentant murderer, the press was able to justify to the public that execution itself was justified as a duty and a way of protecting the values of the Victorian civil sphere. A letter to the Editor of *The Daily News* from the GLPS was used to reiterate the view that the execution was justified as a civil duty and that the Society was '… satisfied with having performed what they regard as a sacred duty, and sustained by many kind opinions from their English friends, [and, given this, they] have resolved not to make any answer to the hostile criticisms of their recent proceedings which have appeared in the press'.[59]

5   Anti-civil Judgements Made in the News Reports

5.1   Müller's Anti-civil Attitudes and Behaviour

In the context of the anti-civil lexicon press and public expressions of shock that the murder was committed in a first-class carriage were compounded by the idea which began to circulate quickly that this was not done by a gentleman, but by someone of the *lower* criminal classes. The press amplified the view that the murder suspect was not, 'one of us' when it characterised the murder as '[one] of the most atrocious crimes that probably ever disgraced this country'.[60] The nature of the murder and the identity of the murderer were seen by some members of the public as particularly horrific 'I sincerely believe that the murder of Mr. Briggs was a real willful murderer and a most awful murder of modern times committed in a first class carriage. I feel deep horror for such crime under such circumstances'.[61] The reaction by *The Daily News* was to tendentiously call for greater differentiation and segregation of the different classes: 'Let every carriage be in this way fitted up according to its class'.[62]

Sensational headlines such as 'Murder in a First Class Carriage',[63] 'Atrocious Murder in a First Class Railway Carriage',[64] 'Atrocious Murder in a First Class London Railway Carriage',[65] Murder in a First Class Carriage',[66] 'Atrocious Murder in a First Class Railway Carriage',[67] 'Atrocious Murder in a First Class London railway carriage'[68] contained an anti-civil judgement which sought to distinguish between the behaviour and attitudes of those who might perpetrate such a crime and the civilised 'we'. In common with moral panics, the behaviour and attitudes of 'types of people' were unfairly conflated with other negative associations. In this way, a violation of the sanctity of the first-class carriage by 'someone like' Müller was partly explained by the press and the public as symptomatic of a wider range of social and cultural problems. As we have seen, this was not however a straightforward task due to Müller's quiet and calm demeanour.

The idea that unexpected strangeness, unusual behaviour or appearance was a sign of guilt materialised in the early anti-civil reports of Müller's so-called escape to America and his subsequent capture and arrest. For *The Times*, though, it was perhaps easier to make the case that Müller's lack of calculation signalled his stupidity rather than to try to reconcile the contradictions in his behaviour. 'A criminal of more than ordinary intellect, and provided with abundant means, might perhaps employ them to his advantage. The man bewildered by his own act, or blinded by a conviction that it has had no witnesses, is unable to calculate even the everyday operation of the powers society now has at command. Comparing what a calm observer might imagine a man flying for his life could do to effect his escape with all he forgets, or overlooks, or neglects, it really seems as if a great crime has a stupefying effect and leaves an average intelligence less than its average acuteness'.[69] The Illustrated London News concluded that 'His own movements had produced the handwriting on the wall which ensured his doom',[70] echoing the view by a member of the public in a letter to the Home Secretary, that 'very nature of thieves more generally led to their 'mad fatality'.[71] The Evening Standard referred to Müller as a 'wretched creature' and 'consummate booby', '... a journeyman tailor, not less well educated than most German workmen of his class, sufficiently social in his habits, surrounded by all the influences that are though most sure to repress the savage instincts, if not to develop the better attributes of man, who is yet so absolutely in the moral condition with a Papnan or a Zooloo that he suffers himself to be tempted by the mere desire of possessing a shining bauble',[72] and his 'audacity in exhibiting these articles [received in his exchanges at the pawnbroker] does certainly seem remarkable'.[73]

The press's anti-civil focus on Müller's behaviour and attitudes, in particular his concern with his appearance and liking for jewellery, was remarked upon as something unusual and as unexpected behaviour for someone of his class. There was a certain Schadenfreude in some reports where this vanity was seen to be his undoing. Reynolds's Newspaper pointed out well before Müller had been arrested or tried that 'As far as the evidence has yet been collected against Muller, there is little doubt that he owes the discovery of his complicity in the murder to his reckless conduct and vanity'.[74] The fact that Müller owned jewellery was also criticised as having sinister undertones, 'he had in his possession a very handsome gold watch and massive chain, by no means according with his position or the money at his command'.[75] Tendentiously the reporting indicated that having expensive jewellery was not appropriate to a person of his class. In this context, an observation made by Jonathan Matthews, the cab driver, was reported as evidence of Müller's guilt because, although he 'had a watch of his own, ... it is a singular fact that he openly expressed his dissatisfaction with it, and actually, with unaccountable candour, announced his determination to replace it by another at somebody else's expense',[76] the implication being that that he may well be the type of person who would attack someone in order to acquire property. In this way, Müller's behaviour was assessed to be overbearing and inclined to violence. According to *The Preston Chronicle*, it was remarked on that on more than one occasion he 'said, "I don't like this watch; I will see a nice watch some day, and I will have it' and that 'Matthews states that this remark was made with a particular emphasis, and was accompanied by a forbidding look'.[77]

Anti-civil judgements by the press emerged through its reporting of information that emphasised Müller's obvious guilt, often through a descriptive style reporting which contained quotations or insights taken directly from depositions and trial transcripts which were at the time also reprinted at length or even in full.

Uncertainty about the true nature of Müller's character and his quiet disposition in the context of anti-civil judgements actually served to make Müller more not less sinister, not helped by the reporting that Matthews, the cab driver, and his family had referred to Müller as having a 'morose and jealous disposition'.[78] *The Dublin Evening Mail* reported that a labourer called Callaghan observed Müller at the docks before he sailed for the USA and said that Müller was 'so queer that one would think he has done some murder or other. He must have done something'.[79] The idea of Müller having a sinister side to his nature as well as an inappropriate interest in jewellery designed for those of a higher class status meant that the exchanges of jewellery and Müller's actions up to leaving for the USA were regarded as in and of themselves as self-evidently 'dodgy'. From there it became easier in parts of the press to assume that Matthews's observation that there was 'something sinister in his look and violent temper'[80] might be an accurate character reference, despite the fact that other dock workers observed that 'Müller had scarcely the appearance of a murderer'.[81] The problem of Müller's complex character was later contemplated by *The Evening Standard* which observed that, 'It has been commonly held that crime sharpens the wits; and as commonly that in one educated under the restraints and in the habits of civilised life there will generally be found to be some proportion between the motive of a crime and its gravity. Both of these tenets are thoroughly upset in the case of Muller'.[82]

Nonetheless, despite later moments of reflection, the press soon after the murder had begun to emphasise that lurking beneath Müller's civilised surface was a dark side to his behaviour. The press lent more weight to observations from witnesses reprinted from depositions which emphasised an unstable character, reporting that 'as the engagement to Miss Matthews progressed, he became more and more violent in his disposition, until at length, acting under the advice of her friends, the young woman wrote to Muller telling him she would no longer keep his company, and saying he was a murderer in intention, who she would have nothing to do with'.[83] Similarly, 'While this engagement lasted Muller evinced a morose and jealous disposition; if the young woman spoke to any other man it goaded him almost to madness, and on one occasion he swore if she spoke to a man again he would murder her. As the engagement lengthened Muller became more violent'.[84] Evidence of Müller's anti-civil behaviour and attitudes reported in the press directly from witness statements alluded to his likely guilt and these rather random observations were reprinted and circulated in the newspapers before the case came to court. Some of his behaviour on the ship to America was seen to point to his guilt, 'The cook of the vessel, who either slept with Muller or in the next berth, voluntarily stated to the captain that Muller, during the voyage, seemed to sleep very unsoundly, often waking with a start, or talking in his sleep, exclaiming "whose there!" "take your hands off!" and similar expressions denoting a very perturbed mind'.[85]

In the context of the anti-civil lexicon of identity, Müller's behaviour was always cast as being suspicious and he was variously portrayed as desperate whereby he must be watched at all times, 'Muller was not allowed the most remote chance of escape, not even by the desperate act of suicide, which was considered possible from what had become known of the man's character',[86] or as too cheerful, 'During the voyage he has appeared indifferent, if not cheerful. He has been engaged in reading Dickins's works'.[87] Müller's cheerful disposition was reported on with disapproval as it too seemed to emphasise his guilt. Routine reporting about the sleeping and eating habits of prisoners at the time meant that the press picked up on Müller's liking for food. His good appetite was interpreted to signal that he was not in the slightest bit concerned about what he had done. During his confinement in Newgate, he was seen to have 'conducted himself with the same air of coolness and indifference to his position that has characterised him from the very moment of his apprehension'.[88] Contrarily the same behaviour that was judged through a civil lexicon to be dignified and respectable was also in different articles judged by the same newspapers as possible indications of guilt, 'when [Müller] underwent the operation with the most perfect composure, maintaining all the sullen indifference he had exhibited during the morning'.[89] Problematically for Müller a general theme emerged through the use of the anti-civil lexicon. Reports from the police or his jailors about his liking for food and his quiet character were agreed upon in the press as a cause for concern and out of kilter with someone who had committed such an 'atrocious' crime. Consequently, when Müller 'seemed quite cool and collected, though somewhat downcast, and made a hearty meal of the food offered him on his arrival'[90] he was criticised for his behaviour. The Illustrated *London News* disapprovingly reported that 'He ate and drank during the voyage, as if nothing had occurred; and read "Pickwick" and several periodicals'[91] and The *Lloyd's Weekly London Newspaper* similarly reported that 'He ate, drank, and slept well, read the "Pickwick Papers" and laughed heartily over them'.[92]

His behaviour was frustrating for the press which seemed to be searching for behavioural signs of his guilt and so the fact that 'he is reserved and incommunicative, without, however, being in the least morose … He eats and sleeps well',[93] was reported unanimously as inappropriate behaviour for a guilty man (the assumption was that he was guilty). It had already been noted earlier that 'On being told the charge against him [when arrested in the USA) he turned "ghastly white", but soon recovered his self-possession, or a sullen demeanour that appeared like it'.[94] This strand of disapproval continued throughout the lead-up to and during his trial. On arriving for the Magistrate's hearing at Bow Street Police Court in London, it was reported that 'The prisoner jumped from the carriage in a light and gay manner, but the increased pallor of his countenance told that he fully comprehended the position in which he was placed'.[95] When Müller appeared to improve in spirits and demeanour once he had been charged and incarcerated, *The Times* commented disapprovingly, 'the prisoner continues cool and collected, and to eat and sleep well. He is even much improved in appearance since this conviction. His countenance, which at times during the trial was pale and careworn, is said to have assumed its wonted hue and expression, and altogether he is described as being in high health'.[96] The fact that he had not said much to his parents was also remarked upon as inappropriate, 'His father and mother and sister, it is said, reside in Saxe Weimar. He wrote a letter to them a few days ago. It was in German, and in it he only slightly alluded to the crime of which he has been convicted, without saying either that he was innocent or guilty'.[97]

Moreover, Müller was also characterised as untrustworthy and evasive 'and in the habit of making boastful and untrue statements about himself and his doings' (Knott 1911: xxxiii).[98] One provincial newspaper observed that, 'Whether he was in the habit of drinking, or how the circumstances arose, Muller would never divulge, but some months ago he got into a broil with some women or woman, and lost his watch and chain'.[99] This unsubstantiated prejudicial statement was followed up in the same article with the telling expectation and hope that while that 'No trace whatsoever has been found of the watch, [in reference to Thomas Briggs' watch which Müller was implied to have stolen to replace the one he had lost] itself, and it may be fairly expected, and for the ends of justice hoped, that Muller has it still in his possession'.[100]

Müller's behaviour, his vanity, greed, lack of respectability, untrustworthiness and evasive behaviour were assessed as exhibiting nonconformity with the prevailing moral, social and cultural expectations of the time. Both Müller and his chief witness for the prosecution, the cab driver Jonathan Matthews were judged to be dishonest or unreliable: 'Mr Matthews, with no disrespect be it said, is a London cabman, and nothing more'[101] and was regarded as nothing more than an 'illiterate cabman'.[102] The theme of the stupidity, inadequacy or the lack of credibility of the lower classes was also evident in the anti-civil judgements made about some of the witnesses for Müller's defence. 'Stupid and confused as these witnesses were, they created an impression in court that they were speaking what they believed to be the truth'.[103] The strongest anti-civil commentary was reserved for those witnesses who were prostitutes and claimed to have seen Müller very close to the time of the murder. Their testimony and its reception in court were picked over and judged with disapproval. In particular, Müller's alibi attracted a disapproving judgement based on what was deemed to be the prostitute's immoral behaviour, even though her statement was clear. 'Next came the alibi, about which so much previous curiosity had been excited, and upon which the hopes of the defence mainly rested. A miserable old woman, a keeper of a lodging house, "for ladies who received gentlemen" was put up in the box to avow in the face of the world her participation in a trade of which even she felt evidently ashamed. But although she spoke with the suppressed tones of a self-convicting Pariah, her evidence was singularly clear and collected'.[104] '"Miss" Eldred, the female "friend" of Muller',[105] 'was then sworn, and was the object of general curiosity. She was a pale dissipated, and very plain looking woman of about thirty years of age, and had still enough of womanhood left in her to feel shocked at her position and to be unable to answer the questions put to her except in whispers'.[106] The idea that these women were so shamed by their profession that they could barely speak or that they were too stupid to make a reliable statement was used successfully by the prosecution to discredit them. The press coverage was complicit in their portrayal of them as 'non-acceptable' witnesses and in their negative assessment of the quality of their testimonies.

5.2 Non-compatibility: The Anti-civil Behaviour of the Press: Some Self-Criticism

One of the most intriguing aspects of the reporting of the murder was the way in which the press was divided among itself about its relationship to public sentiment. Some newspapers charged other newspapers with anti-civilly whipping up mob tendencies. *Lloyd's Weekly*, for example, reflected on both the press's and the public's insatiable appetite for any type of information about the murderer, 'The railways station is besieged; the telegraphic wires are set to work. A later edition must issue – for the German tailor has spoken a few more words, and has eaten a few crumbs of bread and cheese!'[107] *Lloyd's Weekly London Newspaper*, without any sense of irony about the part it had played itself, was quick to condemn the activities of the press as well as the detectives and police who had added to public confusion about the case and contaminated public sentiment, claiming that 'it is impossible to condemn too severely the freedom with which the Muller gossip, and questions and answers of detectives, connoisseurs in murders, and policemen, have been given to the public'.[108] Most opprobrium was directed at 'The penny-a-liners [which] endeavoured to satisfy the appetite of the multitude on Monday morning, by keeping Muller under their powerful microscopes throughout Sunday; but the public maw was insatiate'.[109] Public sentiment was also judged in anti-civil terms and heavily criticised as mawkish and inappropriate. 'The court was crammed with privileged people; and upon the bench, beside the judge sat the heir to the throne of Italy, come specially to regale himself with a sight of the poor, accused tailor's features. So the great and the humble – the scholar and the ignoramus – were alike interested in him. The heir to the crown had the same strong desire that inflamed the breast of the costermonger who had been waiting and fighting the street since sunrise'.[110] Taking an anti-civil and moralising tone, *Lloyd's Weekly London Newspaper* declared tendentiously that, 'This appetite for murder news is a most demoralising one, and we are sorry to find that it exists in all classes, from the heir apparent to the throne to the heir apparent to a fruit-stall. It is strong in France, as well as in England, and it shows itself in its most revolting forms when the end of the murder's tragedy is at hand'.[111] This interest by the public was not seen as acceptable 'our volatile and impressionable community immediately went mad with excitement'.[112] The excitement in the murder case was also seen to lead to unacceptable behaviour and 'At the Euston-square station of the London and North-western railway the crowd was really fearful, and as the quarter to three o'clock train approached excitement overruled all propriety'.[113] It seemed as if the press disowned the very public sentiment that it had amplified and inspired. The crowd became a mob (a strongly political term then) and criticism abounded about the anti-civil nature of it. This rationale was straightforward: the salacious and unseemly excitement and the excessive public interest in Müller's conviction was viewed as being the response of uneducated masses, closely aligned to the lower and criminal classes. The mob or 'hungry crowd'[114] was to be found at Müller's arrival in America, where 'The excitement among the German population of New York is immense'.[115] The same excitement was seen in Liverpool as well as in London during the exercise of the different judicial proceedings and finally at the time of his execution. With regard to the preparations for his execution *The Times* reported, 'The shouts and obscene remarks as the two upright posts were lifted into their places were bad enough, but they were trifles as compared with the comments which followed the slow efforts of the two labourers to get the cross-beam into its place ... The propriety of such an amusement at such a time admits of question, to say the least, even among such an audience'.[116]

The allegedly lawless and voyeuristic mob were often described in the newspapers in strongly anti-civil terms as 'clamouring, shouting, and struggling with each other to get as near to the gibbet as the steaming mass of human beings before them would allow.... It was literally and absolutely nothing more than the sound caused by knocking the hats over the eyes of those well-dressed persons who had ventured among the crowd, and while so "bonneted" stripping them and robbing them of everything. None but those who looked down upon the awful crowd of yesterday will ever believe in the wholesale, open, and broadcast manner in which garrotting and highway robbery were carried out'.[117]

The mob was not only lawless, but also godless, and 'Some one attempted to preach in the midst of the crowd, but his voice was soon drowned amid much laughter'.[118] This behaviour was described in detail and tendentiously judged as shameful and profoundly anti-civil, as Müller 'died before such a concourse as we hope we may never see again assembled either for the spectacle which they had in view or for the gratification of such lawless ruffianism as yesterday found its scope around the gallows'.[119] As 'The greater part of the rough mass moved off, leaving the regular execution crowd to take their early places',[120] the press further commented that 'the crowd could be seen in all the horrible reality in which it had been heard throughout the long wet night'.[121] Overall, the mob was seen as contaminating civil procedures and by association reinforced the view that their response to the execution of Müller was implicated in an anti-civil threat to 'us'. Although the press had reflected on its own part in contributing to the public's interest in the Müller case, it did not go so far as to blame itself for inciting people to action. Here the press took a step back from genuine self-criticism.

5.3 Civil Intolerance: Müller as an Anti-civil Threat to 'Us' and the Non-compatibility of the 'Other' with 'Our' Civil Society

The idea that the behaviour and attitudes connected with the murder were contaminating civil space was emphasised in the context of the anti-civil lexicon of non-compatibility when the press amplified not only the problematic nature of this crime, but laid great emphasis on the difference between the civil 'we' and the perpetrator. In this vein, claims were made that this murder was different from other murders and that this meant that the punishment for the murderer should be all the greater. 'As this man's guilt is deeper and darker than the guilt of common murderers so it seems right and fitting that his punishment should include elements of mortal anguish beyond any penalties which they can inflict … the concentrated agony … of the dock, the condemned cell and the Scaffold'.[122]

In parallel to the outrage about the nature of the murder, Müller's status as an outsider attracted anti-civil judgements based upon the fact that Müller was a German immigrant and therefore presumed to be different. *The Evening Standard* reflected on the fact that the 'sensational' character of 'this horrible business' was exacerbated because 'a foreigner had been concerned in the murder'.[123] As *The Daily News* put it 'All the circumstances attending this horrible business have partaken of the "sensational" character. The frightful nature of the crime, committed within three minutes and a half in a railway carriage – the complete novelty of the outrage in this country (a fact which in itself suggested the probability, generally expressed at the time, that a foreigner had been concerned in the murder)'.[124] Headlines such as 'Another Murder by a German'[125] amplified the dangers of difference when it referred to an unrelated crime a few days after Briggs was murdered. It was written before Müller had been formally arrested or tried and was set in the fourth column of the newspaper directly underneath the larger headline 'Capture of the murderer of Mr Briggs'.[126] It was seen necessary to point out that 'Muller reads English with some difficulty and writes it badly. He was for some time in the German army. At the departure of the prisoner there was little or no popular demonstrations, though at an earlier period threats of violence had been made among the German population'.[127] This particular article included three references to Müller's background (if his lack of English proficiency is counted) and underlines the idea that because he did not speak English fluently he was unlikely to be intelligent. The observation made in several newspapers that Müller '… is not an intelligent man, and writes badly',[128] referred to his writing in English not in German, the quality of the latter was never ascertained. There was also an implication that German people may resort to violence rather than succumb to civilised English procedures and processes. *The Times* in its important column 'From Our Own Correspondent' made a point of observing that at Müller's departure from New York on the Etna 'there was little or no popular demonstration, though at an earlier period threats of violence had been made among the German population'.[129] What these threats were or when they were issued was not specified in the column.

When referring to an associate, it was also pointed out superfluously that this 'friend of his, [was] a German'.[130] The regular reference to Müller's nationality was sometimes connected in the news with some aspects of Müller's physical appearance or attitude, with *Reynolds's Newspaper* exhibiting some surprise in its observation that, 'In short he struck us as merely a weak undersized German lad, perhaps sentimental and conceited, but with none of those conditions which we should look for in a ruffian and a murderer'.[131] It was remarked upon that 'As the man is seen in the sixpenny cards that have been hawked about the streets of London and which have no doubt contributed materially to the prejudice against him, he is represented with the countenance of a ruffian and the frame of a prize-fighter, whereas in fact he is a thin undersized German lad such as we see everyday in the well known German bands'.[132] Alongside judgements about his nationality 'Müller [was seen] as representative of some particular group the foreigner, the fiend, the lower class, the criminal, the brute or even the innocent victim or the ignorant pawn somehow caught up in a web of coincidental circumstances' (Fox 1998: 295). A case in point from The Examiner was cited approvingly by *Lloyd's Weekly London Newspaper* when it acerbically dismissed a character reference by the GLPS that Müller was fond of children. For the Examiner, a weekly Sunday paper, this reference was seen as irrelevant and it responded with the observation that, 'so was Corder, who barbarously murdered Maria Martin'.[133]

The press's judgement of Müller extended into an anti-civil criticism of his apparent lack of remorse or, as noted above, a desire for repentance. In the context of the US extradition hearing and the UK hearings and criminal court trial, some reporting focused on Müller's lack of emotion as a sign of a lack of remorse: 'The examination took place in the United States District Court-room, which was thronged with persons who evinced the greatest interest in the proceedings, and who anxiously sought for a view of the accused, the latter sat beside his counsel, with an unmoved countenance and a calm demeanour, apparently the most uninterested and unaffected person in the densely crowded court'.[134] The fact that 'Muller showed no signs of emotion',[135] and appeared 'quite unmoved'[136] here was seen as evidence of his lack of regret. A news article in the New York Herald, reported verbatim in *The Evening Standard*, opined that Müller's lack of emotion showed his lack of remorse as 'indifference or callousness, or remarkable self-possession'.[137] For both papers, the public shared the same need for an indication that Müller was sorry for his crime and 'The court was thronged with spectators anxious to obtain a view of the accused',[138] but 'The prisoner, on entering accompanied by his counsel, appeared totally indifferent to the charge against him'.[139] On hearing the jury's verdict, it was remarked with some surprise that 'The prisoner, whose only indication of emotion, even at this terrible crisis of his fate, was seen in the slight involuntary twitching of his firmly compressed upper lip, replied "I have nothing to say before judgment"'.[140] Once the verdict and the sentence were given, Müller's seeming lack of remorse was taken to be an indication of his difference from the 'civilised' British public and an indifference to British civil values. The judgement was that 'They know that men capable of such crime as Muller's are not prone to make confession to a good chaplain or a sheriff, and are as likely as not to die with a "lie upon their lips"'.[141]

When Müller did confess at the very last minute, just before he was hanged, the press made the self-righteous assertion that it had been right all along in considering Müller to be guilty (even though many of the newspapers had expressed numerous doubts). In a letter, Dr Cappel (see Sect. 4.2) had stressed the idea that 'this resolution was formed only at the last moment is quite in keeping with the firmness of his strange character, which kept steadily to a denial of the crime with friend and enemy until the very last glimmering of hope had disappeared'.[142] In its anti-civil reporting of Müller's confession, rather than being relieved about his expression of remorse (see Sect. 4.3), the press instead picked up on the idea of Müller's confession being a last resort rather than emanating from a genuine desire to express regret. Accordingly, the press reflected that 'Up to the last evening he had not shown the slightest inclination to confess the crime of which he has been convicted'.[143] The expedient nature of Müller's confession was emphasised: 'it will be seen that the convict fenced with the questions as to his guilt down to the latest moment of his existence, and that it was not until that the last ray of hope had fled that he confessed'.[144] Confidence in Müller's guilt empowered *The Daily News* to quickly make anti-civil judgements about the GLPS's lack of compatibility with what it saw to be wider public sentiment. It also noted that the GLPS's request for a stay of execution until further evidence could be explored was not appropriate or necessary. 'It is no fault of the German Protection Society, or of the benevolent enthusiasts who concurred in acquitting MULLER after his sentence that he did not die "with a lie upon his lips." It seems as if they had almost persuaded the miserable man that he was innocent until the great darkness was actually looming upon his soul'.[145]

5.4 Civil Intolerance: Anti-civil Reports as Alterity: Müller the German and the Nature of the Mob

Political events in Europe and imperial chauvinism had generated a narrow civil outlook towards strangers and foreigners reflected in anti-civil reports that emphasised alterity and we have seen that Müller's nationality was prominent in the press coverage as soon as he was named a suspect. The Illustrated *London News* observed that it was 'curious that, with the strong anti-German feeling which the success of audacious Austria and predatory Prussia has excited, the murderer should be a German'.[146] When expressing civil intolerance the press accused and stigmatised Müller precisely because of his German nationality. In part, the attitude was similar to the reaction in England to the Whitechapel murders in the 1880s (some twenty years later) where the press coverage and public opinion revealed deep racist sentiments evident in a moral superiority that believed that an Englishman would not be capable of committing such a heinous crime. *Reynolds's Newspaper* in its lead article on 24 July 1864 illustrated a casual racism in its observation that 'while democracy and liberalism are kept in subjection, our rulers will not be greatly concerned though thousands of railway and Road House murders, by German and other ruffians, were to be perpetrated every year, without a trace of their authors ever being discovered – always providing the murderous and plundering ruffians will have discrimination enough to confine their assaults to persons and property of the poor plebian orders'.[147] Here the reporting conflated Germans 'ruffians' and violent crime. *Reynolds's Newspaper*[148] expressed further casual racism in its observation that 'even though when travelling by rail, or walking the high road and the streets, we should be in constant danger of having our hearts pierced, or our brains beaten out, by the daggers and spiked "life preservers" of Germans and other ruffians'.[149] Concerns about Müller's strength and ability to commit the murder because of his slight stature were explained away in the context of alterity as a hidden strength that must have been acquired as a German youth as he was likely to have participated in particular types of strength-building exercises. When his slight appearance was first noted in the press, there were speculations that as a German he should be stronger though than most young men, being used to the kind of exercises that 'the young men of his class'[150] take part.

Müller's characteristics and appearance were cast in the press in a sinister light: 'Franz Muller is short, but firmly knit, and with a very determined lower jaw. Like most Germans he is fair – rather weak-looking in complexion – but this effect is contradicted by his solid head. His expression is not pleasing; his light blueish grey eyes are set far back in his head, and he has a downcast look, but his forehead is high, his head is well balanced, and his mouth is not coarse. His hands are large and muscular; he is in tolerably good condition, and in certain lights in the court has a pugilistic appearance'.[151] The descriptions of Müller's appearance were used to imply a set of unpleasant and unacceptable values 'eyes blue, but very small, and deeply set in his head, while his mouth is decidedly repulsive, from its extreme width and protuberance, impressing one with the idea of dogged obstinacy and vindictive relentlessness'.[152] As Müller's 'German' appearance was increasingly portrayed as grotesque it also became more like that of an archetypal murderer. In other words, it was believed that despite his small stature he was entirely capable of murder. Müller's physical appearance also led to some peculiar observations such as 'During the trial his counsel had made repeated references to his want of physique, but his appearance at that time, with his expanded chest, his large, massive, sinewy hands, folded on the dock, and his peculiar determination of which the closely-compressed lips were indicative, must have gone far to neutralize their theory in this respect'.[153] Even Müller's rather unremarkable choice to buy an altered and cut down top hat was seen as an indication of something foreign and therefore suspicious,[154] 'it will be remembered that the hat found in the railway carriage was a foreign shape, although made by an English manufacturer. These two facts taken together seem to indicate that the murderer was not an Englishman'.[155] Fox (1998: 287) goes so far as to argue that 'it is clear from their criticism of the trial that German and other European newspapers considered Müller's nationality to be far and away the decisive factor in the guilty verdict'. While this may be overstated, given the existence of civil reporting about Müller outlined above, it is evident that the anti-civil judgements expressed against Müller allowed the press to have moments when it spoke of Müller in terms of pure alterity. One such instance occurred after his body was removed from the scaffold and *The Times* chose to refer to the body rather than to Müller himself. The words are dehumanising and to contemporary eyes rather shockingly expressed: 'It had died publicly; the surgeon had certified to its shameful death'.[156] Equally shocking is the fact that a cask or death mask was made of his head which had also been phrenologically examined.[157] In its comments on this examination, *Lloyd's Weekly London Newspaper* spared Müller no pity: 'Müller's head, taken from the cast after the execution ... as a whole is by no means of the low criminal type ... It is certainly indicative of deep craftiness – the most unsafe of characteristics. ... It indicates also much covetousness of property'.[158]

Once Müller had confessed, elements of the press were specifically critical of the GLPS. The sense of *Schadenfreude* in parts of the press was tangible with the press duly endorsing British values of fairness thereby denouncing 'The more rabid portions of the German press, which so industriously denounced our criminal procedure and impugned our juries, may now drop the subject'.[159] The idea that before his trial 'Muller at once rose to the rank of a hero',[160] partly due to intense press coverage that reflected upon every piece of circumstantial evidence was now recast as a damning indictment of 'do-goodism'. Whereby 'It is almost piteous to contemplate the utter discomfiture which has availed all who went out of their way to prove a man innocent who has nevertheless owned himself guilty. Those were not a numerous class, as we gladly admit; but they were a busy, loquacious lot; and though we can respect the conscientious scruples of those who failed to appreciate the full force of the evidence against the prisoner, and who desired to see some rather obscure points more fully cleared up, yet we have very little to say for those who acted on the policy of Deutscher Rechtsschutz Verein, displaying a determination to see only one side of the question, as if the interests of society were but a feather-weight in comparison with the life of a convicted murderer'.[161] Those who had questioned the circumstantial nature of the evidence were rebutted accordingly: 'But for the tolerable certainty that crime will be detected and punished, what would become, this very day, of all the treasures of the capital and centre of the world's wealth and industry? Do philanthropists who set their wits to work to defeat justice ever ask themselves this simple question?'[162]

Having reflected on and sought to increase the public's interest in the story, the press also condemned the behaviour of a voyeuristic public in terms of alterity. Here the press sought to distance its own and its readers' identity from the behaviour of 'the mob'. In parallel to focusing on the behaviour of the crowds the press also stressed the mob's alien composition. The 'dismal crowd of dirty vagrants'[163] were represented as a seething mass of humanity, among whom 'were very few women; and even these were generally of the lowest and poorest class … The rest of the crowd was, as a rule, made up of young men, but such young men as only such a scene could bring together – sharpers, thieves, gamblers, betting men, the outsiders of the boxing ring, bricklayers labourers, dock workmen, German artisans and sugar bakers, with a fair sprinkling of what may almost be called as a grade as any of the worst there met – the rankings of the cheap singing-halls and billiard-rooms, the fast young gents of London… There can be only one thing more difficult than describing this crowd, and that is to forget it'.[164] In the context of the anti-civil lexicon of alterity, the *behaviour* of the mob became less important than the actual *nature* of it from which the newspapers sought to distance themselves and their readers: 'The mob was not guilty of many remarkable and unaccustomed acts of brutality; but there was the stone heart, the brazen face, and the cursing and blaspheming ... Gathered before that black scaffold were myriads of upturned faces all hardened and distorted, and cankered with the vices, the crimes, and the hard living, and the ignorance that, to our shame, still deface the body social'.[165] From here it was a simple step to describe the mob in sub-human terms as insects [166] and animals, 'a thick, dark, noisy fringe of men and women settled like bees around the nearest barriers, and gradually obliterated their close white lines from view',[167] as 'the dismal crowd, ... seemed to writhe and crawl among themselves'.[168] The anti-civil picture that was painted was stark. The animalistic nature of the mob was contrasted with civilised British identity and found wanting. When Müller arrived at Bow Street in September—'a cry of "there he is," and a mixed confused howl – something between a groan and a howl, was raised',[169] and 'When the trembling wretch appeared upon the scaffold there was a cry of hate – a cry loud and deep; - a howl of vengeance at the very gates of death! A more shocking, a more degrading spectacle this to our civilization'.[170] Concerns about the degradation of civilisation led some to speculate about the harm that public execution may do to a civilised culture, considering that 'while it cannot be proved that any good can come from drawing the scum of a great city to see a malefactor hanged in a public place, it is capable of demonstration that much harm might be prevented by removing such spectacles from the public gaze'.[171] So, when 'The Paris "Nation" writes of the recent execution of Latour. The crowd remained dumb with stupor, and could not imagine a man insulting death when so near to it ... The writer hits the mark – "such blood does not purify – it sullies"'.[172]

Ultimately for the press it was Müller as an anti-civil force of some elemental kind that was utilised to explain events: he was fundamentally disposed to anti-civil behaviour and in this was demonstrated alterity from the civilised man. In support of this were claims about class, nationality, behaviour and appearance combined with a constant pandering to public sentiment in evocative and emotional terms—until such times as the public turned into a mob, demonstrating its own lack of humanity. In the absence of modern medical and psychological concepts or any sophisticated criminological techniques or developed social theory to explain Müller's actions, the press came up with the fact that while not evil and not without humanity and some semblance of decency he was simply and naturally inclined to anti-civil behaviour because of who and what he was. This appeal to his ultimate nature rendered him, from a Victorian civilised point of view, an alien of a profound and unsettling kind.

6 Summary

In its protection and preservation of the values of middle-class identity and British civil life (its benchmark position being that of the civilised public represented in and through the archetypal gentleman-professional) the press made a range of civil and anti-civil judgements in parallel in the reporting of the murder. In so doing it displayed a consistent form of hypocrisy in the range of contradictory judgements that were made and which largely remained unexamined and uncorrected. It was only able to accord favourable civil judgements to Müller when he exhibited English/British civilised behaviour. When making anti-civil judgements about Müller and the mob, the press was all too easily drawn into casual racism and snobbery, which often degenerated into strongly tendentious criticisms of foreigners as well as of the civil status generally of the lower classes. Overall those who spoke and got to speak as upholders of the civil orthodoxy were the respectable 'we' whose views, in the context of the invariant civil concern of identity, embodied a rejection of change in the class system, the way status was ascribed and the mores associated with respectability and correspondingly advocated firm ways of dealing with what they perceived as anti-civil behaviour.

Notes

1. I duly focus on the collection of group memberships that define the individual and the recognition that an individual actually has several selves that correspond to widening circles of group membership and that in different social contexts an individual may be triggered to think, feel and act on the basis of different levels of self (Turner et al. 1987). In other words, I am concerned with the civil aspects (which subsumes matters of history, race, gender, place, religion sexuality identity) and the politico/economic aspects (which subsumes matters of power and economic

standing) of identity expressed via membership of diverse associational groups since these are the loci of questions about the levels of discrimination and prejudice which arises against those who do not share the same associational group identity. Civil identity is therefore what an individual perceives can be defined as the 'us' and the 'we' associated with any group membership and stands in contradistinction to the 'them' of other groups. It is the extent to which there is a differentiation between group identities (between us/them) and more specifically, the way in which this is reported that results in a civil or an anti-civil prominence in news reporting that concerns me.

2. Article 20(2) of the International Covenant on Civil and Political Rights (ICCPR) requires states to prohibit hate speech. This requirement does not include all negative statements towards national groups, races or religions, but if a statement constitutes incitement to discrimination, hostility or violence, it must be banned. Incitement to genocide is specifically recognised now as a crime under international law.

3. Though as Cohen (1972) well understood for some news outlets some social categories remain persistently used as the basis for vilification and moral panics. These include (a) Young, Working Class, Violent Males; (b) School Violence: Bullying and Shootouts; (c) Wrong Drugs: Used by Wrong People at Wrong Places; (d) Child Abuse, Satanic Rituals and Paedophile Registers; (e) Sex, Violence and Blaming the Media; (f) Welfare Cheats and Single Mothers; and (g) Refugees and Asylum Seekers: Flooding our Country, Swamping our Services. These categories—clusters of social identity—are the basis from which the news media amplify and distort genuine issues and areas of political and social life into various forms of 'panic discourses'. The astonishing thing is how little these have changed over time.

4. Civil identity formation is highly complex and the individual's engagement with the news media is only one small part of their exposure to ideas and values and it is for this reason that the news is not identity forming per se. The news however resonates with different aspects of identities and the idiosyncratic things that make us unique.

5. For example, the UK's tabloid press coverage of Brexit constantly frames the UK's decision to leave the EU and subsequent negotiations in 'them and us' terms.

6. A recent study has shown that British coverage of migration in some of the country's newspapers is the most aggressive and divisive in Europe (see Berry 2016).

7. In the 1860s, the Church was influential both inside the government and within royalty and held seats in the House of Commons and the House of Lords. It also ran schools and universities and was promoted

through rapid church building programme occurring in 1851 (Inglis 1963).
 8. The urge to improve society and a belief in progress and duty was central, whether it be through education, technological development, religious instruction, temperance societies, enhanced planning through the development of model towns such as Saltaire in West Yorkshire, sanitation reforms, prompted by the Public Health Acts 1848 and 1869 and the development of charities and relief organisations such as the Salvation Army (1865) and numerous charities, often with a strong religious fervour, run mainly by middle-class women.
 9. Charles Dickens's mid-Victorian literature masterfully captures the plight of those caught up in the horror of factory conditions, brutal poverty and the temptation to criminal activity as a means to survive, as well as the hypocrisy and carelessness of the middle and upper classes towards the urban poor. His character Ebenezer Scrooge represents the typical lack of social empathy tinged with fear of the growing urban poor.
 10. Between 1851 and 1891, the numbers of Germans living in London tripled in size to 26,920. The German population was made up of 'businessmen, scientists, and political refugees as well as tradesmen and labourers. The largest single occupational group were those involved in the east London sugar refining industry', and 'the greatest residential concentration was in an area of Stepney which became known as "little Germany"' (London Metropolitan Archives, Information Leaflet Number 23 Published August 2001 updated December 2008 and June 2010).
 11. *Lloyd's Weekly London Newspaper*, 1 January 1865: 6.
 12. See also Waddington (2013). Fears about diseased meat from German were mixed with hostility that reflected anxieties and antagonisms between Britain and Germany.
 13. *The Times*, 19 July 1864: 7. Much of this was reprinted verbatim in regional newspapers.
 14. *The Preston Chronicle* and *Lancaster Advertiser*, 23 July 1864: 2.
 15. *The Huddersfield Chronicle*, 23 July 1864: 7.
 16. *The Huddersfield Chronicle*, 23 July 1864: 7.
 17. *The Huddersfield Chronicle*, 23 July 1864: 7.
 18. *The Huddersfield Chronicle*, 23 July 1864: 7.
 19. *The Times*, 11 July 1864: 9.
 20. *The Evening Standard*, 11 July 1864: 4.
 21. *The Evening Standard*, 11 July 1864: 5.
 22. *The Times*, 11 July 1864: 9.
 23. 'Murder in a First Class Carriage' (*Cork Examiner*, 11 July 1864: 2); 'Atrocious Murder in a First Class Railway Carriage' (*Western Daily Press*,

12 July 1864: 3); 'Atrocious Murder in a First Class London Railway Carriage' (*Newcastle Journal*, 12 July 1864: 3); 'Atrocious Murder in a First Class Railway Carriage' (*Western Daily Press*, 12 July 1864: 3); 'Horrible Murder in a Railway Carriage' (*London Evening Standard*, 11 July 1864: 5); 'Railway Carnage' (*Swindon Advertiser* and *North Wilts Chronicle*, 11 July 1864: 3); 'Murder in a Railway' (*Morning Post*, 11 July 1864: 5); 'Atrocious Murder of the North London Railway' (*London Daily News*, 11 July 1864: 6); 'Horrible and Atrocious Murder in a Railway Carriage' (*Sherbourne Mercury*, 12 July 1864: 4); 'Atrocious Murder in a Railway Carriage' (*Liverpool Mercury*, 12 July 1864: 7); 'The Perils of the Rail' (*Western Daily Press*, 12 July 1864: 2).
24. *Liverpool Daily Post*, 12 July 1864: 5.
25. *The Daily Telegraph* and *Courier*, 13 July 1864: 5.
26. The Illustrated *London News*, 5 November 1864: 453.
27. *The Daily News*, 11 November 1864: 2.
28. *The Times*, 20 September 1864: 9.
29. *Lloyd's Weekly London Newspaper*, 31 July 1864: 7.
30. *The Daily News*, 22 July 1864: 5.
31. *The Daily Telegraph*, 28 October 1864: 2.
32. *The Times*, 20 September 1864: 9.
33. *The Evening Standard*, 7 November 1864: 4.
34. For Example, see *The Evening Standard*, 8 November 1864: 6.
35. *The Daily Telegraph*, 13 July 1864: 12.
36. *The Daily News*, 22 July 1864: 5.
37. *The Times*, 5 November 1864: 9.
38. *The Times*, 15 November 1864: 9.
39. *Lloyd's Weekly London Newspaper*, 24 July 1864: 7.
40. From a close reading of newspaper accounts, police reports, letters from the public, extradition, inquest and court transcripts as well as other published accounts of the story by Knott (1911), Fox (1998), and Colquhoun (2011), it is evident the character of Müller actually remains difficult to ascertain and that views were divided.
41. *The Daily News*, 27 September 1864: 3.
42. *The Times*, 15 November 1864: 9.
43. *Lloyd's Weekly London Newspaper*, 25 September 1864: 5.
44. *The Evening Standard*, 31 October 1864: 4.
45. *The Times*, 5 November 1864: 9; *The Times*, 7 November 1864: 10.
46. *The Times*, 15 November 1864: 9.
47. *Reynolds's Newspaper*, 18 September 1864: 3.
48. *The Daily News*, 31 October 1864: 6. The same words were used verbatim by *Reynolds's Newspaper*, 6 November 1864: 6.
49. *The Daily Telegraph*, 14 July 1864: 4.

50. For example, the system of governance known as the British Raj in India 1858–1947 was typically understood and represented as bringing enlightenment to a benighted people; a view notably shared by John Stuart Mill.
51. *The Daily Telegraph*, 14 July 1864: 4.
52. Letter from Jane Tanner (undated) received by the Home Office 14 November 1864 (HO 12/152/63401). Letter from George Beresford (undated) received by the Home Office on 14 November 1864 (HO 12/152/63401).
53. *The Daily News*, 22 November 1864: 9.
54. *The Times*, 15 November 1864: 9.
55. *The Times*, 15 November 1864: 9.
56. *The Times*, 15 November 1864: 9.
57. *The Times*, 15 November 1864: 9.
58. *The Evening Standard*, 15 November 1864: 4.
59. *The Daily News*, 23 November 1864: 5.
60. *The Times*, 11 July 1864: 9.
61. Letter from M. Williams dated 9 November 1864 sent to the Home Office (HO 12/152/63401).
62. *The Daily News*, 9 August 1864: 6.
63. *Cork Examiner*, 11 July 1864: 2.
64. *Western Daily Press*, 12 July 1864: 3.
65. *Newcastle Journal*, 12 July 1864: 3.
66. *Cork Examiner*, 11 July 1864: 2.
67. *Western Daily News*, 12 July 1864: 3.
68. *Newcastle Journal*, 12 July 1864: 3.
69. *The Times*, 9 September 1864: 6.
70. The Illustrated *London News*, 5 November 1864: 454.
71. MEPO 3/76, 13 July 1864 (signature not clear).
72. *The Evening Standard*, 9 September 1864: 5.
73. *Lloyd's Weekly London Newspaper*, 24 July 1864: 7.
74. *Reynolds's Newspaper*, 24 July 1864: 5; the same phrase was used by *The Daily Telegraph*, 22 July 1864: 3.
75. *The Daily News*, 20 July 1864: 5.
76. *The Preston Chronicle* and *Lancashire Advertiser*, 23 July 1864: 2.
77. *The Preston Chronicle* and *Lancashire Advertiser*, 23 July 1864: 2.
78. *Lloyd's Weekly London Newspaper*, 24 July 1864: 7.
79. *The Dublin Evening Mail*, 25 July 1864: 3.
80. *The Preston Chronicle* and *Lancashire Advertiser*, 23 July 1864: 2.
81. *The Dublin Evening Mail*, 25 July 1864: 3.
82. *The Evening Standard*, 9 September 1864: 5.
83. *Lloyd's Weekly London Newspaper*, 24 July 1864: 7.

84. *The Times*, 21 July 1864: 11.
85. *The Times*, 9 September 1864: 7. Also reported verbatim in *The Daily News*, 9 September 1864: 5.
86. *The Times*, 9 September 1864: 6.
87. *The Times*, 16 September 1864: 7.
88. *Reynolds's Newspaper*, 23 October 1864: 5.
89. *The Times*, 9 September 1864: 7; *The Daily News*, 9 September 1864: 5.
90. *The Times*, 9 September 1864: 7.
91. The Illustrated *London News*, 17 September 1864: 279.
92. *Lloyd's Weekly London Newspaper*, 18 September 1864: 12.
93. *The Times*, 5 November 1864: 9.
94. *The Times*, 9 September 1864: 6.
95. *The Daily News*, 19 September 1864: 6.
96. *The Times*, 7 November 1864: 10.
97. *The Times*, 7 November 1864: 10.
98. George Knott was a barrister-at-law who edited a book entitled the 'Trial of Franz Müller' (1911) based on trial transcripts and from which he derived his assessment of Müller's character.
99. *The Preston Chronicle* and *Lancashire Advertiser*, 23 July 1864: 2.
100. Ibid.: 2.
101. *The Daily News*, 27 September 1864: 3.
102. *The Evening Standard*, 31 October 1864: 4.
103. *The Daily Telegraph*, 31 October 1864: 2. Referring to two witnesses for the defence, Mrs. Jones and Miss Eldred.
104. *The Daily News*, 31 October 1864: 6, reprinted verbatim in *Reynolds's Newspaper*, 6 November 1864: 6.
105. *The Daily News*, 31 October 1864: 6.
106. *The Daily News*, 31 October 1864: 6.
107. *Lloyd's Weekly London Newspaper*, 25 September 1864: 1.
108. *Lloyd's Weekly London Newspaper*, 25 September 1864: 1.
109. *Lloyd's Weekly London Newspaper*, 25 September 1864: 1.
110. *Lloyd's Weekly London Newspaper*, 25 September 1864: 1.
111. *Lloyd's Weekly London Newspaper*, 25 September 1864: 1.
112. *The Daily Telegraph*, 13 September 1864: 2. Referring to the announcement in the press that the sailing ship, Victoria had arrived at America with Müller on board.
113. *Lloyd's Weekly London Newspaper*, 18 September 1864: 12.
114. *The Times*, 15 November 1864: 9.
115. *The Evening Standard*, 16 September 1864: 4.
116. *The Times*, 15 November 1864: 9.
117. *The Times*, 15 November 1864: 9.
118. *The Times*, 15 November 1864: 9.

119. *The Times*, 15 November 1864: 9.
120. *The Times*, 15 November 1864: 9.
121. *The Times*, 15 November 1864: 9.
122. *The Liverpool Mercury*, 12 July 1864: n.p., also cited in Colquhoun (2011: 107).
123. *The Evening Standard*, 19 September 1864: 4.
124. *The Daily News*, 20 September 1864: 5.
125. *The Evening Standard*, 20 July 1864: 5.
126. *The Evening Standard*, 20 July 1864: 5.
127. *The Daily News*, 17 September 1864: 5.
128. *The Evening Standard*, 16 September 1864: 4.
129. *The Times*, 16 September 1864: 1.
130. *The Daily News*, 20 July 1864: 5.
131. *Reynolds's Newspaper*, 6 November 1864: 6, reprinted verbatim from *The Daily News*, 31 October 1864: 6.
132. The word 'bands' refers to the numerous German musicians who emigrated to the UK and who were welcomed. *Reynolds's Newspaper*, 6 November 1984: 6, reprinted verbatim in *The Daily News*, 31 October 1864: 6.
133. *Lloyd's Weekly London Newspaper*, 'Guilty or Not Guilty', 20 November 1864: 1.
134. *The Times*, 13 September 1864: 10.
135. *The Times*, 7 September 1864: 9.
136. *The Daily News*, 19 September 1864: 6.
137. *The Evening Standard*, 9 September 1864: 5.
138. *The Times*, 12 September 1864: 7.
139. *The Evening Standard*, 12 September 1864: 4.
140. *The Times*, 31 October 1864: 7.
141. *The Daily News*, 15 November 1864: 4.
142. *The Daily News*, 22 November 1864: 9.
143. *The Times*, 7 November 1864: 10.
144. *The Times*, 15 November 1864: 9.
145. *The Daily News*, 15 November 1864: 4.
146. Illustrated *London News*, 23 July 1864: 91.
147. *Reynolds's Newspaper*, 24 July 1864: 1.
148. *Reynolds's Weekly Newspaper* was founded in 1850 and by 1864 it was a very successful Sunday newspaper, especially in the North of England, with a radical working-class approach combined with sensationalism.
149. *Reynolds's Newspaper*, 24 July 1864: 1.
150. *Morning Post*, 31 October 1864: 4.
151. *The Daily News*, 20 September 1864: 5.
152. *The Times*, 9 September 1864: 7.

153. *The Times*, 31 October 1864: 7.
154. Rather ironically the cut down top hat became a fashion icon among young men who began to copy the design which became known as the Müller cut down.
155. *The Times*, 13 July 1864: 11.
156. *The Times*, 15 November 1864: 9.
157. There is no further detail available as to who undertook the phrenological examination—it is possible that it was done by the surgeon who confirmed Müllers' death—and who made the cask/death mask.
158. *Lloyd's Weekly London Newspaper*, 20 November 1864: 5.
159. *The Evening Standard*, 15 November 1864: 4.
160. *The Daily Telegraph*, 13 September 1864: 2.
161. *The Evening Standard*, 15 November 1864: 4.
162. *The Daily News*, 15 November 1864: 4.
163. *The Times*, 15 November 1864: 9.
164. *The Times*, 15 November 1864: 9, reprinted verbatim in *Lloyd's Weekly London Newspaper*, 20 November 1864: 5.
165. *Lloyd's Weekly London Newspaper*, 20 November 1864: 1.
166. Similarly and recently insect metaphors have been used in the context of debates about immigration. In July 2015, then Prime Minister of the UK, David Cameron was widely reported for referring to people attempting to enter the UK via Calais in France as 'a swarm of people coming across the Mediterranean, seeking a better life, wanting to come to Britain'. Although criticised by various news media (Elgott and Taylor 2015; Walton and Ross 2015) he defended the use of this terminology as not dehumanising. Katie Hopkins, in a column published in *The Sun* on 17 April 2015, described migrants as cockroaches.
167. *The Times*, 15 November 1864: 9.
168. *Lloyd's Weekly London Newspaper*, 20 November 1864: 5.
169. *The Evening Standard*, 26 September 1864: 4.
170. *Lloyd's Weekly London Newspaper*, 20 November 1864: 1.
171. *Lloyd's Weekly London Newspaper*, 20 November 1864: 1.
172. *Lloyd's Weekly London Newspaper*, 25 September 1864: 1.

Bibliography

Becker, H. S. (1963). *Outsiders: Studies in Sociology of Deviance*. Tampa: Free Press.

Berry, M. (2016, March 14). *British Media Coverage of Refugee and Migrant Crisis Is the Most Polarised and Aggressive in Europe*. JOMEC School Blog. http://www.jomec.co.uk/blog/new-report-finds-british-media-coverage-of-refugee-and-migrant-crisis-is-the-most-polarised-and-aggressive-in-europe/.

Byrne, B. (2007). England—Whose England? Narratives of Nostalgia, Emptiness and Evasion in Imaginations of National Identity. *The Sociological Review,* 55(3), 509–530.

Cohen, S. (1972). *Folk Devils and Moral Panics.* London: Routledge.

Colquhoun, K. (2011). *Mr. Briggs' Hat: A Sensational Account of Britain's First Railway Murder.* London: Little, Brown.

Cornell, C., & Hartmann, D. (1998). *Ethnicity and Race: Making Identities in a Changing World.* London: Sage.

Dinc, P. (2016). *Collective Memory and Competition over Identity in a Conflict Zone: The Case of Dersim* (PhD thesis). The London School of Economics and Political Science (LSE).

Elgott, J., & Taylor, M. (2015, July 30). Calais Crisis: Cameron Condemned for 'Dehumanising' Description of Migrants. *The Guardian.* https://www.theguardian.com/uk-news/2015/jul/30/david-cameron-migrant-swarm-language-condemned.

Fox, W. (1998). Murder in Daily Installments: The Newspapers and the Case of Franz Müller (1864). *Victorian Periodicals Review,* 31(3), 271–298.

Hampton, M. (2004). *Visions of the Press in Britain, 1850–1950.* Urbana and Chicago: University of Illinois Press.

Hogg, M. A. (2006). Social Identity Theory. In P. J. Burke (Ed.), *Contemporary Social Psychological Theories* (pp. 111–136). Palo Alto, CA: Stanford University Press.

Hogg, M. A., & Abrams, D. (1988). *Social Identifications: A Social Psychology of Intergroup Relations and Group Processes.* London: Routledge.

Inglis, K. (1963). *Churches and the Working Classes in Victorian England.* Routledge: Routledge & Kegan Paul.

Jenkins, R. (2000). Categorization: Identity, Social Process and Epistemology. *Current Sociology,* 48(3), 7–25.

Johnson, P. (1993). Class Law in Victorian England. *Past & Present, 141,* 147–169.

Kellett, J. R. (1969). *The Impact of the Railways on Victorian Cities.* London: Routledge & Kegan Paul.

Knott, G. (1911). *The Trial of Franz Müller.* https://archive.org/stream/trialoffranzmull025046mbp#page/n9/mode/2up.

Mathieson, C. (2015). *Mobility in the Victorian Novel: Placing the Nation.* Basingstoke: Palgrave Macmillan.

Mayhew, H. (1864). *German Life and Manners as Seen in Saxony at the Present Day: With an Account of Village Life--Town Life--Fashionable Life--Married Life--School and University Life, &c., of Germany at the Present Time.* London: W. H. Allen.

Tajfel, H., & Turner, J. C. (1979). An Integrative Theory of Intergroup Conflict. In W. G. Austin & S. Worchel (Eds.), *The Social Psychology of Intergroup Relations* (pp. 33–37). Monterey, CA: Brooks/Cole.

Thompson, F. M. L. (1988). *The Rise of Respectable Society: A Social History of Victorian Britain 1830–1900*. Cambridge, MA: Harvard University Press.
Turner, J. C. (1975). Social Comparison and Social Identity: Some Prospects for Intergroup Behaviour. *European Journal of Social Psychology, 5*(1), 1–34.
Turner, J. C., Hogg, M. A., Oakes, P. J., Reicher, S. D., & Wetherell, M. S. (1987). *Rediscovering the Social Group: A Self-Categorization Theory*. Oxford, UK: Blackwell.
Waddington, K. (2013). We Don't Want Any German Sausages Here! Food, Fear, and the German Nation in Victorian and Edwardian Britain. *Journal of British Studies, 52*(4), 1017–1042.
Walton, G., & Ross, T. (2015, August 15). *David Cameron Insists Describing Migrants as a 'Swarm' Wasn't 'Dehumanising'*. https://www.telegraph.co.uk/news/politics/david-cameron/11804861/David-Cameron-says-describing-migrants-as-a-swarm-wasnt-dehumanising.html.

CHAPTER 7

The Reporting of the Murder and the Invariant Civil Concern of Legitimacy

1   THE SCOPE OF THE INVARIANT CIVIL CONCERN OF LEGITIMACY

Concerns about what is legitimate[1] are in various ways linked to the concept of authority. For the purposes of this book, authority is understood in two ways. First, with regard to the strength of moral codes which are derived from and recommend codes of conduct, mores and norms, values and traditions, natural justice and therefore by extension legitimate both who we are and what constitutes acceptable or unacceptable behaviour and right or wrong actions. Second and with regard to institutions, authority is understood as stemming from formal power, formal laws (de jure) and justice, rights and accountability. Both kinds of authority can be scrutinised but in different ways. The first kind of authority, which is in some ways expressed informally by the press, concerns itself with civil identity and anti-civil alterity.[2] The second kind of authority can be formal, legalised or institutionalised and is best understood by examining how the news media report the relationship between the civil sphere and non-civil spheres and correspondingly the legitimacy of claims and counterclaims between these different spheres and their respective concerns to promote certain conflicting values.

With regard to the non-civil spheres, concerns about legitimacy mainly (but not exclusively) relate to the legitimacy of the state and the extent of its authority and power. For Williams (2005), meeting the basic legitimation demand (BLD) is what distinguishes a legitimate state from an illegitimate state and correspondingly, legitimate from illegitimate power and authority. The BLD is met when there is an '"acceptable solution" to the first political question' (ibid.: 4) of 'how to create order out of mayhem' (Hawthorn 2005: xii), or alternatively expressed, when the state can justify its power in a manner deemed acceptable by its subjects/citizens, which, in turn, raises the matter of consent. For Locke, the legitimacy of authority resides in the transfer of elements of personal authority to the state in a consensual manner. Accordingly, he argues that individuals must give their tacit or express consent to a 'social contract' that obligates[3] them to obey the laws of the state. Today, we might put the matter more simply. First and negatively, legitimacy is bestowed upon the state by subjects/citizens not engaging in revolutions and anti-state violence, or more positively by subjects/citizens confining themselves to politically and civilly agreed forms of endorsement and protest if they think that state activity transcends agreed boundaries of legitimate authority. The point being that the BLD is concerned with what is 'acceptable' and what is regarded as an acceptable civil life. In short, where state authority stops being legitimate is when it betrays civil values or oversteps civil boundaries.

With regard to the civil sphere, concerns about legitimacy are mainly expressed with regard to the regulatory institutions of civil society which, in the context of the invariant civil concern of legitimacy, include the activities of the law which are separate from the communicative institutions of the factual media. Legal proceedings and processes, questions of accountability and transparency as well as the maintenance and supervision of democratic procedures require that regulatory institutions provide formal criteria—laws, codes of conduct, regulatory frameworks and guidelines—and that they are adjudicated upon by an independent judiciary, tribunal or governing body. The willingness and ability of the regulatory and communicative institutions to sometimes work together enable the law to scrutinise the communicative institutions, and the communicative institutions to scrutinise and hold accountable the legal institutions and for public opinion to be freely expressed[4]; all facilitate the interaccountability of civil society institutions and public trust in them.

In order to decide what is legitimate and what is not, whether legal procedures are followed and whether laws are fairly applied, civil scrutiny needs to be undertaken. Civil scrutiny needs to include the actions and activities of both civil society's own institutions, but must extend to the actions and activities of the non-civil spheres themselves

(Alexander 2006). This entails judgements about the effectiveness of the law, justice, liberty, democracy and rights and guides the placement of public trust through an emphasis on transparency and openness of decision-making and the accountability of power holders and institutions. When such scrutiny is undertaken, it is determined whether or not what we judge and hold to be 'our' standards of legality and justice are applied and maintained and whether or not power is being used reasonably and fairly. Accordingly, such scrutiny can either lead to the approval of the legitimacy of authority or the disapproval of it, within both the civil sphere and the non-civil spheres. The ability of the non-civil and civil institutions to work fairly and effectively on behalf of citizens has, in modern liberal democratic societies, been seen to entail the giving and withholding of public trust and of a public warrant for action. In the case of the actions of the non-civil sphere, civil society, in theory at least, is able to withdraw its public warrant.

Scrutiny of both the civil and non-civil spheres is therefore undertaken in part by the factual media.[5] The extent to which the factual media can scrutinise and also help citizens to evaluate the activities of regulatory institutions and the authority or power held by non-civil actors is crucially dependent on its own independence from such power.[6] The invariant civil concern of legitimacy is therefore to some degree institutional in outlook as it (a) scrutinises institutions and formal arrangements of power and (b) expects that such scrutiny can lead to changes in law that correct a perceived lack of acceptable legitimacy. As such, the civil 'we' fights its claims both in and through the factual media as well as through legal procedures. In other words, a mature civil society always has at its disposal two civil institutions that can increase the demands for legitimacy and define the extent of acceptability: the law and the factual media. When civil scrutiny is undertaken in and by the news, the news engages in civil and anti-civil judgements about matters pertaining to the invariant civil concern of legitimacy by expressing trust and distrust, or approval or disapproval of the actions of civil and non-civil institutions. More specifically, the reporting of and engagement with the invariant civil concern of legitimacy by the news media assumes a view of legitimacy which involves the creation of an imaginary civil consent.[7] This civil consent, in turn, operates as a benchmark against which news reporting takes its own position. In this way, news carries its own normativity in relation to what is deemed to be legitimate and not legitimate.

2 NEWS LEXICA OF THE INVARIANT CIVIL CONCERN OF LEGITIMACY

The engagement with the invariant civil concern of legitimacy in news reports is linked to 'what will withstand civil scrutiny' and to the giving and withholding of public trust. Although the invariant civil concern of legitimacy must necessarily be underpinned by jurisprudence and civil societies that value the fairness of the law and legal process to produce justice, it is the bestowing and withdrawing of legitimacy of these activities by the communicative institutions (news and public sentiment) that is at particular issue in the context of the invariant civil concern of legitimacy.

The language of legitimacy is about how events conform to our held and felt sense of 'what is best for us', 'what cost does this entail and for whom', 'what is right and wrong', 'what is just and unjust', 'what can we justify', 'what is seen to be fair' and so on. In the process of doing so, the news responds, in different ways, to what is constantly debated (and publicised) by the regulatory civil institutions of civil society. In this way, the news is able to bestow and withdraw legitimacy both positively and negatively: positively by exposing perceived corruption, injustices, unwarranted attacks upon our civil way of life and by helping to bring about progressive changes and reform to civil life; negatively by endorsing repressive activities that in some way or another undermine our extant civil freedoms and values. Both point to the fact that the ability of the news to make civil and anti-civil judgements about the legitimacy of what others say or do is a very potent aspect of its civil power.

With this in mind, it is possible to identify both a civil and anti-civil lexicon that the news uses in its reporting of the invariant civil concern of legitimacy.[8]

The civil lexicon of legitimacy (see Table 1, p. 215) is found where the focus in the news is on solidarising and approving legitimate (democratic) authority, where it emphasises and endorses the need for accountability in the intentions and actions of civil and non-civil institutions and where it calls for the need for transparency and openness in their actions through a questioning of their actions, intentions and possible outcomes.[9] In short, the civil judgements made are those that endorse extant civil values or promote change in accordance and consistent with those particular values in civil society. This occurs for example where

Table 1 The civil lexicon of the invariant civil concern of legitimacy in the news cycle

Civil lexicon	*Expressions of the civil lexicon of legitimacy: The focus is on approving or withdrawing legitimacy through civil scrutiny that is solidarising*
Legitimate authority evidenced through accountability, scrutiny, transparency and openness	• Emphasises and endorses the need for scrutiny of the authority of both civil and non-civil institutions • Emphasises and endorses the need for accountability in the intentions and actions of civil and non-civil institutions • Emphasises and endorses the need for transparency and openness in the intentions and actions of civil and non-civil institutions • Exposes non-legitimate activities • Exposes illegality, corruption, attempts to deceive, vested interests • Grants approval if non-civil institutions and their actors are seen to be acting in the interests of civil society through the direct descriptive use of their quotations and transcripts • Emphasises the desirability of public trust in civil institutions that hold power • Emphasises the values of democracy
Law	• Scrutinises and evaluates existing law and legal processes • Evaluates the civilising effects of law and endorses its reasonable nature • Emphasises civil tensions within existing law that need to be addressed • Exposes civil inconsistencies and unfairness in the law • Endorses or calls for a need to change existing law for civil purposes
Justice	• Emphasises the need for justice • Entails oversight to ensure that justice is done and fair treatment has been received • Expects a guarantee of equal civil freedoms and civil liberties for all • Ensures that injustice is exposed • Supports the view that attacks on civil freedoms and liberties merit the issue of a civil warrant for action for the pursuit and protection of greater civil rights and traditional rights (custom and practice) • Endorses civil protest, civil action, petitions, campaigns and public mobilisation for equal rights and freedoms

legitimate authority is found wanting, corruption is revealed and vested interests and non-legitimate activities are exposed as not acting in the interests of civil society. In these cases, change may well be demanded in the news. Where legitimacy and authority are seen to be accountable, open to scrutiny and transparent, the civil responsibility of the news media may simply involve the confirmation of existing and seemingly uncontested arrangements through the endorsement of existing law and an overseeing that justice is done.

The civil lexicon of the law involves the scrutiny and evaluation of existing law and legal processes. This entails scrutiny of the actions and outputs of non-civil sphere actors, the lawmakers (the civil value of the laws that are in force and which come into force), the law enforcement agencies (the way in which evidence is gathered and its quality, which is assessed and reported as information comes to light during official hearings, inquests and court cases), through to the activities of the regulatory institutions of the civil sphere themselves, namely the fairness and reasonable nature of legal processes of inquests, extradition orders, court cases, the actions of juries and their verdicts. The civil lexicon of law assesses and evaluates the civilising effects of law. Civil tensions within existing law and/or inconsistencies and unfairness may be identified and need to be addressed. If so, this may lead to a call for a change to existing law for civil purposes. Where existing law is found wanting due to legal procedures, these too are exposed. In either case, the civil lexicon of law requires civil scrutiny and in the end a civil judgement, which reveals what is and is not regarded as law-like and legitimate.

The civil lexicon of justice emphasises the need for justice and entails oversight to ensure that justice is done and fair treatment has been received and that there is a guarantee of equal civil freedoms and civil liberties for all. If injustice is suspected, concern is expressed and injustice is exposed. Where civil freedoms and liberties are attacked or undermined, there may be an issue of a civil warrant for action for greater civil rights and traditional rights (custom and practice) as well as an endorsement of civil protest, civil action, petitions, campaigns and public mobilisation. Though under certain circumstances, which affect civil liberties, the dynamic of civil scrutiny and civil judgement may be suspended by the news media. This usually entails the state pronouncing a 'state of exception', 'state of war', 'national security', 'national emergency', 'natural disaster' and more recently 'terrorist attack'. Special circumstances may require civil liberties to be restricted. Demands to restrict these do not originate in the civil sphere but in the political sphere. Thus far, history shows that when such special circumstances arise the mainstream factual media in the West has mostly complied. The news lexicon is one of non-solidarising legitimacy which emphasises and endorses the authority of non-civil institutions and activities in the civil spheres to ensure greater national or personal security. Such actions can include for example that the right to free movement may be temporarily suspended after a terrorist incident, that inconvenient security measures to prevent terrorism are put in place. Measures such as these were adopted for example, in the aftermath of the attacks on the Boston Marathon in April 2013, the Paris attacks in November 2015 and with the judgement to shut down the centre of Brussels in February 2016, Westminster Bridge in London in March 2017 and Manchester city centre in May 2017 and so on. These types of decisions are generally uncontested in the news media and seen as necessary and proportionate to protect national security. Instead of questioning these decisions, the focus of reporting is largely on the perpetrators and their motives, the victims and their suffering and the need to resist actions that would change our 'civil cultures'. In short, in the face of a direct attack on 'our way of life', there is often initially a call from both within and outside civil society for the need for retributive justice via legitimate intervention by the non-civil spheres—even where this may involve dispensing justice without a majority civil endorsement for a while. Here the lexicon may reflect the view that a loss of common civil rights is desirable under certain circumstances and a corresponding acceptance of such loss necessary. In such circumstances, the news media accept (explicitly or implicitly) that there is a need for some secrecy in the intentions and actions of non-civil institutions for the protection of common national interests and personal security and that extra measures such as the need to be searched when entering public buildings or being required to carry identity cards might be put in place. These measures appear to be incontestable for a while because we cannot be sure of the nature and extent of the threat. The legitimacy of the public to decide and object to the use of such powers is dismissed against what at the time must surely be the trump card—personal and collective safety and national security (see Chapter 8). Here an incursion into the civil sphere may not be deemed to be civil in character, but is not rejected overtly in the news media and within public sentiment because of other considerations that come into play as different experts are brought in to frame and contextualise events. For a while, at least the legitimacy of the non-civil authorities to act may override those voices that protest that such actions are excessive and are an attack on civil freedoms and liberty.

In contrast, the anti-civil lexicon the news uses in its reporting of the invariant civil concern of legitimacy can be summarised accordingly (Table 2).

The focus of the anti-civil lexicon is always on the non-solidarising. The emphasis is on anti-civil values, the promotion of non-civil programmes and policies, partisan antagonism towards civil institutions, endorsement of questionable authority as well as vengeful and angry calls for justice. The deployment of the anti-civil lexicon is grounded in an emphasis upon the failure of civil society to meet our best interests and needs and is often presented in highly individualistic terms.

Table 2 The anti-civil lexicon of the invariant civil concern of legitimacy in the news cycle

Anti-civil lexicon	Expressions of the anti-civil lexicon of legitimacy: The focus is on the withdrawal of legitimacy and is non-solidarising
Legitimate authority	• Expresses a cynical view of the legitimate authority of the civil and non-civil institutions • Authorises and inflames a lack of public trust • Negates the need for transparency, scrutiny or accountability of power holders in their actions against others • Calls for and endorses a lack of public trust in what has been deemed, without due civil scrutiny, to be 'non-legitimate' • Is iconoclastic, but may fail to replace discredited authority with a civilly endorsed alternative • Emphasises a lack of public trust in what has been deemed to be the 'non-legitimate' other
Justice	• Advocates and dispenses justice without a civil warrant • Speculates about guilt or innocence • Gives implicit or explicit approval and even endorsement of the importance of liberty for some but not others • Explains, justifies and even endorses the suspension of democratic processes against some but not others • Overlooks laws or changes to law that seek to control or constrain 'others' without a civil warrant for such control • Provides implicit or explicit acceptance of the creation of spaces of exception, camps, building of walls and boundaries or areas where rights are suspended • Condemns calls for civil protest, civil action, petitions, campaigns, public mobilisation

The anti-civil lexicon of authority is designed to engender doubt, suspicion, fear or anger about formal, legalised or institutionalised legitimacy and authority. It especially seeks to excite public sentiment on these matters—particularly so via the amplification of the event or issue and the use of the tendentious news style. As such, the anti-civil lexicon of authority can support or inflame anti-establishment public sentiment in ways that can undermine civil and political cultures. It can appear to authorise and legitimate a lack of public trust in civil and non-civil institutions and is, in essence, designed and deployed to persuade. It is both the factual media of undisguised partisan news and the more subtle news of promoting disguised vested interests, where it can more easily masquerade as objective, factual and unbiased while promoting partial truths by using information selectively. Instead of emphasising and endorsing the need for accountability in the intentions and actions of civil and non-civil institutions and calling for the need for transparency and openness in their actions, the anti-civil lexicon of authority serves to reduce the need for detailed civil scrutiny. It reduces public trust in what becomes the non-legitimate other and allows newly legitimated but unscrutinised views to be endorsed. In this case, the extent to which the news media undertake their legitimate responsibility is diminished.[10]

The anti-civil lexicon of justice is also non-solidarising and is found where the news media act as the quasi-judicial or sentencing authority. It is a lexicon of speculation over guilt or innocence and what is right or wrong, what constitutes fairness and who deserves it, and appeals to those that do not support due process. It is the news acting as an advocate of particular verdicts or punishments in the absence of safe evidence and recommending anti-civil outcomes in the name of natural justice. Such anti-civil sentiment in news reporting also serves to settle what is justice and what is due to 'criminals' in highly selective and inconsistent ways.[11] On the one hand, the news may frame approval for laws which control or constrain civil liberties while on the other hand such liberties may be appealed to when protecting or promoting a cause close its own heart. Nowhere is this more so than in cases of freedom of expression. Equally, the press may demand prosecution for some and actively promote the innocence of others, demanding harsh sentences for some while complaining of harsh sentences for others. In some of its parts, the news media can adopt an anti-civil lexicon of justice that can simultaneously question the legitimacy of law and the inviolability of law; believe in the one and only original meaning of the constitution and yet support its flexible interpretation; believe in the jury system and yet find it antiquated and irrelevant; support habeas corpus and human rights but not for all. In short, it gives and withholds matters of legitimacy inconsistently and sometimes incoherently.

3   The Context of Legitimacy of the Murder: The Authorities

Irrespective of whether the law is derived from norms or from moral fiat, whether it is constitutionally circumscribed or not, the civil legitimacy of the application of the law is derived from the public's perception of fairness. How fair things were in the Müller case was consistently derived from press and public judgements concerning the conduct of the police, lawyers, the Home Office and the press itself. Specifically, it was examined and judged whether they conducted themselves throughout the case in accordance with the application of traditional 'English justice'. The civil warrant of legitimacy could only be accorded if the public was convinced that this was the case. In essence, the public needed to be convinced that the legitimate authorities followed what English justice 'stood for', what it represented and what it symbolised to others—namely the English as civilised and fair-minded. Thus, the case of the Thomas Briggs murder was not simply a matter of the observance of criminal law, or of the correct application of the 'Offences against the Person Act of 1861',[12] but of being able to make the judgement that what should have been done was indeed done. And this was of paramount concern to both the press and the public at the time of the murder and manifest in the way that the press deployed the lexicon of the invariant civil concern of legitimacy for much of the time with regard to the authorities.

In 1864, police investigation through the application of organised detection was a relatively new phenomenon. A new type of police inspector, the detective, had been created in 1842 by Richard Mayne, who by 1864 was the Police Commissioner of the Metropolitan Police. Originally, there were eight police inspectors that formed the new detective branch. They were plain clothed and their specific remit was to investigate and solve murders. One of the best known of these was Detective Inspector Jack Whicher, who had investigated the murder of three-year-old Saville Kent in 1860, a case which would become known as the Road Hill House murder. The Road Hill House case was widely covered in the national press and became especially notorious when Saville Kent's half-sister, Constance Kent, was arrested. She claimed her innocence and was released without trial. The case was mired in class politics with Whicher being cast in the role of the working-class lad who seemingly did not know his place, while Constance Kent was deemed to be a middle-class lady of refinement. Public sentiment was with Constance Kent and not with Whicher or the detective branch. The fact that Constance Kent subsequently confessed to murder in 1865 did little to restore public confidence in this relatively new form of policing. There was in fact a Victorian appetite for playing the 'armchair detective' and advising the police and writing into the press with their opinions and ideas about how to solve the crime, which had become more notable in 1855 in the case of the Rugeley Poisoner,[13] and was also very evident in the case of the murder of Thomas Briggs in 1864. As is still the case with high-profile murder cases, the senior investigating officer, Detective Inspector Tanner, came under immediate press and public scrutiny in the days that followed his murder. The detection of the perpetrator was to prove a stressful event, both aided and hampered by an increasingly anxious and critical press and public. As all the transcripts from witness statements, the extradition hearing and later from all the court proceedings, were reprinted in many of the newspapers, the public was able to review the detectives' processes and evaluate their evidence over and over in the depositions of the witnesses, the Coroner's report, the extradition hearing and the statements made for the defence and the prosecution. In the absence of any form of legal[14] or press guidelines about the use of such material and how it might influence the case and the trial, the press could virtually make of the evidence what it wished. Furthermore, at that time, the justice system in England prohibited Müller from speaking in his own defence, as defendants on murder charges (and their spouses) were seen to be 'incompetent witnesses', leaving his testimony to be delivered by his defence. It was not until 1865 that legal revisions to this way of regarding evidence statements by witnesses and the accused were first considered. In the end, in the absence of forensic science, Müller was convicted on circumstantial evidence drawn in large part from witness statements which had been gathered by the detectives and published in the press.

The passing of a sentence of death following a guilty verdict for murder was seen as legitimate, but there were growing differences in public opinion about public hanging. The Home Secretary was caught in a balancing act between the calls for the abolition of capital punishment voiced by Charles Dickens, Thomas Carlyle and other public intellectuals in the 1840s and an apparently insatiable public appetite for retribution and spectacle. Questions were raised about the effectiveness of public hanging as a deterrent and the House of Lords Select Committee had considered its legitimacy and value in 1856 and recommended private rather than public executions, a recommendation that was not put into practice. Concerns about the validity of public hanging as a deterrent to those who might commit a capital offence gained in strength through the 1860s and the Royal Commission on Capital Punishment 1864–1866 recommended the ending of public hangings and parliament passed the Capital Punishment (Amendment) Act on the 29 May 1868—a decision that was too late to spare Müller from the public spectacle.[15] The Act required that 'Judgment of death to be executed on any prisoner sentenced on any indictment or inquisition for murder shall be carried into effect within the walls of the prison in which the offender is confined at the time of execution'.[16]

4 Civil Judgements Made in the News Reports

4.1 Legitimate Authority of the Detectives and the Legal System

The activities of the detectives and the legal system were used by the press as routine sources of information about the murder of Thomas Briggs. A good deal of newspaper coverage utilised verbatim transcripts of proceedings in the descriptive news style of reporting to cover the extradition hearing in New York on 26–27 August 1864, the magistrate hearing in the Bow Street Court in London on 19 September 1864 and the proceedings of the inquest and the verdict of the Coroner's jury of 'wilful murder' against Müller on 26 September 1864, as well as the trial at the Central Criminal Court in London, 27–29 October 1864.[17] A typical approach was taken by *The Daily Telegraph* which reported that, 'The following facts may now, we think be taken for granted, on evidence which there is no printed factual reason to distrust'.[18] *The Evening Standard* reported that the 'adjourned inquest on the body of Mr Briggs, who was so brutally murdered in a carriage on the North London Railway on the 9th inst., was resumed before Mr HUMPHREYS this morning. A detailed report of the proceedings will be found in our columns'.[19] Often, the press also printed verbatim the full deposition taken from witnesses.[20]

Letters written by Detective Inspector Tanner to his senior officer while travelling to and from America (July–September 1864) were also a source of information for the press and used to provide detailed fact-based accounts of the processes of arresting Müller and the extradition hearing. They included references to the negative comments about the extradition treaty of 1842 between Britain and America made by the Counsel for the Defence, Chauncey Schaffer.[21] The way this material was used in news reports revealed a good deal of press approval for the British detectives, who while also being criticised were simultaneously regarded as civil actors.[22] Accordingly, the material was constantly updated by the provision of detailed accounts of the police's activities at all stages of the investigation. Additional information that provided colour was taken directly from police letters which revealed intimate details such as, 'A rug and bolster were given him, for which he [Müller] thanked the officer, saying "You are very kind; the police are very kind, particularly Mr. Tanner".[23] The humane treatment of Müller was emphasised in the reporting: 'Inspector Kerressey and Sergeant Clark had charge of the prisoner, who has been kept in the sick bay or hospital, of which he has had the range. He has never been in irons'[24] and 'He would extremely dislike to do anything bearing even the appearance of a desire to withhold from the unfortunate man any privilege or right that belonged to him'.[25] Much of this information was printed without comment or any additional material. The UK press also reprinted verbatim articles from the American press and used these for a while as a routine source with comments such as, 'The following … details … are furnished by the New York journals, files of which, up to the 27th inst., have been received'.[26] In providing so much information, the press was responding to what it judged to be in accordance with public sentiment and its insatiable appetite for more news, and should the public be in any doubt about the level of its own interest, it was consistently emphasised in the press reports that the murder was of great importance to the public. From the outset, newspaper reports were adamant that it was in the public interest that the murderer must be caught and caught very quickly. It also became of paramount concern and legitimate that the murderer must be dealt with effectively by the authorities[27] and the decision of Sir George Grey, the Home Secretary, that the 'memorial [from the GLPS following the sentence of execution] did not warrant his interfering with the verdict of the jury' was reprinted uncritically in full in several newspapers.[28]

The rich source of material provided by the police, and the fact that it was republished in a way that was uncritical and official, allowed the press to provide a constant flow of information that formed a civil endorsement of the activities of the detectives and their industrious attempts to solve the crime as quickly as possible. Ample evidence was given to the readers who were reassured that, 'Up to the time of this being written the detectives, under the direction of Mr Inspector Kerressey, are instituting every possible inquiry with a view of detecting the guilty parties, and it is hoped that before long some clue will be obtained which may lead to their apprehension',[29] and in the same vein, 'Up to the time of this being written, the detectives under the direction of Mr Inspector Kerressey, were resolutely making every possible inquiry'.[30] The commitment of the detectives' time and efforts to catch the perpetrator and to protect 'us' was approvingly noted, 'Up to the late hour last evening the officers engaged in the endeavour to unravel the mystery which has hitherto surrounded the circumstances of the perpetrator of the atrocious crime'.[31] Readers were further approvingly told that 'Superintendent Harris and Inspector Tanner, with a heavy staff of detectives, were engaged until midnight in following up the track of the murderers, and in the course of a few hours it is expected that the officers will be successful in their efforts'.[32] The commitment of the detectives was reiterated several times over the first few days following the murder, and it was noted that they were 'using every possible exertion to effect the capture of the guilty parties'.[33] It was soon reported that the police had an idea who the perpetrator was and that, 'The police believe that the man is already known to them, and they are following him up with great perseverance'.[34] The pressure placed on the detectives to resolve the crime was high and the press and public endorsement of their legitimacy were based upon an anticipation of success and premised upon the view that they were clearly acting in the interests of civil society. The detectives were praised for their experience and their meticulous approach, 'Mr. Williams, Mr. Tanner, and the most experienced detectives both of the metropolitan and city forces are actively engaged in pursuing the most rigid inquiries into the circumstances of the murder, and no stone will be left unturned by them which may tend to bring the murderer to justice'.[35] The press endorsed the detectives' competence that had rendered 'it impossible for Muller to escape, upon arrival in New York'[36] due to 'The most complete arrangements [that] have been made to effect Muller's capture on the arrival of the Victoria'.[37] In the press's civil judgement, 'the police took their measures with well-grounded confidence'[38] and 'Muller was not allowed the most remote chance of escape'.[39]

Optimism about the likely success of the detectives involved a continual account of their activities which were reported daily and in detail even when there was little of substance to reveal, 'During the whole of yesterday the police were entirely employed in following up a track which, although at the moment involved in some obscurity, is likely to lead to most important results. At present it would be premature to indicate the precise nature of the clue which has been obtained'.[40] Nonetheless, rather prematurely readers were told that 'The exertions made by the police were partially rewarded yesterday by the discovery of a rather important clue'.[41] Readers were equally reassured that 'A very lengthy report from the officers in charge of the case was sent into Sir Richard Mayne last night, containing some very important information that we hope to be able to give to our readers to-morrow'.[42] *Lloyd's Weekly Newspaper* strongly expressed its belief in a successful outcome and the abilities of the detectives, saying that, 'We trust heartily that this crime is now in a fair way of being traced home to its perpetrator. There is a clue, and a tolerably clear one, which we leave the police to follow'.[43] In the few days, following the crime both the importance and atrocious nature of the crime and the pressing need to capture the perpetrator meant that the press was actually urging the detectives to do so quickly and accordingly their every move was followed. The sentiment here is solidarising and the public was encouraged to trust the press which was working closely (on its readers' behalf) with the detectives in order to produce a successful outcome.

As the investigation developed, the press began to take a more questioning approach to the activities of the detectives and the need for the latter's accountability to the public was more greatly emphasised. Although the tone remained optimistic and the sentiment was still one of a civil endorsement of their authority, the news reports became more qualified. 'Later Particular, from the Globe - TUESDAY - The police have not yet succeeded in apprehending the ruffian or ruffians who committed the murder on the North London Railway on Saturday night, but it is reported that they have hit upon a "particular line of enquiry"'.[44]

Through this slightly less praiseworthy approach, trust in the success of the detectives was replaced by a hope for their success: 'The following details of the circumstances attending to the recovery of the chain are authentic and may possibly lead to the detection of the parties engaged in the perpetration of the atrocious crime'.[45] The by now qualified success of the detectives was noted, 'Reporting From the Times of Wednesday, The exertions made by the police were partially rewarded on Tuesday by the discovery of a rather important clue'.[46]

However, enthusiasm for the detectives and trust in their ability returned to that of an unqualified endorsement once the perpetrator was identified. The excitement and belief in the legitimacy of the work of the detectives were once again restored and apparent. The hasty preparation of Detective Inspector Tanner and his team for the voyage to America and the support of the Home Office for the trip were reported as a deserved outcome of all their hard work; the pursuit of Müller was now legitimate, desirable and necessary. 'Success attended the inquiries, and a person ... identified as Müller was ascertained to have left London four days ago in a ship bound direct for New York, which usually averages 19 days in the journey, and which, having left the Downs many hours before the inquiries... Government resources were at once asked for and granted'.[47] The Home Secretary's response was seen by the press as important in 'lessening the chances of Muller's escape, Sir George Grey and the police commissioners resolved to procure a second warrant against him, supported by additional evidence, and again endorsed by the American minister, to be sent out by the mail packet leaving Liverpool this morning (Saturday), and which is one of the best on the line'.[48] A successful outcome was anticipated with confidence, 'Although beyond the momentary reach of the police, the measures taken for his apprehension are certain to be attended by a successful result'.[49]

Once the detectives had left the UK in their steamboat, there was only patchy reporting with information derived from a few snippets from the New York newspapers and letters from Detective Inspector Tanner to his superior officer, which were released by the police.[50] Through these sources, particularly Tanner's letters, the public was reassured that 'The most complete arrangements have been made to effect Muller's capture upon his arrival of the Victoria, a special steam vessel being kept in readiness, with steam up night and day, to start the moment the Victoria is sighted, in order that the pilot-boat may be anticipated, lest by any mischance information should reach Muller that the officers of justice are on his track - it being feared that he might in desperation seek by suicide to evade justice'.[51] Given that 'The New York police, in conjunction with the English detectives, have made every arrangement to arrest Muller at his arrival',[52] the detectives were seen as up to the task as 'the police took their measures with well-grounded confidence',[53] being so well prepared that it would 'render it impossible for Muller to escape, upon arrival in New York, [and] a private circular was placed in the hands of all New York pilots … as soon as the Victoria was signalled the detectives boarded her, and Muller was placed under arrest'.[54] Through efficient action 'Muller was not allowed the most remote chance of escape'.[55] The capture of Müller was viewed as a great success by the news media as well as an excellent exercise in international cooperation between the UK detectives and the American authorities. It was reported in *The Daily News* that 'The New York Herald publishe[d] a correspondence between Inspector Tanner and Superintendent Kennedy, the former returning thanks for the attention, advice, and assistance he received during his visit; also for the valuable assistance of officer Tiernan, and inclosing [sic] for him a gratuity of £10'.[56] *The Daily News* also reprinted part of the correspondence between Inspector Tanner and Superintendent Kennedy, 'Permit me to return my sincere thanks, both to yourself and Mr. Inspector Carpenter, for the attention, advise [sic], and assistance that have been given to me during my visit to New York to arrest the man Muller for the murder of Mr. Briggs, in London; and I beg to assure you that I shall ever have a grateful remembrance of your kindness… - acknowledgement of letter by Kennedy follows'.[57] *The Daily News* put the matter this way 'the details of the murder of MR BRIGGS raised the natural feeling of abhorrence for the criminal suspected of the deed, and facilitated the ends of justice. The English officers found everyone perfectly ready to assist them the Federal authorities the New York police and the harbour pilots, all gave a willing and most effectual aid'.[58]

News about the outcome from the extradition hearing, which ruled that Müller should be returned to the UK for a trial, was viewed with approval by all the news media. The endorsement of the detectives was fulsome and unequivocal, 'The police are now in possession of facts which place beyond doubt that the hat worn by Mr. Briggs on the night he was murdered, and of such importance was this considered that, at the request of the commissioners of police, Mr. Briggs, the younger, accompanied Inspector Kerressey, by the second… steamer, the more effectually to complete the evidence necessary for the extradition of Muller'.[59] There was no doubt about the legitimate authority of the detectives to apprehend Müller as 'All the proceedings of the American authorities appear to have been perfectly fair and impartial'.[60] That the whole exercise deserved civil endorsement was not in doubt, especially given that 'The hat and watch of the murdered gentleman were found in the possession of Muller so far as justifying the great exertions made for his capture; for whether guilty or not, the safe custody of the man who possessed these mute witnesses of a horrible crime was an end worth attaining at any cost and trouble'.[61] Praise for the detectives once back in the UK was unconditional, 'The detectives were immediately on the alert, and finally their patience was rewarded',[62] and as 'Inspector Tanner left the station he was cheered lustily',[63] concluding after the trial that 'In this case, the attention bestowed on every incident, from the first discovery of the murder to the close of the trial, will not have been in vain'.[64] On this reading, '... the blood hounds of the law'[65] had succeeded and Muller had been 'Hunted down at last'.[66] Within the context of the civil lexicon, the metaphor of the hunting dog, while emphasising the tenacity, capability and effectiveness of the detectives, reduced Müller to the status of a fleeing animal in fear for its life. The message from the press was that the public and the press were right to have placed their trust in the non-civil sphere actors from the detective force and the Home Office. The brief transition of the detectives from non-civil sphere actors (state law enforcers) to actors of the civil sphere was evident when for a moment they were even regarded as, 'the English officers of justice'.[67]

4.2 Law: The Press's and the Public's Approval of the British Legal System and Trial Proceedings

In the context of legitimacy, the scrutiny, evaluation and endorsement of the effectiveness of law and the legal processes were evident in reports emphasising and endorsing the reasonable nature of the legal processes that were followed. The legal skills of the lawyers were noted approvingly regardless of their message, the eloquence of Müller's defence lawyer in America was commended,[68] 'How admirably logical was Mr. Chauncey Shaffer',[69] but also the capabilities of the Solicitor General in his reply to Müller's case for the defence in the criminal court were greatly admired as 'a masterpiece of legal dissection'.[70] Special admiration was reserved for the Solicitor General's performance, 'It was in the dissection of the *alibi* that the honourable and learned gentleman most successfully showed his readiness, skill, and acumen. With excellent taste he avoided the temptation which a more vulgar practitioner would not have been proof against, and did not seek to influence the jury by a single word relative to the degraded characters of the *alibi* witnesses. He took their facts as facts, and with extraordinary dexterity endeavoured to show that they were the strongest confirmation of his case'.[71] For the *Daily News*, these skills paid off and 'The depreciation of the whole *alibi* case by the use of the single epithet "*alibi clock*", was at once felt by the whole court'.[72] The idea that English law would inevitably be successful in (while operating reasonably and fairly) bringing a criminal to account was expanded on at length in the London Illustrated News, which reflected on the idea that murder did 'bring home to us one of the most impressive lessons of the history of crime. It is this; that men cannot wholly disentangle themselves from the traces of their past actions … For weeks past he has been talking of emigrating to America, and thither, a few days after the murder, he has sailed, without a shade of suspicion upon him… And now, mark how the minutest traces of Muller's recent life, wholly unconnected as they were with his crimes, reappear in damning evidence against him'.[73] The 'deadly skill' of the prosecution was emphasised as something which had a legitimate purity of purpose requiring consummate and legitimate skills, so 'Muller kept his seat and looked perfectly composed whilst the Solicitor-General was thus weaving the web of death round him'.[74] The press was at pains to emphasise the propriety of the proceedings, 'The extraordinary trial, so ably conducted and so patiently heard',[75] comprised a 'jury who tried him [that] were most impartially chosen'.[76] Procedures were followed that ensured that Müller wasn't disadvantaged, with the 'investigation … accordingly adjourned to the following day, in order that counsel for the prisoner might be employed'.[77] *The Times* remarked that, 'Whatever view might be taken of the case, it would be but an act of simple justice to allow counsel for the defence an opportunity to examine the testimony adduced against the unfortunate client'.[78] As Müller 'had no means of attaining legal assistance, counsel was assigned him by the court'.[79] The peaceful nature of the law in contrast to the violent activity perpetrated by the murder was emphasised, lending weight to its civilising purpose, 'The calmness, the patient carefulness, and the impartiality with which the trial of the culprit has been conducted must add to the satisfaction with which the Englishmen regard its issue. From first to last administrative or judicial step has been taken of which the accused could make a reasonable complaint … The facts, however, and the facts only, thoroughly sifted as they were, condemned the accused'.[80] The reasonable nature of the processes of the English legal system was widely emphasised in a number of ways. Müller's decision to waive his right to have a mixed jury composed of English and German citizen in the view of *The Daily Telegraph* 'was undoubtedly a wise one'.[81] The idea that the accused was innocent until proven guilty was given prominence, and in the context of Müller's arrival back in the UK, the *Daily News* reported that 'The accused was a foreigner, a German by birth, who had a few days since arrived on these shores in the ordinary course of transit. When any man thus lands here he is presumed to be innocent of any crime. The law throws around him that shield of presumptive innocence, and he is secure; and that power which sends forth fleets and armies, and which on this occasion is embodied in your Honour, is here to shield and defend him from any violation of that principle'.[82] *The Times* also emphasised the civilised nature of the English legal process, 'If there is any disposition on the part of his country men to regard the impending trial from the point of nationality, we would merely observe that had an Englishman been arrested in Germany on such an accusation we should all heartily desire he might be dealt with in strict accordance with the weight of the evidence against him, to whatever decision the proofs might lead'.[83] Given that 'He was defended, owing to the generosity of his compatriots in this country, by all that legal ability and ingenuity,[84] Müller's endorsement of and belief in the fairness of the English legal system was welcomed'. When the 'constable told him that all government prosecutions were conducted at Bow-street. He replied, "well it is of no consequence. I shall get justice wherever it is"'.[85] Following the sentencing of Müller, the press reflected that, 'There has never been the slightest indecorum or disorder in the court, crowded though it has always been, and the approaches to it have always been kept clear for the passage of witnesses and other persons having legitimate business there. The trial was conducted in a manner so well calculated to impress a spectator with the majesty of the law and the dignity of its administration in this country, and no one present could have failed to be struck with the solemnity with which the inquiry was invested from beginning to end'.[86]

According to the press, Müller spoke approvingly of English law though what he actually said was disputed. *Lloyd's Weekly Newspaper* noted that in fact although 'the "actual words" uttered by Muller after his sentence are under discussion',[87] the paper still goes on to quote 'one who was accommodated with a seat in the dock'[88] who reported Müller as saying after the sentence of death was passed, 'I wish to say I am satisfied with my trial, I knew this would come, because it is the English law'.[89] *The Times* reporting on Müller's alleged words a week earlier appeared to be more certain about Müller's response, which it quoted as, 'I should like to say something. I am, at all events, satisfied with the sentence which your Lordship has passed, I know very well it is that which the law of the country prescribes'.[90] Relatively comfortable in their assessment of the propriety of the trial, an admonishment was issued by the *Daily News* to the GLPS which had been working to first prove Müller's innocence and then, following the guilty verdict, to delay the execution so that further investigation might be undertaken. The GLPS was admonished and directed to recognise the legitimacy and authority of English law, 'Now that the fruitlessness of the efforts made to save MULLER'S life is apparent … with regard to Englishmen, we may expect that they will not only acquiesce in, but as far as may be necessary, support the administration of the law'.[91] *The Daily Telegraph* advised its readers that following the public hanging of Müller, 'we must still think that with its brief agony of to-day a great crime was legally expiated'.[92] For *The Times*, the issue was that the swift and successful execution of the law might well have acted to prevent others from others engaging in such a crime as 'there is an actual and a virtual incompleteness in the legal proceedings of the case; but the task of the executive has been most thoroughly performed. As soon as the track of the criminal was discovered not an hour was lost. Considering the immense distance to be traversed before the police could be sure that the fugitive had not by some chance escaped, justice has been really "swift in its arrest." The means now at the disposal of authority, if evil doers ever make any rational estimate of consequences, might well stay their hands before the deed is accomplished'.[93] For *Lloyd's Weekly London Newspaper*, leading with the headline 'Condemned to Death', support for the civil institutions of the law and the press to conquer wrongdoing was unequivocal, 'It is the conviction of murder that will be a lesson to evil-doers, showing them, as it does, how the law, with its preset machinery, aided by the world wide publicity of the press, can, in these days, battle the deepest laid schemes, and bring the most subtle-witted criminal to judgement'.[94] In this, 'the awful presence of Authority, and the majesty of Law, without which the whole order of society would relapse into barbarism, and our boasted civilisation sink into savagery'[95] were seen to be vital elements of civilised society. After Müller's execution, the press was still reassuring its readers, reporting that 'It is understood (according to the Observer of yesterday), that a communication has been made by the Secretary of State to the judges who presided at the trial, with reference to the case, as to their opinions of the verdict. It is customary in all cases of capital convictions for such an application to be made, and it is said that both the Lord Chief Baron and Mr. Baron Martin, in reply, stated that they considered the evidence entirely conclusive, and that they saw no reason to doubt the propriety of the verdict',[96] especially given that readers 'would shudder at the thought than an innocent man was in danger'.[97]

In the context of the civil lexicon, the judgement of the press was straightforwardly an endorsement of extant civil values regarding the police and the courts, but it also revealed something else. Namely (and perfectly consistently) that legal proceeding could be improved to fit more closely to the 'reasonable' nature of English Law and that they could become more civil and more legitimate. This was, however, by no means a universally held view. Convinced about the soundness of the judicial proceedings, the *Daily News* referred to the case against Müller as being 'not a chain which breaks at its weakest point ... [but] a solid pyramid of facts, rising to an apex of conviction'.[98] *The Times* was slightly more cautious in its views about the certainty of the chain of circumstantial evidence. Nonetheless, it sought to reassure readers that the right decision had been reached, reporting that although 'we may never know the precise circumstances of the deed, that Franz Muller committed it is a certain as any human conclusion can be ... The result of the whole investigation made it impossible for the jury to return any verdict but Guilty'.[99]

However, Müller's comment that, 'I have not been convicted on a true statement of the facts, but on a false statement'[100] and several inconsistencies in the detectives' work that came to light during the trial were picked up by the press. For example, 'the shopman was taken by Mr. Beard into the convict's cell, in the presence of the Governor, but Muller, it is said, did not recognize him, nor did the stranger recollect having seen the convict before'.[101] Disapproval of the attempt to wrongly connect Müller to other crimes was also evident in the reporting, 'an attempt has been made to connect Muller with the murder of the young woman Emma Jackson, which took place in a house of ill fame in George-street … from some alleged similarity in personal appearance between him and the man, a foreigner, who had accompanied her to the house, and who was last seen in her company'[102] and 'This is not the first time a convict under sentence of death has had other murders laid to his charge. It is somewhat common practice in the case of noted criminals'.[103] Concern about the making of assumptions about Müller's guilt had briefly been expressed by *The Daily Telegraph* when it reflected that, 'It has been assumed – but, as we think, erroneously – that the evidence just received from America respecting Franz Muller conclusively proves his guilt'.[104]

Legal inconsistencies and seeming unfairness raised questions and doubts 'in the minds of all who see and know how fallable [sic] is human law'.[105] Qualms about the effectiveness of the law as a civilising force and in particular the extent to which public hanging could be seen as a deterrent against further criminal acts were also raised 'The gallows as a moraliser is at best a rough one. It is not, as a general rule, supposed to address the educated and refined, but to preach its bitter lesson to the hordes of lesser criminals, it draws around it to see a greater criminal die'.[106] Despite press and public relief that Müller finally confessed at the gallows, which for many justified the execution, the idea of a public hanging as an uncivilised and unsuitable mode of punishment in an enlightened and more progressive modern era was a subject for discussion and contestation. The *Evening Star* questioned the English legal system, endorsing the need to change existing law for civil purposes asserting that, 'it is surely worthy of most serious consideration whether a regard to the character of English justice does not demand further inquiry'.[107] *The Daily Telegraph* remarked that 'It may be impractical, "Utopian" and "sentimental" and so forth, to hope that capital punishment will be abolished in our time; but at least we suppose there is nothing to be censored in the wish that it could be, and that the first example of maintaining the sacredness of life might be met by the law itself'.[108]

As we saw in Chapter 6, the public spectacle of Franz Müller's execution created a sensation. The conduct of the public at the execution was extensively reported and condemned in the press as being little better than that of a lynch mob marked by drunkenness and fighting. Many members of the crowd were reported to have shouted out 'Hats off' as

Müller was 'dropped and executed'.[109] *Reynolds's Newspaper* reported on the 'uselessness' of public hanging, asserting that 'The class of half-brutes, half-fiends, who are only restrained from the commission of vile and violent deeds through the influence of terror, have become so inured to the spectacle and contemplation of the gallows that it has ceased to have any terror for them'.[110] These half-brutes and half-fiends[111] were portrayed by *Reynolds's Newspaper* as a threat to civilised society and as an insensate and degenerate public that has retained a capacity for murder despite the fearful example of a public execution. This provided a somewhat convoluted way for a radical newspaper to disavow the legitimacy of public hanging. This lack of legitimacy accorded to public hanging was not because of its barbaric nature, or the voyeuristic spectacle it accorded, but rather because it was seen by some of the other newspapers as ceasing to be a deterrent. 'Hence, while it cannot be proved that any good can come from drawing the seam of a great city to see a malefactor hanged in a public place, it is capable of demonstration that much harm might be prevented by removing such spectacles from the public gaze'.[112] The crowd that gathered at Müller's hanging was described as one 'hungry' for excitement, full of 'vagrants' who '"bonneted" and sometimes garotted, and always plundered any person whose dress led them to think him worth the trouble'.[113] Among the crowd, 'there were very few women; and even these were generally of the lowest and poorest class'.[114] In short, those of a civil disposition (the civil 'we') found such events 'abhorrent'.[115] In the condemnation of public hangings as an entertainment spectacle rather than a deterrent, the press was largely in accordance with a more liberal form of public and political sentiment that was developing at the time,[116] with *Lloyd's Weekly Newspaper* remarking that 'Every public execution is an injury done to public morals'.[117]

One last point needs to be made with regard to the civil judgements made by the press. The disquiet over the legitimacy of Müller's treatment did somewhat undermine the parallel strands of civil endorsement of the police and legal proceedings, and therefore, it should be noted that for public and press alike, the fear that an innocent man might have been hanged was at the same time roundly offset by a civil endorsement of the law and its civilising effects.

The reliability of the formal proceedings of the legal institutions and the possibility that the law might well act as a deterrent were also weighed against the possibility that not all evidence had come to light, so it is perhaps not surprising that the *Sunday Times*, reflecting on the trial and Müller's execution, sought to reassure its readers that Müller had 'repeatedly stated that he had a fair trial'.[118] The issue of whether Müller had a fair trial leads us to the question of justice and how it was assessed and reported.

4.3   Justice: The Press's Relief and Self-Scrutiny

The civil lexicon of justice was also used to express misgivings about the possibilities of injustice towards Müller and doubts about his guilt which, it must be noted, were reported alongside declarations of certainty that justice had been done. Leading up to his execution, Müller's lack of a confession was disquieting, particularly his comment that 'I would indeed confess, had I committed it, if for the sake of my parents only, that they should not think I could die with a lie on my lips'.[119] Müller's declaration of his innocence made in 'this solemn assertion, and all the evidence which the German society had managed to scrape together, had at the end of last week unsettled the public mind as to the condemned convict's guilt'.[120] The civil tensions within existing law and legal procedures needed to be addressed because, although fair 'A case like this … is disquieting to the conscience. We see by it how confident men may be, how conscientious as jurymen and judges, and yet how far from the truth. We see, in short that it is not safe to take human life, even where the very strongest circumstantial evidence seems to fasten guilt upon the accused'.[121] Problematically, 'circumstantial evidence had convicted the wrong man before and that this was a failure of justice and is disquieting to the conscience'.[122] Not only were the judges and jury not infallible there was also the problem that although 'Muller was tried fairly by a jury; … he was hooted and prejudged before he was tried. The public anger lusted after an object: and while Muller was on his way back from America, it had been fixed upon him'.[123] A letter from a member of the public in a newspaper clipping in the Home Office files expressed reservations about the sentence of death, 'After all, Muller has nothing but circumstantial evidence against him'.[124] The writer went on to say 'let it not be forgotten that many and many a time before the apparent indications of evidence just as clear have been proved to be altogether wrong'. The letter, in common with observations in several other newspapers,[125] cited an example of when a fatal mistake was made. 'The circumstantial evidence against Eliza Fenning, some fifty years ago, was as least as strong as that against Muller. Yet, in the opinion of some of the ablest judges and lawyers of our time, Eliza Fenning was innocent of the crime for which she was executed'.[126]

In the press's and in the public's calls for justice and fair treatment for Müller, doubts were expressed about the quality of the counsel for the defence. Concern was also expressed that Müller may have suffered an injustice that went to the heart of the criminal justice system.[127] *The Evening Standard* expressed concern that the Solicitor General, who had the last word, undermined the strength of the defence statement. 'Had Mr. Serjeant PARRY relied upon his own eloquence, and addressed the jury with his customary pathos, without giving the Solicitor General the advantage of speaking the last word before the summing up, there would have been a far better chance for the prisoner than that which presented itself after the crushing reply for the Crown'.[128] *The Daily Telegraph* was more critical remarking that 'the singularly able but unsatisfactory speed in which Serjeant PARRY endeavoured to obtain the acquittal of his client',[129] meant that 'it was felt that the defence for the prisoner was fatally inconclusive'.[130] Similarly critical *The Evening Standard* commented that 'the witnesses for the defence strengthened the case for the prosecution, and the wretched attempt at an *alibi* fastened the noose round the prisoner's neck',[131] 'and throughout the case neither the prosecution nor the defence seemed to present any great elements of strength'.[132] *The Daily Telegraph* questioned the quality of the evidence remarking that 'In fact, it is difficult to avoid the impression that both the prosecution and the defence are conscious of certain flaws in their respective briefs, and are more anxious to conceal their weakness than to exhibit their strength',[133] concluding two days later that 'The defence was virtually based on the hope that they might feel too perplexed to come to any decision'.[134] In this vein, the *Daily News* observed that, 'A reservation of defence is always a sign of weakness; and in this case the tenor of the cross-examination of witnesses for the prosecution showed that it was weaker than ordinary'.[135] *The Daily Telegraph* also reported that, 'One story is good till the other side is told, and during the course of yesterday's investigation the prosecution had it pretty well their own way. In fact, if we may borrow a cricketing metaphor yesterday was the innings of the prosecution and it was not for the interest of the defence to bowl out most of their adversary's batters'.[136] After sentencing, but two weeks before the execution, the newspaper went on to express its doubts about the verdict. 'The sole fatal certainty is that, though we may have got at the truth, we have not got at the whole truth; and with nothing less will the public mind rest absolutely contented ... it is probable that the public will find a lurking doubt whether we have at present got to the bottom of the mystery'.[137] *Reynolds's Newspaper* went further and openly disputed the soundness of the verdict, asking in a front page headline 'Is Muller the murderer of Mr Briggs?', outlining the concerns that 'should Muller be executed before the doubts which now harass the public mind have been dispelled', there will be 'myriads who believe that he has been judicially murdered'.[138] The article devoted a paragraph to the problems regarding the evidence against Müller and provided a list of innocent people who had been wrongly executed. Six days after Müller's confession and execution, *Lloyd's Weekly London Newspaper* ran the front page headline, 'GUILTY OR NOT GUILTY?'.[139] The article was portentous in tone, implying that there had been too quick a rush to execute Müller. *Lloyd's Weekly London Newspaper* was in synch with public sentiment which had been calling for greater due diligence. There had been numerous letters to the Home Office[140] from the time of the guilty verdict and Müller's sentencing (29 October 1864) and his execution (14 November 1864) as well as letters published in newspapers.[141] Speaking on behalf of the public, the newspaper pointed out that 'The people at a distance – impartial readers who know the case only through the newspapers ... hoped that time would be given to the believers in Muller's innocence to search their case in his favour fully out, and to give him the benefit of every doubt they could raise. The idea was agony to every right-thinking mind, that a man, whom many believed to be innocent was about to suffer an ignominious death at the hands of the common hangman'[142] and earlier it had been observed by *Illustrated London News* that in fact 'The manner in which the crime was traced to him [Müller] is curious'.[143]

Despite these misgivings following the trial and the guilty verdict (but prior to Müller's confession), the same newspapers through their discursive styles of reporting also provided assurances that justice had been done through due process and that the verdict was indeed the correct one. 'We now know, and the countrymen of the condemned man also know, that there ought not to rest on the mind of any human being the shadow of a doubt that on the night of the 9th of July last Muller ... committed this crime'.[144] For *The Times*, 'The evidence for the prosecution was clear, positive, and unshaken by all the efforts of the prisoner's counsel, the evidence for the defence not only did not exculpate him, but rather tended to increase the probability of his guilt'.[145] For *the Illustrated London News*, 'It [was] satisfactory to find the atrocity brought home to the delinquent, even under circumstances peculiarly favourable to his escape, by evidence of all but invincible force'.[146] Reassurance offered to the readers about the safety of the verdict,[147] with the *Daily News*, assuming the role of overseer of justice, offering congratulations on the way in which justice had been dispensed and emphasising the desirability of public trust in the civil and non-civil institutions that brought Müller to account in a way that accorded with esteemed civil values. As far as that newspaper was concerned, 'He was well befriended: he was defended by most able counsel; the jury was selected with care; the judges were such as we might be proud to put forward as the representatives of the judicial bench; and the verdict was that of a unanimous court'.[148] In particular, that English justice should be seen to be infallible was important to the press. *The Daily Telegraph* was at pains to point out that 'The discovery of the murderer of Mr. Briggs is a matter of great moment; but there is an object which is even more momentous and that is the due administration of English justice'.[149] A belief in the soundness of the judicial system was expressed strongly and with confidence: 'No prudent jury would convict a man simply on the ground that the narrative of his supposed guilt is reconcilable with known circumstances: nor even on the ground that the hypothesis of his guilt is more probable than any other'.[150] Later, those who had questioned the fairness of English justice were offered the reassurance that 'The harsh censures which have been passed on English justice in the present case will recoil on the hands of their authors. No prisoner ever entered the dock with surer guarantees of a fair and impartial trial than did FRANZ MULLER on the 27th of October'.[151]

Though in the interest of fair play to the press, it needs to be noted that it went to some length to point out that prejudices against the prisoner might arise and should be guarded against: 'for the sake of English justice and fair play, we must exhort the public, who actually include the jurymen, by whom the prisoner will be tried, not to be led away in this matter … In the first place, we refer to the by no means uncommon mistake which allows the natural indignation excited by a crime of peculiar atrocity to create a prejudice against the prisoner at the bar'.[152] The claim that 'We are anxious that this wretched man should not be condemned on mere surmise, but only on the clearest and most certain testimony'[153] also exhorted the public to be part of the fair-minded process and to avoid prejudice and cast itself as 'judicious observers of this remarkable trial'.[154] The civil 'we' who were judicious observers were seen as active citizens, who were keen to oversee that justice was done. 'We do not refer to those who resign themselves to a passive and unintelligent approval of whatever the courts decide. There is an active, rational, and useful occurrence of public opinion in the processes of criminal justice which it is most desirable to recognise and guard from perversion'.[155] Furthermore, and again in the spirit of fairness, the press portrayed the GLPS in its endeavours to support Müller as fair-minded and correctly tenacious. It was also reported before Müller's trial that 'The society state, it is said, they have a clear case of alibi for Muller',[156] and that since 'the trial and conviction of Franz Muller for the murder of Mr. Briggs, the German Legal Protection society, who, notwithstanding the verdict of the jury, will hold to their belief of the prisoner's innocence in respect of the crime, have continued their investigations with unremitting assiduity.[157] In this, 'The members of the society, in their zeal that their unfortunate countryman should be properly defended, are only anxious that he should have the means of proving, if possible, his innocence, and the observations at the meeting of the utter abhorrence entertained of the foul crime and its perpetrator exhibited an anxious wish that should the guilt be clearly brought home justice should have its due'.[158] This was particularly the case given 'that there are a good many links wanting before the evidence will be sufficient to bring home the charge conclusively to the prisoner'.[159] Equally fairly reported was their meeting with the Home Secretary 'to have an interview with Sir George Grey [The Home Secretary], on his return to town, to urge a commutation of the sentence'.[160] *The Times* printed an appeal from the GLPS in its newspaper, 'The committee of the German Legal Protection Society beg the powerful aid of your journal in making known to the English public the fact that their committee will sit in permanence at Boyd's Hotel … until the answer to their memorial has been received from the Secretary of State. The committee are stimulated to make this special appeal by the circumstance that important evidence … as they believe, to exonerate their countrymen has presented itself almost at the last moment before the presentation for their memorial'.[161] The reporting of the GLPS and the provision of space for it to express views that were contrary to that of the jury and much of public sentiment, allowing dissent to be expressed. This was consistent with *The Times*'s earlier comment that 'It is satisfactory to know that, though poor and personally friendless, he had all the advantages that money and friends could procure. The Germans in London took up his cause with zeal, and he was defended by able and experienced counsel. But no real defence was possible'.[162] The *Daily News* responded to the evidence offered by the GLPS in its Memorial to the Home Secretary and the changing public mood, reporting two days before the execution that 'the dissentient minority is rapidly increasing' although, as if to reassure itself and its readers, asserted, without any sound empirical evidence that, '[T]he majority no doubt hold as firmly as ever their belief in Muller's guilt'.[163]

Supporting the premise that justice had been done, the last minute confession of Müller was met with great relief and was seen to legitimate the sentence and remove any doubts about injustice. *Lloyd's Weekly London Newspaper* summed up the press and public mood in its report that 'Happily, Muller confessed before he met his death. Had he gone stubbornly before his God with his great sin unconfessed upon his head, there would have been very many people in this country, and abroad, who would have said that it was possible he was a martyr to an overwhelmingly fatal concurrence of circumstances'.[164] Similarly, *The Daily Telegraph* was relieved that justice had been served, 'Muller has confessed. The relief which this announcement has brought to millions must be regarded as some proof of the uneasiness which arises from the necessity of taking life for life, when justice can only be satisfied by probabilities amounting to such cogent argument and demonstration as would suffice to rule our ordinary affairs'.[165] For *The Times* 'His quiet and almost instantaneous death cut short what might have been a full confession. The mere details, however, matter not; enough, at last, was disclosed to show that the sentence of mankind was right'.[166] A sense of relief was also echoed by the *Daily News*, 'that he has confessed is at least as sensible a relief to those who felt convinced of his guilt as to those who persisted in declaring that his death would be a sacrifice; an expiatory sacrifice to a painstruck public, to a baffled police, and an unjust tribunal'.[167] The value of the public execution as a legitimate form of the exercise of justice was expressed at some length in *The Daily Telegraph* which articulated the view that we are 'Hoping believing indeed, that the life taken in the chill air of this November dawn is not sacred thing, an immortal life, we must allow that there is in that final satisfaction of justice, for a crime which threatened to remain a mystery, something profoundly imposing and terribly satisfactory'.[168] The path to justice was not straightforward, but had been served nonetheless and to 'look back far away from the scaffold to-day, and, all along, the road seems plainly marked out with the limping footsteps of justice'.[169]

But relief that justice had been done also elicited a more strident view, one that, although civil in intent, sought to quieten the doubts of all those who had, quite rightly, been free to express them. *The Evening Standard* was keen to emphasise the value of the confession, seeing it as something which would put an end to unwelcome misgivings in order that the civil conscious would be clear, 'the simple confession of solitary guilt possesses one great element of practical value; it stops the clamour of a party whom no other kind of evidence would convince, and we are very glad it comes through the hands of a minister who is himself a German, otherwise the actual confession itself might be disputed'.[170] *The Daily News* issued a stronger warning to those who had fallen into the temptation to attempt to act as judges thereby undermining the proper exercise of legitimate civil justice when it said 'Let us hope it may be a lesson to that distorted national sentiment which identifies itself with a convicted felon; a lesson to amateur judges of criminal appeal; a lesson to philanthropists who, in their abundant tenderness for the assassin, take no account of his victim, and forget that self-preservation is the first law of society as of the individual'.[171] The confession was indeed an important end stop, and speaking on behalf of public sentiment, *The Evening Standard* asserted that 'the public would doubtless have been bored with a heap of maudlin nonsense about the possible hanging of an innocent man, and blockheads would not have been wanting to impugn the moral validity of the sentence by which MULLER was given over to the executioner'.[172] Nonetheless, as *The Evening Standard* observed after Müller's execution, justice of course had been served and yet there remained a little mystery about the case: 'There is no possibility of disputing his guilt, but a certain amount of mystery yet remains undispelled'.[173] Following Müller's confession, the *Daily News* was more acerbic in its views about those who had tried to say that justice had not been done, noting that 'Public discussion is happily free in this country, and there is no subject which is exempt from inquiry. Many persons object to our practice of trying prisoners, and others to our habit of dealing with persons convicted of capital crimes. The field of argument is open to them; but there is one course which is not open, although it has on this occasion been clandestinely entered upon: they have no right to embarrass and obstruct the administration of justice in the supposed interest of any theory'.[174]

The role of the press in reporting the story in the context of legitimacy was not immune from self-scrutiny. Two months before Müller's trial, *The Daily Telegraph* took a civil tone when it pointed out that 'The oath of the juryman requires that he should give his verdict according to the evidence, and nothing else ought to guide him, but in a case in which tongue and pens have been so busy as in that of Muller, it is almost beyond hope that the jurymen should be absolutely without prejudgment; and certainly the perusal of the leading articles which speak of his conviction in the optative mood is not conducive to impartiality'.[175] Similarly without any sense of self-reflection, *Lloyd's Weekly London Newspaper* pointed out that 'It is unfair towards a prisoner to permit his talk with the detective, or the policeman, to be handed to reporters for the satisfaction of the morbid appetite of the crowd. The accused is made to criminate [sic] himself by confused and conflicting statements, while retailers of gossip about him are left free to create a strong prejudice against an untried man, by publishing his unguarded sayings and doings'.[176] The *Sunday Times* took a more self-righteous position in its criticism of some other newspapers, in a way that is reminiscent of today, entreating the respectable press to take more responsibility in its coverage. 'We hope our contemporaries will now fulfil theirs [duty], by abstaining from all such comments as might have a tendency to bias that jury either in favour of or against the prisoner. The scandalous manner in which some of the cheap papers have discussed the question of Muller's guilt or innocence has elicited the reprehension even of foreign journalists'.[177] Similarly, *Lloyd's Weekly London Newspaper* expressed the view that 'The untried man is, before the law, innocent. Then why should he be kept under the microscope of the penny-a-liner from the moment of his capture until he is tried? On Monday morning last, every newspaper was choked with details about the sleep, the food, the manner, and the talk of Muller'.[178] *The Daily Telegraph* took an equally tendentious moral tone, 'We do not remember to have seen the case against an unconvicted man so distinctly prejudiced, nor can we recall a greater violation of the constitutional rule which forbids public expressions of opinion on merits of causes pending before the judicature.[179] In this way, the press (a month or so before the trial) emphasised the possibility of injustice and that the wrong man may have been accused. This brought to the readers' attention that 'In fact, the mystery still remains as intricate as ever. On the one side you have a number of coincidences, utterly impossible to account for by any satisfactory explanation, which bring home the crime to the prisoner; on the other, you have the almost complete absence of motive, the difficulty of comprehending how the assault could ever have been perpetrated in so brief a period, and above all, the fact that the prisoner's whole conduct and demeanour, from the time when the offence was perpetrated to the present day, have been inconsistent with all past expectations of the manner in which criminals are apt to behave themselves'.[180]

Parts of the press also reflected on its responsibility not to unduly influence public sentiment, cautioning its readers with the rather pious comment that, 'we should be disregarding the rule which we laid down for ourselves to the discussion of this memorable trial if we presupposed any positive opinion on such incomplete evidence as is now before us'.[181] This was particularly notable as *The Daily Telegraph*, in common with all of the press, did indeed go on to speculate and express both civil and anti-civil sentiment about Müller's innocence or guilt in other parts of its coverage. *The Daily Telegraph* openly assured its readers that although 'We know certain events affecting MULLER which occurred at the time of the murder of Mr. BRIGGS, but we do not know directly that the one man was ever in the presence of the other: therefore, in order to convince MULLER, we have to invent a story which shall not only accord with all the known facts, but shall accord with them much more probably than any other story that could possibly be suggested'.[182]

Some members of the public were not at all convinced by *The Daily Telegraph*'s frequent hypocritical moralising. Someone who signed himself/herself 'DUPLEX' and was published in *The Evening Standard* criticised *The Daily Telegraph* for its *volte-face* regarding assumptions about Müller's innocence and guilt, concluding that 'If Muller is acquitted, thanks to the *Telegraph* of September 8; and if he is hung equal thanks for the lead of 20 July. That is what I call being prepared for all emergencies'.[183] After Müller's trial, *The Daily Telegraph* printed a letter to its editor which expressed alarm that 'The ordeal to which he [Müller] has been submitted has been far more severe than that applied in ordinary cases. Instead of starting with the assumption that a man is innocent till he is proven guilty, the vox populi, had but with few exceptions, at first sight declared Muller guilty'.[184] *The Daily Telegraph* reported that 'independently of the GLPS report,[185] of which the second part has yet to be published, a pamphlet has been found, entitled, "Franz Muller. Thou shalt do no murder!" containing a number of remarkable statements, which if capable of proof, would certainly suggest the necessity of further investigation'.[186] A letter signed by someone using the pseudonym WILL WATCH admitted that his knowledge and ability to assess the situation was limited and he expressed his disquiet that '… it is not at all improbable that … some important facts may be overlooked. My knowledge of the details of this horrible occurrence, and of the subsequent facts that have been elicited, have been entirely derived from the newspaper report'.[187] Indeed, *The Daily Telegraph* admitted two days later that 'The published story of the murder of Mr. Briggs has been told in a manner so fragmentary that it is at present impossible to form that connected and precise idea of it that would be requisite in a judicial examination'.[188]

5 ANTI-CIVIL JUDGEMENTS MADE IN THE NEWS REPORTS

5.1 Legitimate Authority: The Withdrawal of Public Trust in the Detectives

The views of the public regarding its lack of trust in the ability of the detectives successfully to bring a murderer to justice were expressed in letters to the Home Office and to the newspapers—a fact noted in the press, that 'Inspector Kerressey and the other detectives employed in the case have been inundated with letters from all parts of the country, making suggestions for tracing the murderer. One gentleman suggests that by way of discovering the number of persons implicated in the affair the number of first class tickets issued for the train in which the murder was committed should be ascertained, and that everyone who travelled by it should send in their names. At the station at Bow there is a large collection of hats of all shapes and sizes found all over London since the murder and the police have received the names of doubtless the most innocent individuals who returned home hatless or with a black eye on the night in question. These matters are only important in showing the amount of interest taken in the affair out of doors'.[189] Detective Inspector Tanner in particular was in the spotlight[190]—a situation which Colquhoun (2012: 48) likened to being akin to 'sitting at the narrow end of a mighty funnel into which the public were pouring their insinuations, suspicions and fears'. Little reticence was exercised by those who wrote to the Chief Commissioner, Sir Richard Mayne, to offer the police advice about how best to solve the crime and to earn the trust of citizens. In these letters in the Metropolitan Police Archives, dating from July 1864 to January 1865, the general public offered a broad range of advice such as, '… had the police at once called in the aid of a dog of the bloodhound species, the hat left in the carriage of the murder might have proved of the highest value'.[191] Others went further in their investigative advice suggesting that 'an examination of the tickets received at the different stations on the line to see if there is any blood on them'[192] would be a sensible course to follow. Another questioned 'how does he [Mr Tanner] account for the disappearance of the hat worn by the deceased, and the finding of one, proof beyond the doubt not his, in the same compartment of the carriage?'[193] In an unsigned letter printed in *The Evening Standard*, the author bemoaned what he or she perceived to be a lack of common sense exhibited by the authorities, announcing that, 'I have been much surprised that no allusion has been made during the recent trial of Muller to the fact of the hat found in the railway carriage fitting him or not. Surely it has been placed upon his head'.[194] One member of the public claimed that 'I have every reason to think that I can assist in bringing the real murderer of the late Mr. Briggs to justice',[195] while another was concerned enough to write that 'I cannot discover any proof whatever throughout the whole case to satisfy me that Muller really was the murderer of Mr Briggs'.[196] *The Daily Telegraph* declared itself specifically to be on the side of the detecting public when it 'claimed' for the press the merit of 'enlisting the whole people in the cause of the officers of justice'.[197] In the process of discrediting the detective police force, *The Daily Telegraph* went so far as to call for 'making the entire nation a detective for the nonce'.[198]

The need for a quick resolution to the crime, expressed by the press via an anti-civil lexicon, served to undermine 'confidence in the supremacy of law'[199] as it was seen in this context to be too slow and pedestrian given that 'a murder may remain a mystery and its perpetrator escape with impunity'.[200] Speaking on behalf of the public, the *Daily News* reported that 'a most fervent desire was expressed that the perpetrators of the atrocious crime would be brought to justice'.[201] The murder was, it was reported, 'the topic of conversation in all circles'.[202] The press fed a public appetite to undertake the work that the incompetent detective force appeared to be incapable of. Within two days of the murder, it was declared that 'Nothing, we regret to say, has up to the present time, been discovered as to the perpetrators of this diabolical crime',[203] and 'No additional facts of any importance about this horrible affair have transpired since yesterday'.[204] Indeed, the case was in some respects 'involved in greater mystery than ever'[205] because 'The police have little further clue to the murderer'.[206] *Reynolds's Newspaper* was scathing about the police, saying that 'The more Sir Richard Mayne and his men have been weighted in the balance of public opinion and found wanting. Either as preventives or detectives of great atrocities. We give this verdict as the result of our careful study of the records of crime and of police … for many years past'.[207] The paper went on to proclaim that 'It is quite certain that neither Sir Richard Mayne nor his men will be entitled to any pride in their behaviour in this matter',[208] concluding that 'the police have been utterly useless'.[209] Just over a week after the murder, the reporting took a despairing tone given that 'Up to a late hour last night the police had not succeeded in tracing the murderer … the police are endeavouring to trace this man, but as some time has elapsed it seems rather a hopeless case'.[210] *Reynolds's Newspaper* concluded that 'In this, as in other cases, Sir Richard and his creatures resembled a pack of bewildered fox-hounds who had lost the scent'.[211] In this vein, without any cited evidence, *Lloyd's Weekly London Newspaper* reported that 'The police seem to feel that after their many failures of late years the present case puts them on their trial, and that if their exertions are not rewarded with success it will be a blot on the detective police system of this country'.[212]

Even after the detectives had left to pursue Müller to America and the extradition hearing had been successfully completed, the coverage of the detectives' activities, which via the civil lexicon had expressed a great deal of optimism and excitement, also contained anti-civil asides in the same reports. *The Evening Standard* expressed its concern that it was 'to be hoped that no mistake will be made, or has been made, in the hasty getting up of the case, and that – always supposing the man to be guilty – sufficient evidence will be forthcoming to satisfy the New York magistrates, and justify them in acting upon the terms of the extradition treaty with this country'.[213] This concern was founded on the basis of rumours that had been circulating: 'Since the commencement of the pursuit there have been rumours in circulation that the English officers awaiting the arrival of the Victoria at New York had not in their possession all the evidence necessary, or that they might have secured, had their departure from this country not been so hurried. It is to be hoped that those rumours are unfounded, or that, if correct, the defect has ere been remedied by the foresight of the home authorities, and by the dispatch to New York of everything requisite to complete the chain of evidence'.[214]

The lack of trust in the police was also expressed in letters from the public to the newspapers. In one letter addressed to the Editor of the *Sunday Times*, it was stated that 'no apology is needed for addressing you in continuation, on the subject of the incapacity of the police, especially as facts elicited since your last publication tend to place that incapacity in still more glaring light'.[215] In another letter to the same newspaper, the writer pointed to the fact that 'some apparent difficulties in Muller's case, that have in a measure been caused by the incapacities of the police'.[216] A reprint of a letter in a column entitled 'German view of the Muller Case' stated that 'In our opinion the chief reproach should be laid at the door of the police'.[217]

The dismissal of the detectives as incompetent sits strangely alongside the use of the civil lexicon to almost slavishly follow and approve of their activities. The anti-civil lexicon does, however, provide space for unfounded speculation and opinion. The requirement for fast news updates from those involved in a slower official process is of course one of the aspects of journalism, beautifully captured in many fictional books and films, where the tenacious journalist is nothing but a nuisance, a vulture feeding off other people's misery and a thorn in the side of officials. While such journalism is indeed required to feed a 'hungry news machine', in the context of the anti-civil lexicon, speculation can give rise to damaging exaggeration or inaccuracies, that can have long-term consequences for the exercise of justice and fairness—something that was picked up on by some elements of the press in 1864. Without a credible or authoritative external source of information, it is possible to invent or import another more strident and interesting one to fill its place, as *Lloyd's Weekly London Newspaper* recognised: 'Although we have nothing of interest from the police, we may, nevertheless, have something to communicate to the public which they will read with certain interest; and to these bare statements of ours it may be pardonable to add a little by way of speculation and hypothesis'.[218] What followed was full of qualifying words such as 'very likely', 'it is probable', which revealed that not only did the press admit it was reliant on the police as sources of information, but that it had a relatively honest way of flagging up some of its own speculation. In contemporary news reporting, the demands of immediacy, competition from other news suppliers and the requirement to constantly update and refresh information place greater pressure on reporters continuously to provide material that will keep their audiences' interest, with the likelihood that it reduces their impulse to signal any uncertainty about the veracity of their reporting to their audiences.

5.2 Justice: The Press Investigation and Trial of Müller

The press itself took on the role of a detective and its news reports can be seen as testimonies to its own efforts to solve the crime. In fact, in order to keep the public interested, it variously encouraged the public to be fearful or fascinated by the crime, thereby generating stronger interest and greater desire for the crime to be solved. While this intensifying interest was driven by the press itself, it was also reported as evidence of the public's interest in the story. One of the effects of this type of circular amplification was that the press created for itself the need to generate more copy. This in turn led the press to speculate about how the crime was committed, 'If a man meditated a robbery and a murder on the line of the railway between the city and Hackney-wick and desired to adopt a plan which would render his safety at all possible, a careful examination of the line would be an obvious precaution, and no spot could be selected which could give a better chance of escape than that of which the murder of Mr Briggs was actually committed'.[219] *Lloyd's Weekly London Newspaper*, taking upon itself to act as a detective, concluded that 'There is one fact of which we are quite satisfied, by the sickening evidence of the blood outside the carriage: it was anything but a lifeless body that was thrown or thrust out upon the line. The last fierce blow was given as the victim struggled on the outer step. Very likely he had used his stick'.[220] Speculation about the nature of the crime, as well as the character/nature of Müller himself, provided interesting copy and filled newspaper columns, a requirement which has only grown over the years as a 24/7 news cycle increasingly and extensively demands new and interesting copy to move the story on. *The Daily Telegraph*, which notably switched its judgements about the innocence or guilt of Müller regularly, found it difficult to reconcile Müller's appearance and behaviour with the crime he was accused of committing. 'if judgment had to be formed on probabilities along, the balance of evidence, so far on his conduct both before and after the date of murder is concerned, would be strongly in favour of the suspected man'.[221] *The Daily Telegraph* later acknowledged that many different stories had been told which were likely to confuse the public, but nonetheless went on to add to it with further consideration of the evidence, 'The public has been so puzzled and bewildered by a multitude of fragmentary stories, that our simple statement as to the effect of the evidence is likely to cause cavil'.[222] The inappropriateness of their own newspaper as regards the weighing up of evidence and the production of theories went, so it appears, quite unnoticed by the paper. This was in spite of its earlier moralising to the contrary, going on to observe that, 'We believe, however, it is the common experience of our courts of justice, that criminals suddenly captured either make no defence, or make up some story which is demonstrably untrue'.[223] Convinced of Müller's guilt, *The Daily Telegraph* had earlier declared that 'the burden of proof rests with the defence',[224] but in the press, Müller was already convicted of murder, 'That the man just captured on board of the Victoria packet-ship is really the assassin of the unfortunate Mr Briggs appears hardly to admit of a doubt'.[225] The anti-civil lexicon was used largely to convict Müller as guilty before the trial had even taken place. In the case of the invariant civil concern of identity, his characteristics and strangeness were discussed in detail (see Chapter 6), whereas in the invariant civil concern of legitimacy he was labelled as the murderer as soon as his identity was released. That the press assumed the authority to make such a judgement was problematic as it appears to have helped to shape public sentiment up to the trial. Headlines such as 'Discovery of the murderer',[226] 'Discovery of the Murderer – His flight to America'[227] and 'DISCOVERY OF THE MURDERER OF MR BRIGGS'[228] were common across national and regional newspapers within two weeks of the murder when the name of the suspect was released by the police. The press was quick to condemn the suspect as the killer, as 'Very little doubt can be felt, after certain facts which transpired yesterday afternoon, that the police are now on the track of the man who murdered Mr. Briggs',[229] similarly 'Very little doubt, if any, can now be felt by the most sceptical, that the murderer of the ill-fated Mr, Briggs has been discovered'.[230] *The Times* expressed a desire that the suspect would be found in the possession of the missing watch, to put an end to speculation and allow a conviction to take place, 'No trace whatever has been found of the watch itself, and it may be fairly expected, and for the ends of justice hoped, that Muller still has it in his possession, and that it will be found upon him, so as to constitute and undoubted link in the chain of evidence'.[231] The expression of certainty of guilt was reinforced via small snippets of information appearing in the press for several weeks after Müller had travelled to New York. *The Daily News* reported that 'the captain detailed the second mate of the vessel to keep Muller under his immediate surveillance, though without, if possible, exciting his suspicion that such was the case. This the mate did, but as the vessel came near the light ship an excursion boat came alongside, and, seeing the name of the vessel, some person shouted out: "How are you, Muller, the murderer?"'.[232]

Speculation about Müller's motives required the development of theories to fit with the certainty that he was without doubt the killer, *The Times* observed that 'To the second transaction he seems to have been driven by want of money, and it left another clue to his proceedings in the interval between the deed of which he is accused and his embarkation'.[233] Despite Lloyd's weekly comments about the press intrusion on 25 September, on 11 September 1864 the same paper had reported on the preparations for the arrest referring conclusively to 'the man who may safely now be called the murderer of Mr. Briggs'.[234] The only conclusion that was drawn in the press as Müller arrived in Liverpool on 16 September 1864 was that 'The evidence that has been adduced shows clearly and conclusively that the prisoner is guilty of the murder of Mr Briggs, with which he is charged'.[235] Following the Coroner's jury's verdict of 'wilful murder' (which did not determine by whom the murder had been committed), the *Daily News* concluded that, 'The further the case goes the more the evidence is piled up against the prisoner, and the sharp decisive way in which this coroner and the coroner's jury dealt with it yesterday morning at Hackney very fairly represents the popular feeling. The verdict of that jury was wilful murder' against the prisoner.[236] A member of the public writing to the *Sunday Times* just over a month before Müller's trial perhaps summarised the then prevailing anti-civil mood when he wrote about 'a quoted article from some silly country paper, apparently written for the nonce, and perhaps to order; an absurd view from one "correspondent" keeps the "idea" of possible innocence alive'.[237]

In the anti-civil lexicon of legitimacy, the support for Müller by the GLPS, whose Memorial to the Home Secretary was reprinted in most newspapers, was seen to be unnecessary and destabilising. For example, the *Sunday Times* commented that 'As we predicted, efforts are being made to induce Sir George Grey to advise her Majesty to reprieve the murderer of Mr Briggs. The German Legal Protection Society deserves great credit for the zeal with which the defence of Müller was conducted; but we cannot approve the course of action on which they have now entered. We do not see, in the first place, now a reasonable doubt can be entertained of the guilt of the condemned man; and secondly, the *national* aspect given in the agitation for the commutation of his sentence seems, to us, to rob it of much of the authority it might otherwise claim'.[238] With the use of the anti-civil lexicon, the press took a partial rather than an impartial approach to the forthcoming court case. There are both assertion of guilt and an implicit endorsement of the importance of civil liberties and justice for some but not others, and importantly, it was explicitly non-solidarising in its intent. The sentiment derived from the idea that English law is above scrutiny, negating the need for transparency or accountability of power holders in their actions against others. The GLPS memorial outlined in some detail particular areas of doubt with regard to the evidence presented at the trial, raising doubts as to Müller's guilt. The efforts of the GLPS were met with exasperation in some quarters with the *Daily News* observing that 'The Germans, we fear, will not be convinced that their countryman has not been murdered'.[239] The day after Müller's execution *The Evening Standard* commented that 'We hope the German Legal Protection Society is now satisfied',[240] the tone of which conveyed a desire for the GLPS to desist in its unconstitutional efforts on Müller's behalf. The implicit criticism also pointed to *The Evening Standard*'s view that such activity may cause unrest and in this way the newspaper was seeking to shut down any further civil protest and draw a line under the whole affair.

6 Summary

It was in the context of the invariant civil concern of legitimacy that the press was at its most undecided and changeable, and because of this, it occasionally provided fragmentary and confusing coverage. On the one hand, it was at great pains to emphasise the legitimacy, fairness and civil nature of English authority, law and justice by endorsing their civil value, embracing public sentiment about the need for fairness and support for the underdog, while simultaneously rejecting the need for any major structural changes, other than that the death penalty should be undertaken in private (although the views on why this should be the case varied). On the other hand and with sometimes breathtaking hypocrisy, the press argued that Müller was denied a fair trial because of the nature of the press coverage. The press undermined the efforts of the detectives, undertook speculation about the case, and condemned Müller as the murderer before his trial. In its fragmentary and confusing coverage, the press was non-solidarising and protected existing inequalities and did not meaningfully scrutinise the biases in the processes of authority, law and justice. It rejected institutional change and thereby endorsed the status quo in civil society. Such reforms that were spoken about—trial procedure and public execution—were firmly contextualised by an overall endorsement of the authorities responsible for introducing them.

Notes

1. On the distinction between justice and legitimacy and their relationship, see Hampton (1998), Buchanan (2002), Rawls (1993, 1995), and Peter (2017).
2. Authority in this way is linked to both the invariant civil concerns of identity and legitimacy and accordingly the news's engagement with this form of authority could be analysed with regard to both identity and legitimacy. I have chosen, for reasons of clarity, to examine the authority of informal norms through identity (see Chapter 6).
3. For Locke (1967 [1690]), such an obligation is not absolute or unconditional, matters of conscience, issues of tolerance and the observation of certain basic rights provide for a discursive space for debating and on occasions rejecting state commands. Thus, for Locke, any 'contract' that exists between 'us' and the state is in principle revisable.
4. Principles about the importance of civil scrutiny of the legal institutions by the news media and their important role in communicating public sentiment can be drawn from the case law of the European Court of Human Rights—an important example of this is the case Semik-Orzech v Poland, No. 39900/6, 15.11.11. (particularly para. 52).
5. Also Alexander (2006) and Weber (2013 [1968]).
6. On this see Chapter 3.
7. It is imaginary because 'not everyone shares the same legitimacy beliefs at the same time' (Geuss 2008: 36). Disagreement about how politicians rule, the content of policies, the values and actions of power holders and office holders and so on are all continuously disputed and, as Geuss (ibid.) points out, 'the beliefs that lie at the base of forms of

legitimation are often as confused, potentially contradictory, incomplete, and pliable as anything else' (ibid.).
8. See Crossley and Harrison (2013, 2015).
9. An example of this is the case brought to the UK High Court by two citizens—Gina Miller and Dier Dos Santos—who questioned whether the government could trigger art. 50 TEU to start the process of leaving the EU unilaterally without an Act of Parliament. On 3 November 2016, three senior judges of the High Court of England and Wales ruled in favour of Miller and Dos Santos leading to an appeal by the government which it lost in the Supreme Court in January 2017. Following directly on from the High Court ruling, on 4 November 2016, *The Daily Mail* newspaper in condemnation of the judges' ruling led with the headline 'Enemies of the People'.
10. The UK's media's tit-for-tat style of reporting in the build-up to the UK referendum (23 June 2016) meant that strong slogans and memorable facts (whether factually true or not) gained traction in mediated debates with insufficient challenges being made to effectively cover the more nuanced and less newsworthy elements of Brexit.
11. The European Court of Human Rights case, Craxi (No. 2) v Italy, No. 25337/94, 17.7.03, para. 65 urged the press to 'abstain from publishing information which is likely to prejudice, whether intentionally or not, the right respect for the private life and correspondence of the accused persons'.
12. How far the conduct of the Müller trial influenced the subsequent debates concerning the Criminal Justice Act of 1865 is a matter of conjecture, though reform of criminal procedure had been contested before the murder of 1864 and as such the trial could only at most have confirmed what reformers were already arguing, that trial procedure discriminated against the defendant.
13. In this case, Dr. William Palmer was tried and convicted of using strychnine to poison his friend John Cook and was executed by public hanging in 1856.
14. In the UK, for example, the Contempt of Court Act 1981 was specifically introduced to codify some aspects of the existing common law offence of contempt of court. The principles applied to contempt by publication within the Act seek to balance the right of a defendant to a fair trial with the right of publishers to freedom of expression. Defendants' rights are most likely to be prejudiced through revelations about previous convictions, implying guilt through any other suggestion that he or she is guilty, providing information that he or she is of bad character or dishonest in other ways or supplying any evidence seeming to link the accused directly to the crime of which he or she is

accused. This has a direct implication for the reporting of court cases and is mainly covered by defamation law and libel laws (see Dodd and Hanna 2012), which were very strict until a four-year civil campaign in the UK helped to bring about the Defamation Act 2013 which received Royal Assent on 25 April 2013 and came into force on 1 January 2014 and which reformed English defamation law on issues of the right to freedom of expression and the protection of reputation. The Act changed the criteria for a successful claim, claimants now had to show actual or probable serious harm before suing for defamation in England or Wales.

15. The last public hanging in England took place at Newgate on the 26 May 1868, three days before its abolition. The Murder (Abolition of Death Penalty) Act 1965 was made permanent on 16 December 1969.
16. The Capital Punishment (Amendment) Act 1868 Section 3 also allowed that others may be present at hangings that were no longer open to the public: 'Any justice of the peace for the county, borough, or other jurisdiction to which the prison belongs, and such relatives of the prisoner or other persons as it seems to the sheriff or the visiting justices of the prison proper to admit within the prison for the purpose, may also be present at the execution'. In practice, this meant that the sheriff of the county in which the execution took place had the discretion to admit newspaper reporters.
17. It went unremarked (at the most it was simply reported as an acceptable descriptive fact) that the justice system in England in 1864 prohibited Müller from speaking in his own defence. The process to change this began in 1865, a year after the trial, but it was not fully implemented until 1889.
18. *The Daily Telegraph*, 27 September 1864: 4.
19. *The Evening Standard*, 18 July 1864: 4.
20. For example, the full transcript of the depositions taken was printed *The Evening Standard*, 23 July 1864: 6.
21. Inspector Tanner reported from New York to Sir Richard Mayne, in a letter dated 28 August 1864 (Evening) in which he confirmed that 'yesterday the first trial examination of Müller took place when the Commissioner decided that it was a case in which he should certify for a warrant of extradition, it will be seen by the newspapers which I send after by this mail that strong language was used by the prisoner's counsel in reference to England and the applause it gained' (MEPO 3/75).
22. See also Chibnall's (1981: 208) discussion of the social history of crime reporting and his study of newspaper articles from the 1830s and 1860s which are scathing about the detective forces.
23. *The Daily News*, 20 September 1864: 5.

24. *The Daily News*, 17 September 1864: 5.
25. *The Daily News*, 13 September 1864: 5.
26. *The Daily Telegraph*, 9 September 1864: 2.
27. 'But the government will surely now, after so fearful an occurrence as that on Saturday night, feel themselves bound to interfere …' (Letter to the Editor, from J. Heron Maxwell, printed in *The Times*, 13 July 1864: 11).
28. *Lloyd's Weekly London Newspaper* reprinted the whole Memorial on 13 November 1864: 7 under the heading 'Presentation of the German Society's Memorial'. On the same page, the newspaper reported verbatim sections of the German Legal Protection Society's case without comment, using a descriptive style of reporting. The paper also reprinted a letter from Mr. Parker, the Solicitor for the presentation of the German Legal Protection Society's Memorial in which he quoted directly saying: 'Surely under these circumstances, no very great harm can result from a thorough investigation taking place before the man is hung, seeing that he cannot be restored to life, however innocent he may afterwards turn out to be' (*Lloyd's Weekly London Newspaper*, 13 November 1864: 12). The letter from the Home Office to Thomas Beard announcing this decision from H Waddington was reprinted in full on page 12. The whole memorial was also reprinted verbatim on page 7 on the same day, with page 7 devoted entirely to the preparations and submission of the memorial. The memorial was also printed in full in other newspapers: *The Daily Telegraph*, 12 November 1864: 3; *The Times*, 11 November 1864: 5; *Reynolds's Newspaper*, 13 November 1864: 3; *The Daily News*, 11 November 1864: 2.
29. *The Times*, 11 July 1864: 9.
30. *The Stirling Observer* and *Midland Counties Advertiser*, 14 July 1864: 5.
31. *The Daily News*, 13 July 1864: 3.
32. *The Evening Standard*, 14 July 1864: 5.
33. *The Daily News*, 12 July 1864: 3.
34. *The Times*, 14 July 1864: 9.
35. Supplement to the *Sheffield and Rotherham Independent*, 16 July 1864: 12; The Western Gazette, 16 July 1864: 5. There was a lot of reporting in the descriptive news style when it came to the press's and the public's opinion of the police. Examples include: 'In the opinion of many of the police the meeting between the murderer and his victim in the railway carriage was not accidental' (*The Westmorland Gazette* and *Kendal Advertiser*, 16 July 1864: 6); 'the police having got a description of the watch and gold eye-glass forwarded it to the police stations in the metropolis, with the facts of outrage and then proceeded to examine minutely the carriage in which the crime was committed' (The Leicestershire Mercury, 16 July 1864: 6).

36. *The Times*, 8 September 1864: 7.
37. *The Times*, 22 August 1864: 12.
38. *The Times*, 22 August 1864: 12.
39. *The Times*, 9 September 1864: 6.
40. *The Evening Standard*, 13 July 1864: 2.
41. *The Times*, 13 July 1864: 11.
42. *The Times*, 13 July 1864: 11.
43. *Lloyd's Weekly London Newspaper*, 17 July 1864: 7.
44. *The Kendal Mercury*, 16 July 1864: 6.
45. *The Evening Standard*, 14 July 1864: 6.
46. *The Kendal Mercury*, 16 July 1864: 6.
47. *The Daily News*, 20 July 1864: 5.
48. *The Times*, 23 July: 7.
49. *Lloyd's Weekly London Newspaper*, 24 July 1864: 5.
50. Inspector Tanner was at pains to show that he was in great readiness for the arrival and arrest of Müller. He reported the arrival of Superintendent Kerressey in New York and was pleased to confirm that he had brought 'further depositions' with him. Tanner also reported that on his 'arrival I placed myself in communication with Mr. Edwards, the Counsel here, who will render me all assistance in his power; he advises me to place myself also in communication with Mr. Kennedy the Chief of Police here which I have done' (9 August 1986, MEPO 3/75, received by the Metropolitan Police on 25 August 1864). Although the Victoria did not arrive in New York until 24 August 1864, on 19 August 1864, Tanner wrote that 'we keep a strict watch night and day' (MEPO 3/75) and on 26 August 1986, Superintendent Kerressey wrote to Sir Richard Mayne to inform him 'that the ship Victoria arrived in the Bay at 9 pm 24th. She was immediately boarded .... The prisoner is going before the Commissioner this morning' (MEPO 3/75).
51. *The Times*, 22 August 1864: 12.
52. *The Illustrated London News*, 27 August 1864: 206.
53. *The Times*, 22 August 1864: 12.
54. *The Times*, 8 September 1864: 7.
55. *The Times*, 9 September 1864: 6.
56. *The Illustrated London News*, 17 September 1864: 279.
57. *The Daily News*, 17 September 1864: 5.
58. *The Times*, 9 September 1864: 6.
59. *The Daily News*, 8 August 1864: 2.
60. *The Times*, 9 September 1864: 6.
61. *The Evening Standard*, 6 September 1864: 4.
62. *The Times*, 9 September 1864: 7.
63. *The Times*, 19 September 1864: 7.

64. *The Times*, 31 October 1864: 6.
65. *The Daily Telegraph*, 13 September 1864: 2.
66. *The Daily Telegraph*, 13 September 1864: 2.
67. *Lloyd's Weekly London Newspaper*, 28 August 1864: 1.
68. The transcripts of the trial show that Mr. Chauncey Schaffer's defence of Müller was notable for the fact that he made no reference to the charge against him. Rather, he made strong criticism, to loud applause, of the British 'for their flagrant iniquity in regard to the ship "Alabama," which had been destroyed in the previous June, and said that by our own treachery and gross misconduct we had made any Extradition Treaty a dead letter'.
69. *The Illustrated London News*, 17 September: 283.
70. *The Daily News*, 31 October 1864: 6.
71. *The Daily News*, 31 October 1864: 6.
72. *The Daily News*, 31 October 1864: 6.
73. *The Illustrated London News*, 5 November 1864: 453.
74. *The Daily News*, 31 October 1864: 6.
75. *The Times*, 31 October 1864: 6.
76. *Lloyd's Weekly London Newspaper*, 6 November 1864: 6.
77. *The Times*, 9 September 1864: 7.
78. *The Times*, 13 September 1864: 10.
79. *The Times*, 9 September 1864: 6.
80. *The Illustrated London News*, 5 November 1864: 454.
81. *The Daily Telegraph*, 28 October 1864: 2.
82. Daily News, 13 September 1864: 5.
83. *The Times*, 9 September 1864: 6.
84. *The Illustrated London News*, 5 November 1864: 454.
85. *The Times*, 20 September 1864: 9.
86. *The Times*, 31 October 1864: 7.
87. *Lloyd's Weekly London Newspaper*, 6 November 1864: 6.
88. *Lloyd's Weekly London Newspaper*, 6 November 1864: 6.
89. *Lloyd's Weekly London Newspaper*, 6 November 1864: 6.
90. *The Times*, 31 October 1864: 7.
91. *The Daily News*, 14 November 1864: 4.
92. *The Daily Telegraph*, 14 November 1864: 4.
93. *The Times*, 9 September 1864: 6.
94. *Lloyd's Weekly London Newspaper*, 6 November 1864: 1.
95. *The Daily News*, 15 November 1864: 4.
96. *The Times*, 7 November 1864: 10.
97. *The Daily News*, 14 November 1864: 4.
98. *The Daily News*, 5 November 1864: 4.
99. *The Times*, 31 October 1864: 6.

100. *The Times*, 31 October 1864: 7.
101. *The Times*, 5 November 1864: 9.
102. *The Times*, 5 November 1864: 9.
103. *The Times*, 5 November 1864: 9.
104. Daily Telegraph, 8 September 1864: 5.
105. *The Daily Telegraph*, 14 November 1864: 4.
106. *The Times*, 15 November 1864: 9.
107. *Evening Star*, 10 November 1864: 1.
108. *The Daily Telegraph*, 15 November 1864: 2.
109. *The Times*, 15 November 1864: 9; *Lloyd's Weekly London Newspaper*, 20 November 1864: 5.
110. *Reynolds's Newspaper*, 20 November 1864: 1.
111. Given that the lesser charge of manslaughter did not exist at the time, all those who killed for whatever reason could easily be classified in the same way as brutes and fiends.
112. *Lloyd's Weekly London Newspaper*, 20 November 1864: 1.
113. *Lloyd's Weekly*, 20 November 1864: 5; *Reynolds's Newspaper*, 20 November 1864: 6.
114. *Lloyd's Weekly*, 20 November 1864: 5.
115. Ibid: 5.
116. As was evident both in the press and in the letters the public sent to the Home Secretary, for example, the Morning Star Newspaper (11 November 1864, page number not visible) tendentiously appealed for the death penalty to be commuted as 'the chain of circumstantial evidence against Müller ... has not been sufficiently identified to warrant any great reliance upon that alone' (H012/15263401). A letter from Matthew Ecclesfield to the Home Secretary on 3 November 1864 asked that 'his life may be spared in case his innocence may transpire' (3 November 1864, H012/15263401). An anonymous writer expressed concern about the need for execution, public or otherwise, because 'Even if Müller is guilty and escaped punishment in this world, there is a God above who will avenge the death of Mr Briggs' (11 November 1864, Letter B, H012/15263401), another wrote that 'whatever the guilt death should not be the pain' (10 November 1864, Letter B, H012/15263401). Professor Clare wrote that 'all executions should be stayed', until the deliberations relating to capital punishment were made public (8 November 1864, H012/15263401). In 1868, the Parliament passed the Capital Punishment (Amendment) Act which allowed the sheriff of the county in which the hanging was to take place to decide whether or not to admit reporters to cover the hanging. In effect, the public, in many cases, was still able to read the details of the execution.

117. *Lloyd's Weekly London Newspaper*, 20 November 1864: 1.
118. *The Sunday Times*, 6 November 1864: 8.
119. *Lloyd's Weekly London Newspaper*, 20 November 1864: 1.
120. *Lloyd's Weekly London Newspaper*, 20 November 1864: 1.
121. *Lloyd's Weekly London Newspaper*, 20 November 1864: 1.
122. *Lloyd's Weekly London Newspaper*, 20 November 1864: 1.
123. *Lloyd's Weekly London Newspaper*, 20 November 1864: 1.
124. The clipping does not have an author's name, but is filed among numerous newspaper clippings and letters from the public to the Home Secretary, Sir George Grey in file HO12/152/63401 in the National Archives in Kew, London, UK.
125. *Reynolds's Newspaper*, 2 October 1864: 4.
126. HO12/152/63401.
127. An anonymous letter writer to the Home Office summed up some of this sentiment when he/she said that 'Franz Müller had a most unfair trial arising from the … prejudices which jurymen and judges have against the Germans' (1 November 1864, Letter A, H012/15263401).
128. *The Evening Standard*, 31 October 1864: 4.
129. *The Daily Telegraph*, 31 October 1864: 4.
130. *The Daily Telegraph*, 31 October 1864: 2.
131. *The Evening Standard*, 31 October 1864: 4.
132. *The Evening Standard*, 31 October 1864: 4.
133. *The Daily Telegraph*, 29 October 1864: 2.
134. *The Daily Telegraph*, 31 October 1864: 4.
135. *The Daily News*, 27 September 1984: 3.
136. *The Daily Telegraph*, 28 October 1864: 2.
137. *The Daily Telegraph*, 31 October 1864: 4.
138. *Reynolds's Newspaper*, 13 November 1864: 1.
139. *Lloyd's Weekly London Newspaper*, 20 November 1864: 1.
140. The public's desire to both criticise and help the police was particularly evident in the numerous letters still held in the Metropolitan Police and Home Office files which led unsurprisingly to many false leads and wasted police time (see MEPO 3/75 and 3/76). The stream of letters to the Home Secretary were numerous. There was a letter to the Home Secretary, dated 15 November 2015 (a day after Müller's execution) from a Professor Clare who asked for an answer to his previous letter. Sir George Grey had responded in writing on the back of the letter against the Home Office receipt stamp of 16 November, 'Tell him that there's been a great number of letters' (first bundle, HO12/152/6301). There was also a letter from the man who said in his dreams he, not Müller, 'was the murderer' (undated letter, received by the Home Office on 14 November, first bundle, HO12/152/6301). Others pointed out

'the discrepancies in the convict's statements of the manner in which he became possessed of the murdered man's property' (letter dated 9 November 1864, received by the Home Office on 10 November 1864, from a Mr. A Byde, second bundle, HO12/152/6301). Another wrote in to explain the 'reasons why he could not as a jury have sentenced a verdict of guilty' (letter dated 9 November 1864, received by the Home Office on 11 November 1864, from Charles Poyser, second bundle, HO12/152/6301). Another wrote in to express the hope 'that the execution of the sentence will be postponed in order that further inquiry may be made' (letter of 9 November 1864, received by the Home Office on 10 November 1864, second bundle, HO12/152/6301) and 'a humble Memorial from an Advocate', called for 'further inquiries' (a Memorial submitted to the Home Secretary and received on 10 November 1864 from James Aytoun, Advocate, second bundle, HO12/152/6301).

141. Letter from Louis Blanc in response to a letter he received from the German Legal Protection Society addressed to the Editor of the *Daily News*. 'I cannot say that I am convinced of the prisoner's innocence; but this much I will say, that important points appeared to me doubtful. Now, holding as I do that, in any case whatever capital punishment ought to be abolished, because a kind of punishment which is irretrievable implies a judge who is infallible, I earnestly wish your efforts to obtain a reprieve may prove successful. ... Were I an Englishman, I would insist on such a thorough sifting of all the facts which after the condemnation of Muller our committee have brought to light. ... I cannot help regretting that the English public at large should not seem more keenly alive to the necessity of dispelling all doubts that might hang on this horrible event', *The Daily News* (10 November 1864: 3). See also a letter to the Editor of *The Daily News*, signed T.H. BRENDES, 'He certainly does not seem the man who infringed them on the night of the murder, which continues to be involved in as much mystery as ever. That this should be the case after the trial is over is certainly discouraging; but is it not better to know it and to make all necessary efforts in furtherance of the ends of justice, than to execute an unfortunate man, whose innocence is believed in by many, and may be proved yet. ... I do not belong to those sentimentalists who advocate the abolition of capital punishment ... But the convicted man doomed to die on the 14th instant presents a marked contrast to anything resembling that class of criminals, and therefore I beg to conclude with a renewed appeal in his favour to the powerful assistance which is in your hands to render', *The Daily News* (9 November 1864: 2).
142. *Lloyd's Weekly London Newspaper*, 20 November 1864: 1.

143. *The Illustrated London News*, 23 July: 87.
144. *The Times*, 31 October 1864: 6.
145. *The Times*, 31 October 1864: 6.
146. *The Illustrated London News*, 5 November 1864: 454.
147. *The Times*, 7 November 1864: 10.
148. *The Daily News*, 14 November 1864: 4.
149. *The Daily Telegraph*, 25 July 1864: 4.
150. *The Daily Telegraph*, 25 July 1864: 4.
151. *The Daily News*, 14 November 1864: 4.
152. *The Daily Telegraph*, 8 September 1864: 5.
153. *The Daily Telegraph*, 27 September 1864: 4.
154. *The Evening Standard*, 31 October 1864: 4.
155. *The Daily News*, 14 November 1864: 4.
156. *Daily News*, 17 September 1864: 5.
157. *Lloyd's Weekly London Newspaper*, 6 November 1864: 7.
158. *The Times*, 15 September 1864: 11.
159. *Lloyd's Weekly London Newspaper*, 25 September 1864: 12.
160. *The Daily News*, 4 November 1864: 3.
161. *The Times*, 11 November 1864: 5.
162. *The Times*, 31 October 1864: 6.
163. *The Daily News*, 12 November 1864: 4.
164. *Lloyd's Weekly London Newspaper*, 20 November 1864: 1.
165. *The Daily Telegraph*, 15 November 1864: 2.
166. *The Times*, 15 November 1864: 9.
167. *The Daily News*, 15 November 1864: 4.
168. *The Daily Telegraph*, 14 November 1864: 4.
169. *The Daily Telegraph*, 14 November 1864: 4.
170. *The Evening Standard*, 15 November 1864: 4.
171. *The Daily News*, 15 November 1864: 4.
172. *The Evening Standard*, 15 November 1864: 4.
173. *The Evening Standard*, 15 November 1864: 4.
174. *The Daily News*, 14 November 1864: 4.
175. *The Daily Telegraph*, 8 September 1864: 5.
176. *Lloyd's Weekly London Newspaper*, 25 September 1864: 1.
177. *The Sunday Times*, 2 October 1864: 2.
178. *Lloyd's Weekly London Newspaper*, 25 September 1864: 1.
179. *Daily Telegraph*, 8 September 1864: 5.
180. *The Daily Telegraph*, 27 September 1864: 4.
181. *The Daily Telegraph*, 27 September 1864: 4.
182. *The Daily Telegraph*, 25 July 1864: 4.
183. *The Evening Standard*, 9 September 1864: 8.

184. Letter to the Editor of *The Daily Telegraph*, signed 'A LAWYER', 1 November 1864: 2.
185. This refers to the investigations by the German Legal Protection Society in order to produce the Memorandum submitted to the Home Secretary to request a stay of execution and to bring a further interpretation of the circumstantial evidence. The investigations were published as a two-page report in full in *The Daily Telegraph*. The first part was published on 7 November: 5, the second on 10 November: 2 and the concluding part on 12 November 1864: 3.
186. *The Daily Telegraph*, 7 November 1864: 5.
187. *The Daily Telegraph*, 23 July 1864: 5.
188. *The Daily Telegraph*, 25 July 1864: 4.
189. *The Times*, 13 July 1864: 11.
190. The focus on the senior investigating officer by the public and the press was and still is central to high-profile murder cases. Press interest can be useful to both the police and the press if but the press can turn against police decisions and become extremely critical if it appears that a mistake has been made or if the case isn't moving on quickly enough. Examples are the 1970s case of Chief Constable George Oldfield and more recently the Portuguese police investigation into the disappearance of Madeleine McCann.
191. MEPO 3/76, 13 July 1864, entitled 'The Railway Murder', signed 'A fellow of the Royal Geographical Society'.
192. MEPO 3/76, 11 July 1864 (signature not clear).
193. Letter written by A. M. 18 July and published in *The Times* on 19 July 1864: 7.
194. *The Evening Standard*, 2 November 1864: 6.
195. Letter signed 'Catholic Priest' sent to the Home Office, 11 November 1864, Letter K (H012/15263401).
196. Letter signed by 'Edward' sent to the Home Office, 11 November 1864, Letter I (H012/15263401).
197. *The Daily Telegraph*, 13 July 1864: 4.
198. *The Daily Telegraph*, 13 July 1864: 4.
199. *The Times*, 7 September 1864: 8.
200. *Morning Post*, 21 July 1864: 4.
201. *The Daily News*, 12 July 1864: 3.
202. *The Evening Standard*, 12 July 1864: 4.
203. *The Evening Standard*, 11 July 1864: 4.
204. *The Times*, 12 July 1864: 11.
205. *The Evening Standard*, 18 July 1864: 7.
206. *The Times*, 19 July 1864: 7.
207. *Reynolds's Newspaper*, 24 July 1864: 1.

208. *Reynolds's Newspaper*, 24 July 1864: 1.
209. *Reynolds's Newspaper*, 24 July 1864: 1.
210. *The Times*, 18 July 1864: 9.
211. *Reynolds's Newspaper*, 24 July 1864: 1.
212. *Lloyd's Weekly London Newspaper*, 17 July 1864: 7.
213. *The Evening Standard*, 6 September 1864: 4.
214. *The Evening Standard*, 6 September 1864: 4.
215. *The Sunday Times*, 31 July 1864: 4.
216. *The Sunday Times*, 25 September 1864: 4.
217. *The Daily Telegraph*, 15 November 1864: 3.
218. *Lloyd's Weekly London Newspaper*, 1864: 7.
219. *Lloyd's Weekly London Newspaper*, 24 July 1864: 5.
220. *Lloyd's Weekly London Newspaper*, 17 July 1864: 7.
221. *The Daily Telegraph*, 10 August 1864: 4.
222. *The Daily Telegraph*, 8 September 1864: 5.
223. *The Daily Telegraph*, 8 September 1864: 5.
224. *Daily Telegraph and Courier*, 24 October 1864: 4.
225. *The Evening Standard*, 9 September 1864: 5.
226. *The Times*, 20 July 1864: 9.
227. *Lloyd's Weekly London Newspaper*, 24 July 1864: 5.
228. *The Daily Telegraph*, 20 July 1864: 3.
229. *The Daily Telegraph*, 20 July 1864: 3.
230. *Lloyd's Weekly London Newspaper*, 24 July 1864: 5.
231. *The Times*, 20 July 1864: 9.
232. *The Daily News*, 9 September 1864: 5.
233. *The Times*, 9 September 1864: 6.
234. *Lloyd's Weekly London Newspaper*, 11 September 1864: 7.
235. *The Times*, 13 September 1864: 10.
236. *The Daily News*, 27 September 1864: 3.
237. *The Sunday Times*, 25 September 1864: 4.
238. *The Sunday Times*, 6 November 1864: 2.
239. *The Daily News*, 14 November 1864: 4.
240. *The Evening Standard*, 15 November 1864: 4.

Bibliography

Alexander, J. (2006). *The Civil Sphere*. Oxford: Oxford University Press.
Buchanan, A. (2002). Political Legitimacy and Democracy. *Ethics, 112*(4), 689–719.
Chibnall, S. (1981). Chronicles of the Gallows: The Social History of Crime Reporting. *The Sociological Review, 29*(1), 179–217.

Colquhoun, K. (2012). *Mr. Briggs' Hat: A Sensational Account of Britain's First Railway Murder.* London: Little, Brown Book Group.

Crossley, J. G., & Harrison, J. (2013). The Mediation of the Distinction of "Religion" and "Politics" by the UK Press on the Occasion of Pope Benedict XVI's State Visit to the UK. *Political Theology, 16*(4), 329–345.

Crossley, J. G., & Harrison, J. (2015). Atheism, Christianity and the British Press: Press Coverage of Pope Benedict XVI's 2010 State Visit to the UK. *Implicit Religion, 18*(1), 77–105.

Dodd, M., & Hanna, M. (2012). *McNae's Essential Law for Journalists.* Oxford: Oxford University Press.

Geuss, R. (2008). *Philosophy and Real Politics.* Princeton: Princeton University Press.

Hampton, J. (1998). *Political Philosophy.* Boulder: Westview Press.

Hawthorn, G. (2005). *Thucydides on Politics: Back to the Present.* Cambridge: Cambridge University Press.

Locke, J. (1967 [1690]). *Two Treaties of Government* (P. Laslett, Ed.). Cambridge: Cambridge University Press.

Peter, F. (2017). Political Legitimacy. In E. N. Zalta (Ed.), *The Stanford Encyclopedia of Philosophy.* https://plato.stanford.edu/archives/sum2017/entries/legitimacy/.

Rawls, J. (1993). *Political Liberalism.* New York: Columbia University Press.

Rawls, J. (1995). Reply to Habermas. *The Journal of Philosophy, 92*(3), 132–180.

Ryan, A. (2012). *The Making of Modern Liberalism.* Princeton: Princeton University Press.

Weber, M. (2013 [1968]). *Economy and Society, Vol. 2.* (G. Roth & C. Wittich, Eds.). Berkeley, Los Angeles, and London: University of California Press.

Williams, B. (2005). *In the Beginning Was the Deed: Realism and Moralism in Political Argument.* Princeton: Princeton University Press.

CHAPTER 8

The Reporting of the Murder and the Invariant Civil Concern of Risk

1 The Scope of the Invariant Civil Concern of Risk

Risk can be understood in two ways: first, it can be measured scientifically and analysed rationally, particularly in relation to such things as health, financial and environmental risks. Second, it can focus on individuals' and groups' perceptions of risk 'to them' and their corresponding rational-emotional relationship to risk. In the context of the civil power of the news, it is the second type of risk I am interested in. Research into the second type of risk has been varied and crosses several disciplines, mainly the social sciences: psychology, psychometrics,[1] anthropology, sociology[2] and cultural studies as well as some more recent integrated interdisciplinary approaches made necessary by the complexity of some types of risks.[3] The most relevant of these approaches for understanding the news's engagement with the invariant civil concern of risk are the anthropological, sociological and cultural ones as they address when, if and how press and public engagement with particular types of risk arises. Also relevant is the extent to which news coverage emphasises or suggests the possibility of danger or risk and how degrees of certainty or uncertainty in the face of risk are expressed. The specific focus in this chapter is on how the news media engages with the invariant civil concern of risk through civil and anti-civil judgements made about it.

It is important from the outset to point out that the relationship between the factual media and public engagement with risk is a fluid one. One attitude survey of sixteen nations which focused on news reporting about the environment showed that 'mass media are influential but not all powerful ... but notably that as news coverage of the environment increases (or decreases), the public becomes more (or less) alarmed about environmental hazards' (Mazur 2006: 1; Sampei and Aoyagi-Usui 2009). Public attitudes to risk[4] are influenced to some extent by the news media which play a role in shaping understandings of and responses to risk (Eldridge 1999; Hansen 2000; Reilly 1999; Wales and Mythen 2002) and depending on how the risk is reported there is the possibility of generating 'moral panics'[5] (Cohen 1972; Ericson et al. 1987; Hall et al. 1978). Critcher (2003: 131) has argued that 'modern moral panics are unthinkable without the media' meaning that the media's engagement with risk can lead to 'risk amplification'[6] (Kasperson et al. 1988). A list of risk perception factors provided in a 2002 Nieman Report[7] was extrapolated from over two decades of risk research and focuses on particular elements of risk. Some of these are particularly relevant to the invariant civil concern of risk in terms of how the news and public sentiment coalesce and respond to each other with regard to a sense of greater or lower risk such as: trust versus lack of trust of those informing us and protecting us; if a risk is one we voluntarily undertake ourselves or is imposed upon us; if it is natural or man-made; chronic (long-term) or catastrophic (immediate); familiar or new; whether we feel we have control or no control over the risk. Other elements may exacerbate or reduce risk, such as how bad the outcome is likely to be (the dread factor); how easy or difficult it is to understand the nature of the risk; and specifically the extent to which uncertainty is explained. Greater sensitisation to particular stories may be increased if groups or individuals have already had experience of or been involved in something similar such as being caught up in a disaster, violence or become victims in an act of terrorism.

For Giddens (1994), modernity is double-edged, creating more opportunities for people to feel secure, but also extending the realm of uncertainty. One form of such extension is the 'globalisation' of risk, which in turn can produce two types of risk. The first is risk generated from a greater physical interconnectivity, for example, the international transport of nuclear waste or the emergence of a pandemic. The second type of risk is generated through virtual interconnectivity which brings with it the risk of, for example, financial and commodity markets crashing. Both entail the possibility of events that can affect millions of people. Equally, for Giddens (1994: 4) new risks constantly arise from the nature of modern social organisation and the emergence of what he calls 'abstract systems' of control such as markets, bureaucracies and knowledge-based patterns of social behaviour. These 'abstract' threats involve such things as arcane systems of science, globalised markets, advanced forms of social monitoring, international agencies and, increasingly, government bureaucracies. All of them produce a situation where we experience distant occurrences having an effect on proximate events.

For Giddens, risk goes to the heart of an individual's very identity. It involves a felt loss of control and ability to adequately respond to hazards and threats primarily because those who are responsible for mitigating and/or responding to risk are perceived to be incapable of effective action because they are deemed to be too remote or indifferent (the latter is usually attributed to the diminishment of the local in the face of the global). Consequently, the 'challenge to individuals is to construct and reconstruct their own identity, which is no longer given for them by traditional institutions and cultures, but are constantly at risk' (Shaw 2001: 9). What replaces these institutions and cultures, according to Giddens, is in fact these very distant and abstract systems themselves which, while often claiming to be minimally risky or seeking to control risk, paradoxically produce the conditions whereby an 'awareness of risk seeps into the actions of almost everyone' (Giddens 1991: 112). Giddens's view can be summarised as one that emphasises the particularly risky nature of high modernity due to the breakdown of traditional institutions, the diminishment of civil society and its displacement by abstract systems and globalising forces, the remoteness of expert thinking and the institutionalisation of risk. In short, we can point to the sociological fact that we might call 'a preoccupation with risk' and its intrusion into daily life.

Beck's understanding of risk society (1992a)[8] is also relevant to understanding the way the news articulates the invariant civil concern of risk in the sense that there are from time to time heightened concerns about certain types of risk. This happens when individuals and social groups are preoccupied with negative perceptions about, for example, the risk of accidents or technological failure and errors, or when ecological disasters strike, the plausibility of imminent social disintegration, or the possibility of professional mistakes that result in scientific disasters and catastrophes (Beck 1995). To this, we would now add, among other things, the fear of terrorist attacks and extreme weather. Beck's analysis of 'risk' relates to the antecedent concept of personal and societal 'security' (Giddens 1990, 1991). Beck's conceptualisation of the risk society recognised the role of media in the social development of 'risk consciousness' (e.g. Beck 1992a: 23, 132f.) and in particular at a theoretical (and ideal) level he envisaged them as providing a space for the social contestation and criticism of risk (Cottle 1998).[9] Certainly, organisations like eco/bio-protest groups have been very effective in their use of the factual media. As a result, public awareness of risk has increased and, correspondingly, the public has become increasingly informed. Equally civil activism with regard to environmental hazard is now presumed and anticipated by politicians, policy makers and planners and the involvement of the factual media (local or otherwise) is regarded as axiomatic. Indeed Murdock et al. (2003) and Tulloch (2000) believe that the news does influence public perceptions and responses and that it has, as such, a role to play in disputes of what constitutes risk. It is therefore easy to understand the battle for the news media's attention waged by groups who have opposite versions of risk.

It is impossible to single out a particular causal connection between news and risk perceptions due to the complexity of human perceptions[10] and behaviour as well as the variety of influences that come to bear on attitudes and reactions to risk. However, analyses of the relationship between the news media and risk have been well established in factual media research and scholarship (Adams 1992; Allan et al. 2010; Beck 1992a, b, 1995, 1997; Beck et al. 1994; Cottle 1998; Friedman et al. 1986; Kitzinger 1999; Sandman 1988).[11] The focus of this research has expanded over time to include a range of factual media from citizen journalism (Mythen 2010) to science journalism. What unites the various approaches in research and scholarship is the analysis of the way risks are selected for reporting in the news media and the ways in which expert views on scientific, environmental, health-related and security-related are used.[12] The staple of the research is how the news media chooses experts and constructs the meaning of risk. Kitzinger (1999) put the matter clearly by arguing that the news media's attention to risk is highly selective, although one thing is clear and agreed upon: stories that contain risk are often highly newsworthy because they provide a mystery, highlight a possible exposure of something of value to danger, signal the possibility that something highly negative or unexpected will happen or has occurred. Such stories have all been identified as having news value.[13] A news story that contains ingredients that make people more fearful is likely to be more newsworthy and journalists themselves recognise the value of stories that scare people, and 'to most journalists, those are the elements of a great news story, even if the actual risk involved is insignificant ... the emotional aspects of risk stories are so appealing to journalists, too often at the expense of caution and balance' (Ropeik 2002). More recently a former investigative journalist (Lashmar 2013: 69) refuted the idea that journalists simply amplify risk in a way that is purely driven by news providers themselves, arguing that 'news production can on occasion be a bottom-up rather than a top-down process, particularly when the reporter identifies a new zeitgeist-defining event' which then nonetheless makes the event or issue of even more interest to the public and likely to receive high levels of coverage.

To take a more anthropologically inclined approach to risk, risk is constructed across the intersections of history and culture[14] which, as Douglas and Wildavsky (1982) pointed out, can be best understood as having four particular aspects.[15] These combined describe both the degree to which an individual's life is limited by externally imposed factors and the degree to which a group of people's commitment to a particular group drives or restricts them in thought and action. This risk culture approach encompasses the idea that identity-formation significantly influences the ways people perceive and take risks (Denscombe 2001; Mitchell et al. 2001; Tulloch and Lupton 2003) and importantly recognises the temporal specificity of risk where what might be seen as a risk in one era or location may no longer be so viewed at a different time or in a different place (Tulloch and Lupton 2003). Individuals have therefore come to be seen to be influenced by their cultural context, building up their own risk-related knowledge in ways that necessarily relate to sometimes contradictory knowledge systems that compete or are different through different stages of life and in different situations. Crucially, as the factual media well understand, the position and positioning of expert knowledge is vital for helping individuals to evaluate risk, even though it is only one source of information among a variety of points of reference that individuals draw upon as they build up their individual and private knowledge based on their own experiences during their life (MacGill 1987).

Perceptions of risk exist at different levels: personal (me), immediate group (a few of us), wider belongings (you, all), the civil and inclusive 'we' up to everyone and everything (annihilation). Correspondingly, it is no surprise to note that the perception and extent of risk affect attitudes and dispositions, group-level anxiety and social atmospheres (see Waldron 2012)—and unsurprisingly, the news covers events as entailing risk that can span any or all of these three states. Today perceptions of and claims about the extent of risk have become a major topic for social media especially in terms of exposing concealed risk and strategies for minimising risk. Given that the relationship between social media and news organisations has evolved into one of competitive mutual attentiveness (see Chapter 3), risk remains a key topic for the news which can now be received and recycled faster than ever before. Reciprocity of interest and use is, however, not without its problems. The news's engagement with the invariant civil concern of risk can expand or contract an individual and/or a group's sense of what constitutes 'high risk' or 'low risk' to them depending on the 'believability' of the news item they have engaged with. Significantly though, when the news engages with the invariant civil concern of risk in its reporting it typically focuses on what can be called civil risk. By doing so, it joins the gap between individual concerns and those of a more general 'public', which arise and connect around events that threaten 'our way of life',[16] which may influence public attitudes to risk.[17] It is civil risk that I am concerned with and to which I now turn.

2   News Lexica of the Invariant Civil Concern of Risk

The key elements of the invariant civil concern of risk are about how 'we' (including the scale of 'my' personal concerns) worry about things and people who may threaten 'my' and 'our' own world. Our sense of belonging and solidarity is in some part derived from the risk we perceive it faces and needs to confront. It is as a result of the determination of the scale of risk that the civil sphere is variously open or closed, adaptable or rigid, irredentist or forward-looking. Risk simply affects the meaningfulness of things and our capacity for collective action. As such the expression in the news of the invariant civil concern of risk spans the highly irrational as well as the instrumental and logical rationalism of what we do about the risk confronting us. Both are dependent on information we receive and choose to believe and again the news's packaging of expertise is crucial. It is possible to identify specific kinds of lexica that the news

Table 1 The civil lexicon of the invariant civil concern of risk in the news cycle

Civil lexicon	Expressions of the civil lexicon of risk: The focus is on overcoming the threat of risk and is solidarising in response to risk
Civil empowerment	• Emphasises and explains the need to take some risks to increase civil freedoms • Empowers the public to make informed decisions for themselves and safely and knowingly to place their trust in particular organisations and actors in the face of particular types of risk or threats and sanctions, and endorses non-civil intervention where it is needed to maintain civil life • Calls for recognition and communal endorsement for exemplary acts of bravery or protection of civil life
Reassurance	• Explains fully the nature of risk(s) and gives reassurance about any increased security's role in reducing risk • Puts the nature of risk into a wider context • Explains the scale and extent of the risk • Attempts to reduce fear and dread • Emphasises vigilance but stresses the need for normality in the face of risk, threat and danger • Expresses relief that risk has been mitigated
Civil defiance against risk	• Emphasises the need to embrace unfamiliarity, to deliberately extend public trust to strangers/others • Emphasises the need to regain control over risk and shows how to produce order and certainty from disorder and uncertainty • Emphasises the virtue of not being threatened by difference • Emphasises the need to develop a solidarising and inclusive sentiment rather than retrenchment and exclusion as a means to protect 'our way of life' • Refuses to be undermined by danger and risk and stresses that there is a virtue in carrying on 'as normal'

uses in its reporting of the invariant civil concern of risk and these can be summarised accordingly (Table 1).

Civil empowerment arises from the news media's ability to make a civil judgement in relation to when and how it is necessary and desirable to take risks in order to increase civil freedoms. These civil judgements may relate to a breakthrough in particular types of technological, medical or scientific discovery, but importantly, and more relevant to the analysis of civil power in this book, civil empowerment manifests itself when the public itself is empowered through the news media to feel it can safely and knowingly place its trust in particular organisations and actors in the face of particular types of risk or threat. The ability of the news media to sanction and endorse non-civil intervention where it is needed to maintain civil life is expressed in the civil lexicon of risk in ways that span the descriptive and banal commentary that often accompanies non-civil sphere activity, through to the endorsement and praise of it. Here there is a hailing of heroic civil action in the face of catastrophe and crisis. In order for the work of the non-civil spheres to be endorsed by the news media as acting on civil society's behalf, the intentions of those non-civil actors have to be judged to be civil and solidarising. The civil judgements made by the news media in this way can be used to reassure civil society both of the legitimacy of the views and actions of certain non-civil actors (the State, its institutions of law enforcement, the government, police, religious leaders, experts, see Chapter 7) and also as a mechanism to empower the public to safely and knowingly place its trust in particular organisations and actors in the face of particular types of risk or threat and under different and varying sets of circumstances. The ability of the news media to make civil judgements in this way is a powerful one as it also indicates the scope and limitation of trust which should be accorded (and for how long) to those actors. Civil reporting in the lexicon of risk is solidarising and it seeks to express an agreement of feeling and sentiment around issues, events, actions and viewpoints which are seen to serve (at that particular moment) a common interest. Such civil empowerment is directly related to its kindred outlook of civil endurance.

The civil lexicon of risk also emphasises the security and endurance of the world we find ourselves in. It consists of claims that 'we' must endure, exist or survive with normative 'claims of worth' and that it is fitting that our way of life endures, survives and persists. These two claims both emphasise what today is called sustainability. They also focus on the need to take some risks if we are to progress, and progress here can include the increase of civil liberties and the advancement of certain civil and social programmes. These claims made in the news lexica downplay the idea that 'others' are always a threat, or that technological progress is always risky. Such claims seek to empower the public's capacity for 'feeling' safe to make 'informed decisions' about what risks it faces and about what particular organisations and actors it places its trust in the face of particular types of risk or threat.

Where the emphasis is on extending civil hospitality to others and perceiving there to be no risk in doing so, there is an overt expression of the desire to embrace and welcome unfamiliarity rather than being threatened by difference. Where a risk has manifested itself as a significant threat or where a threatening event has taken place, the civil lexicon is used to be as reassuring as possible about the nature of risk, its content and its extent to individuals or groups. Such reassurance normally and where possible proceeds by more fully explaining the scale and extent of risk after a particular type of event has occurred. For example, a nuclear power station accident can generate reassuring coverage of how safe 'our' power stations are; a terrorist attack will elicit the news to show 'how prepared we are', or how we are able to militate against terrorism through civil solidarity that prevents 'our way of life' from being damaged and so on. The use of the civil lexicon may well emphasise vigilance while stressing the desirability of a return to normality in civil life (implicitly suggesting a return to 'normality' and traditional civil values in the future is possible). Equally the lexicon throws some degree of responsibility back on the viewer or reader by emphasising personal choice with regard to making decisions about what it is safe and what it is not. One exception to all of this should be noted: like any language, the civil lexicon can be used duplicitously, for example, in cases of special pleading (usually for more resources for a particular agency where the resources are said to be needed because of how unprepared we are). This is not always easy to spot.

There may even be an expression of defiance in the face of risk. Here the civil lexicon moves beyond empowerment and reassurance to place an emphasis on a more proactive response, namely the need to embrace unfamiliarity and to deliberately extend public trust to those who might normally be treated with caution; that is outsiders and others. It emphasises the virtue of not being threatened by difference. Such a mindset serves to prevent labelling, stereotyping or scapegoating in a panicked response to risk or threat. In this way, an emphasis is placed on gaining control over risk without losing the civil dimensions of 'who we are'. Through a measured response to risk, there is an emphasis on how to produce order and certainty from disorder and uncertainty. There is an implicit or explicit refusal to be undermined by danger and risk, by carrying on 'as normal', but importance is placed on the need to develop a solidarising and inclusive sentiment rather than resorting to retrenchment and exclusion as a means to protect 'our way of life'. Defiance represents calls for a more proactive attitude to those matters that threaten 'our way' of civil life. A refusal to be undermined by danger and risk may endorse short- or even longer-term non-civil intervention whereby praise may be given for exemplary acts of bravery by non-civil sphere actors whose actions protect civil life. Overall, these types of civil reports are more soothing and reassuring and reduce the sense of risk by engendering a solidarising sentiment that downplays the impetus to overreact, to seek scapegoats or to panic.

In stark contrast, the anti-civil lexicon of risk is non-solidarising and can be summarised accordingly (Table 2).

In the context of the anti-civil lexicon of hostility, distrust and suspicion in the face of risk, there is an amplification of the sense of fear, dread and sometimes terror. Such amplification can develop through an emphasis on the dangers of scientific, medical, technological and

Table 2 The anti-civil lexicon of the invariant civil concern of risk in the news cycle

Anti-civil lexicon	Expressions of the anti-civil lexicon of risk: The focus is on the menacing nature of risk and its alien quality
Hostility, distrust and suspicion	• Amplifies the sense of fear, dread and terror • Emphasises the dangers of scientific, medical, technological and engineering developments • Emphasises the probability of attack or threat from others and focuses on 'extreme otherness' • Emphasises what or who is unwelcome • Makes links between terrorism, radicalism, militancy and judgements are made about what is evil • Endorses retaliation (eye for an eye) as the best means to ensure safety • Emphasises the dangers arising from the beliefs and actions of others
Disempowerment	• Emphasises and amplifies what is unknown or unknowable • Emphasises vulnerability • Emphasises uncertainty • Stresses the random and arbitrary nature of danger • Amplifies the scale of risk and the likelihood of catastrophe • Emphasises the lack of personal control over risks and that there is no reliable way of controlling particular risks • Emphasises threats to civil security from within civil society and from outside • Emphasises that preventative systems are not working or are not in place because of the random nature of risk • Evokes and endorses excitement and voyeurism

engineering developments, but also through a stress on the probability of attack or threat from others. Where those threats or attacks have already occurred and where more may be anticipated, there may be an endorsement of retaliation (a call for 'an eye for an eye') as the best means to ensure safety.[18] Links may be made between notions of enemy, terrorism, radicalism and militancy and be combined with anti-civil judgements such as evil, wicked or profoundly immoral. These may enter into discussion of quotidian matters, such as migration and, as we have seen in 2016 in the case of the Presidential election in the USA and in the case of the referendum which resulted in the UK voting to leave the EU, can easily be appropriated implicitly or explicitly in the rhetoric of formal politics and electioneering. Such an emphasis on the dangers arising from the beliefs and actions of others is based on anti-civil judgements of what or who is unwelcome and who or what is seen to be a threat.[19]

The anti-civil lexicon of the invariant civil concern of risk is found in news reports that amplify the perception of risk and express alarm about the activities, beliefs and attitudes of others. In so doing, the lexicon is used to express retrograde attitudes and endorse retrograde actions. It plays to hostility, suspicion and distrust of others and of bodies of knowledge (science, technology, engineering and sometimes medicine) and of proposed solutions. At a more reified level, things or groups suspected of heightening risk or perpetuating danger may be referred to as 'alien', 'evil' or 'monsters'. Risk amplification is also a feature of the use of this lexicon and is undertaken by a news organisation when it decides to endlessly address a certain risk in increasingly alarmist terms thereby often conflating mainstream views with more heterodox outlooks. The amplification of fear towards particular risks can lead to a reduced sense of civil agency in terms of controlling and managing risk and to the generating of uncertainty and fear.

Unlike the civil lexicon that does not seek to hide the scale of risk, but is explanatory and solidarising in its expressions of it, the anti-civil lexicon is pessimistic in tone and raises the question for citizens or individuals whether 'any of us can ever be safe again?' The scale of risk may be amplified, catastrophe is (often wrongly) described as imminent, threats to security appear unmanageable (or require extreme and draconian measures without clear explanation of the evidence to support the risk calculation), and the random and arbitrary nature of danger is emphasised and sometimes exaggerated. The idea of a changing and frightening world in the anti-civil lexicon is one that is disempowering. It stresses the lack of public agency or of the possibility of effective control.

The anti-civil lexicon of disempowerment emphasises and amplifies what is unknown or unknowable. In this way, it stresses uncertainty and appeals to the random and arbitrary nature of danger and scales of likelihood of catastrophe. It emphasises that there are threats to civil security from within civil society and from outside. In this way, a sense of vulnerability is highlighted and the lack of reliable control over risks is emphasised by indicating that preventative systems are not working or are not in place. Thereby a feeling that 'no one is safe' is engendered.

3 The Context of Risk of the Murder: Railway Travel

The risks we think we face can often be derived from versions of our civil identity and our concern for legitimate authority and the exercise of power. In the former case, the press has consistently concerned itself with who might 'swamp us', 'attack our way of life', 'exploit us' and so on. Equally, it has been consistently quick to interpret legitimate authority against what it regards as our civil rights. More directly risk is couched in terms of what are deemed by public sentiment and the press to be significant direct and immediate hazards (spanning political, economic, environmental, technological and medical aspects). And of course there is always the threat of one or more forms of moral hazard. In short, risk is derived from many different sources. But as noted above, it always amounts to a diminishment of our civil security, a re-evaluation of our civil values and measures to mitigate risk that we find tolerable and acceptable (even if that entails the loss of some civil rights that we are required to trade away). In the context of the murder of Thomas Briggs, risk (in this case violence against an innocent respectable person) was identified as having two sources: technology (railway travel) and identity (the failure of the railway to effectively segregate the classes). In this context, the murder of Thomas Briggs in 1864 resonated strongly with concerns about the disadvantages of social, political, scientific and economic progress and reform.

Within the press's coverage were expressions of anxiety and disagreement about what actually constituted progress and the fear of its effects upon the human psyche (Fox 1998) as well as the nature of threats to established and privileged ways of life. The rapid growth of the railway in

Victorian Britain was both a symbol of progress and of terrifying risk. On the one hand, people were able to commute and travel faster and further than ever before. On the other, it brought risk in two main ways: first, risk associated with train travel itself and second, the fear of the changes that were taking place within Victorian society; a society which exhibited a form of 'societal entropy, in which "each change is ever for the worse"' (Fox 1998: 278). Although being able to overcome the constraints of distance meant that individuals were able to commute to work and to live away from the dirty and noisy industrial city centres, frighteningly it also meant that people from 'outside' could also more easily travel and enter into previously protected middle-class enclaves. A desire to be removed from the industrialised squalor of the cities had resulted in the UK in migrations of the new middle class to suburban locations from the 1850s. These migrations were partly created in London through the squeezing out of large numbers of people to make way for the new railway transport system, resulting in the destruction of whole working-class neighbourhoods and leading to the requirement for cheaper travel for workmen to come back into the cities on trains (Hylton 2015: 28). There was a rise between 1859 and 1874 of tickets sold for third-class travel 'from 49.3% to 76.66%' (ibid.: 29) alongside a decline in second-class ticket sales. By 1864, middle-class spaces were increasingly becoming susceptible to working-class migrations near to their borders (Baker Whelan 2010) and by then far more people were travelling in third class than in first class. The fear of the third class, perceived as the criminal class, coming into middle-class respectable neighbourhoods, to commit a crime and then 'be able to make a swift getaway' (Hylton 2015: 67) meant that the reality of the shifting margins of the expanding city and the difficulty of establishing secure, permanent and impermeable boundaries fuelled middle- and upper-class anxieties about the sanctity of their own spaces. These spaces were increasingly futile attempts to be geographically distinct from the criminal classes and were psychologically and materially linked to a Victorian middle- and upper-class moral imaginary of a respectable and peaceful life; one in which wealth was generated through hard work, an imaginary, it turned out, that was fragile.

Concerns about the railways elicited responses in fictional and factual writing. For some, the expansion of the railways was seen as vandalism. The satirical magazine Punch ironically recommended St. Paul's Cathedral as a potential station in 1863 as 'the centre to which all railway lines should end' (Simmons 1991: 167). The destruction of the countryside was of particular concern to those artists and poets who had contributed to the imaginaries of generations of middle- and upper-class British people of beautifully expressed visions of England as a green and pleasant land which the rush of working-class visitors would destroy through their lack of appreciation of the aesthetics of beauty. For many critics of the time such as William Wordsworth and Matthew Arnold, the rush to accumulation of wealth was to place material concerns above aesthetic and moral ones and Ruskin observed that it is a 'fool [who] always wants to shorten space and time' (Newsome 1998: 31). For him, railways represented 'destructions of all wise social habit or possible natural beauty, carriages of damned souls on the ridges of their own graves' (Hylton 2015: 148 quoting a letter from Ruskin to *The Times* in 1887). Concerns about the destructive force of the railways were also referred to in literature such as George Eliot's Middlemarch (Mathieson 2015) and in Dickens's The Uncommercial Traveller where he 'bemoans the impact of the railways on the Rochester of his childhood' (Hylton 2015: 170) and Elizabeth Gaskell's Cranfield where Captain Brown was killed by 'them nasty cruel railroads' (Newsome 1998: 31).

The risks of travel by train were undoubtedly high and numerous accidents were systematically and graphically recorded,[20] but despite the well-founded fears about exploding boilers and derailments, broken axles, collisions, pollution of the atmosphere, destruction of the countryside and the less well-founded fears about being made unwell by the speed and noise of the trains, or setting houses alight from the sparks from passing trains, the mid-1800s are often described as the golden age of the railway across many parts of the world.[21] Passengers, it appeared, were generally more than happy to take a calculated risk to take advantage of the new freedoms that the railways brought, taking day trips to the seaside and venturing further afield than ever before (Hylton 2015). In addition, the ability to travel to find work meant employment and the possibility of a more secure life for some, but it also meant unemployment and poverty for others as traditional cottage industries and ways of life were replaced by mechanised and more efficient means of production.

The risk to the safety of first-class passengers from the growth in the use of the same mode of transport by a variety of people was militated against through the specific structure and deliberate segregation of railway compartments. No movement between the different carriages on the train was possible, a situation that also contributed strongly to the sense of risk of being trapped alone with an assailant with no means to escape. In 1860, the murder of the French Chief Justice, Judge Poinsot who was robbed and shot in a first-class carriage on a train bound for Paris had encouraged British writers and journalists to reflect about their unease regarding the safety of railway travel (Colquhoun 2011; Hylton 2015). In the UK until 1864, there had been no high-profile physical assaults in a first-class railway compartment, although other attacks had been attempted as a member of the public reminded, the Police Commissioner, Sir Richard Mayne, in a letter that recalled that 'an outrage was committed on the North London railway at precisely the same spot in a similar manner but not with the same frightful consequences as the recent one because the man only stunned his victim, stole his watch and jumped off the carriage himself'.[22] The murder of Thomas Briggs in a first-class compartment in 1864 served to increase feelings of risk which undermined a belief in middle-class security and the idea that wealth and hard work could buy safety. In this context, the police and the detectives, to whom both the press and the public accorded uneven levels of trust and respect in the 1860s (Chibnall 1981) were expected to reinstate a certain feeling of safety and security by quickly solving the murder.

4 Civil Judgements Made in the News Reports

4.1 Civil Empowerment as the Mitigation of Risk

The press and the public both demonstrated a sense of civil empowerment in their calls upon the public authorities to act immediately. There was evidence of a tendentious and campaigning tone in the news articles which called for measures to be taken to ensure such a horrendous crime could not happen again. This was echoed in the small number of letters from the public that the newspapers chose to print. The fact that the government should respond seemed self-evident given that the 'government does already interfere in many regulations as affecting railways and, still more, steam vessels, and my present proposition would only be carrying interference a little further and in a wholesome advance'.[23] A letter writer to the Editor of *The Daily Telegraph* asked 'why not have saloon carriages … which are open the whole length of the carriage'[24] and a letter to the Editor of *The Daily News* pointed out that 'The appalling murder committed with at least temporary impunity on a line of the metropolitan railway by which thousand travel to and from the City every day, has very naturally raised the question as to how the travelling public, including not only nine-tenths of the metropolis, but a large proportion of the whole community, may be protected in future from exposure to such fearful risks'.[25] The author who signed himself or herself R.N.B. went on to emphasise the necessity of 'fitting communication system – perhaps in the form of an outside ledge which guards could use - in order to ensure that the compartments are not completely isolated from the guards or each other'.[26] Another writer reflected on 'The complete isolation of travellers on a railroad between station and station officers offers to dangerous men facilities for the gratification of any sudden criminal impulse. After all that has occurred it will be an inexcusable and indelible disgrace to those who administer the affairs of railway management to allow of the continuance of those facilities a moment beyond the time for such mechanical changes as the safety of travellers renders indispensable. It is in the power of the directors to make crimes of violence on a railway journey all but impossible; when they will be convinced that to do so will serve their interests as much as it will conduce to the comfort and confidence of the public?'[27] Equally, in a Letter to the Editor of *The Daily News* signed A.M., reprinted under the header 'Safety in railway travelling', the writer proposed some solutions, 'SIR, - Many suggestions have been made as to the best means of preventing outrage in railway carriages, and it may be useful at this stage to examine the different plans proposed with this view. These may be divided broadly into two classes'. The letter writer referred to these as (1) better means of communication between the victim and the guard of the train, and (2) allowing the guard access to each compartment, also rather bizarrely by a ledge on the outside of the carriage. A.M. went on to observe that they 'have unintentionally stumbled on what is, in fact, the gist of the whole question. Privacy and security are incompatible'.[28]

In the context of civil empowerment, the detective work that was being undertaken was a key source of information for the press which was presented to the public as a way of helping to mitigate threats to public safety and likely to be the most successful way of protecting civil life. When the detectives/police were endorsed by the press as competent it empowered the public to make informed decisions for themselves from trustworthy information that was provided to them via the press. In this vein, the public was reassured that the detectives were 'resolutely making every possible inquiry'[29] and 'following [Müller] up with great perseverance',[30] so that 'no stone will be left unturned by them which may tend to bring the murderer to justice'.[31] The press positioned itself as working closely with the police to quickly produce a successful outcome: 'We trust heartily that this crime is now in a fair way of being traced home to its perpetrator. There is a clue, and a tolerably clear one, which we leave the police to follow'.[32] The use of the 'we' speaks for the newspaper and its public and lends authority to the press's judgement that 'Although beyond the momentary reach of the police, the measures taken for his apprehension are certain to be attended by a successful result'.[33] Calls for recognition and communal endorsement for exemplary detective work to protect civil life were evident in the press's own endorsement of the diligent inquiries being made by the detectives. The public was advised that 'A very lengthy report from the officers in charge of the case was sent into Sir Richard Mayne last night, containing some very important information that we hope to be able to give to our readers to-morrow'.[34] For *The Times*, the engagement of the public as well as its own relationship with the police on the public's behalf had clear civil benefits as 'There can be no doubt that the interest with which great crimes are followed is beneficial, by the facilities for detection which results from the whole public being acquainted with the facts as well as the police'.[35] When the press's endorsement of the detectives waned somewhat because of a lack of result (see Chapter 7), the press simply explained the nature of the risk to the public, namely that the perpetrator was still at large, 'The police have not yet succeeded in apprehending the ruffian or ruffians who committed the murder on the North London Railway on Saturday night'.[36] Such straightforward information, that implied it was only a matter of time before the murderer was caught, empowered for a time the public to decide for itself whether being patient with the detectives was at this stage of events a risk worth taking in order to guarantee future security. In this context, the press emphasised the idea that there was still via the detectives a reliable way of controlling risk.

4.2 Reassurance Through the Detectives and the Press

The civil lexicon of risk in the context of reassurance was used to emphasise the importance of retaining and returning to normality as far as possible and an expression of relief when risk was reduced or mitigated. 'A great feeling of relief will be experienced this morning when it is announced that a clue has at last been found to the murder of the late Mr. Briggs'.[37] 'The *Globe* of Wednesday night, remarked:—The conclusive evidence which has come to light, pointing out the man, Franz Muller, as the actual murderer of Mr Briggs has produced throughout the city and the metropolis a feeling of intense satisfaction and relief'.[38] Indeed, it was observed that 'London and the world at large will be thankful that such a clue has at last been found in the track of the murderer of the late Mr. Briggs as to leave no doubt that the miscreant will be brought to justice'.[39] By addressing the nature of risk and putting it into a wider context, the need for increased security or the intervention of non-civil sphere actors in civil matters was articulated in an attempt to reduce fear or dread. The public was swiftly advised that their fears that a murderer may escape 'were at last set at rest by a telegram from Sandy Hook on Wednesday evening, the 24th inst., about 6 o'clock announcing that the Victoria was then entering the lower bay'.[40]

The public was also reassured by that the press that although a need for vigilance needed to be emphasised, risks could be dealt with and faced down. The story of a near encounter with a shady character on the London railway three weeks after the murder of Thomas Briggs was reported as an alarming incident, but as one where the threat was overcome and that victimhood was not inevitable, 'More frightened than hurt.—Mr. Thomas Beard, the well-known solicitor of Basinghall-street, on Tuesday last [encountered a man on a train]. On arriving at Snaresbrook Mr. Beard made a communication of what had occurred … so thoroughly convinced is he that a murderous outrage was purposed, and was only not committed through his own caution and watchfulness'.[41] Reassurance also entailed a belief in the effectiveness of public hanging as a deterrent to dissuade others from perpetrating such crimes, 'if evil doers ever make any rational estimate of consequences, might well stay their hands before the deed is accomplished'[42] and it is 'likely to be brought home to the perpetration in a manner that will be a fearful warning to wrongdoers'.[43] The papers reassured their readers that, 'The crime was one of a nature which, while others are punished, could not be allowed to escape by an sense of indulgence'.[44] When Sir George Grey, the Home Secretary responded to the GLPS Memorial by refusing to grant a stay of execution, he was careful to emphasise the value of the jury, the safety of the verdict and the appropriateness of the punishment. He concluded that the new evidence brought did not 'warrant his interfering with the verdict of the jury'. It is interesting to note that his refusal to intervene with the judgement of the jury or the civil institution of the law was reprinted in full in several newspapers[45] without criticism or comment. The implicit civil judgement here was a reassuring one namely that the public need not worry that the wrong person had been caught. In short, there was no chance that the perpetrator was still at large. The capture and punishment of the criminal were seen to allay more than just public fears; it was also necessary to ensure a return to normality where the disruptive forces that threatened social stability and public confidence could be held in check. The press, safely secure in the knowledge that justice had been done, reassured its readers that 'The crime, undetected, would have operated to repeat itself, and it is impossible to foresee the extent to which it might have disorganised the daily mechanism of commercial life. Happily, this dark prospect has passed away, and the avenging hand of justice has dissipated a host of highly disagreeable fears'.[46]

4.3   Civil Defiance for 'Our Way of Life'

In the case of the murder of Thomas Briggs, the press was susceptible to the emotional feelings of safety, kinship, warmth and hospitality that form within bounded communities. In the context of the civil lexicon of risk, this sense of community was deliberately extended as the press reassured itself and its readers that it was possible to ensure a protection of 'our way of life', and that we must not lose sight of British 'fair play' or our civil values of fairness and hospitality. In the spirit of fairness and hospitality, *The Daily News* apologised for the intensity of the public's interest in Franz Müller, excusing it as something which was needed to protect 'ourselves', rather than a mawkish interest. It noted that 'Many may deplore, but none can quarrel, with the intense anxiety of the public to gain a passing glimpse of the man whose name has been uppermost in every man's mouth for two months past',[47] to which *The Evening Standard* added a note of civil defiance, that given some of his more civil qualities (see Chapter 7) 'we cannot but wish that he might have proved himself innocent'.[48] Equally, the observation that 'Unquestionably he has behaved well, and now that his guilt is so distinctly proved we cannot but feel that in this unpretending and unprepossessing looking youth there must be a greater depth of character than was originally supposed'[49] elicited a sense of pathos and was an attempt to understand this particular convicted criminal in civil terms despite the pressures to bring the feelings of risk and insecurity and uncertainty to an end. Although the newspapers, and by extension their readers, were encouraged to endorse their own civil interests, their civil defiance against those who 'might harm us' was in some cases played out generously and hospitably via the use of the civil lexicon which allowed for reflection and shame about the behaviour of some elements of the press which 'discussed the question of Muller's guilt or innocence … [and] elicited the reprehension even of foreign journalists',[50] because 'it is impossible to condemn too severely the freedom with which the Muller gossip, and questions and answers of detectives, connoisseurs in murders, and policemen, have been given to the public'.[51] From this kind of reflective civil perspective, 'it was impossible not to feel some sympathy for the wretched human animal far away from home and kindred, and frowned upon by hundreds of hostile strangers'.[52] The sense of our own security in our civil values allowed the press to extend some civility while simultaneously exhibiting civil defiance in the secure knowledge that those who wish to harm 'us' can be defeated.

Although a fear of travel and a sense of risk were articulated, public sentiment and the civil judgements made by the press as time passed more strongly emphasised the need collectively to regain control and to push the authorities harder overcome the problem—to show civil defiance.[53] Both the press and some of the public expressed a belief that change was desirable, possible and should be pushed for asking defiantly 'how long we are to endure the present scandal of our railway arrangements'.[54] A letter to the editor of *The Evening Standard* entreated further action, 'SIR - you very properly call, in your leader of today upon the railway companies to adopt some effectual means to protect, as far as is practicable, railway travellers from murder and assault'.[55] A press campaign developed and joined in the criticism and call for action. The Illustrated *London News* was strident in its criticism of the railway management, arguing that 'The complete isolation of travellers on a railroad between station and station offers to desperate men dangerous facilities for the gratification of any sudden criminal impulse. After all that has occurred it will be an inexcusable and indelible disgrace to those who administer the affairs of railway management to allow of the continuance of those facilities a moment beyond the time required for such mechanical changes as the safety of travellers render indispensable'.[56] The same paper went on to observe that 'It is in the power of directors to make crimes of any violence on a railway journey all but impossible: when will they be convinced that to do so will serve their interests as much as it will conduce to the comfort and confidence of the public?'.[57]

The press recognised these difficulties but nonetheless called for action, 'No doubt it is a difficult problem to solve. Even in France, where everybody is watched by some official, it has been found impossible to prevent crime in railways, That however, does not exonerate us from making an effort to reduce the amount of crime to a minimum. … At the present the first duty of the state is to bring the criminal to justice, and the state has shown that it is fully alive to its duty',[58] given that 'From the number of outrages which from time to time have occurred in first-class railway carriages, it earnestly behoves us to seek for some remedy',[59] another wrote that 'Your article into-day's paper in reference to the insecurity of railway travelling in some cases to single individuals causes me to ask the question why our carriages are not constructed on the plan prevalent in Switzerland? These, forming large saloons, all connected, are most comfortable and safe; each passenger being in immediate communication with the guard, who in the course of the journey walk down the centre of all carriages to collect the tickets. In such carriages no such foul murder as is now the talk of the city could be perpetrated, nor would a defenceless lady be helplessly left to the vile persecution of any scoundrel who may be happen to be shut up with her for an hour or two. The advantages of such carriages in case of accident are also very apparent'.[60]

5   Anti-civil Judgements Made in the News Reports

5.1   Hostility, Distrust and Suspicion

Hostility towards Franz Müller as well as distrust and suspicion of foreigners and ruffians were emphasised in the anti-civil lexicon of risk. *The Evening Standard* was concerned that 'a foreigner had been concerned in the murder'[61] as was *The Daily News* which felt that 'the complete novelty of the outrage in this country … [suggested] that a foreigner had been concerned in the murder'[62] and headlines such as 'Another Murder by a German',[63] served to fuel hostility and suspicion of others. The idea that 'every carriage' should be 'fitted up according to its class'[64] emphasised the desire for segregation from those who might cause harm. Such distrust extended to fellow passengers, 'You remark in your leading article this morning on the late murder that "without the means of communicating with the guard we are almost at the mercy of fire, collisions, and fellow-passengers."'[65] Indeed, 'The idea of being shut up with a madman has frightened sane persons'[66] and 'Men would—as, in fact, before a clue to the murderer was found, men did—confront each other in railway carriages with savage suspicion, and social confidence "on the line" would have been rudely shaken'.[67] *The Burnley Gazette* captured this suspicion and distrust well when it speculated that, 'While humanity is influenced by vicious persons, and men are animated by a spirit of greed or feelings of brutality, … there is something very saddening in the reflection that a man cannot journey from his place of business to his domicile in the country, without standing in jeopardy of being assailed by a lawless ruffian and having his skull battered'.[68] Hostility and fear of unknown assailants were emphasised 'The schoolmaster is alarmed, the policeman is everywhere, the securities for persons and property challenge comparison with the most advanced countries, and yet the inoffensive citizen is as exposed to the brigand and the assassin as he would be in Naples, Algiers or South America'.[69]

Distrust and suspicion of the dangers of technological progress meant that the Victorian traveller was told by the press that he or she had to consider carefully the convenience of the railways and their necessity in modern life against the dangers from the risks they brought. The frightening image of the train hurtling in the dark through the wild area of Bow in London was highlighted as a particularly risky undertaking, with *The Daily News* pointing out that 'It is notorious that in that particular locality [Hackney-wick] there are often congregated some of the worst and vicious gangs in the metropolis, and skirmishes on the platform are not of unusual occurrence'.[70] In the context of hostility, distrust and suspicion of others, the need for segregation of passengers was judged to be as essential as it is the English who, unlike the 'Americans that live and move and have their being in crowds and congeries',[71] prefer to 'retire from view', travelling 'at most with only a few fellow-travellers'.[72] The letter writer who signed themself only as R.B.N. wrestled with the need to mitigate risk of seclusion against the fear of being forced to travel with others which brought with it the problem of losing privacy and seclusion. The concerns about the safety of travel in compartments designed to protect the upper classes and the idea someone could so casually be attacked reinforced the idea that citizens' abilities to mobilise and look after themselves and each other was diminishing and suspicion, hostility and distrust were increasing.

5.2 Disempowerment of the Public

In the reporting of the murder, it became apparent that the public was viewed by the press as nothing more than passive spectators who had become somewhat voyeuristic in their appetite for news about Franz Müller. In this context, risks to the public or to society itself were presented as threatening and were reported in a ghoulish and mawkish manner for entertainment purposes, but with no reassurances or sense of agency for the public encouraged. The murder was classed tendentiously as one of the 'most atrocious crimes that probably ever disgraced this country',[73] and such exaggeration served to escalate the sense of violation of and risk to an already fragile middle-class sense of security.

Like many contemporary reports of crime, press reports engaged in the use of sensational language to indicate the corrosive and hidden dangers lurking within society and to emphasise that these were getting worse: 'It would almost seem as if human depravity were an increasing epidemic – a canker eating its way in every walk and rank of life. Its aspects vary with kaleidoscopic rapidity, but with each change is ever for the worse, and each revelation reveals a darker and more complicated picture. Yet it is seldom the public are startled by so fearful a disclosure as the horrible murder which took place on Saturday on the North London Railway'.[74] The nature of the murder of Mr Briggs was compared unfavourably to the horrors of the writings of Poe, evoking terror and a sense of dark and fearsome dangers hidden from view, but nonetheless likely to strike at any time. 'Of late we have supped full of horrors. The very air is dark with the shadow of crime; even the tales in which EDGAR ALLAN POE loved to group together all the workings of his morbid and gloomy imagination grow lame and commonplace when compared with the actual and proved realities of our police reports and coroners' inquests'.[75] Once the press had set the scene regarding the nature of the murder, it was an easy step to declare that public interest in the crime was intense (and driven by fear). The press further drove up the public's interest through sensationalist and entertaining reporting. The press wrote about the public's interest as being rather unpleasant, 'The excitement created by this murder is growing daily more and more intense'[76] and that it 'would be impossible to convey any adequate idea of the excitement which prevails in the neighbourhood of the murder',[77] because 'No event has excited such intense interest among the public, for years past, as the murder on the North London Railway'[78] and 'The public interest in this horrible affair seems rather to increase than abate'.[79] In this way, the public were cast as helpless spectators to the increasing dangers of railway travel.

As the pressure to catch the murderer grew, anti-civil judgements were frequently made about the lack of control over the risks to the travelling public. A particular emphasis evident in this line of reasoning was the idea that the detectives did not have the expertise to solve the murder successfully, thereby leaving the public exposed to the murderer who may strike again. This wasn't helped by the observation made by *Reynolds's Newspaper* that despite best efforts 'Crime keeps pace with civilization; and every invention devised for the benefit of man we find can be perverted, by the depraved ingenuity of educated and civilised scoundrels, to promote human misery, and to render the destruction of life and property'.[80]

When the press took up its role of pushing the police hard on behalf of the public (in response to the press's view that the public had a high level of interest and fear relating to this crime), it was, as we've seen in Chapter 7 often hostile in its judgements. In the context of the invariant civil concern of risk, it was more so, 'Once more Sir Richard Mayne and his men have been weighed in the balance of public opinion and found wanting. Either as preventatives or detectives of great or atrocious crimes they are now proved to be miserable failures'[81] as 'Up to the time of our going to press, the murder or murderers were still at large'.[82] In the context of the invariant civil concern of risk, this judgement was not based so much on the detectives' activities in relation to this particular crime, but arrived at through a retrospective analysis of past murders that had not been solved. The idea that the crime had been committed with impunity was of concern, with *The Times* remarking that, 'It is somewhat singular that about six years ago an attempted robbery and assault was made in a train passing the same spot. The thief jumped out and would have escaped if he had not injured his knee in falling. Great surprise has been expressed that so fearful a murder should have been committed merely for the sake of an old fashioned watch and chain ... and many persons are of the opinion that the objective of the murderer was not merely robbery'.[83] *The Evening Standard* was also hostile, 'Judging from the police reports, Life in London is getting rather an agreeable thing to those who like purchasing a little excitement at the rice of constant exposure to danger. ... Crimes of violence are becoming increasingly common and, what is even more alarming, their perpetrators not unfrequently [sic] escape with complete impunity'.[84] It went on to comment that 'We are afraid to say how many murders have come to light within the last year or two in which the criminals have escaped pursuit, while some detected and punished crimes have left an enduring sense of insecurity upon the public mind'.[85] Concerned that the perpetrator would not be caught, the public was told that this 'has very naturally raised the question as to how the travelling public, including not only nine-tenths of the metropolis, but a large proportion of the whole community, may be best protected in future from exposure to such fearful risks'.[86] 'It is somewhat singular too, that the perpetrator of the outrage, who must have been covered with fresh blood, should have been able to pass unnoticed by the persons about the station, and the ticket collector'.[87] In other words, the public should be afraid of the skill of the murderer and his ability to evade detection and at the same time be aware of their own vulnerability because of the random and arbitrary nature of the murder. 'There are fears that are very general in the public mind; and which, we are bound to say, the Legislature has done little, by more rigorous railway legislation to abate …The most fearful of travellers must consign himself to the mercies of railway management, or he must "abide in his den"'.[88] The arbitrary, unknown and random nature of risk was exaggerated, as was the uselessness of the authorities in the face of risk, amplifying a sense of helplessness in the face of threat and heightening both fear and dread. For *the Burnley Gazette*, part of the horror was that 'this [occurred] in a public railway carriage where the sound of his voice [Mr. Briggs's voice] should have aroused hundreds to his assistance'.[89] Alarmingly, 'There is no ground for supposing that personal enmity or revenge had anything to do with the murder of Mr. Briggs, or that any other elderly gentleman with a gold watch-chain might not have been singled out for the same fate. This is a very serious aggravation of a murder, considered in its effect on public security'.[90] The idea that this could happen to anyone was amplified, 'There are few of us who are conscious that others have special reasons to wish for our death but all of us are liable to find ourselves in positions where we might easily be murdered for the sake of a purse or a gold watch'.[91] The danger to each of 'us' is that such risks and threats are capricious, posing a threat not only to each individual 'like us', but also to society in general and that this sudden and arbitrary crime suggested a common danger. In this respect, the murder was seen as a new type of threat to the safety of 'us', a point emphasised by *The Daily Telegraph* when it asserted that if 'we', by which it meant a 'civilised we', can be murdered in a first-class carriage, 'we can be slain in our church pews or at our dining room tables'.[92] *The Times* emphasised that 'it is plain that no man is safe from assassination, no woman from rape, as long as people are left … with the impossibility of making known their situation'.[93] The amplification of risk in this way is a non-solidarising sentiment which serves to destabilise and disempower while divisively disaggregating a civil 'we' from unknown and unnamed others.

In these ways, risk and threat were reported as arbitrary and unpredictable in terms of their actual outcomes making the world seem more uncertain and risky and the nature of the crime and the threat of it amplified.[94] Press reports dwelt upon the uncertain nature of risk and the impossibility of predicting when it might happen to you if you were to find yourself in the wrong place at the wrong time. Indeed, several years later *The Times* reported that a murder 'which was perpetrated in a carriage of the London and Brighton Railway Company on Monday afternoon is of a sort to startle and fill everyone with misgiving. The violent death which has befallen Mr. Gould might befall anyone who is infirm or wealthy enough to be singled out by a deliberate assassin'.[95] The idea that Thomas Briggs was 'murdered in a place in which, of all others, he might have considered himself safe'[96] meant that 'The first question every man asked his neighbour on hearing of this tragedy of ten minutes, was: "Who then is safe, even in the busiest streets of London, by day or by night?"'[97] It is not surprising that the outcome of this amplification of risk and fear was a rise in public anger. The public whipped up into a state of excitement and anxiety was then somewhat starved of news as the detectives pursued Müller across the Atlantic. As the public waited for his ship to arrive, it was told that 'it may be stated that it is exceedingly probable that no news will be received for a month or five weeks'.[98] When information was finally made available, the press demeaned the public's appetite to see Müller, criticising the dangerous spectators who simply 'lusted after an object' noting disapprovingly that 'the anger of the mob was not hushed. It had been lashed into an uncontrollable storm. Such storms, which are never stirred by truth and justice, waken and demoralize the body social'.[99] The judgement was that 'There is something very demoralizing in the violent fits of anger which shake the public judgement now and then. There is danger also. Carlyle, in his Essay on Voltaire writes: "A wise man has well reminded us that, in any controversy, the instant we feel angry, we have already ceased striving for truth, and begun striving for ourselves." The public anger is a fear for self: it was so in the case of Muller'.[100] In fact, the press had whipped up public concern and interest through its early assertions that '… no man is safe in a first class carriage',[101] and it continued to feed public anxiety with a variety of other stories about the danger of railway travel, 'Fearful railway collision',[102] and 'The Perilous journey on a railway'.[103] The idea of the train hurtling through the undeveloped parts of the metropolis in the dark was constructed to engender greater levels of fear in its readers. The regional press was at pains to emphasise that, 'The part of the North London line where the outrage took place is perhaps freer from public view than any other portion of the railway'[104] and that 'the district through which the railway passes in the neighbourhood of Bow is somewhat of a wild one',[105] and 'to a very great extent unbuilt upon, and just such a place as a person intent upon such an attack would select to carry out his purpose'.[106] Headlines such as 'PERIL OF RAILWAY TRAVELLING'[107] were used to emphasise heightened danger arising from both the context of the murder and the nature of the crime and as if that wasn't enough, the reader was reminded that 'If railways are to make the means for crimes of violence like this, they will become a curse instead of a blessing in the country'. An unfathomed mystery of the French railway murder was recalled to readers minds by the assassination of Mr Briggs,[108] to emphasise that his murder 'must rank among the most atrocious on record, if the atrocity of crimes be measured either by the wickedness which they betray or by the terror which they inspire, was committed near the Victoria-park on Saturday night'.[109]

The public was told by the press that it was understandably fearful, 'One thing certain is that the outrage has created no little alarm among the many thousand travellers who daily use the line'[110] and was reminded, in case the travelling public had not already thought of it that 'A railway carriage is a place where we are cut off for a time form all chance of assistance, and this feeling helplessness in case of emergency has been a bugbear to many nervous travellers, male as well as female'.[111] Again and again the public was told how to be afraid and what to be afraid of; in some cases it was the speed with which the murder was committed, 'It is the rapidity of the incident, and the fact that the deed was done on a frequented line of road, that creates unwonted alarm in the public mind'.[112] In other cases, it was the fact this type of atrocity had happened before and so easily happened again, as 'The spot where Mr Briggs was thrown out of the train is about the same place where a similar outrage was committed some four or five years since'.[113] Other related stories were co-opted to emphasise, without any evidence, the likelihood of recurrence, 'Another scene in a railway carriage is reported',[114] there had been another 'Outrage upon a lady in a railway carriage',[115] and yet 'Another rascal in a railway carriage'.[116] Stories of unnerving incidents were reported, 'Alarming incident in a railway carriage'—'the recollection of the recent horrible murder on the same line of railway rendered him almost powerless'.[117] The travelling public was repeatedly informed that they were disempowered and unable to assess their own security, 'we are face to face with a fact which brings home to our minds, with the utmost force, the perils of railway travelling as at present conducted … For railway carriages are now the scenes of very shocking crimes and offences'.[118] Attention-grabbing headlines such as, 'The perils of the railway',[119] were used to tendentiously alert readers out of London that 'The whole country has been aroused by the truly horrible murder on the North London line … no railway crime has made so profound an impression'.[120] In the context of the anti-civil lexicon of disempowerment, the public lost control over the risk that it was facing. The emphasis placed by the press on what is unknown or unknowable and uncertain highlighted the vulnerability of the public in the face of random and arbitrary danger. At the same time, excitement and voyeurism were encouraged by the press, inflaming public interest while simultaneously reminding it that preventative systems were not in place and that no one was in fact safe.

6 Summary

It was in the context of the invariant civil concern of risk that the press was at its most campaigning and tendentious in its reporting of the murder. Such campaigning though was often nothing more than a call for certain specific (minor) changes. These were apparent in both its civil and anti-civil news reporting. Civil news reporting supported the public's calls for improvements in the railway system as well as perversely endorsing the civil value of public hanging as a deterrent (while also disputing its legitimacy, see Chapter 7). In its civil reporting of risk, the press assuaged risk and insecurity by emphasising Müller's guilt before his trial by saying that 'the murderer had been caught' (an approach that is also anti-civil in terms of justice in the context of legitimacy, see Chapter 7) and by promoting the idea that public interest in Müller was a natural response to the question of how to redress and mitigate risk. Anti-civil news heightened the public's sense of fear and disempowerment, justifying improvements to railway transport as a means of achieving greater segregation of 'them' from 'us' in order to keep 'us' safe, as well as emphasising the requirement to be suspicious of foreigners and wary of the lower classes. Middle- and upper-class concern and interest in the murder were justified as a natural response to risk, while 'lower-class' interest was deemed mawkish and representative of its lack of moral outlook. Overall the general character of the news reports emphasised a perceived need to do something (to enact change) in order to keep 'us' safe. Such changes did not require a radical approach but rather were grounded in an extension of the available political and public mechanisms for change at the disposal of the authorities and it was left to the authorities to enhance personal security and to minimise the social level of perceived risk.

Notes

1. Psychological understandings of risk focus on the idea that people use cognitive heuristics in sorting and simplifying information which leads to biases in comprehension; an idea developed further in psychometric work, particularly in the work of Slovic (2000, 2001, 2010).
2. Influential theories of sociological risk research such as the Risk and Culture approach (Thompson and Wildavsky 1982; Thompson et al. 1990) and Beck's (1992a, b) Risk Society approach moved the focus towards understanding risk as expressed in organisations or in social groups; also Douglas (1994).
3. An example of such a 'complex risk' is climate change. Helgeson et al.'s (2012) five-factor model sees the public risk perceptions of climate change as multidimensional, resulting from a combination of cognitive, emotional, subconscious, socio-cultural and individual factors. The more a person experiences the feeling of dread or terror, the higher its perceived risk.
4. The Social Amplification of Risk Framework (SARF) has enabled the examination of connections between technical assessments of harm and public perceptions of risk (see Kasperson et al. 1988; Kasperson and Kasperson 1996; Pidgeon et al. 2003) and is based on the way in which risk events interact with individual psychological, social and other cultural factors.

5. See Miller et al. (1998) for a critical assessment of 'moral panics'.
6. See Pidgeon (1997) for an assessment of amplification theory.
7. Also see Ropeik (2002).
8. Beck emphasises the way in which modern societies have ceased to be characterised by inequalities of wealth and income (although these inequalities continue to exist) to societies whose main problems are environmental hazards such as nuclear and chemical pollution, which themselves generate new inequalities that are only partially related to those of income and wealth.
9. Beck has been criticised for his rather cursory engagement with the literature of communication and a rather hasty engagement with the effects of mass media, largely ignoring substantial research into audiences (Wilkinson 2001).
10. Or as Chernobrov (2016: 584) puts it, it is the case that 'in perception of any political event there are multiple "Je Suis"', which may come together in response to perceptions of certain types of risk. Here we see individuals come together to form a civil 'we' while holding their own individualised connection to a particular news event and their own perceptions of it as a risk.
11. The reporting of risk has changed over time (Kitzinger 1999). Although, several early studies suggest that the news media pay increasing attention to scientific uncertainty and have been instrumental in generating public concern about particular threats (Goodell 1987; Peters 1995), news reporting has also been shown, at times, to avoid the emphasis of 'risk' in favour of offering reassurance (Schanne and Meier 1992).
12. For critique and analysis of a range of ways that risk stories are covered by the news media in a selective way (prioritising the views of some experts over others) see Boyce (2007), Stallings (1990), and Kitzinger and Reilly (1997).
13. Galtung and Ruge (1965), Harcup and O'Neill (2001) point to aspects of risk-related news value such as negativity (see also Boyce 2007).
14. This orientation towards understanding risk as a socially constructed historical and cultural phenomenon has extended to focus on emotion and the aesthetic where 'quasi-membership is as likely to be collective as individual' and 'their concern is less with utilitarian interests than the fostering of the good life' (Lash 2000: 47) and on the idea of positive risk (Lupton and Tulloch 2002; Tulloch and Lupton 2003).
15. Douglas and Wildavsky (1982) argue that differing risk perceptions can be explained by referring to four viable ways of life which correspond to four distinct cultural biases that exist within the same social group, institution or nation: hierarchy, egalitarianism, individualism and fatalism.

16. For example, Columbine and Virginia Tech shootings, 9/11, the Madrid bombings, 7/7, the Hillsborough disaster, Hurricane Katrina in 2005, the Indian Ocean earthquake and tsunami (2004), Fukishima (2011), the Boston Bombings (2013), the disappearance of Malaysian aeroplane MH370 (2014) and the shooting down of Malaysian aeroplane MH17 over Ukraine (2014).
17. See Eldridge (1999), Hansen (2000), Reilly (1999), and Wales and Mythen (2002).
18. The idea that retaliation is a means to ensure safety is based on the idea that safety is the public's primary concern and that unless 'corrective' action of some kind is undertaken we can anticipate a less safe future. The point being that such anticipation is usually made in anti-civil news reporting without supplying sufficient evidence since underpinning this type of anti-civil judgement is a focus on retrenchment, emphasising problems which are anticipated to happen, and highlighting a concern with a risky future (Giddens 1999) rather than a factual explanation of the present.
19. The anti-civil reporting of 'threats' focuses on targets and victimhood, justifiable suspicion of others, uncertainty due to the random and arbitrary danger of the threat posed, the menacing and alien quality of threats and their scale and uncontrollable nature. The anti-civil reporting of 'threats' basically encourages civil intolerance in the guise of vigilance.
20. The many railway accidents were graphically retold in publications such as *The Illustrated London News*, Punch, and the daily newspapers. The Household Narrative of Current Events (a twopenny monthly publication of national and international news which was published from April 1850 to December 1855) had a special segment on 'Accidents and Disasters'.
21. British-made rails were exported in the 1840s to France, Belgium, Italy, Austria, Denmark and Canada and in the 1860s to India to begin construction of the Delhi railway. Similarly in the USA, the so-called railway mania began in the late 1820s with most North and Mid-West cities connected by the mid-1860s.
22. Letter to Sir Richard Mayne, signed A.M. Burghes, received by the Metropolitan Police on 13 July 1864. MEPO 3/75.
23. Letter to the Editor, from J. Heron Maxwell, printed in *The Times*, 13 July 1864: 11.
24. *The Daily Telegraph*, 14 July 1864: 2.
25. *The Daily News*, 21 July 1864: 5.
26. Letter signed RNB in *The Daily News*, 21 July 1864: 5
27. *The Illustrated London News*, 5 November 1864: 454.

28. *The Daily News*, 9 August 1864: 6.
29. *The Sterling Observer* and *Midland Counties Advertiser*, 14 July 1864: 5; see also *The Times*, 11 July 1864: 9; and *The Daily News*, 13 July 1864: 3.
30. *The Times*, 14 July 1864: 9.
31. Supplement to the *Sheffield and Rotherham Independent*, 16 July 1864: 12; *The Western Gazette*, 16 July 1864: 5.
32. *Lloyd's Weekly London Newspaper*, 17 July 1864: 7.
33. *Lloyd's Weekly London Newspaper*, 24 July 1864: 5.
34. *The Times*, 13 July 1864: 11.
35. *The Times*, 31 October 1864: 6.
36. *The Kendal Mercury*, 16 July 1864: 6.
37. *The Daily News*, 20 July 1864: 4.
38. *The Preston Chronicle* and *Lancashire Advertiser*, 23 July 1864: 2.
39. *The Hereford Times*, 23 July 1864: 12.
40. *The Times*, 9 September 1864: 7.
41. *The Times*, 29 July 1864: 12.
42. *The Times*, 9 September 1864: 6.
43. *The Times*, 31 October 1864: 6.
44. *The Daily Telegraph*, 14 November 1864: 4.
45. *Lloyd's Weekly London Newspaper*, 13 November 1864: 12.
46. *Illustrated London News*, 5 November 1864: 454.
47. *The Daily News*, 20 September 1864: 5.
48. *The Evening Standard*, 31 October 1864: 4.
49. *The Evening Standard*, 31 October 1864: 4.
50. *The Sunday Times*, 2 October 1864: 2.
51. *Lloyd's Weekly London Newspaper*, 25 September 1864: 1.
52. *The Daily News*, 31 October 1864: 6. The same words were used verbatim by *Reynolds's Newspaper*, 6 November 1864: 6.
53. Although vigilance may be called for, the emphasis was on carrying on as normal, on finding a solution to the problem rather than being overcome by it. Similarly, following the attacks in Paris in November 2015 the BBC (2015) reported 'Defiant French businesses carrying on' whilst Time Magazine noted 'After a night of terror and chaos, Parisians found themselves caught between wishing life could go on as normal and fear that the bloodshed was not yet over' (Najekal 2015). In short, civil defiance arises by working together to protect 'our way of life' and refusing to be overwhelmed by danger and risk.
54. *Lloyd's Weekly London Newspaper*, 17 July 1864: 7.
55. *The Standard*, 18 July 1864: 6. The letter has no signature but is from 25 Pembroke Road, Kensington and dated 12 July 1864.
56. *The Illustrated London News*, 5 November 1864: 454.

57. *The Illustrated London News*, 5 November 1864: 454.
58. *The Kendal Mercury*, 16 July 1864: 6.
59. *The Burnley Gazette*, 16 July 1864: 4.
60. Letter published in *The Daily News*, 13 July 1864: 3.
61. *The Evening Standard*, 19 September 1864: 4.
62. *The Daily News*, 20 September 1864: 5.
63. *The Evening Standard*, 20 July 1864: 5.
64. *The Daily News*, 9 August 1864: 6.
65. Letter to the Editor from J. Heron Maxwell printed in *The Times*, 13 July 1864: 11.
66. *Reynolds's Newspaper*, 17 July 1864: 3.
67. *Illustrated London News*, 5 November 1864: 454.
68. *The Burnley Gazette*, 16 July 1864: 4
69. *The Daily Telegraph*, 14 July 1864: 4
70. *The Daily News*, 12 July 1864: 3.
71. *The Daily News*, 21 July 1864: 5.
72. Ibid.
73. *The Times*, 11 July 1864: 9.
74. *The Daily Telegraph*, 12 July 1864: 4.
75. *The Daily Telegraph*, 12 July 1864: 4.
76. Supplement to *The Sheffield and Rotherham Independent*, 16 July 1864: 12; *The Era*, 17 July 1864: 5.
77. Supplement to *The Sheffield and Rotherham Independent*, 16 July 1864: 12; *The Western Gazette*, 16 July 1864: 5.
78. *The Daily Telegraph*, 14 July 1864: 4.
79. *The Times*, 13 July 1864: 11.
80. *Reynolds's Newspaper*, 17 July 1864: 1.
81. *Reynolds's Newspaper*, 24 July 1864: 1.
82. *Lloyd's Weekly London Newspaper*, 17 July 1864: 12.
83. *The Times*, 12 July 1864: 11.
84. *The Evening Standard*, 23 November 1864: 4.
85. *The Evening Standard*, 23 November 1864: 4.
86. *The Daily News*, 21 July 1864: 5.
87. *The Times*, 12 July 1864: 11.
88. *Lloyd's Weekly London Newspaper*, 3 July 1864: 1.
89. Ibid.
90. *Reynolds's Newspaper*, 17 July 1864: 3.
91. *Reynolds's Newspaper*, 17 July 1864: 3.
92. *Daily Telegraph* and *Courier*, 13 July 1864: 5.
93. *The Times*, editorial, 13 July 1864: 10.
94. See Gardner (2009) for an analysis of risk-taking by the travelling public post 9/11.

95. *Reynolds's Newspaper*, 3 July 1881: 1.
96. *Reynolds's Newspaper*, 17 July 1864: 4.
97. *Lloyd's Weekly London Newspaper*, 6 November 1864: 1.
98. *The Daily News*, 22 July 1864: 5.
99. *Lloyd's Weekly London Newspaper*, 20 November 1864: 1.
100. *Lloyd's Weekly London Newspaper*, 20 November 1864: 1.
101. *The Kendal Mercury*, 16 July 1864: 6.
102. This occurred on the West Midland and Taff Vale Extension railway at Pontypool-road on 27 August, where 'all the passengers were thrown together with great violence and many of the were severely cut about the hand, legs and various parts of the body'. The front-page column also mentions other collisions and railway accidents. *Lloyds Weekly Newspaper*, 28 August 1864: 1.
103. *The Daily Telegraph*, 12 July 1864: 3.
104. Supplement to *The Sheffield and Rotherham Independent*, 16 July 1864: 12.
105. *The Belfast News-Letter*, 13 July 1864: 4.
106. *The Leicestershire Mercury*, 16 July 1864: 6.
107. *Reynolds's Newspaper*, 17 July 1864: 3.
108. *Lloyd's Weekly London Newspaper*, 6 November 1864: 1.
109. *Reynolds's Newspaper*, 17 July 1864: 3.
110. *The Western Gazette*, 16 July 1864: 5.
111. *Reynolds's Newspaper*, 17 July 1864: 3.
112. *The Kendal Mercury*, 16 July 1864: 6.
113. *The Stirling Observer* and *Midland Counties Advertiser*, 14 July 1864: 5.
114. *The Kendal Mercury*, 16 July 1864: 6.
115. *The Kendal Mercury*, 16 July 1864: 6.
116. *The Era*, 17 July 1864: 5.
117. Report about Mr. Beard, Solicitor feeling threatened by the presence of a man holding what appeared to be a weapon or bar of some sort. The encounter passed without incident. *The Sheffield Daily Telegraph*, 29 July 1864: 5.
118. *The Kendal Mercury*, 16 July 1864: 6.
119. *The Kendal Mercury*, 16 July 1864: 6.
120. *The Kendal Mercury*, 16 July 1864: 6.

Bibliography

Adams, W. (1992). The Role of Media Relations in Risk Communication. *Public Relations Quarterly Winter, 37*(4), 28–32.

Allan, S., Anderson, A., & Petersen, A. (2010). Framing Risk: Nanotechnologies in the News. *Journal of Risk Research, 13*(1), 29–44.

Baker Whelan, L. (2010). *Class, Culture and Suburban Anxieties in the Victorian Era*. London: Routledge.

BBC. (2015, November 16). *Paris Attacks: Defiant French Businesses Carrying On*. https://www.bbc.co.uk/news/business-34828546.

Beck, U. (1992a). *Risk Society: Towards a New Modernity*. London: Sage.

Beck, U. (1992b). From Industrial Society to Risk Society: Questions of Survival, Social Structure and Ecological Enlightenment. *Theory, Culture & Society, 9*(1), 97–123.

Beck, U. (1995). *Ecological Politics in an Age of Risk*. London: Polity Press.

Beck, U. (1997). *The Reinvention of Politics*. Cambridge: Polity Press.

Beck, U., Giddens, A., & Lash, S. (Eds.). (1994). *Reflexive Modernization: Politics, Tradition and Aesthetics in the Modern Social Order*. Cambridge: Polity Press.

Boyce, T. (2007). *Health, Risk and News*. New York: Peter Lang.

Chernobrov, D. (2016). Ontological Security and Public (Mis)recognition of International Crises: Uncertainty, Political Imagining, and the Self. *Political Psychology, 37*(5), 581–596.

Chibnall, S. (1981). Chronicles of the Gallows: The Social History of Crime Reporting. *The Sociological Review, 29*(1), 179–217.

Cohen, S. (1972). *Folk Devils and Moral Panics*. London: Routledge.

Colquhoun, K. (2011). *Mr. Briggs' Hat: A Sensational Account of Britain's First Railway Murder*. London: Little, Brown.

Cottle, S. (1998). Ulrich Beck, "Risk Society" and the Media: A Catastrophic View? *European Journal of Communication, 13*(1), 5–32.

Critcher, C. (2003). *Moral Panics and the Media*. Milton Keynes, UK: Open University Press.

Denscombe, M. (2001). Critical Incidents and the Perception of Health Risks: The Experiences of Young People in Relation to Their Use of Alcohol and Tobacco. *Health, Risk & Society, 3*(3), 293–306.

Douglas, M. (1994). *Risk and Blame: Essays in Cultural Theory*. London: Routledge.

Douglas, M., & Wildavsky, A. (1982). *Risk and Culture*. Berkeley: University of California Press.

Eldridge, J. (1999). Risk, Society and the Media: Now You See It, Now You Don't. In G. Philo (Ed.), *Message Received: Glasgow Media Group Research 1993–1998* (pp. 3–20). Harlow: Longman.

Ericson, R. V., Baranek, P. M., & Chan, J. B. L. (1987). *Visualising Deviance*. Toronto: Toronto University Press.

Fox, W. (1998). Murder in Daily Installments: The Newspapers and the Case of Franz Müller (1864). *Victorian Periodicals Review, 31*(3), 271–298.

Friedman, M., Dunwoody, S., & Rogers, C. (Eds.). (1986). *Scientists and Journalists: Reporting Science as News*. New York: Free Press.

Galtung, J., & Ruge, M. (1965). The Structure of Foreign News. *Journal of Peace Research, 2*(1), 64–91.

Gardner, D. (2009). *Risk: The Science and Politics of Fear*. London: Virgin Books.

Giddens, A. (1990). *The Consequences of Modernity*. Cambridge: Polity Press.

Giddens, A. (1991). *Modernity and Self-Identity: Self and Society in the Late Modern Age*. Cambridge: Polity Press.

Giddens, A. (1994). *Beyond Left and Right: The Future of Radical Politics*. Cambridge: Polity Press.

Giddens, A. (1999). Risk and Responsibility. *The Modern Law Review, 62*(1), 1–10.

Goodell, R. (1987). The Role of Mass Media in Scientific Controversy. In T. Engelhardt & A. Caplan (Eds.), *Scientific Controversies: Case Studies in the Resolution and Closure of Disputes in Science and Technology* (pp. 585–598). Cambridge: Cambridge University Press.

Hall, S., Critcher, C., Jefferson, T., Clarke, J., & Roberts, B. (1978). *Policing the Crisis*. London: Macmillan.

Hansen, A. (2000). Claims Making and Framing in British Newspaper Coverage of the Brent Spar Controversy. In S. Allan, B. Adam, & C. Carter (Eds.), *Environmental Risks and the Media* (pp. 55–72). London: Routledge.

Harcup, T., & O'Neill, D. (2001). What Is News? Galtung and Ruge Revisited. *Journalism Studies, 2*(2), 261–280.

Helgeson, J., van der Linden, S., & Chabay, I. (2012). The Role of Knowledge, Learning and Mental Models in Perceptions of Climate Change Related Risks. In A. E. J. Wals & P. B. Corcoran (Eds.), *Learning for Sustainability in Times of Accelerating Change* (pp. 329–346). Wageningen: Wageningen Academic Publishers.

Hylton, S. (2015). *What the Railways Did for Us: The Making of Modern Britain*. Stroud: Amberley Publishing.

Kasperson, R. E., & Kasperson, J. (1996). The Social Amplification and Attenuation of Risk. *Annals of the American Academy of Political and Social Science, 545*, 116–125.

Kasperson, R. E., Renn, O., Slovic, P., Brown, H. S., Emel, J., Goble, R., et al. (1988). The Social Amplification of Risk: A Conceptual Framework. *Risk Analysis, 8*(2), 177–187.

Kitzinger, J. (1999). Researching Risk and the Media. *Health, Risk & Society, 1*(1), 55–69.

Kitzinger, J., & Reilly, J. (1997). The Rise and Fall of Risk Reporting: Media Coverage of Human Genetics Research 'False Memory Syndrome' and 'Mad Cow Disease'. *European Journal of Communication, 12*(3), 319–350.

Lash, S. (2000). Risk Culture. In B. Adam, U. Beck, & J. Van Loon (Eds.), *The Risk Society and Beyond: Critical Issues for Social Theory* (pp. 47–62). London: Sage.

Lashmar, P. (2013). The Journalist Folk Devil. In C. Critcher, et al. (Eds.), *Moral Panics in the Contemporary World* (pp. 51–72). London: Bloomsbury Academic.

Lupton, D., & Tulloch, J. (2002). 'Risk is Part of Your Life': Risk Epistemologies Among a Group of Australians. *Sociology, 36*(2), 317–334.

MacGill, S. (1987). *Sellafield's Cancer-Link Controversy: The Politics of Anxiety.* London: Pion Press.

Mathieson, C. (2015). *Mobility in the Victorian Novel: Placing the Nation.* Basingstoke: Palgrave Macmillan.

Mazur, A. (2006). Risk Perception and News Coverage Across Nations. *Risk Management, 8*(3), 149–174.

Miller, D., Kitzinger, J., Williams, K., & Beharrell, P. (1998). *The Circuit of Mass Communication: Media Strategies, Representation and Audience Reception in the AIDS Crisis.* London: Sage.

Mitchell, W., Crawshaw, P., Bunton, R., & Green, E. E. (2001). Situating Young People's Experiences of Risk and Identity. *Health, Risk & Society, 3*(2), 217–233.

Murdock, G., Petts, J., & Horlick-Jones, T. (2003). After Amplification: Rethinking the Role of the Media in Risk Communication. In N. Pidgeon, R. Kasperson, & P. Slovic (Eds.), *The Social Amplification of Risk* (pp. 156–178). Cambridge: Cambridge University Press.

Mythen, G. (2010). Reframing Risk? Citizen Journalism and the Transformation of News. *Journal of Risk Research, 13*(1), 45–58.

Najekal, N. (2015, November 14). 'France Is a Catastrophe': Life in a City Gone Still. *Time Magazine.* http://time.com/4112907/paris-terror-attacks-isis-survivors/.

Newsome, D. (1998). *The Victorian World Picture.* London: Fontana.

Peters, H. (1995). The Interaction of Journalists and Scientific Experts: Co-operation and Conflict Between Two Professional Cultures. *Media, Culture and Society, 17*(1), 31–48.

Pidgeon, N. (1997). *Risk Communication and the Social Amplification of Risk.* London: Report to the Health and Safety Executive.

Pidgeon, N., Kasperson, R., & Slovic, P. (Eds.). (2003). *The Social Amplification of Risk.* Cambridge: Cambridge University Press.

Reilly, J. (1999). Just Another Food Scare? Public Understanding of the BSE Crisis. In G. Philo (Ed.), *Message Received: Glasgow Media Group Research 1993–1998* (pp. 129–145). Harlow: Longman.

Ropeik, D. (2002). *Journalists Can Be Seduced by Aspects of Risk* (Nieman Reports).https://niemanreports.org/articles/journalists-can-be-seduced-by-aspects-of-risk/.

Sampei, Y., & Aoyagi-Usui, M. (2009). Mass-Media Coverage, Its Influence on Public Awareness of Climate-Change Issues, and Implications for Japan's National Campaign to Reduce Greenhouse Gas Emissions. *Global Environmental Change, 19*(2), 203–212.

Sandman, P. (1988). Telling Reporters About Risk. *Civil Engineering, 58*(8), 36–38.

Schanne, M., & Meier, W. (1992). Media Coverage of Risk: Results from Content Analysis. In J. Durant (Ed.), *Museums and the Public Understanding of Science* (pp. 142–168). London: Science Museum Publication.

Shaw, M. (2001). The Development of the Common Risk Society. *Society, 38*(6), 7–15.

Simmons, J. (1991). *The Victorian Railway*. London: Thames & Hudson.

Slovic, P. (2000). *The Perception of Risk*. London, UK: Earthscan.

Slovic, P. (2001). *Smoking: Risk, Perception, and Policy*. London: Sage.

Slovic, P. (2010). *The Feeling of Risk: New Perspectives on Risk Perception*. London, UK: Earthscan.

Stallings, R. A. (1990). Media Discourse and the Social Construction of Risk. *Social Problems, 37*(1), 80–95.

Thompson, M., & Wildavsky, A. (1982). A Proposal to Create a Cultural Theory of Risk. In H. C. Kunreuther & E. V. Ley (Eds.), *The Risk Analysis Controversy* (pp. 141–165). Berlin: Springer.

Thompson, M., & Wildavsky, A. (1986). A Poverty Distinction: From Economic Homogeneity to Cultural Heterogeneity in the Classification of Poor People. *Policy Sciences, 19*(2), 163–199.

Thompson, M., Ellis, R., & Wildavsky, A. (1990). *Cultural Theory*. Boulder: Westview Press.

Tulloch, J., & Lupton, D. (2003). *Risk and Everyday Life*. London: Sage.

Tulloch, M. (2000). The Meaning of Age Differences in the Fear of Crime: Combining Quantitative and Qualitative Approaches. *The British Journal of Criminology, 40*(3), 451–467.

Waldron, J. (2012). *The Harm in Hate Speech*. Cambridge, MA: Harvard University Press.

Wales, C., & Mythen, G. (2002). Risky Discourses: The Politics of GM Foods. *Environmental Politics, 11*(2), 121–144.

Wilkinson, I. (2001). *Anxiety in a Risk Society*. London, UK: Routledge.

CHAPTER 9

The Reporting of the Murder as Type 3 Civil Boundary Maintenance: The Rejection of Change and the Endorsement of the Status Quo in Civil Society

1 Introduction

Two points need to be made here. The first is a methodological point and concerns the reaggregation of the analysis undertaken in Chapters 6–8. The second is more of a sociological point and concerns the nature of the cardinal types of civil boundary maintenance with regard to what kind of civil boundaries the press overall ultimately endorsed and the relevance (if any) this endorsement holds for the wider socio-historical background in which the murder of Thomas Briggs was set.

First, throughout the book I have argued that the civil power of the news resides in its proximity to both the ideal of news journalism (see Chapter 2) and the circumstances of the real and practical task of undertaking news journalism (see Chapter 3). This civil power is manifest in the quotidian and practical way the news reports our invariant civil concerns (identity, legitimacy and risk) and how these, when combined, reveal the boundaries we wish to place and maintain around civil society with regard to whom and what we regard as civil and anti-civil. It has also been noted that in order to get to the point where we can say with any degree of authority what exactly the cardinal type of civil boundary maintenance is, it is necessary first to disaggregate each invariant civil concern in the news reports analysed to deal with each one separately, as was done in Chapters 6–8. This disaggregation is methodologically unavoidable and justified for the following reason: it enables us to understand how each particular invariant civil concern contributes to the constituent dimensions of the civil power of the news by revealing: (a) how the news constantly engages with each one of these concerns in its reporting; (b) how the news prioritises and evaluates each of these invariant civil concerns in any given news report; (c) how the news responds and appeals to public sentiment in terms of how each of these invariant civil concerns is perceived by the press in its reporting to be a public priority (or not); and (d) how in different ways the news *points to* what cardinal type of judgement concerning civil boundary maintenance is eventually arrived at. Consequently, disaggregation is methodologically forced upon us even though it risks appearing to be bleaching out the way in which our invariant civil concerns naturally overlap in news reports. In order to ameliorate such risk, it is a necessary next step to reaggregate how the invariant civil concerns have been reported. This reaggregation is the only way to reveal what cardinal type of civil boundary maintenance about a particular issue or event is endorsed and advocated. Correspondingly and in order to determine the particular cardinal type of civil boundary maintenance the press coverage of the murder adopted, a final methodological step is necessary.

This final step consists of combining the following: (a) the civil and anti-civil judgements made for all three invariant civil concerns; (b) the type of news style adopted (discursive, descriptive and tendentious) and the nature of the responses; and (c) the different appeals to public sentiment that were made throughout the reporting of the Thomas Briggs murder. As such a reaggregated account has three intertwined themes that combine through lexical analysis to reveal the basic structure of the civil narrative told by the press in relation to any one issue or event. Although news styles (as noted in Chapter 4 and in the diagram on methods in Chapter 5: Introduction to Part II), have the additional quality of allowing us to determine the way a news report looks and feels, how news reports are laid out and designed and to what extent their para-textual qualities (photographs, diagrams, drawings, etc.) play a role in determining the type of cardinal boundary maintenance ultimately endorsed. News styles are not neutral in terms of their wider rhetorical content, construction and aesthetic design, as we noted (in Chapter 4, Sect. 5) news styles accord with readers' affective and rational disposition as well as with their degree of concern towards a particular subject. In short: their civil outlook. This final methodological step therefore enables us to provide an overarching understanding and account of the justificatory reasoning that leads to the identification of the cardinal type of civil boundary maintenance ultimately endorsed and advocated in the news coverage of the Thomas Briggs murder.

Second, as laid out in Chapter 4, Sect. 4, there are three cardinal types of civil boundary maintenance:

- Type 1 is the *endorsement of civil values* and the *promotion of change* in accordance and consistent with those values in civil society
- Type 2 is the *endorsement of anti-civil values* and the *promotion of change* in accordance and consistent with those values in civil society
- Type 3 is *the rejection of change*: the *endorsement of the status quo* in civil society

Each of these cardinal types of civil boundary maintenance represents the overall assessment that is made in the news. It is derived from and simultaneously represents an amalgam of civil and anti-civil judgements as well as values, normative views and outlooks in a particular setting. This overall assessment contributes to both the rational and emotional elements of public sentiment and exists as a form of civil orthodoxy about what boundaries we seek to place around ourselves and which ones are endorsed and, implicitly or explicitly, advocated. Within the context of this specific case study, we return to the relationship between news and public sentiment set in this case in the historical circumstances of 1860s mid-Victorian England[1]; circumstances that have by historians been variously described as a time of: imperialism, laissez-faire, political and social reform on behalf of 'ordinary people', the origin of the gradual emergence of new forms of industrialism and rising wages, widening class divisions in quality of life (especially education, health care and leisure), the application of gains made through popular (and radical) politics, political chaos, the emergence of a secular and scientifically inspired culture and the emergence of a widespread literary middle-class culture alongside an extensive working-class popular culture, a time of slowly emerging claims on behalf of non-English national identities across the UK and even a time of widespread anxiety and fear. All of these circumstances are subject to historical debate and it is not the intention here to join in these debates but simply to draw attention to the particular historical assessments of life in England in the 1860s insomuch as they provide an indication of the complexity of the historical background to the analysis of the reporting directly related to the murder of Thomas Briggs.

Consequently, this historical background is only approached and addressed through what was said and alluded to by the press itself (and in the letters written by the public) and represents what was seen and judged to be of importance to its readers in mid-Victorian England with regard to their invariant civil concerns. Importantly, the case study is used to make both a sociological argument and a judgement about the nature of the civil boundary maintenance that was endorsed and advocated by the press covering the murder. The nature of this civil boundary maintenance can only be discerned by looking at what was civilly endorsed (Sects. 2.1 and 2.2) and what was anti-civilly endorsed (Sects. 2.3 and 2.4).

2 The Cardinal Type of Civil Boundary Maintenance Endorsed by the Press Covering the Murder: The Rejection of Change and the Endorsement of the Status Quo in Civil Society

2.1 The Civil Endorsement of the Status Quo in Civil Society

The civil endorsement of maintaining the status quo was arrived at through a narrative in which identity was summarised in the archetypical status of the murdered Thomas Briggs. He became the emblematic figure and the trope used for speaking about the middle classes in two ways: first, in the foreground of the press coverage was his gentleman-professional middle-class standing and second, in the background and extended from the reports of his standing were concerns for the well-being of the middle class in general which was summarised as consisting of the 'civilised public'. Supporting this, and in order of priority for the press, was the civil narrative of risk and legitimacy. The former was exemplified through concerns for middle-class public safety and the latter through using the coverage of the murder to confirm the reputation and standing of English policing and justice.

2.2 The Civil Narrative of the Civilised Public

As a result of reaggregating the findings of Chapters 6–8, the overwhelming impression gleaned from the civil endorsements made in the news reports and letters was that the interests of the mid-Victorian gentleman-professional middle class were of paramount importance. Its interests were assumed by the press to be the very bedrock of civility itself and the only accepted form of associative life; one that was quintessentially and traditionally English. A sixty-nine-year-old chief clerk at a City of London bank was thus transformed into a vehicle of symbolic meaning. What he symbolised (as noted in Chapter 6, Sect. 4.1) was a powerful form of Victorian civil rectitude. He was, according to the press reports, simultaneously a loyal, diligent hard worker, a devoted family man, a conscientious churchman, affable and kind as well as the head of a large family. Above all, he was esteemed and respected. He had a large circle of admiring friends and was deemed to be the epitome of the 'civilised public'. In essence, he came to be seen as someone of whom 'in the courtesies of social life no one could better play his part'.[2] He became the archetypical civilised Victorian middle-class gentleman-professional of unimpeachable and irreproachable character.

Equipped with this 'civil archetype', the press ensured that all the invariant civil concerns were cast in the form of a particular socio-economic group's culture, self-interests and values. It was the gentleman-professional middle class's social codes and mores as well as their classificatory schemes and social distinctions that provided the reporting milieu and background context for how the news reports of the murder were written. These then were the taken-for-granted elements of a 'way of life' that provided the civil outlook that dominated the news coverage of the murder. This is not to imply a narrow-minded bigotry in the news coverage, but rather a consensus that such a way of life was entirely capable of preserving the 'best' while at the same time accepting the need for progressive (and gradual) reforms. It was a way of life capable of encouraging and rewarding self-improvement (here again Briggs's background of educational progress and hard work since leaving school at sixteen was exemplary). It was certainly not a way of life blind to the social evils and horrors of the day, though it was conservative in disposition. Like any other 'way of life', it was replete with its own internal contradictions, none more so than in the repetitive claim that what suited this way of life was cast as being 'in the public interest'. An example of this was the use of the language of 'public safety' to mean nothing more than meeting the specific interests of the gentleman-professional middle class and more widely the middle class generally. Here matters of public safety and the management of urban space simply meant that personal safety needed to be guaranteed for two specific reasons: first, to enable the gentleman-professional middle class to travel safely through newly opened up (by the railways) urban and suburban areas and second, and following the issuance of such guarantees, to allow all members of the middle class to travel safely. In other words, the term and idea of 'public safety' were used in a particularly exclusive way—the safety of the professional gentleman and a more general but still exclusive way—the safety of the middle class per se. In either case, no thought was given in the press to improving the travelling conditions of those non-middle-class people whose livelihood depended to some extent on public transport such as members of the industrial working class, journeymen traders or itinerant agrarian labourers. Consequently, the murder of Thomas Briggs meant that the right of the gentleman-professional middle class (and by extension all members of the middle class) to travel safely was perceived to have been breached, and it was felt that something that should have been taken for granted had become something that was now at risk. This risk was all the more shocking because one of the most routine and mundane features of gentleman-professional middle-class life had become dangerous, so because a systemic feature of life—safe travel to and from work (or increasingly for leisure)—had been lost someone or some authority had to be seen to be managing the interests of the gentleman-professional middle class in the name of the public safety for all members of the 'civilised public'. Supporting such concerns was the press's deliberate adoption of a largely tendentious news style. This type of writing placed at the fore of its concerns both public safety and personal risk. More specifically, the murder was treated as evidence of the fact that the risks and dangers now faced by the middle class were very tangible and real and could occur in any place that was hitherto regarded as safe. In other words, the murder had the potential of becoming a middle-class civil crisis.

However, the status of the murder as a full-blown civil crisis was pre-empted by a stream of reassuring 'insider information' that was continuously and constantly reported in the news coverage of the murder. As we know from studies of contemporary news media, the accurate use of sources can define the public status of a piece of news journalism[3]; namely how reliable it is—it was the same in mid-Victorian England. The historian Lucy Brown (1985: 276) argues that the public desire for news was 'connected with the public appetite for inside news, and the assumption that a true view of the situation could only be obtained through confidential hints from those in the know'. As for those 'in the know' (mainly the police and the Home Office) what they were actually reported as knowing was that the murder was not indicative of a civil crisis, but was an exceptional and shocking incident that could be more than adequately contained and dealt with through the implementation of some minor modifications to railway travel. At the same time though, this 'shocking incident' served as a way to remind everyone, despite some criticisms of aspects of it, of the standing of English policing and justice to be both effective and fair. 'Insider' knowledge thus provided two principal informal guidelines: (a) the 'civilised public' should be made even more safe when using public transport and (b) English policing and justice were second to none. These two guidelines would influence the way the news ultimately judged the civil implications of the murder. Negatively, there was no need for a comprehensive set of civil changes designed to promote civilly inclusive public spaces or greater social cooperation across class divides. Such measures were precluded by 'those in the know' and remained (mainly) ignored in the coverage of the murder. Positively, improvement should and would be undertaken with regard to the use of the railways by the middle class and ultimately the institutions of English policing and justice showed themselves able to underwrite such safety by ensuring that perpetrators were brought to account. The murder did not reach the societal standing of pointing to the need for wholesale civil changes simply because the authorities were not unduly shaken in their belief that this 'exceptional incident' did not merit undue concern. As such, the language and the narrative adopted by the press ultimately endorsed the view that the authorities were capable and effective and fully appreciated the civil implications of the issue—the need of the 'civilised public' eventually to be reassured. This was partly achieved by taking up the cause of both greater railway travel safety for the 'civilised public' and some discussion about amendments to trial procedures and changes aimed at putting a stop to public executions.

The cause of railway travel safety was undertaken by a press that mainly used the letters of the public (mainly written by members of the middle class itself) to campaign for greater security for railway travellers—though by railway travellers it of course meant middle-class railway users. Through these letters, the press let the middle class speak. This provided the press with greater legitimacy (based on a presumed endorsement by the middle class) to actively and tendentiously endorse the need for actions to be taken to ensure such a horrendous crime could not happen again and correspondingly to guarantee the protection of passengers from assault and murder. While the press acknowledged that the introduction of the changes necessary to meet higher standards of safety would be difficult and that safety could never be completely guaranteed, it also joined the voices campaigning for specific features of railway safety that could be implemented relatively easily by railway management. Importantly, it was the railway management rather than the government that was tasked by the press with undertaking these specific changes. The changes the press and the public highlighted were the provision of easier communication (especially ways of alerting others to danger) between compartments or more radically, the abolition of compartments in favour of saloon-like carriages (following the Swiss example). It was argued that turning carriages into saloons would ensure that passengers could talk to the guards more easily and that the train guards, in turn, had a much better view of what was going on and would therefore be able to intervene in situations that required them to. It appeared that ultimately for the press, securing safe railway travel meant that safety was slightly more important than privacy—though not more important than the strict demarcations and classifications between middle-class travellers and other travellers. The press constantly acknowledged and accepted the need for clear segregation between passengers since the English who, unlike the 'Americans that live and move and have their being in crowds and congeries',[4] prefer to 'retire from view', travelling 'at most with only a few fellow-travellers'.[5] The leitmotif: 'Let every carriage be in this way fitted up according to its class ...'[6] was endorsed by the press as a means of maintaining social distinctions with the acknowledgement that some degree of privacy could also be supported by ensuring 'fellow travellers' enjoyed greater safety when being surrounded by like-minded members of the civilised public. The implicit code of conduct suggested that civilised disattendability would be the benchmark for balancing privacy and saloon-type seating arrangements.

In endorsing the standing of English justice, it was recognised in the press that the English legal system could be improved by two legal reforms: first, to allow the defence to speak last. As noted above, in Chapter 7, at the time of Müller's trial it was the prosecuting Solicitor General who spoke last and summed up. This gave rise to the view among the public (and was reported in the press) that the role and case made by the defence counsel was undermined and that this could be seen as 'unfair' to the defendant. Second, that public executions were contested as a means of deterrent as well as being problematic as public spectacles. Although this was very much part of public discussions and sentiment before the murder and on the brink of parliamentary approval, and thus regarded by some as increasingly likely and by many as an 'already acceptable' viewpoint (see Chapter 7, Sect. 3), the problematic nature of public hanging, as opposed to the more civil practice of private hanging, was raised quite often in the press's reporting of the trial. Interestingly, the press reinforced and emphasised the call to abolish public executions because it would reduce the attendant chaos and show the world that English justice was civil and firmly rejected the spectacle. The press's position in relation to public executions was made evident through the predominate use of the tendentious news style that emphasised the way public executions could potentially disrupt public safety. Public executions were decried as uncivilised events and should therefore be ended, if for no other reason than that they brought the uncivilised together and gave them the opportunity to become a mob of rioters (see below). These two potential improvements to the legal system could, for the press, potentially further enhance the civil nature and international standing of English justice and its criminal system and both received either endorsement or no criticism in the reporting.

Neither the suggestions about improvements to railway travel nor the implicit endorsement of legal reforms were particularly radical, or for that matter especially politically controversial. Indeed, at the most they were minor adjustments to the status quo, which was also accompanied by an overall sense in the press of satisfaction with the status quo. The status quo represented a unique English way of going about things which was undoubtedly still to be admired and preserved. In short, what can be seen is an overall conservative view with a strongly inward-looking press which presented a mid-Victorian middle-class view that was simultaneously self-serving and yet also concerned about the way justice was perceived to have been done, namely with basic decency.

The press was convinced and satisfied with its own civil role, though on occasions (and as noted in Chapter 7, Résumé) the press confusingly argued that Müller was denied a fair trial while at the same time condemning him as guilty prior to the trial. Ultimately though the press displayed a self-belief that it had reported matters fairly and any self-doubts it had about its own role were quickly resolved and dealt with in a clear discursive and ultimately decisive way. When considering its own decency and the manner and conduct of its own reporting the press noted, with a good degree of hypocrisy in some cases (see also Résumé), that it had not succumbed to the public's appetite for sensationalism and it had not reported the murder in a way that would agitate the mob. Any misgivings about the legitimacy of the proceedings or even Müller's guilt were reported next to confident assertions that the trial and sentence were fair and just and that the press had, in its reporting, conformed to the standards of mid-Victorian decency. Even when the press engaged in bouts of self-reflection, it convinced itself of its own fair-mindedness and civil value. By deploying a systematic use of the descriptive style of news reporting—through reprinting court transcripts, deliberations and legal argument verbatim—the press had done its duty revealing to the civilised public how English justice proceeded. For the press in its reflections, this was evidence of its own impartiality and fair-mindedness as well as evidence that the English justice system 'had nothing to hide'. The press's judgement of itself was that it had reported the murder in such a way that the 'high reputation' of English justice had been maintained and accordingly it could unequivocally endorse the civilised public's faith in the English legal system as well as by and large, its reporting in the press. In short, by reporting the processes of English justice and finding them to be reputable it simultaneously endorsed the civilised public's faith in the press's own civil standing as an institution of the civil sphere which holds other civil and non-civil institutions to account. Any residual moments of meaningful self-doubt finally evaporated once English justice had declared its verdict and had decided on Müller's guilt. As far as the press was concerned when Müller was hanged, the case came to a close, although the press did allow itself to express relief along with the public once Müller confessed, even though to date the precise meaning of what he said is still not clear. The press's final verdict, which was echoed in the vast majority of newspapers, was that 'We now know, and the countrymen of the condemned man also know, that there ought not to rest on the mind of any human being the shadow of a doubt that on the night of the 9th of July last Muller … committed this crime'. In this sentiment, the press endorsed the police, English justice and its legal system and at the same time derived its own civil legitimacy from its support for what has been described above as 'Victorian rectitude', with its narrow mind-set of the Victorian middle-class and its rejection of anything non-English.

2.3 The Anti-civil Threats to the Status Quo in Civil Society

The anti-civil threats identified as challenging mid-Victorian civil society and the preservation of the status quo were reported in the newspapers via a narrative that saw the invariant civil concerns accordingly. With regard to (a) identity and associated risks, Müller was depicted as the exact opposite to Briggs, although like Briggs he became an archetypical representative symbol of his class, namely the uncivilised working class,[7] and of foreigners, both of whom were viewed as pre-civil and inclined to natural forms of incivility and criminality. Accordingly, the press adopted a widespread use of the tendentious news style to explicitly advocate the view and to reinforce the idea that the uncivilised public and the civilised public were of two completely different natures that bore no commonalities. With regard to (b) legitimacy and associated risks, they were combined in an endorsement of the ending of public executions to limit the opportunities for public lewd behaviour, displays of indecency, drunkenness and petty criminality and (most worryingly) mob violence. In short, out of fear rather than out of civil respect for the 'criminal' and arising from this the press revealed a palpable fear of and distaste for the mob. As *Lloyd's Weekly London Newspaper* put it, 'The mob was not guilty of many remarkable and unaccustomed acts of brutality; but there was the stone heart, the brazen face, and the cursing and blaspheming … Gathered before that black scaffold were myriads of upturned faces all hardened and distorted, and cankered with the vices, the crimes, and the hard living, and the ignorance that, to our shame, still deface the body social'.[8] This twofold focus of the news reporting ensured that the anti-civil narrative was simply about the uncivilised public, its ethical (un-)worth, its character and primordial nature and how it stood in contra-distinction to the civilised public.

2.4 The Anti-civil Narrative of the Uncivilised Public

Rectitude manifests itself through an undisputed belief in the righteousness of a particular form of ethical life which itself is manifest in certain traditions, customs, practices and habits which, in turn, are adhered to in a conservative spirit of attachment. This totality and assemblage of values generate what Hegel called 'Sittlichkeit'—a conventional moral outlook that forms the basis of political life, family life and civil association.

Notwithstanding differently from Alexander (2006), Hegel understood the institutional and associative nature of the civil sphere as instrumentally geared to our self-interests.[9] The concept of Sittlichkeit (as an agreed comprehensive and rigorously followed ethical rectitude) captures something of the press's outlook when confronted with what it perceived to be anti-civil; namely, in this case, assaults by the uncivilised public on the civilised public. To this end, and as noted in Chapter 6, Müller's behaviour, his vanity, greed, lack of respectability, untrustworthiness and evasive behaviour were all seen to be out of synch with the prevailing moral, social and cultural expectations of the time. In this, we have the essence of the charge against Müller: he was everything that Briggs was not. He was the archetype of the uncivilised behaviour of the representatives of the uncivilised public, namely the lower 'criminal' classes. When describing or judging Müller and several of the witnesses, the press constantly referred in one way or another to four themes: property, intellectual inferiority, lack of morals and Müller's foreignness (all relating to lower-class status). These four themes provide the structure of the anti-civil narrative of identity and to a lesser extent associated risks as it sought to depict the uncivilised public in its true light—that is in terms of the nature of the threats it posed to the civilised public's way of life.

Regarding property, the two dominant tropes were: (i) the space of the first-class carriage in which the murder took place was the property of this civilised public and Müller had no right to be there; and (ii) the jewellery that Müller displayed an 'inappropriate' interest in or owned—'he had in his possession a very handsome gold watch and massive chain, by no means according with his position or the money at his command'.[10] With regard to intellectual inferiority, Müller was judged by *The Evening Standard* to be a 'wretched creature' and a 'consummate booby', 'a journeyman tailor, not less well educated than most German workmen of his class, sufficiently social in his habits, surrounded by all the influences that are though most sure to repress the savage instincts, if not to develop the better attributes of man, who is yet so absolutely in the moral condition with a Papnan or a Zooloo that he suffers himself to be tempted by the mere desire of possessing a shining bauble',[11] and none of the reporting supported the idea that Müller had an intellectual ability. As for the trial itself, it revealed a population of the illiterate, the stupid and the confused that stood in its entirety (irrespective of whether they were for the defence or prosecution) opposed to the civilised public. The following judgement summarises what the press thought: 'Stupid and confused as these witnesses were, they created an impression in court that they were speaking what they believed to be the truth'.[12] The prosecution witness 'Mr Matthews, with no disrespect be it said, is a London cabman, and nothing more'[13] and as nothing more than an 'illiterate cabman'.[14] The entire brigade of witnesses was like Müller: deemed to be unintelligent. For lack of morals, the strongest anti-civil commentary was directed at those witnesses who were prostitutes. They were reported as being deeply ashamed of themselves or too stupid to be believed. They were denizens of a disgusting world who, if associated with, brought with them automatic pollution and condemnation—to the point that for Müller it was as though things would have been better if his defence had not brought 'such people as these' into consideration. They were so tainted that they could never be the source of a legitimate alibi. Finally, the identity narrative of the uncivilised public was completed when Müller's foreignness was considered. Xenophobia was not uncommon in the early and mid-Victorian period with the Irish suffering the most blatant and violent forms of discrimination. As for the Germans, the Victorian period saw a vacillation between open admiration of the kind that Thomas Carlyle (1885 [1836]) displayed, all the way to alarm and fear of an increasingly expansionist Bismarck-led Prussia. Despite uncertainty over a Prussian-inspired greater German identity, the Second Schleswig War (with Prussia and Austria pitted against Denmark) led the *Lloyd's Weekly London Newspaper* to say on 1 January 1865 that: 'most people saw, in this German invasion of Denmark, the beginning of a European war … The Germans … were bent on the conquest of the dutchies. They advanced under cover of shameless subterfuges and falsehoods, and their bearing was so defiant and insolent, it was hardly possible to believe that peace could be maintained with them… The German invaders showed their customary cruelty and bravado. Their numbers, and not their courage, had given them the victory'.[15] With effortless extension, Müller was equally both defiant and insolent, both cruel and cowardly and full of German bravado. The point was simply that as a member of a foreign cruel and barbaric class, he had found his natural home in the uncivilised lower criminal class of London. *The Illustrated London News* said without irony that it was 'curious that, with the strong anti-German feeling which the success of audacious Austria and predatory Prussia has excited, the murderer should be a German'.[16] Müller's foreign identity mattered, and as we have seen above, it mattered not only to the English press but also the European press where the common perception was that it was Müller's nationality that was on trial rather than anything else.

In essence, foreigners were to be feared not only for their indigenous uncivilised characteristics but because the uncivilised foreigner could so easily find a home or be accommodated by criminal elements of the uncivilised public. The risks were clear: like will find like and criminality is a common cause for both the uncivilised foreigner and the local criminal. Neither respect property, both are intellectually inferior (they are brutish), both morally empty and both equally alien to the civilised public's way of life. In short, they pose an easily identifiable risk to civil life.

Overlapping the above concerns for identity and associated risks were the supporting themes of legitimacy and associated risks. With regard to risks, it was the illegitimacy of the mob and the risk of riot that most commonly attracted comment from the press (Chapter 8). Its concerns centred on the fact that Müller was executed in public and those who showed up to watch the spectacle were nothing other than the uncivilised public turned into a mob whose behaviour 'degraded civilisation' and trampled over the precepts of a 'civilised culture'.[17] The occasion of the execution became an opportunity for the press to show its distaste for the mob and its fear of riots. Indeed, the *Times* insisted that 'how the mob of yesterday behaved must be told'.[18] And in true Hobbesian spirit, the *Times* and the press more widely expressed the view that what was most fearful for any form of civil association was chaos and that defence against the forces of chaos is only effective when the solidarising strength of the civil contract, that a 'civilised public' has with itself, enables it to secure and maintain order—if this meant dispensing with public executions so be it.

For the press of the mid-Victorian 1860s, chaos was greatly feared. As noted above, it tendentiously reported that it was typical for the mob to cause chaos. The fear of the murder trial precipitating a riot was never very far away. Rioting had a long history in Victorian England, though by 1864 it was becoming increasingly difficult to riot in a sustained way or revolutionary manner. The metropolitan police force was established in 1830, and by 1856/1857 there were treasury subsidised police forces across the country. Governments were also increasingly unafraid to use the army to repress civil disorder. The press's distaste for the mob per se (the ultimate symbol of chaos) was palpable. The mob was represented as a seething mass of humanity drawn from the lowest and poorest class, consisting of the dregs of society, the shiftless and the feckless. One list identified the following as belonging to the mob: 'sharpers, thieves, gamblers, betting men, the outsiders of the boxing ring, bricklayers labourers, dock workmen, German artisans and sugar bakers, with a fair sprinkling of what may almost be called as a grade as any of the worst there met – the rankings of the cheap singing-halls and billiard-rooms, the fast young gents of London... There can be only one thing more difficult than describing this crowd, and that is to forget it'.[19] The distaste for the mob did not directly relate to its actual behaviour; indeed, it was recognised that at some points the mob was relatively restrained. More important was its nature and how its nature stood out in sharp relief to the 'civilised public'. If the 'civilised public' was the epitome of a desirable way of life and Thomas Briggs its doyen then the mob was, to cite a report in *Lloyd's Weekly Newspaper*[20] 'cankered with the vices, the crimes, and the hard living, and the ignorance that, to our shame, still deface the body social'.[21] From here, it was a simple step to describe the mob in sub-human terms and to liken it to insects and animals; that is 'a thick, dark, noisy fringe of men and women settled like bees around the nearest barriers, and gradually obliterated their close white lines from view',[22] as 'the dismal crowd, ... seemed to writhe and crawl among themselves'.[23] The anti-civil picture that was tendentiously painted was stark. The animalistic nature of the mob was contrasted with civilised British identity: the mob was an illegitimate gathering that posed a risk to personal and public safety.

Ultimately for the press, the anti-civil narrative consisted of explaining identity and legitimacy in terms of the associated risks. This came down to a very simple set of prejudices—first, the uncivilised can find common cause that transcends national identity in crime and second, the uncivilised can act collectively both as rioters and as a mob on public occasions. Primarily the former threatens personal safety, the latter public order. Both are a threat to a civilised way of life and both should be dealt with by the rigorous application of the law and constant vigilance. The anti-civil narrative emphasised how public space was easily threatened and turned into somewhere unsafe for the civilised public as well as how the civilised status quo was threatened.

2.5 The Civil and Anti-civil Narratives Combined

Overall the civil narrative of the civilised public and the anti-civil narrative of the uncivilised public combined to generate a civil orthodoxy which manifested itself in news coverage which in turn endorsed the view that both narratives vigorously supported a civil ideal and yet promoted the political power of certain state office-holders, mainly the Home Office and the police force and the civil power of the judiciary. Civil pressure groups were few and the most prominent was given short shrift, notably the German Legal Protection Society (Deutscher Rechtsschutz-Verein, also referred to in the UK as the German National Verein). The judgement made was quite simply that current levels of civility were sufficient for a civilised and just society, and also that anti-civil threats could be adequately dealt with and accordingly readers essentially thought that the status quo should be maintained and preserved. In other words, the murder brought forth no demands for radical changes, no cry of immediate redress and any necessary reforms that the trial and sentence revealed were in fact already being dealt with (legal reform and the ending of public executions) and this was to be welcomed as managed progress. To repeat the point (made in Chapter 4, Sect. 4) what emerged from the coverage was the belief that what was currently agreed to be civil, the social narrative with regard to the constitution of the private, the public, or what was taboo was right and did not require change and that established forms of behaviour and manners were both functional and aesthetically acceptable and endorsable. Consequently, despite the contradictory and somewhat hypocritical reporting in the press, the existing normative order was not challenged and the civil society portrayed reflected a middle-class microcosm, whereby the press reduced English society to a dominant upper and lower middle class with an essentially segregationist outlook. The press displayed the view that the murder, for most people, didn't represent an appropriate opportunity to engage in social reform, but rather required a vigorous endorsement of the status quo to protect current ways of life.

Notes

1. The emphasis on England is deliberate. As Hoppen (1998: 513) notes in 1841, 80.2% of the British and 55.7% of the UK population lived in England, by 1901 it was 82.5 and 73.6% respectively.
2. *The Huddersfield Chronicle*, 23 July 1864: 7.
3. Today official sources are adept at working with the press; less so in mid-Victorian England where in some cases there existed among some politicians and civil servants the belief that talking to the press undermined the proper workings of parliament and government. By the 1860s, the importance of the use of authoritative sources and unofficial briefings

was becoming more and more widely recognised and cultivated, perhaps in part due to the example set by Lord Palmerston (Prime Minister, June 1859–October 1865) who constantly used the press for his own political purposes.
4. *The Daily News*, 21 July 1864: 5.
5. Ibid.
6. *The Daily News*, 9 August 1864: 6.
7. The actual phrase working class is rarely used in the newspapers rather terms like lower classes, criminal classes, labourers, travellers and artisan workmen were used in an inferential way and usually in opposition to the descriptions of the 'civilised public'.
8. *Lloyd's Weekly London Newspaper*, 20 November 1864: 1.
9. According to Hegel (1967 [1821]), civil society is organised through three elements: a 'system of needs' (market-based and rule-governed relationships based on the recognition of mutual interdependency); 'the administration of justice' (the enforcement of rights especially property rights through a legal system) and 'the police and corporations' (respectively a public body supporting the administration of justice and those associations concerned with the promotion of public benefits).
10. *The Daily News*, 20 July 1864: 5.
11. *The Evening Standard*, 9 September 1864: 5.
12. *The Daily Telegraph*, 31 October 1864: 2. Referring to two witnesses for the defence, Mrs. Jones and Miss. Eldred.
13. *The Daily News*, 27 September 1864: 3.
14. *The Evening Standard*, 31 October 1864: 4.
15. *Lloyd's Weekly London Newspaper*, 1 January 1865: 6.
16. *The Illustrated London News*, 23 July 1864: 91.
17. *Lloyd's Weekly London Newspaper*, 20 November 1864: 1.
18. *The Times*, 15 November 1864: 9.
19. *The Times*, 15 November 1864: 9, reprinted verbatim in *Lloyd's Weekly London Newspaper*, 20 November 1864: 5.
20. *Lloyd's Weekly London Newspaper*, 20 November 1864: 1.
21. *Lloyd's Weekly London Newspaper*, 20 November 1864: 1.
22. *The Times*, 15 November 1864: 9.
23. *Lloyd's Weekly London Newspaper*, 20 November 1864: 5.

Bibliography

Alexander, J. (2006). *The Civil Sphere*. Oxford: Oxford University Press.
Brown, L. (1985). *Victorian News and Newspapers*. Oxford: Clarendon Press.
Carlyle, T. (1885 [1836]). *Sartor Resartus: The Life and Opinions of Herr Teufelsdröckh*. New York: John B. Alden.

Hegel, G. W. F. (1967 [1821]). *Hegel's Philosophy of Right* (T. M. Knox, Trans. with notes). Oxford: Oxford University Press.
Hoppen, K. T. (1998). *The Mid-Victorian Generation: 1846–1886*. Oxford: Oxford University Press.

CHAPTER 10

Résumé

1   Why a Résumé?

I said in the introductory Chapter 1 to Part I (as well as in the Introduction to Chapter 9) of this book that the civil power of the news resides in two things: (a) its relationship to public sentiment and the way the news subsequently reports our invariant civil concerns of identity, legitimacy and risk and (b) how these invariant civil concerns are assembled and understood in the form of civil and anti-civil judgements which contribute to the type of boundaries we place around civil society with regard to whom and what we regard as civil and anti-civil. The aim of the book was to prove this postulate. In so doing, it has covered a wide range of areas and arguments. I am mindful of this in terms of the demands I have made upon the patience and forbearance of the reader. And so, following the example of the philosopher Philip Pettit, I offer up a brief résumé of the basic intellectual claims and argumentative movements made during the course of this book. In other words, I am only concerned here with two things: the theoretical and the methodological underpinnings of my arguments, specifically the basic reasoning behind the arguments made in Part I and Part II of this book.

Part I

2 Background and Key Insights

Based on the sociological and philosophical insights of Jeffrey Alexander's civil sphere theory, this book attempts to provide both a coherent and consistent explanation of the nature of the civil power of the news. This indebtedness to civil sphere theory explains the critically important assumptions I make about the civil sphere—that it is analytically its own area of sociological inquiry, fundamentally institutional in form, essentially communicative and discursive in nature, instantiated in the real as simultaneously a normative and contested realm of outlooks, views, rules and laws—which are all directly derived from this theory. Based upon these assumptions is the argument that the news engages with our invariant civil concerns of identity, legitimacy and risk. These concerns are, I claim, a universal feature of life in all civil spheres and are nothing other than aspects of human nature and the basic categories of concern whenever people turn their attention and thoughts to the kind of associative life they find themselves in, that they want and that they value. The societal expression of these concerns is to be found among other things in public sentiment which the news inextricably attends to in determining how and what it ultimately reports on.

3 The Ideal, the Real and the News Cycle

The institutional nature of the news has within itself an ideal of how news should be undertaken. It is an ideal that espouses the value of accuracy, sincerity, truth telling and objectivity all of which are supposed to combine to form the basis for receiving the warrant of public trust in the news. It is a powerful ideal and one that still has traction today in the education and training of journalists, the paraphernalia of prizes and awards journalists give themselves and the myths and fictional stories that are told or made about journalists doing their job. The civil ideal of news has a normative force which, as I said in the summary to Chapter 2, influences, shapes or reinforces preferences, choices, values, opinions and above all the civil norms we endorse as they express our invariant civil concerns. Undermining the application of this civil ideal are political and commercial pressures, understood in Chapter 3 as the exercise of state and commercial power. Both state power and commercial power diminish the civil ideal of news and they do so in a variety of ways that span the pursuit of influence through: partisan reporting and/or commercial control, agenda setting through editorial control and by adjusting choices and expectations by systematic misrepresentation and the eschewing of journalistic integrity. The ideal and the real contest each other in mainly antagonistic ways—though occasionally in agonistic ways—in the competition between different newsroom cultures and correspondingly in how newsrooms variously engage with public sentiment. This engagement exists in the news cycle described in Chapter 4 according to its universal and timeless features:

1. Our invariant civil concerns are well understood in terms of the cultural disposition and dominant outlook in any particular newsroom by news editors, news journalists and relevant others.
2. A newsroom declares an event to be a news event, that is an event which is deemed to be of public interest and of relevance to our invariant civil concerns.
3. The news event is judged to be predominantly civil or anti-civil and is reported in one of the three ways (discursively, descriptively or tendentiously).
4. The news report ultimately endorses one of three cardinal types of civil boundary maintenance:
    (a) the endorsement of civil values and the promotion of change in accordance and consistent with those values in civil society.
    (b) the endorsement of anti-civil values and the promotion of change in accordance and consistent with those values in civil society.
    (c) the rejection of change and the civil or anti-civil endorsement of the status quo in civil society.
5. The news report, through its particular endorsement of a certain cardinal type of civil boundary maintenance, re-engages with public sentiment further fuelling the need for the news continuously to attend to our invariant civil concerns.

The news cycle never stops and the news always reports certain news events in accordance with how the newsroom and its culture make its civil or anti-civil judgements and what cardinal type of boundary maintenance it endorses. In this way, the news exercises its civil power as it helps to determine the normative and associative character of civil life. Through its use and endorsement of one of the three cardinal types of civil boundary maintenance, news reports in effect provide a version of a particular type of civil setting and in so doing influence the civil and anti-civil judgements we make and the type of civil boundary maintenance we value and want.

Part II

4 The Key to Part II: A Practical Demonstration of a Methodology Through a Case Study

If Part I is a theoretical account of the civil power of the news, Part II is a practical account—that is a practical demonstration of how the civil power of the news can be methodologically approached and subsequently revealed. Part II seeks to show the following: First, that when considering the civil power of the news, we are dealing with a timeless phenomenon which is part of the deep architecture of news. By this I mean that wherever there exist news services and people who are concerned with the nature and quality of civil life, the two are timelessly linked in the same way. Second, that the civil power of the news can be studied empirically in diverse socio-politico and cultural settings. Both of these two points are addressed through a certain methodological approach which attends to the architecture of the news where that architecture is understood as the way news reports deal with our invariant civil concerns and the type of cardinal civil boundary maintenance that these concerns come to endorse. Specifically, such a methodology must go through two phases: first, disaggregating the invariant civil concerns addressed and prioritised within news reports in order to determine the nature of the news's civil and anti-civil judgements and second, reaggregating these civil and anti-civil judgements to capture which one of the three types of cardinal civil boundary maintenance was ultimately endorsed.

The methodological approach to the disaggregation of the invariant civil concerns in the news reports analysed is premised on the fact that each of these invariant civil concerns has its own language and specifically its own lexicon (see the lexical tables Chapters 6–8). This lexicon is used in news reports in variously explicit and implicit ways and serves any one of the three styles of news reporting (discursive, descriptive and tendentious) equally well. Civil and anti-civil judgements can be just as forcefully made in any particular style of news reporting. Naturally enough, the newspapers and news reports looked at generally had within them more than one invariant civil concern, several lexical codes and sometimes more than one style of reporting, as well as being accompanied to varying degrees by direct appeals to public sentiment and claims made to represent public concern. Nevertheless, as pointed out in Chapter 5 (Introduction to Part II, Sect. 2) in 'A note on method', the information from each newspaper article was disaggregated into the different categories to form a separate document which then formed the body of evidence [quotations] which in turn underpins the analysis under each of the lexical headings in Chapters 6–8. Reaggregation, again as pointed out (in Chapter 5, Introduction to Part II, Sect. 2 in 'A note on method'), occurred when the analysis of the civil and anti-civil judgements made for all three invariant civil concerns, the appeals to public sentiment and the styles of news reporting were brought together in order to determine what cardinal type of civil boundary was endorsed and promoted by the press and the public (Chapter 9).

5   What the Case Study Points to

The case study was chosen to exemplify the fact that newsrooms then and now are similar in their way of exercising their civil power and that the architecture of this power is always the same—consisting of civil and anti-civil judgements accompanied by an endorsement of a certain type of boundary maintenance. None of this disputes the significance of technological change and the immiserating circumstances (globally) that serve to impede free and independent news journalism. The point here is that wherever there is a civil sphere or aspirations to develop one, the role of the news media is important in terms of its civil power. Quite simply, it can exercise this power liberally or illiberally, in solidarising or divisive ways, judicially and with a concern for justice, or in a partisan manner with a concern for the sectarian promotion of political or commercial power. It can have integrity or be supine. In all cases and in all circumstances if we accept, with Alexander, that the civil sphere is instantiated in the real and that the quality of civil associative live has its own ceaseless concerns, even when it is most oppressed and repressed, then the news will attend in some way or another to those ceaseless and invariant civil concerns and be a force for securing civil liberties or not. In this, modern newsrooms are no different to mid-Victorian ones, and that is also the point of choosing this case study.

6 A FINAL REMARK

Though this book deals with the news's circumstances found mainly in emerging, maturing and mature democracies, it needs to be noted that civil society is always an incomplete project and that contestation over its development and nature is perennial. Democracies can slip backwards as much as oppressive states and repressive states can move forward. As such, there exist no guarantees as to the role the institution of news finds itself required to play, nor as to it being progressive in nature. The news occupies a space of ceaseless contestation between the competing forces of civil diminishment and its own capacity for civil resistance. To put it in the terms I used to open the arguments of this book, the attractiveness of the civil ideal of news journalism has not been eradicated, nor has editorial integrity been completely undermined or overwhelmed though there is no doubt that the civil diminishment of the institution of news is in some parts of the world gaining momentum or at worst is almost complete. And yet, civil resistance survives and where it does the expression of the news's civil power is priceless.

Author Index

A
Aalberg, T., 53
Abrams, D., 164
Adams, W., 268
Agamben, G., 22
Aldridge, M., 53
Alexander, J., 3–8, 13, 14, 17, 18, 20, 22, 33, 47, 53, 54, 75, 92, 94, 109, 113, 212, 252
Allan, S., 54, 136, 268
Altheide, D.L., 117, 118
Altick, R.D., 161
Anderson, A., 268
Anderson, B., 14
Anderson, C.W., 95
Aoyagi-Usui, M., 266
Arkell, H., 156
Ashman, I., 24, 84
Azocar, C., 136

B
Bachmann, I., 23
Bachrach, P., 93
Baker, C.E., 96
Baker Whelan, L., 277
Bakker, P., 84
Baldwin, T., 82, 93
Ball, J., 87
Bantz, C., 119
Baran, S., 119
Baranek, P.M., 266
Baratz, M.S., 93
Bardoel, J., 117
Barnett, B., 24
Barnett, S., 55
Beall, J., 23
Beck, U., 267, 268, 293, 294
Becker, H.S., 164
Bell, A., 137
Bennett, D., 92
Bentham, J., 20, 52, 165
Berezin, M., 21, 23
Berg, C., 136
Berkowitz, D., 119
Berry, M., 202
Betz, M., 56
Billig, M., 23
Blaagaard, B., 84
Blackburn, S., 37

Blumler, J.G., 21, 83
Boczkowski, P.J., 117
Boghossian, P., 40
Bohman, J., 21
Bols, P.D., 119
Borger, M., 84
Born, G., 53, 117
Bourdieu, P., 90
Boyce, T., 294
Boyle, K., 24
Boyles, J.L., 95
Branston, G., 136
Brock, D., 93
Brown, L., 152, 308
Brown, W., 23
Brunetti, A., 45
Bruns, A., 23
Buchanan, A., 252
Buckalew, J.K., 118
Buckingham, D., 92
Burke, E., 52
Burns, T., 118
Butler-Breese, E., 92
Butsch, R., 136
Byrne, B., 176

C
Canter, L., 83, 84
Carey, J., 48, 120
Carlson, M., 72, 95
Carlson, T., 92
Carlyle, T., 52, 222, 290, 315
Carter, C., 136
Cassidy, W.P., 23
Chabay, I., 293
Chan, J.B.L., 266
Chernobrov, D., 110, 294
Chibnall, S., 150, 279
Christians, C., 55
Clyde, R.W., 118
Coddington, M., 95

Cohen, A., 15
Cohen, J., 21
Cohen, S., 202, 266
Coleman, S., 83
Collingwood, R.G., 53, 132
Colquhoun, K., 156, 204, 207, 244, 279
Cornell, C., 164
Corner, J., 68, 92, 136
Cornia, A., 57
Cottle, S., 45, 268
Couldry, N., 90
Cranfield, D., 161
Crawford, E., 92
Critcher, C., 266
Crossley, J.G., 124, 253
Curran, J., 53, 56, 68, 81, 136
Cushion, S., 21

D
Dahl, R.A., 92
Dahlgren, P., 55, 73, 74, 90, 117, 118
Davies, G., 53
Davies, K.H., 92
Davies, N., 82
Davis, A., 119
De Keyser, J., 83
Delaney, D., 15
Delanty, G., 23
Denscombe, M., 269
Deuze, M., 117, 118
Dewey, J., 10, 20, 21, 116
Diamond, M., 160
Dickens, C., 203, 222
Dimitrova, D.V., 119
Dimmick, J., 81
Dinc, P., 164
Dixon, T., 136
Dodd, M., 254
Domingo, D., 24, 84

Douglas, M., 269, 293, 294
Dowell, B., 94
Dryzek, J.S., 21
Dunn, J., 55
Dunwoody, S., 268
Durkheim, E., 13, 14, 22
Dworkin, R., 96

E
Eagleton, T., 54, 84
Edelman, M., 94
Edwards, M., 33
Eldridge, J., 266
Elgott, J., 208
Elliott, P., 119
Ellis, R., 293
El Zahed, S., 83
Ensor, R.C.K., 161
Entman, R., 73
Epstein, E.J., 117, 118
Epstein, S., 14
Ericson, R.V., 119, 266
Erikson, K.T., 13

F
Farinosi, M., 24
Feaster, J., 81
Festenstein, M., 21
Fink, K., 95
Fishkin, J., 21
Fishman, M., 117
Fletcher, R., 17
Foer, F., 96
Fontenot, M., 24
Forde, K.R., 32
Foucault, M., 109
Fox, W., 93, 148, 162, 178, 195, 198, 204, 276, 277
Franklin, B., 75

Friedman, M., 268

G
Gálik, M., 97
Gallagher, A.H., 24
Galtung, J., 120, 137, 294
Gans, H.J., 117
Gardner, D., 297
Garton-Ash, T., 86, 90, 112, 137
Gauthier, G., 39, 40
Geuss, R., 19, 113, 137, 252
Ghersetti, M., 81, 84
Giddens, A., 137, 266–268, 295
Gieryn, T.F., 95
Gilens, M., 136
Glass, R., 52
Goffman, E., 107
Gold, D., 118
Goldberger, P., 23
Golding, P., 119
Goodell, R., 294
Gordon, E., 156
Grabe, M.E., 119
Graham, A., 53
Grant, J., 21, 22
Green, J., 93
Gregory, D., 22, 23, 131
Guibernau, M., 15
Gunter, B., 92
Guo, L., 83
Gurevitch, M., 83
Gutmann, A., 94
Gynnild, A., 95

H
Habermas, J., 21, 22, 46
Hahn, K.S., 53
Hall, S., 14, 92, 266
Hallin, D.C., 57

Hamilton, James T., 81, 85
Hammond, E., 94
Hampton, J., 252
Hampton, M., 171
Hanitzsch, T., 45, 54, 90
Hanna, M., 254
Hansen, A., 266, 295
Hapgood, F., 96
Harcup, T., 92, 137, 294
Harding, P., 56
Harlow, S., 23
Harris, M., 97
Harrison, A., 35
Harrison, J., 21, 24, 40, 49, 52, 53, 57, 82, 84, 92, 93, 97, 106, 107, 117–120, 124, 129, 137, 253
Hartley, L., 119
Hartmann, D., 164
Hawthorn, G., 212
Hegel, G.W.F., 3, 313, 319
Held, D., 21
Helgeson, J., 293
Hellmueller, L., 24
Helm, D., 53
Hemmer, N., 93
Henrichsen, J., 92
Hermans, L., 84
Hermida, A., 24, 95
Hoffmann, R.J.S., 22
Hogg, M.A., 164
Hoplamazian, G., 81
Hoppen, K.T., 318
Horlick-Jones, T., 268
Horsley, W., 92
Hudson, M., 92
Hylton, S., 277–279

I
Inglis, F., 33, 131
Inglis, K., 203

Iosifidis, P., 57
Iyengar, S., 53, 81

J
Jackson, D., 94
Jacobs, R.N., 92
Jaworsky, B., 94
Jenkins, R., 164
Johal, S., 69, 93, 136
Johnson, P., 173
Jones, P., 23
Jönsson, A.M., 84
Josephi, B., 47, 56

K
Kakutani, M., 72, 82, 85
Kalogeropoulos, A., 17
Kant, I., 20
Karlsen, J., 95
Kasperson, J., 293
Kasperson, R.E., 266, 293
Katovsky, B., 92
Katsirea, I., 56, 57
Kaufhold, K., 24
Kellett, J.R., 174
Kim, J.J., 92
Kitzinger, J., 268, 294
Kleemans, M., 84
Kleis Nielsen, R., 17, 57
Knightley, P., 92
Knott, G., 148, 190
Kovach, B., 43, 45
Krause, N., 21
Küng-Shankleman, L., 117

L
Lachlan, K.A., 24
Laclau, E., 55
Laing, R.D., 137

AUTHOR INDEX 331

Lamont, M., 22
Lang, A., 119
Lash, S., 268, 294
Lashmar, P., 269
Lasorsa, D.L., 24
Lasswell, H., 55
Lee, A.J., 161
Lefebvre, H., 15, 23
Levack, P., 22
Levin, S., 95
Levy, D.A.L., 17
Lewin, K., 23
Lewis, A., 88
Lewis, S.C., 24, 84, 95
Li, Y., 24
Linz, D., 136
Lippmann, W., 20, 21, 35
Lisosky, J.M., 92
Livingstone, S., 92
Locke, J., 3, 212, 252
Luce, E., 74, 80
Luckmann, T., 71
Luengo, M., 92
Lukes, S., 68–71, 73, 78, 91–93, 112
Lund, A.B., 81
Lupton, D., 269, 294
Lynch, J., 68

M

MacGill, S., 269
Manning, P., 119
Mansfield, H., 20
Massey, D., 15, 23
Mathieson, C., 174, 278
Mayhew, H., 175, 176
Mazur, A., 266
Mazzoleni, G., 118
McConnell, S., 24, 136
McManus, J.H., 90
McNair, B., 45, 54
Meier, W., 294

Meyer, E., 95
Mill, J.S., 55, 165, 166, 205
Miller, D., 294
Mitchell, P., 90
Mitchell, W., 269
Mitchelstein, E., 117
Molnar, V., 22
Moran, M., 69, 93, 136
Morley, D., 23
Morozov, E., 96
Mosdell, N.A., 45
Mouffe, C., 55
Mounk, Y., 70
Müller, J.W., 71, 93
Murdock, G., 268
Mythen, G., 266, 268, 295

N

Nair, G., 156
Najekal, N., 296
Newman, N., 17, 23
Newsome, D., 278
Nikoltchev, S., 52
Noelle-Neumann, E., 54
Norris, P., 45
Nussbaum, M., 21
Nye, J., 68

O

Oblak, T., 117
O'Neill, D., 137
O'Neill, O., 35, 39
Orme, B., 56
Örnebring, H., 84
Ostgaard, E., 137

P

Pachucki, S., 22
Pantti, M., 84

Papathanassopoulos, S., 57
Papper, H., 56
Pariser, E., 93
Park, R., 67
Parsons, T., 22
Paterson, C., 73, 92
Paul, C., 92
Paulussen, S., 24, 84
Pendergrass, M.C., 22
Perrin, A., 23
Peter, F., 252
Peters, H., 294
Petersen, A., 268
Pettit, P., 21, 321
Petts, J., 268
Phillips, D., 41
Pidgeon, N., 293, 294
Popper, K., 41
Postman, N., 90
Pottker, H., 54
Pukallus, S., 21, 57, 92, 93, 97
Putnam, R., 21

R
Rabin-Havt, A., 93
Raeymaeckers, K., 83
Randall, D., 106
Rasmussen, P.K., 117
Rawls, J., 53, 252
Reese, S., 119
Rehg, W., 21
Reilly, J., 266, 294, 295
Revers, M., 95
Reynold, A., 24
Richards, I.A., 130
Rieley, A., 156
Robins, K., 23
Robinson, S., 95
Rogers, C., 268

Ropeik, D., 269, 294
Rosengren, K.E., 137
Rosenstiel, T., 36, 45
Roshco, B., 40
Ross, K., 136
Ross, T., 208
Ruge, M., 120, 137, 294
Runciman, D., 94
Rusbridger, A., 87
Ryan, A., 20, 55
Ryfe, D., 117, 118

S
Said, E., 22
Salovaara-Moring, I., 81
Sambrook, R., 45, 54
Sampei, Y., 266
Sande, O., 120, 137
Sandel, M., 14, 21
Sandman, P., 268
Saurugger, S., 21
Schaap, G., 84
Schain, M., 23
Schanne, M., 294
Schiller, D., 54
Schlesinger, P., 14, 80, 117–119
Schmitt, C., 72
Schoeffl, J., 90
Schudson, M., 54, 92, 119, 120
Schulz, W., 54
Schutz, A., 71
Scott, C.P., 131
Seaton, J., 55, 68, 136
Sehl, A., 57
Shaw, M., 267
Sherman, E., 93
Shklar, J., 94
Shoemaker, P., 23, 119
Silverstone, R., 38, 47, 51, 108

Simmons, J., 277
Simmons, J.L., 118
Singer, J., 24, 53, 84
Slavtcheva-Petkova, V., 23
Slovic, P., 293
Smith, P., 22
Smyth, F., 93
Snow, P., 118
Solon, O., 80
Soloski, J., 117
Soroka, S., 53
Sparkes, V.M., 137
Spates, S.A., 24
Spence, P.R., 24
Stallings, R.A., 294
Stanier, J., 92
Starkman, D., 73
Stavelin, E., 95
Steensen, S., 117
Strömbäck, J., 119
Sundar, S., 119
Sunstein, C., 96
Syllas, C., 57

T
Tajfel, H., 14, 164
Taylor, C., 12, 21, 22
Taylor, M., 208
Thompson, D., 94
Thompson, F.M.L., 173
Thompson, J., 92
Thompson, M., 293
Thorsen, E., 94
Thrift, N., 13, 23
Thurman, N., 24
Tocqueville, A., 3, 19, 20, 47, 166
Treré, E., 24
Tuchman, G., 40, 117–119, 136
Tulloch, J., 269, 294

Tulloch, M., 268
Tumber, H., 92, 119
Tunstall, J., 137
Turner, J.C., 14, 164, 201

U
Ugille, P., 24, 84
Urry, J., 23

V
Vaidhyanathan, S., 87
Van Aelst, P., 53
van der Linden, S., 293
Vehkoo, J., 96
Villa, D., 20
Vos, T.P., 23

W
Waddington, K., 203
Wahl-Jorgensen, K., 95
Waldron, J., 20, 96, 113, 270
Wales, C., 266, 295
Wall, M., 83
Wallis, R., 119
Walton, G., 208
Weber, M., 13, 14, 22, 35, 53, 79, 115, 116, 252
Webster, F., 92
Weder, B., 45
Wennberg, H., 23
Westerman, D., 24
Westlund, O., 81
White, D.M., 23
Wigley, S., 24
Wildavsky, A., 269, 293, 294
Wilke, J., 54
Wilkinson, I., 294

Williams, B., 36, 39, 41, 42, 54, 211
Williams, C., 136
Williams, K., 69, 93, 136, 161
Winter, J.P., 137
Winthrop, D., 20
Woods, L., 49, 53, 78, 91
Woodward, K., 14
Wright Mills, C., 92

Y
Yu, J., 23

Z
Zhou, S., 119

Subject Index

A

accidents, railway, 255, 278, 285, 295, 298. *See also* railway travel, nineteenth-century
accountability, 90, 211–215, 218, 219, 225, 251
advertising revenue, 78, 161
Alexander, Jeffrey. *See* civil sphere, the
ALRC. *See* Australian Law Reform Commission (ALRC) 2014 Report
alternative news media, 18
alt right news, US, 72
analysis, content. *See* research method, the
Anti-civil Judgements (ACJ), 3, 12, 36, 52, 108, 110, 114, 117, 121, 122, 125, 129, 135, 151, 153, 155, 156, 165, 184, 185, 187, 190, 193, 196, 198, 201, 213, 214, 244, 265, 275, 285, 288, 295, 304, 305, 323–325
anti-civil narrative of the uncivilised public, 313, 317

archetype, middle-class, 307
aristocracy, 52. *See also* estates, the three
arrests, 159, 171, 227, 250, 256
audience/user/reader, the
   citizen, as a, 24, 45, 50, 65, 68, 78, 83, 84, 91, 105, 136, 178
   consumer, as a marketplace, 65, 66, 68, 78, 82, 84, 90, 91, 132
   trust in the news, and, 37, 38
audience trivialisation, rejecting, 106
Australian Law Reform Commission (ALRC) 2014 Report, 54
authorities, the, 223, 245, 252, 284, 289, 293, 309
   English justice, and applying, 220. *See also* justice system, the contemporary
   police investigation, 220. *See also* detective force
authority, 5, 47, 49, 50, 52, 53, 84, 90, 95, 110, 113, 123, 165, 211–219, 222, 225, 228, 231, 244, 249, 251, 252, 276, 281, 303, 308

B

balance, 16, 36, 43, 44, 50, 53, 54, 76, 85, 130, 166, 170, 197, 246, 248, 253, 288
BBC, 54, 56, 95, 156
behaviour, 13, 14, 33, 67, 69, 108, 118, 124, 127, 164, 169, 170, 173, 190, 211, 246, 248, 267, 268, 313, 314, 318. *See also* Müller, Franz
  mob, 184, 191–193, 199–201, 316, 317
  press, 136, 171, 175, 178, 180, 181, 183–189, 191–193, 199–201, 284, 316
bias, 41, 43, 54, 55, 67, 73, 87, 106, 116, 119, 166, 242, 252, 293, 294. *See also under* trustworthiness of the news
blood type analysis. *See under* detective investigation, the, forensic crime scene analysis
bombings, 295
boundaries
  borders, as, 14, 15, 23, 277
  civil society, of, 3, 8, 14–16, 23, 108–110, 114, 122–124, 126–129, 168, 215, 274, 303, 305, 306, 321, 323
  normative, 13, 15, 108–111, 125, 126, 305, 324
  space as a social construct, 23
  symbolic, 13, 14, 22
boundary maintenance, 8, 91, 109, 114, 129, 130, 304, 323–325
  inclusion and exclusion, 14, 16
  inhuman geographies, 13
Bow, the neighbourhood of. *See* Hackney
Breitbart, 93
Brexit, 202, 253

Briggs, Thomas. *See* murder, events of the
Britain's first railway murder. *See* railway murder, the
British Social Attitudes Report, 2013, 94
bulletins, 72, 131
Buzz Feed, 18

C

Calcutt Reports, 136
Cameron, David, 76
  Calais migrant 'crisis', 208
campaigns, 74, 75, 77, 94, 132, 153, 254, 310
  newspaper, 132
  public, 47, 215, 216, 218, 279, 284, 292, 309
Canary, The, 73
capitalism, 4
Capital Punishment (Amendment) Act 1868, The, 222, 254, 258
carriage compartment, separate, 146
carriages, railway, 145, 149, 174, 182, 185, 194, 198, 203, 204, 245, 255, 278, 280, 285, 286, 289, 291, 292
categories/categorisation. *See* disaggregation; reaggregation
censorship, 89, 116
chain, gold. *See* watch, gold chain and
chain of evidence, 247, 250. *See also* circumstantial evidence
chaos. *See* mob, the
Church, the, 52, 202. *See also* estates, the three
circumstantial evidence, 148, 199, 221, 232, 235
citizen journalism, 17, 45, 83, 84, 268
  gatekeeping role, 23
citizen journalists, 83, 84

SUBJECT INDEX 337

civil boundary maintenance, 16, 107–109, 125, 128, 129, 133, 156, 303–306, 323, 324
Civil Boundary Type (CBT), 133
civil concerns, 3, 11, 17, 122–124, 132, 134, 135, 145, 151, 153, 155, 156, 163, 213, 214, 270, 288, 303, 304
civil ideal of the news, 19, 31–34, 38, 40, 45–52, 65–67, 70–72, 77, 87, 91, 92, 105–107, 128. *See also* liberal ideals of the news; trustworthiness of the news
civility, 5, 6, 10, 11, 18, 31, 34, 46, 47, 50, 113, 115, 127, 178, 284, 307, 318
civil judgements, 133, 145, 176, 182, 201, 216, 222, 225, 234, 271, 272, 279, 283, 284
civil lexicon, 167–17, 188, 214–216, 228, 232, 235, 246, 247, 271–273, 275, 281, 283, 284
civil narrative of the civilised public. *See* middle-class interests, paramount
civil power, 20, 32, 57, 92, 108, 109, 125–127, 134, 145, 214, 271, 303, 318, 325, 326
civil power of the news, 15, 17, 31, 51, 110, 113–115, 133, 150, 155, 265, 322, 324
  public sentiment, and, 3, 9, 16, 109, 128, 134, 145, 304, 321
civil rights, 32, 215–217, 276. *See also* freedom of expression; rights; right to know
civil society
  active civil society, 17, 23
  anti-civil judgements, 12, 108, 109, 114, 121, 122, 134, 321
  civil judgements, 126, 214, 272
  institutions, factual media, 8, 16

  solidary sphere. *See* civil sphere, the
  tyranny, 19, 112
civil sphere, the
  Alexander, Jeffrey, 3, 4, 7, 78, 314, 322, 325
  CSI, 3
  CSII, 3, 4
  CSIII, 3, 8
  democracy, 31, 47, 48, 213
  inclusion and exclusion, 16, 22
  institutions, 6–8, 16, 18, 47, 78, 109, 122, 126, 213, 216, 217, 312, 314, 322
  journalism, and, 16, 31, 47, 48, 78, 325
  office, exercise of, 47
  power holders, 6, 7, 213
  solidarising nature of, 5, 7, 127, 325
Civil War, American, 159
class. *See* social class in the Victorian era
clues, 224–226, 246, 250, 281, 282, 286
coherentism, 54
commercial journalism, 79
commercial power, 65, 67, 68, 70, 78, 79, 91, 323
commercial reality
  anti-civil values, promotion of, 19, 110
communication, 10, 21, 33, 46–49, 55, 67, 109, 115, 118, 232, 256, 280, 282, 285, 294, 310
communication cord. *See* Railways Act, the 1868 Regulation of
communication technology(ies), advances in, 45
  news production, 83, 118
  social media, role of, 18, 55, 67, 82, 115

communicative democracy, 10, 21. *See also* democracy
compartment, railway, 174, 245, 278, 279. *See also* carriage compartment, separate; carriages, railway
conflict, 6–8, 16, 17, 20, 39, 47, 51, 69, 74, 105, 117, 130, 131, 153, 164, 167, 211, 242
Contempt of Court Act 1981, 253
content analysis of the newspaper articles
   civil/anti-civil judgements, public sentiment appeals and news styles collated, 128, 152, 155, 191, 223, 237, 325
   disaggregation of categories, 128, 155, 156, 325
   invariant civil concerns and lexicon labelled, 155, 156, 214, 218, 270, 271, 275, 325
   public sentiment claims located, 155, 325
   reaggregation to establish civil boundary type, 325
   reporting styles pinpointed, 43, 91, 121, 125, 129–134, 151, 155, 156, 187, 222, 237, 312, 325
control, 5–7, 21, 23, 31, 74, 77, 78, 80, 84–86, 88–90, 95, 116, 119, 218, 219, 266, 267, 271, 273, 274, 276, 284, 288, 292, 323
control, editorial, 70, 118, 323
conviction, 156, 158, 185, 189, 192, 231, 232, 239, 242, 249, 253
Coroner's verdict, 148, 222, 250
corruption, 52, 53, 93, 112, 214–216
cosmopolitanism, 13
court, the, 113, 119, 148, 155, 180, 183, 188, 190, 191, 195, 197, 204, 216, 221, 228–230, 232, 238, 239, 249, 251, 253, 254, 312, 315. *See also* Müller, Franz; press coverage of the murder; trial proceedings, Müller's
crime, 95, 149, 150, 153, 157, 158, 161, 173, 177, 178, 183, 185–187, 189, 193–197, 199, 200, 202, 221, 224–226, 228–231, 233, 236–241, 243, 245, 246, 248, 253–255, 277, 279–285, 287–292, 309, 312, 313, 317
crime scene, 146
criminal classes, the, 185, 192, 277, 315, 319
Criminal Justice Act 1865, 253
criminal system, 311
cultural and historical narrative, 13
civil boundaries, 15
Culture, Practice and Ethics of the Press, 95
cut down mode. *See* hat, cut down top

D

Daily News, The, 151, 180, 184, 185, 194, 196, 204–208, 227, 229–232, 236, 238, 240, 241, 245, 250, 251, 254–257, 259–263, 279, 280, 283, 285, 286, 295–298, 319
Daily Telegraph, The, 151, 152, 160, 177, 179, 182, 204–206, 208, 222, 230, 231, 233, 236, 238, 240, 242–245, 248, 249, 254, 255, 257–259, 261–263, 279, 289, 295–298, 319
danger to journalists, 92
death penalty
   Capital Punishment (Amendment) Act 1868, The, 222, 258
   hanging, public, 148, 221, 222
   Murder (Abolition of Death Penalty) Act 1965, 254

SUBJECT INDEX 339

debate, public, 10, 46, 52, 55
Defamation Act 2013, 254
defendant, 221, 253, 310
deliberative democracy, 21, 45. *See also*
  democracy
  social inquiry, through, 10
democracy
  associations, 7, 8, 19
  information as emancipation, 45, 46, 50, 96
  institutions, formal, 19
democratic integration, 4, 5, 11, 18, 34, 46, 47, 50, 115
descriptive news style, use of the. *See* news reporting styles
detective force, 146, 147, 228, 246
  creation of the plain clothed Detective Branch, 157
  Road Hill House murder, the, 220
  Whicher, Detective Inspector Jack, 221
detective investigation, the
  arrest warrant, arrangements for an, 147, 227
  capture and arrest of Müller, 185, 227
  evidence of the clues, 146
  extradition from New York, 148, 159
  forensic crime scene analysis, the role of, 146
  identifying a suspect, 171. *See also* Matthews, Jonathan
  pursuit of Müller, 226
  rewards for information, 226, 228, 246
  search for Müller, 149
detectives
  Kerressey, Inspector, 224, 227, 244
  Mayne, Sir Richard, 159, 220, 225, 245, 246, 279, 281, 288

Tanner, Detective Inspector, 147, 153, 221, 224, 226–228, 244
Whicher, Detective Inspector Jack, 220
Williamson, Inspector Frederick, 158
digital services, 56
digital technologies, 83
disaggregation, 303, 304, 324. *See also under* content analysis of the newspaper articles
discrimination and prejudice, 164, 202
discursive news style, use of the. *See* news reporting styles
disempowerment, 72, 274, 276, 287, 292, 293
disorder, civil, 273, 316. *See also* mob, the
  army, and the, 316
distortion of views, 130

E
ECHR. *See* European Court of Human Rights (ECHR)
emotive language, 132
empiricism, 4, 8, 19, 21, 41, 117, 162, 240
empowerment, 271–273, 279, 280
entertainment, 38, 234, 287
equality, 5, 20, 31, 45, 55, 112
estate, the fourth, 32, 71, 77
estates, the three, 52
ethics, 19, 85, 96
European Broadcasting Union, 53
European Court of Human Rights (ECHR), 54, 97, 252, 253
Evening Standard, The, 151, 179, 186, 187, 193, 195, 203–208, 222, 236, 241, 243, 245, 246, 251, 254–256, 259, 261–263, 283–285, 288, 296, 297, 314, 319

everyday newsroom reality, 19
  civil ideal, the, 19
  commercial pressures, 105
  political power, 70
execution of Müller. *See* hanging, the
expert knowledge, 112, 136, 269
Extradition Treaty, US and Britain's 1842, 223

F
Facebook, 18, 57, 86–88, 94
fake news, 18, 50, 57, 87, 93, 95, 124
fear, 11, 16, 18, 19, 49, 55, 94, 113, 150, 178, 183, 192, 203, 219, 227, 228, 234, 245, 248, 251, 255, 268, 269, 271, 274–278, 280, 282–284, 286–291, 293, 296, 305, 313, 315, 316
Fenning, Eliza. *See* circumstantial evidence
films, 32, 52, 84, 247
fingerprints, 146
Finkelstein Report, 136
focus on senior investigator, public/press, 262
foreigner(s), 193–196, 201, 230, 233, 285, 293, 313, 316
foundationalism, 41, 54
fourth estate, the. *See* estate, the fourth
Fox News, 72
freedom of expression, 45, 48, 49, 52, 66, 86, 88–90, 97, 128, 167, 219, 253, 254
  freedom of speech, 20, 45
  human rights, 45, 96

G
gatekeeping and gatewatching, 23, 67
German immigrants, 159, 175, 193

German Legal Protection Society (GLPS), 148, 160, 179, 184, 195, 196, 198, 223, 231, 239, 244, 260, 262, 318
  Memorial, the German Society's, 149, 240, 250, 251, 255, 282
Germans, 35, 94, 147, 148, 174–176, 183, 186, 189, 191, 192, 194–199, 203, 207, 230, 235, 240, 241, 247, 251, 255, 259, 285, 314, 315, 317
Germany and nationality
  culture and habits, German, 175
  patriotism and empire, 174, 175
  political situation, German, 174
globalisation, 13, 266
GLPS. *See* German Legal Protection Society (GLPS)
gold watch. *See* watch, gold chain and
Google, 57, 80, 95, 106
'good' and 'bad' news, 10. *See also* fake news; inclusion and exclusion; 'real' news
  bigotry, 66, 307
  exclusion, 14, 107, 136, 271, 273
  fairness, 16, 51, 76, 116, 138, 219
  hate speech, 202
  integrity, 31, 66, 77, 326
  objectivity, 18, 38–40, 42–44, 51, 119, 322
  partisanship, 34, 45, 65, 68, 70–73, 219, 323
  racism, 126, 136, 201, 202
  sincerity, 15, 35–38, 322
  speculation, 219
  truthfulness, 36, 38, 40
gossip, 38, 119, 191, 242, 284
Greece, 57. *See also* neo-liberal agendas
greed, 18, 169, 190, 286, 314
Grey, Sir George (Home Secretary), 149, 153, 160, 161, 223, 226, 239, 251, 259, 282

SUBJECT INDEX 341

group identities, differentiation between civil/anti-civil judgements, press, 202
group identity, 202
guilt, 157, 160, 181, 183, 185–189, 193, 196, 218, 219, 233, 235, 238–243, 248–251, 253, 258, 283, 284, 292, 312

H
Hackney, 146, 176, 250
hanging, the, 184. *See also* death penalty; justice system, the contemporary
confession, Müller's last-minute, 183, 240
public conduct condemned by press, 233, 234
public execution, the, 184, 222, 234, 310, 311
hat, cut down top, 148, 157, 198, 208
headlines, 94, 194, 231, 237, 253
High-Level Independent Panel on UN Peace Operations (HIPPO), 56
HIPPO. *See* High-Level Independent Panel on UN Peace Operations (HIPPO)
historical background: 1860s mid-Victorian England, 305, 308, 316, 318
views of, alternative, 161, 305
Home Office files, 153, 235, 259
background context, as, 161
hospitality, 16, 51, 108, 115, 167–169, 171, 180, 181, 272, 283
hostility, 91, 92, 164, 202, 203, 274, 275, 285, 286
human-interest stories, 132
human rights. *See* freedom of expression
hyper-partisan news, 87, 88, 93, 124

hypocrisy
middle- and upper-class, 149, 173, 277, 278, 293
political, 47, 77, 94
press, 201, 252, 312

I
ICCPR. *See* International Covenant on Civil and Political Rights (ICCPR)
ideal, the, 322
ideal and the real, the, 91, 323
ideal of news journalism, the, 31, 34, 303, 326
identification, 4, 164, 171, 305
identity
group memberships, 163–165
perceived risks to identity, today's, 293
self-identity, 163, 165
identity and belonging, 167
ideology, 40, 71, 85, 89, 118, 120, 182
Illustrated London News, The, 151, 186, 189, 197, 204–206, 237, 238, 256, 257, 261, 284, 295, 296, 315, 319
immigrants, 159
impartiality, press, 242, 312
imperialism, 305
incitement to discrimination, hostility, violence. *See* International Covenant on Civil and Political Rights (ICCPR)
inclusion and exclusion, 14, 16, 22. *See also* boundary maintenance; 'we'/'us'/'our'; 'we', the collective
'us' and 'them', 14
incompatibility of privacy and security, railway, 280

independence, editorial, 77, 79, 80, 115. *See also* control, editorial; political power
independence in thought and action, civil, 33
independence of the press, 76, 79, 115
individuality, 96, 112, 163. *See also* identity
inequalities, 51, 67, 92, 164, 252, 294
information, 16, 23, 34–38, 44, 49, 50, 52, 53, 55, 57, 74, 77, 81, 83, 84, 86–88, 114, 118, 119, 133, 145, 155, 161, 187, 191, 216, 219, 222–226, 247, 248, 250, 253, 269, 270, 280, 281, 290, 293, 325
informed judgements, 34, 43
inhuman geographies. *See* boundary maintenance
injustice, 51, 112, 126, 149, 164, 214–216, 235, 236, 240, 242
innocence, 160, 178, 179, 218, 219, 221, 230, 231, 235, 237, 239, 242, 243, 248, 250, 258, 260, 284
insecurity, 114, 137, 284, 285, 289, 292
insiders, 14, 95, 150, 167, 309
institutions (journalism and news media organisations), 4, 7, 13, 19, 45, 56, 94, 117, 119, 122, 123, 168, 212–214, 234, 252, 267, 272, 309
integrity, journalistic, 66, 323
interactive news media environment, 96
International Covenant on Civil and Political Rights (ICCPR), 96, 202
International Journalists' Network, 48
invariant civil concern, the

identity, of, 3, 11, 15, 112, 122, 163, 165, 167–171, 201, 249, 252, 321, 322
legitimacy, of, 111, 113, 123, 151, 214, 215, 218, 220, 249, 251
risk, of, 113, 114, 124, 270, 271, 274, 288, 292
invariant civil concern of identity, scope of, 163
invariant civil concern of legitimacy, scope of, 211–213
invariant civil concern of risk, scope of, 265–267, 270
invariant civil concerns, 11, 15, 18, 19, 78, 108–110, 114, 132, 145, 151, 153, 155, 156, 163, 303, 304, 306, 307, 313, 323, 324, 326
civil activities, 17, 115, 121, 122, 135, 213
non-civil activities, 16, 17, 115, 121–123, 135, 213
invasions of privacy, 54
inverted pyramid approach, the, 41

J
Jack the Ripper. *See* Whitechapel murders, 1880s
journalism, 11, 17, 18, 21, 23, 24, 31, 32, 35, 39, 40, 42, 43, 45–51, 53, 55–57, 66, 68, 71–74, 77–80, 82, 83, 90, 91, 93, 95, 105, 115–117, 129, 150, 153, 155, 166, 247, 303. *See also* news journalism
journalists, 12, 18, 23, 32, 35–37, 39–45, 48, 53, 54, 65, 68, 73, 74, 77, 79, 81–85, 87, 90, 92–96, 118, 120, 121, 128, 130, 136, 170, 172, 182, 242, 247, 269, 279, 284, 322

judgements, civil and anti-civil, 3, 11, 36, 108–110, 114, 117, 121, 122, 125, 129, 134, 135, 151, 153, 155, 156, 165, 201, 213, 214, 265, 304, 305, 321, 323–325
judgements on identity, news reports'
   adoption of British culture, Müller's, 179
   animalistic nature of the mob, 200, 317
   differences emphasised, Müller's, 164
   hospitality extended to Müller, 16, 115, 167, 181, 272
   respectability of Briggs' social standing, 176
   self-criticism, press, 191
   stigmatised for his nationality, Müller, 197
   unacceptable characteristics/ behaviour, Müller's, 171
   violation of the social order, 177
   witnesses discredited as unacceptable, 191
judgements on legitimacy, news reports'
   English law as above scrutiny, 251
   infallibility of English justice stressed, 238
   injustice, misgivings over, 235
   legal system endorsed, 233
   safety of the verdict, reassurances on, 238
   self-scrutiny, press, 242
   speculation on Müller's guilt, 249
   trial proceedings, approval of, 228
   trust in the detectives withdrawn, public, 38
judgements on risk, news reports'
   civil empowerment; authorities exhorted to act, 279
   distrust of technological progress, 286
   exemplary detective work endorsed, 281
   hidden danger sensationalised, 287
   hostility and suspicion of Müller/ Germans, 285
   insecurity and uncertainty, need to end, 284
   public empowerment; by safer train carriages, 279
   suspicion of 'ruffians'/fellow passengers, 285
judiciary, the, 52, 212, 318. *See also* estates, the three
jurisdiction, 159, 254
jury, the, 148, 160, 179, 195, 220, 224, 229, 232, 236, 238, 239, 282, 283. *See also* Müller, Franz; press coverage of the murder; trial proceedings, Müller's
justice, 5, 11, 18, 31, 32, 34, 45–47, 50, 55, 113–115, 123, 153, 160, 181, 183, 190, 199, 211, 213–216, 218–220, 224, 226, 228, 229, 231, 233, 235–238, 240, 241, 244, 245, 247, 249, 251, 252, 254, 260, 281–283, 285, 290, 292, 306, 309–312, 319, 325
justice system, the contemporary, 221, 236, 312. *See also* death penalty
hanging, public, 148
unlawful killing, procedure about, 148

K

Kerressey, Inspector, 223, 224, 227, 244
Kew. *See* National Archives, Kew
killer, the. *See* Müller, Franz

L

language, 20, 31, 67, 70, 90, 92, 109, 112, 114, 127, 130, 132, 167–171, 179, 214, 254, 273, 287, 307, 309, 324. *See also* news reporting styles

law, 7, 8, 49, 82, 94, 95, 97, 123, 148, 158–160, 164, 172, 173, 202, 212–216, 218–220, 228, 231, 233–235, 241, 242, 245, 251, 253, 272, 283, 317. *See also* justice; justice system, the contemporary

Law of War Manual, US Pentagon's, 93, 94

legal reform, 310, 311, 318

legitimacy, 3, 11, 12, 15, 47, 108, 110, 113, 114, 211–220, 222, 224, 226, 228, 231, 234, 242, 250–252, 272, 292, 303, 306, 309, 312, 313, 316, 317, 321, 322

Lenin, 137

letters from the public, 152, 157, 204, 247, 259, 279, 307. *See also* sample, the research

background context, as, 307

Leveson Inquiry, the, 54, 94, 95

Leveson Report, the, 54

lexicon
   lexical analysis, 304
   lexical codes, 155, 325
   lexical tables, 155, 324

lexicon of identity, 169, 188
   civil hospitality, approval of, 167
   civil intolerance, criticism and, 171

lexicon of invariant civil concerns, news. *See* lexicon of identity; lexicon of legitimacy; lexicon of risk

lexicon of legitimacy
   civil action, condemns, 218
   civil institutions, antagonism towards, 218
   democratic rights and liberties, inconsistently allots, 220
   guilt or innocence, speculates on, 218
   justice, emphasises need for, 215, 216
   legal authorities/processes, scrutiny of, 215
   legitimate authority, approval of, 213
   public trust, seeks to diminish, 215, 218, 271

lexicon of risk
   civil defiance endorsed, 284
   empowerment and freedom, risks needed for, 271, 274
   non-civil intervention, judgements as to valid, 272
   reassurance about nature/scale of any risk, 271
   retrograde acts/retaliation endorsed, 274, 275
   risk, overcoming threat of, 271
   threat from others or scientific advances, 275

liberal ideals of the news, 31, 34
   civil values, promoting, 50, 126
   role of the news, democratic; building new democracies, 47; democratic structure, with a, 45; political deliberation, 46; promoting democracy, 45; Protocol on Public Service Broadcasting, 48, 56; public service communication outlook, 48

liberalism, 78, 174, 197

libertarian commercialism
   freedom of expression, and, 86
   media pluralism, and, 88

SUBJECT INDEX 345

techno-media companies, in the, 88
liberty, 31, 55, 85, 95, 116, 123, 165, 213, 218
Lloyds Weekly London Newspaper, 151
Edward Lloyd, 161
lower class, the, 190, 195, 201, 293
lower classes, newspaper term, 319. *See also* criminal classes, the

M
Magistrates Court Bow Street London, 147
maintenance, boundary, 13, 14
manipulation, news, 116
market, the, 4, 5, 66, 68, 136, 165
Marx, Karl, 4, 172
Matthews, Jonathan, 147, 186
Mayne, Sir Richard, 158, 159, 246, 254, 256, 295
media, the
 factual, 8, 16, 48, 56, 68, 71, 79, 80, 92, 94, 136, 212, 213, 217, 219, 266, 268, 269
 mass, 6, 10, 266, 294
media organisations, journalism and news, 7
mediapolis, 51
Metropolitan Police Archives, 245
metropolitan police force, 316
middle class, the, 152, 161, 176, 182, 306–309
middle classes, Victorian, 176, 178, 277, 307, 312
middle-class interests, paramount
 civil crisis averted by 'insider information', 308
 civil role, press, 55, 71, 128, 311
 English justice endorsed, 312;
  public hanging abolition, 184

railway safety cause undertaken, 310; letters, legitimacy through the public's, 309; segregation maintained, 278
migrants, 208
'mirror on the world', a, 153
mob, the, 184, 192, 193, 199–201, 290, 312, 313, 316, 317
nature of, 196, 200
mobility, sociology of, 23
morality, 172
Morning Post, 151
motive for the murder, 250
Müller, Franz
 behaviour consistent with a murderer, 201
 behaviour inconsistent with a murderer, 243
 fairness of the legal system, belief in, 230
 GLPS support, 179
 mixed jury, waived a, 230
 New York, departure for, 194
 prison, treatment in, 223
 sympathy for, 179, 181
murder, events of the, 150. *See also* press coverage of the murder
 clues, 146, 246, 250, 282, 286
 Hackney, 250
 hat, significance of the, 157, 158, 227
 murder weapon, 157
 North London Railway line, 146, 182, 204, 222, 225, 279, 281, 287, 292
 railways, first murder on the Victorian, 146
 robbery as the motive, 146
 victim, Thomas Briggs the, 146. *See also* status quo, endorsement of the

watch, the gold chain and. *See* watch, gold chain and
Murder (Abolition of Death Penalty) Act 1965, 254
murderer(s), 149, 165, 178, 180, 184, 185, 187, 188, 191, 193, 194, 197–199, 223, 224, 237, 238, 244–246, 249–252, 255, 259, 281, 282, 286, 288, 289, 292, 315. *See also* Müller, Franz
notorious murders, 156, 221
murder investigation. *See* detective investigation, the

N

National Archives, Kew, 161, 259
nationality, 145, 164, 171, 174, 194, 195, 197, 198, 200, 230, 316
national security, 49, 50, 216, 217
neo-liberal agendas, 49
suppression of information, 50
news
homologies, 137
narratives, 10, 70, 72, 131, 136, 166
role of the, 32, 45–47, 71, 128, 325
symbolic representations, 32
'public conversation', as, 56
'news' commercial interests, 78, 79
news cycle, the, 10, 12, 72, 75, 108–111, 115, 116, 121, 122, 133, 134, 145, 149, 151, 156, 168, 169, 218, 248, 271, 274, 322, 323. *See also* public sentiment
newsgathering, 39, 80, 83, 107, 119
news ideology, 89
civil ideal. *See* civil ideal of the news
liberal ideals. *See* liberal ideals of the news
trustworthiness. *See* trustworthiness of the news

news journalism, 39. *See also* 'good' and 'bad' news; 'mirror on the world', a
audience, its, 40, 82
awards, professional, 32
codes of practice, 66
customs and practices, 9
democratisation, and, 48
education and training, 47, 56, 322
ethics, 68
gatekeeping role of, 23
gatewatching, 23
impartiality, 85
investigative journalism, 35, 66, 80, 269
objectivity, 39–42
obligation not to deceive, 39
practices, 17, 44, 46, 48, 70, 82
public service ethos, 91
reporting methods, 16, 39, 43
social sciences, and the, 56
standards, 39
values, 53, 66, 78, 91, 129
news journalists, 12, 16, 33, 36, 38, 40–42, 70, 75, 77, 83, 93, 105, 107, 136, 181, 323
fictional representations of, 52
news media independence, 77. *See also* estate, the fourth; freedom of expression
complicit 'lapdog', the, 71. *See also* political power; antagonistic reporting, 72; partisan news, 57, 72, 73; undermining liberal ideals, 71
watchdog role, the; civil news ideal protected, 77; objective inquiry, 71; trustworthiness, 71
yapping dog and hypocrisy, the; anodyne reporting, 75, 76; mutual dependency with

SUBJECT INDEX 347

political power, 77; political events as news media spectacles, 75
news media, mainstream, 53, 57, 84, 87, 136
news media power, 68, 85
  cultural power, 92
  soft power and hard power, 48
news organisations, 9, 12, 24, 36, 39, 52, 55–57, 66, 70, 71, 73–75, 78, 80, 82–85, 87, 89, 95, 107, 120, 128, 129, 270, 275
newspaper revenue, 80
newspapers, 19, 20, 52, 66, 79, 80, 92, 94, 96, 118, 120, 131, 132, 138, 149–152, 155–161, 172, 174–181, 183, 186, 188–192, 194–198, 200, 202–208, 221–226, 231, 234–240, 242, 244, 246–251, 253–263, 279, 281, 283, 284, 288, 295–298, 312, 313, 315, 317, 319, 325
newspapers of the 1860s, 171, 254
  competition for readership, 161
news reporters, 9
news reporting
  civil and anti-civil judgements, 117, 121, 125, 129, 134, 155, 292, 325
  civil boundary type, 125, 155, 325
  styles of reporting, 43, 129–131, 133, 134, 155, 325. *See also* news reporting styles
news reporting style, 'hard', 313
news reporting styles
  descriptive, 129–132, 135, 155, 187, 222, 255, 304, 312, 323, 325
  discursive, 129, 130, 132, 135, 155, 237, 304, 323, 325
  tendentious, 129, 130, 132, 135, 155, 304, 323, 325

news reports, 3, 36, 37, 40, 44, 71, 73, 80, 108, 112, 114, 115, 117, 124, 125, 129–135, 152, 155, 156, 164, 165, 167, 170–172, 214, 223, 225, 248, 275, 293, 303, 304, 306, 307, 323–325
newsrooms
  agenda setting, and, 115, 323
  civil power, exercise of, 324, 325
  competition for audiences, 81, 117
  influence, commercial and political, 105, 106, 108, 115, 325
  judgements, 121, 323
  newsroom subjectivity, 10, 12
  news selection processes, routine, 118
  newsworthiness, 119, 120
  technological developments, 117
news selection
  coverage, 75, 126, 148, 150–152, 156, 166, 179, 222, 265, 305, 307, 317
  criteria, 119
  newsworthiness, 119, 121, 122
  routine practices, 119
  sources, routine, 119
news services, 50, 89, 324
news stories, 15, 49, 114, 118, 121, 124, 128, 153, 166, 170
  focus, 214, 266, 313
  impact of the story, 134
newsworthiness, 119–122, 126, 150
  civil/anti-civil judgements, as, 122, 125, 151
  invariant civil concerns, regarding, 121, 122
New York. *See* Müller, Franz
New York Times, The, 90
nineteenth century, the, 4, 115, 152
North London Railway line, 146

O

objectivity, 18, 34, 38–44, 53, 54, 76, 119, 136, 322
OFCOM Annual PSB Research Report by the Office of Communication (OFCOM), 53
Offences against the Person Act 1861, 220
Oldfield, Assistant Chief Constable George, 262
online news sources, 17
openness, 14, 107, 166, 213–215, 219
opinion and fact, 44, 118
other, the, 167, 169
otherness, 13, 114, 274
outrage, public, 135
outrage in news reports, 131
outsiders, 95, 167, 199, 273, 317.
  See also foreigner(s); other, the; otherness; 'them'/'their'/'they'; 'them' (and 'us')

P

panics, moral, 169, 170, 185, 202, 266, 294
Paris, 2015 terrorist attacks in, 217
Parry, Sergeant, 158
Pew Research Center, 53, 94
police force, the, 318
policemen, 191, 284
political and commercial power, 65.
  See also commercial power; news media independence; political power
  audience/users/readers, 82, 91
  consumers of, 65
  resisting, 106
political power. *See under* news media independence
  agenda setting, 70, 115
  attacks on journalists, verbal, 92, 93
  editorial control, 70
  influence, 70, 71, 79, 115
  violence against news journalists, 70
political reality, 70
  anti-civil values, promotion of, 126
politics, 7, 17, 19, 21, 32, 46, 49, 67, 72–77, 79, 82, 94, 126, 221, 275, 305
post-conflict resolution and/or reconstruction, 48
POT. *See* Public Opinion Tribunal (POT)
poverty, 173, 203, 278
power, concept of, 68
  asymmetrical power relations, discreet, 69
  conflict of interest, as observable, 69
Power Elite, The, 92
practices of news journalism
  civil passions, articulate our, 10
  public opinion, reflecting on, 182
  research, empirical, 9
  research, ethnographic, 9
prejudice, 13, 16, 21, 39, 88, 93, 116, 162, 164, 167, 173, 183, 195, 238, 239, 242, 253, 259, 317
  Müller, against, 242
press, the, 19, 52, 76, 83, 92, 116, 136, 145, 149–151, 153, 155–158, 160, 161, 165, 174, 176–184, 187, 191, 193, 196–199, 206, 211, 219–226, 228, 230–232, 234–236, 238–240, 242–245, 247–253, 255, 258, 262, 276, 279–284, 286–288, 290–292, 303, 304, 306–319, 325
  freedom of, 55
press coverage of the murder, 150. *See also* murder, events of the
  concerns in letters, public, 150
  final verdict by the press, 312

SUBJECT INDEX 349

focus on the murder suspect, increasing, 150
horror and alarm, initial, 149
public engagement, widespread, 149
press response to public sentiment, 165, 288
prison. *See* reform of criminal procedure
privacy, right to, 50, 54
privilege, 6, 90, 131, 172, 177, 182, 191, 223, 276
procedures, civil/legal, 114, 193, 212, 213, 216, 235
PSB. *See* Public Service Broadcasting (PSB)
public debate, 10, 52, 55
public discourse, as an ideal, 74
public empowerment to engage in deliberation, 55
public interest, 7, 20, 32, 37, 53, 54, 66, 95, 106, 130, 135, 192, 223, 287, 288, 292, 293, 307, 323
public opinion, 6, 8–10, 12, 20, 32, 52, 55, 168, 197, 212, 221, 239, 246, 288. *See also* public sentiment
public opinion polls, 7, 34, 128, 135
Public Opinion Tribunal (POT), 9, 20, 32, 52
public safety, 280, 306–308, 311, 317
  civil crisis, middle-class, 308
  professional gentleman/middle classes, 308
public sentiment
  boundary concerns, 304
  civil passions, on, 10, 21
  civil power of the news, 3, 8
  invariant civil concerns, 3, 11, 15, 18, 134, 151, 155
  newsroom subjectivity, grounded in, 10, 12

Public Service Broadcasting (PSB), 48. *See also* neo-liberal agendas
  charters, founding, 48
  values and practices, 48
public sphere, 9, 12, 13, 22, 32, 45, 46, 53, 72, 83, 86, 92, 116
public sphere, Taylor's, 12
public trust in institutions, 123, 212, 219, 238

Q
Quartz, 18
questioning, critical, 5

R
racism, 112, 169, 197, 201
radio, 56
railway murder, the, 177, 262
  events, the. *See* murder, events of the
  sensationalisation in the press reports, 185
Railways Act, the 1868 Regulation of, 156
railway travel, nineteenth-century
  expansion, concerns over, 174
  risks to safety, 114, 276
  safety and accident risks, 267
  saloon carriages, 310
  segregation by unconnected compartments, passengers', 174
  technology, benefits of, 276
rationalism, 270
readers, 20, 39, 49, 73, 128, 129, 150, 151, 159, 161, 162, 171, 172, 178, 199, 200, 224, 225, 231, 232, 235, 237, 238, 240, 243, 281–284, 291, 292, 304, 306, 318

'real' news, 8, 128
reaggregation, 303, 304, 325
reason, public, 9, 53
reciprocity, 5, 11, 18, 34, 46, 47, 50, 115, 270
rectitude, Victorian civil, 307
Reddit, 93
reductionism, 4
reform of criminal procedure, 253. *See also* death penalty
  Criminal Justice Act 1865, 253
regimes, 23, 57, 83, 90
regulatory institutions, 7, 212, 213, 216
rejection of change. *See* status quo, endorsement of the
reporter, 9, 39, 120, 242, 248, 254, 258, 269. *See also* news journalism; news journalists
reporting of the murder, 149, 153, 176, 191, 201, 287, 292
  background context, 307. *See also* authorities, the; Germany and nationality; railway travel, nineteenth-century; social class in the Victorian era
  judgements made in the news reports, 165, 272. *See also* judgements on identity; judgements on legitimacy; judgements on risk–news reports'
research method, the
  background, sociological, 6
  content analysis. *See* content analysis of the newspaper articles
  insights, key, 322
  methodology, 324
  research template. *See* research template
  sample, the. *See* sample, the research
  theoretical underpinnings, 321

research template, 153
  context of the period, 153. *See also* Home Office files; letters from the public; Metropolitan Police Archives
  social background, 22. *See also* social class in the Victorian era
respectability, 168, 173, 176, 178, 190, 201, 314. *See also* rectitude, Victorian civil
responsibility of the news, 216. *See also* news journalism
Reuters Institute Digital News Report, 53
revolutions, 174, 212
reward for evidence, 158
Reynolds Newspaper, 151, 181, 186, 194, 197, 234, 237, 246, 288
Reynold, G.W.M., 161
rhetoric, 45, 90, 96, 275
rights. *See* freedom of expression
right to know, 50, 90
rigour, 39, 40
rioters. *See* mob, the
risk, 3, 11, 15, 50, 108, 111, 113, 114, 124, 130, 151, 153, 165, 265–279, 281, 283–288, 290, 292–294, 296, 297, 303, 306, 308, 316, 317, 321, 322
Road Hill House murder, the 1860. *See* detective force
Royal Commission on Capital Punishment 1864-1866, 222
Royal Commissions, 136
Rugeley Poisoner, the 1855 case of the, 221

S
saloon, 279, 285, 310
sample, the research

SUBJECT INDEX 351

archival files, Home Office, 151. *See also* Grey, Sir George (Home Secretary)
letters to the police, Home Office and press, 151. *See also* Metropolitan Police Archives
newspaper articles on the murder, 151
SARF. *See* The Social Amplification of Risk Framework (SARF)
Scrooge, Ebenezer, 203
scrutiny of the press, 180
secrecy, 49–51, 217
Securities against Misrule, 52, 165
security, feelings of, 11
security or national interest grounds, 46
self-interest, 7, 13, 14, 68, 135, 307, 314
sensationalism, 79, 115, 207, 312
sentence, 148, 149, 152, 179, 195, 196, 219, 221, 222, 224, 231, 233, 235, 239–241, 251, 260, 312, 318
sentiment, public, 3, 8–13, 15, 16, 18, 20, 21, 45, 78, 107–113, 115, 120, 122, 125–128, 134, 135, 137, 145, 150–152, 155, 158, 165, 167, 171, 182–184, 191, 192, 196, 200, 214, 217, 219, 221, 223, 237, 239, 241, 243, 249, 251, 252, 266, 276, 284, 304, 305, 321–323, 325
Silicon Valley, 85, 96
The Social Amplification of Risk Framework (SARF), 293
social class in the Victorian era
moral values, 173
railway system, and the, 173
social imaginary, 12
social inquiry, 10, 11, 21
social media, 18, 55, 57, 67, 80, 82, 86, 96, 106, 112, 115, 116, 135–137, 270
social psychology, 67. *See also* news media power
sociology, 23, 67, 92, 265
solidarity, 4, 5, 7, 8, 22, 31, 33, 95, 108, 114, 135, 270, 273
solidary civil sphere. *See* civil sphere, the
sources, journalists' reliable, 34, 36
space as a social construct, 23
spaces of contested values, 8, 107
standing, Briggs' social. *See* status quo, endorsement of the
state, the, 4, 5, 17, 66, 68, 85, 124, 165, 172, 174, 211, 212, 216, 252, 272, 285
state power, totalitarian/authoritarian, 12, 20, 46, 92
state secrecy, 50
status quo, endorsement of the
status, identity summarised in Briggs'; civilised public's well-being, 306; standing, Victorian middle-class gentleman-professional, 176
status quo, threats to the, 313, 317
legitimacy risk; ending public hangings, 222
steamship, 147, 148
strangers, 181, 196, 271, 284
styles of reporting. *See* news reporting; news reporting styles
subjectivity, 10, 41
Sun, The, 52, 208
Sunday Times, The, 151, 235, 242, 247, 250, 251, 259, 261, 263, 296
suppression of information, 50
suspect, the murder. *See* Müller, Franz

suspicion, 73, 147, 170, 219, 229, 245, 250, 274, 275, 285, 286
symbol of the middle classes, 306
symbol of walls, 222

T
tailor. *See* Müller, Franz
Tanner, Detective Inspector Richard, 147, 153, 221, 223, 226, 244
technological advancements, 13. *See also* newsrooms; railway travel, nineteenth-century
nineteenth-century, 115
television, 55–57, 95
'them' (and 'us'), 14, 109, 202, 293
'them'/'their'/'they', 39, 73, 109, 163, 202, 293
tendentious news style, use of the. *See* news reporting styles
terrorism, 217, 266, 273–275
theories, 13, 249, 250, 293
threat, 14, 48, 50, 73, 114, 150, 153, 170, 193, 194, 217, 234, 267, 271–276, 280, 282, 289, 290, 294, 295, 313, 314, 318
three-dimensional power, 69
three estates, the. *See* estates, the three
tolerance, 13, 16, 51, 52, 167, 168, 173, 252
traditional news media, 17, 85, 96, 121. *See also* alternative news media
challenges, current, 57
train, the, 146, 149, 158, 177, 244, 278, 280, 286, 291, 310. *See also* railway travel, nineteenth-century
transcript, Müller's trial, 187
transparency, 37, 52, 212–215, 218, 219, 251
transport, 266, 277, 278, 293, 308, 309
travel, 173, 174, 276–280, 284, 286, 288, 291, 308–311. *See also* railway travel, nineteenth-century

trial proceedings, Müller's, 228. *See also* transcript, Müller's Trial
circumstantial evidence, 199
defence, Müller's, 148, 190, 228
evidence, 188, 221
inconsistencies, 233
Judge, Lord Chief Baron, 156
prosecution by the Solicitor General, 228, 310
reprieve, requests for a, 161
sentence of death, 148, 235
verdict, the jury's, 195
witnesses, 190, 221
Trump, Donald, 57, 93
election campaign, 2016 US, 153
trust in the news. *See* audience/user/reader, the
trustworthiness of the news
objectivity, 34; partial/provisional reports, 41; subjective reporting, 41
truth telling, 34; accuracy, 35, 36, 322; sincerity, 36, 322
truth, 18, 31, 32, 34–39, 41–44, 49–51, 71, 106, 109, 137, 184, 190, 219, 235, 237, 290, 291, 315
knowledge claims to truth, 54
Turkey, 57. *See also* neo-liberal agendas
TV. *See* television
Twitter, 18, 57, 81
types of civil boundary, 110, 126, 128
types of civil boundary maintenance, 128, 129, 133, 303, 305, 323, 324

U
uncertainty, 41, 137, 159, 248, 265, 266, 271, 273–276, 284, 294, 295
uncivilised public, anti-civil narrative

identity concerns, Müller and the witnesses; foreignness, 314, 315; intellectual inferiority, 314; lack of morals, 314; property, 314
risk and threat to safety; mob and public order, the, 317; riot as threat to safety, 316
UNESCO. *See* United Nations Educational, Scientific and Cultural Organization (UNESCO)
unfairness in the law, 215
United Nations (UN), 32, 56
United Nations Educational, Scientific and Cultural Organization (UNESCO), 48
United States Circuit Court House, New York, 148
UN. *See* United Nations (UN)
updates, fast news, 247
upper class, the, 203, 286
urban poor, the, 203
USA, 43, 55, 57, 72, 93, 94, 159, 174, 189, 275, 295
'us' and 'them', 14

V
verdict, the. *See* press coverage of the murder; trial proceedings, Müller's
Vice News, 18
victim, the murder. *See* murder, events of the
Victoria, the sailing ship, 147
Victorian era, the, 132
Victorians, 172, 173, 182
visual material
  graphics, 81
  photographs, 129, 131, 304
  pictures, 81

videos, 18
voice of the people/public opinion, 71
voices, marginalised, 166

W
walking stick, 157
walls, legitimation for, 23, 218
war, 35, 78, 84, 93, 94, 96, 153, 159, 175, 315
warrant, civil, 113, 215, 216, 218, 220
watch, gold chain and, 146, 147, 158, 186, 289, 314
way of life', 'our, 127, 165, 217, 270–273, 283, 296
wealth, 5, 7, 172, 174, 199, 277–279, 294
weapon, murder, 157
'we', the collective, 19, 177
we-perspective, 9, 21
'we'/'us'/'our', 168, 169
Whicher, Detective Inspector Jack, 220
Whitechapel murders, 1880s, 197
WikiLeaks, 49, 50, 83, 96
withhold information, the state's claim to, 37
witnesses, 81, 147, 157, 158, 185, 187, 190, 191, 221, 223, 228–230, 236, 314, 315
working class, the. *See* lower class, the; lower classes, newspaper term

Y
YouTube, 18

Z
Zeitgeist, 129, 269. *See also* social class in the Victorian era, moral values

Printed by Printforce, the Netherlands